RE-VISIONING PERSON-CENTRED THERAPY

By exploring various ways to assimilate recent progressive developments *and* to renew its vital links with its radical roots, *Re-Visioning Person-Centred Therapy: Theory and Practice of a Radical Paradigm* takes a fresh look at this revolutionary therapeutic approach.

Bringing together leading figures in PCT and new writers from around the world, the essays in this book create fertile links with phenomenology, meditation and spirituality, critical theory, contemporary thought and culture, and philosophy of science. In doing so, they create an outline that renews and re-visions person-centred therapy's radical paradigm, providing fertile material in both theory and practice.

Shot through with clinical studies, vignettes and in-depth discussions on aspects of theory, *Re-Visioning Person-Centred Therapy* will be stimulating reading for therapists in training and practice, as well as those interested in the development of PCT.

Manu Bazzano is a psychotherapist and supervisor in private practice. He has studied eastern contemplative practices since 1980. He is the author and editor of many books, including *Zen and Therapy, After Mindfulness* and *Nietzsche and Psychotherapy*. A visiting lecturer at the University of Roehampton, London, he facilitates workshops and seminars internationally. He is editor of *Person-Centered and Experiential Psychotherapy* and associate editor of *Self & Society*.

'Heretical, subversive, a celebration of precarious uncertainty, and yet radically personal, this book will inspire trainees and new therapists, of any tradition, to save our profession. *Re-Visioning Person-Centred Therapy* expands the scope of Rogers' approach, updating and redeeming in equal measure. The book itself is an instance of its message, diverse, unexpected, gritty and well-argued. If you want to remain comfortable, offering manualised "treatments" to patients in order to retire and die peacefully, then avoid this book.'

> Greg Madison, PhD, non-affiliated international lecturer, writer, Founder of London Focusing Institute

'This book represents a remarkable contribution in the contemporary Person-centred Therapy world. Bringing together both a critique and a call for a reinvention of theory and practice, it takes up Rogers' original proposal and brings it forward, broadening, updating and consolidating this perspective for our times. This results in a fruitful and creative renewal of PCT instigated by authors and practitioners from various parts of the world. Carl Rogers would certainly be proud to read this book.'

> Virginia Moreira, APHETO, Laboratory of Psychopathology and Humanist Phenomenological Psychotherapy, University of Fortaleza, Brazil

'This is a welcome and timely book for anyone interested in person-centred psychotherapeutic work. It takes a completely fresh look at person-centred and experiential therapies by offering critical and innovative approaches to theory and practice, while also sustaining relevance to contemporary therapeutic needs. Particularly distinctive strengths are the transcultural perspectives; the philosophical breadth, which is inclusive of spirituality and political awareness; and the practical applications of theory to practice.'

> Jean O'Callaghan, Convener of the MA Integrative Counselling and Psychotherapy training (BACP accredited) at the University of Roehampton, London, UK

RE-VISIONING PERSON-CENTRED THERAPY

Theory and Practice of a Radical Paradigm

Edited by Manu Bazzano

Routledge
Taylor & Francis Group

LONDON AND NEW YORK

First published 2018
by Routledge
2 Park Square, Milton Park, Abingdon, Oxon OX14 4RN

and by Routledge
711 Third Avenue, New York, NY 10017

Routledge is an imprint of the Taylor & Francis Group, an informa business

© 2018 selection and editorial matter, Manu Bazzano; individual chapters, the contributors

The right of the editor to be identified as the author of the editorial material, and of the authors for their individual chapters, has been asserted in accordance with sections 77 and 78 of the Copyright, Designs and Patents Act 1988.

All rights reserved. No part of this book may be reprinted or reproduced or utilised in any form or by any electronic, mechanical, or other means, now known or hereafter invented, including photocopying and recording, or in any information storage or retrieval system, without permission in writing from the publishers.

Trademark notice: Product or corporate names may be trademarks or registered trademarks, and are used only for identification and explanation without intent to infringe.

British Library Cataloguing-in-Publication Data
A catalogue record for this book is available from the British Library

Library of Congress Cataloging-in-Publication Data
Names: Bazzano, Manu, editor.
Title: Re-visioning person-centred therapy : theory and practice of a radical paradigm / [edited by] Manu Bazzano.
Description: Abingdon, Oxon; New York, NY: Routledge, 2018. | Includes bibliographical references.
Identifiers: LCCN 2018003742 | ISBN 9780815394082 (hardback : alk. paper) | ISBN 9780815394099 (pbk. : alk. paper) | ISBN 9781351186773 (epub) | ISBN 9781351186766 (mobipocket) | ISBN 9781351186797 (ebk) | ISBN 9781351186780 (web)
Subjects: | MESH: Person-Centered Therapy
Classification: LCC RC480 | NLM WM 420.5.N8 | DDC 616.89/14–dc23
LC record available at https://lccn.loc.gov/2018003742

ISBN: 978-0-8153-9408-2 (hbk)
ISBN: 978-0-8153-9409-9 (pbk)
ISBN: 978-1-351-18679-7 (ebk)

Typeset in Bembo
by Taylor & Francis Books

Printed and bound in Great Britain by
TJ International Ltd, Padstow, Cornwall

**Fyodor E. Vasilyuk (1953–2017)
In Memoriam**

CONTENTS

List of contributors	x
Introduction Manu Bazzano	xvi
Tribute to Fyodor E. Vasilyuk Tatiana Karyagina and Fedor Shankov	xxiv

PART I
Some kinds of love: person-centred therapy and the relational dimension — 1

1. Therapy as an accident waiting to happen — 3
   Julie Webb

2. The psychotherapeutic encounter as a political act of micro multitude — 17
   Claudio Rud

3. Beauty and the Cyborg — 28
   Manu Bazzano

4. Walking backwards towards the future: reclaiming the radical roots – and future – of person-centred therapy — 46
   Keith Tudor

5. Ethics and the person-centered approach: a dialogue with radical alterity — 60
   Emanuel Meireles Vieira and Francisco Pablo Huascar Aragão Pinheiro

PART II
The politics of experience   77

6 Dialectics of person and experiencing   79
   Tatiana Karyagina and Fyodor E. Vasilyuk

7 Actualizing tendency, organismic wisdom and understanding
   the world   93
   Salvador Moreno-López

8 Person-centred approach as discursivity and person-centred
   therapy as heterotopic practice   110
   Pavlos Zarogiannis

9 Client-centered: an ethical therapy   128
   Bert Rice and Kathryn A. Moon

10 Experiencing and the person-centred approach   137
   Nikolaos Kypriotakis

11 Experiential-existential psychotherapy: deepening existence,
   engaging with life   151
   Siebrecht Vanhooren

PART III
Person-centred therapy and spirituality   165

12 From the scientific to the mystical in the work of
   Carl Rogers   167
   Michael Sivori

13 Living from the 'formative tendency': 'cosmic congruence'   174
   Judy Moore

14 "A kind of liking which has strength" (Carl Rogers): does
   person-centred therapy facilitate through love?   192
   Peter F. Schmid

PART IV
Person-centred learning and training   209

15 Enter centre stage, the case study…   211
   Deborah A. Lee

16 Sheep of tomorrow   226
   Manu Bazzano

17 What do I know and how do I know it?: theories of knowledge
    and the person-centred approach   237
    Dot Clark

18 The empathor's new clothes: when person-centered practices
    and evidence-based claims collide   247
    Blake Griffin Edwards

PART V
Challenging some aspects of person-centred practice   263

19 Challenging snoopervision: how can person-centered
    practitioners offer new alternatives to the fracturing of the
    person in the supervision relationship?   265
    Zoë Krupka

20 Re-visioning person-centred research   277
    Jo Hilton and Seamus Prior

21 Psychopathology and the future of person-centred therapy   289
    Andrew Schiller

22 Presence: the fourth condition   300
    Sarton Weinraub

23 A place in which everything can go   315
    Darran Biles

24 A person-centred political critique of current discourses in
    post-traumatic stress disorder and post-traumatic growth   330
    Deborah A. Lee

Index   342

CONTRIBUTORS

Manu Bazzano is a psychotherapist and supervisor in private practice. He has studied eastern contemplative practices since 1980. He is the author and editor of many books, including *Zen and Therapy*, *After Mindfulness* and *Nietzsche and Psychotherapy*. A visiting lecturer at the University of Roehampton, London, he facilitates workshops and seminars internationally. He is editor of *Person-Centered and Experiential Psychotherapy* and associate editor of *Self & Society*.

Darran Biles is a writer and therapist who lives and works in Norwich. He originally trained in person-centred counselling and is currently training in embodied-relational therapy and wild therapy.

Dot Clark writes: While on long-term retreat 2008–9, I experienced a profound connection between mystical explorations of the unity of being and the fundamentals of the person-centred approach (PCA). Both traditions call for a particular quality of attention to be paid to whatever is happening in relationship with other people and through being itself. The territory discussed in this chapter was part of the exploration I undertook into the meaning of this experience while a student at the University of Edinburgh. I am in my 60s, living in Fife in Scotland and have been learning about the PCA for over twenty years.

Blake Griffin Edwards is a licensed marriage and family therapist, clinical fellow in the American Association for Marriage and Family Therapy, and clinical supervisor. Blake has held professional roles as a therapist with homeless and foster care youth, at a university counselling centre, in private practice, and for military personnel at a naval base, as a systems consultant and trainer, as an abstract reviewer for AAMFT national conferences, as a contributing editor for GoodTherapy.org, and as an agency clinical director. He is currently a clinical programme manager for a child and family therapy programme at Children's Home Society of Washington and behavioural health champion for the American Academy of Paediatrics in north central Washington state, U.S.A. His writing has been featured at GoodTherapy.org, PsychCentral.com, GoodMenProject.com, and RelevantMagazine.com, as well as in the AAMFT's *Family Therapy Magazine*, the Association for Family Therapy and Systemic Practice in the UK's *Context* magazine, and the American Academy of Psychotherapists' *Voices Journal*.

Jo Hilton is a counsellor, trainer and supervisor. She has an interest in the impact of early life experiences and difficult process. Her background in arts management and promotion is integral to her interest in exploring the interfaces between the arts and research.

Tatiana Karyagina is a senior researcher at the Psychological Institute of the Russian Academy of Education, laboratory of counselling psychology and psychotherapy (Moscow). She is also a trainer and supervisor in training programmes of the Association for Co-Experiencing Psychotherapy. Her PhD thesis (Moscow State University) was devoted to the evolution of the empathy concept in psychology. She is the author of more than a dozen papers on the theoretical and methodological problems of empathy in psychology and psychotherapy. Her scientific and practical interests are experiential psychotherapy and development of empathy for helping professionals.

Zoë Krupka works as a psychotherapist and supervisor, lecturer and writer in Melbourne, Australia. She lectures and supervises research in the Master of Counselling and Psychotherapy programme at the Cairnmillar Institute and writes widely on the intersection of psychology, therapy, politics and public life. You can find her blog at zoekrupka.com.

Nikolaos Kypriotakis has studied physics and has been trained in person-centred and focusing-oriented counselling/psychotherapy (Hellenic Focusing Center, HFC) and in children focusing. Currently he teaches physics and science in a public junior high school and focusing in HFC and is the editor-in-chief of the magazine *Εποχή-Epoché* (*Psychotherapy, Phenomenology, Hermeneutics*). As well as teaching conventional and non-conventional educational objects to children with severe vision problems with the help of Focusing, web administrating and creating e-learning simulations, in recent years, his interest has been captured by the application of the experiential methods of Focusing and Thinking at the Edge (TAE) in educational/school programmes. For two years, he was the General Secretary of the Hellenic Association for Person-centred & Experiential Approach.

Deborah A. Lee is a senior lecturer in Sociology at the University of Nottingham, UK and a trainee psychotherapist.

Kathryn A. Moon is a client-centred therapist and consultant in private practice in Chicago. She has written several articles, co-edited *Practicing Client-Centered*

Therapy: Selected Writings of Barbara Temaner Brodley and collaborated in multiple bibliographic and archival projects, including assisting in making available for research, personal study and teaching, the transcripts of Carl Rogers' therapy sessions.

Judy Moore is former Director of the Centre for Counselling Studies at the University of East Anglia (UEA), Norwich, UK, where she was also for many years Director of the University Counselling Service. She originally trained as a person-centred counsellor in the mid-1980s and taught on UEA's postgraduate diploma in person-centred counselling throughout the 1990s. She subsequently trained in focusing and helped to introduce focusing training and research at UEA and became a Certifying Coordinator of the Focusing Institute. Since retiring from full-time employment at the end of 2013 she continues to supervise PhD students and to publish on person-centred and focusing theory and practice.

Salvador Moreno-López earned a bachelor degree in psychology, a M.A. and a Ph.D. He trained as a humanistic psychotherapist, then specialized in person-centred psychotherapy, the philosophy of the implicit of Eugene T. Gendlin, and focusing-oriented psychotherapy. Currently, he promotes an interdisciplinary dialogue in psychotherapy and the inclusion of the experiential dimension in it. In the late 1970s and early 1980s he participated in several workshops conducted by Carl R. Rogers in the United States, Mexico and Brazil. He has been a university professor in graduate courses in psychotherapy and human development at ITESO University, Universidad Iberoamericana Cd. De México, León and Monterrey, University of Veracruz and Vasco de Quiroga University. Author of three books: *Person-Centred Education* (*La educación centrada en la persona*), *Participatory Learning Guide* (*Guía del aprendizaje participativo*) and *Discovering My Body Wisdom, Focusing* (*Descubriendo mi sabiduría corporal, Focusing*). Author of numerous articles on education and psychotherapy, he is currently director of Focusing Mexico, and promotes the appreciation of the Empathic Listening that Animates the Heart as a cultural project. He has worked as a psychotherapist and consultant for more than 40 years.

Francisco Pablo Huascar Aragão Pinheiro is a Psychologist at the Coordenadoria de Organização e Qualidade de Vida no Trabalho at the Universidade Federal do Ceará (Brazil), and he is a Doctor in Education at the Programa de Pós-Graduação em Educação Brasileira at the same institution. He is currently dedicated to studies on workers' health, and research on the relations between health and the work of early childhood education professors.

Seamus Prior is a Senior Lecturer in Counselling, Psychotherapy and Applied Social Sciences at the University of Edinburgh. He is a practising psychodynamic counsellor. He teaches on professional training programmes and research programmes in counselling, psychotherapy and applied social sciences and supervises masters and doctoral students. He also contributes to the development of ethical research practice among social science doctoral students across the university.

Bert Rice left the practice of law in 1996 to pursue learning opportunities in an elementary school classroom. He has organized and participated in hundreds of large and small person-centred groups. He has written several articles and co-edited *Practicing Client-Centered Therapy: Selected Writings of Barbara Temaner Brodley*.

Claudio Rud is a Psychiatric physician and psychotherapist U.N.B.A. (1969), a psycho-dramatist and founding member of the Argentine Society of Psychodrama (1980), founder and coordinator of Casabierta, an institution dedicated since 1989 to assisting and training in the person-centred Approach. He has been a keynote speaker and Professor for Masters degrees in several Latin American and European Universities. He is author of conference presentations and articles published in journals of international interest (Austria, Germany, England, Spain, Mexico, Colombia), Board Member for the WAPCEPC from 2003 until 2008, President of the Argentine Association of Person-centred Approach and organizer and member of the Scientific Committee of the **V** Psychotherapy World Congress (2005). Currently he is working on philosophical deepening of the foundations of psychotherapeutic practice, fundamentally from the work of Baruch Spinoza

Andrew Schiller is a counsellor currently working for a number of mental health charities. After completing a Bachelor's degree in history from the University of Bristol, he embarked on a career in marketing, working with some of the world's largest corporations. Now retraining as a psychotherapist, Andrew is in the final stages of an MSc in contemporary person-centred psychotherapy at Metanoia Institute.

Peter F. Schmid is founder of person-centred training in Austria and co-founder of both the World Association (WAPCEPC) and the European Network (PCE-Europe). He co-operated with Carl Rogers in the eighties, is a teacher at the Sigmund Freud University, Vienna, psychotherapist and trainer at the Institute for Person-Centred Studies (APG•IPS) in Austria, author and co-editor of 27 books and almost 400 academic publications about the foundations of the PCA and anthropological, epistemological and ethical issues of person-centred psychotherapy and counselling. Peter was a co-founder of the two major international academic person-centred journals: the German language journal *PERSON* and the English language journal *Person-Centered and Experiential Psychotherapies*. Websites: www.pfs-online.at, www.pca-online.net.

Fedor Shankov graduated from Moscow State University as clinical psychology specialist. He gained a Master's degree at Moscow State University of Psychology and Education, individual and group psychotherapy and participated in the co-experiencing psychotherapy training programme. He is a PhD student and researcher at the Laboratory of Counselling Psychology and Psychotherapy, Psychological Institute of the Russian Academy of Education and a counselling psychologist at the International Psychological Centre, Moscow.

Michael Sivori is curriculum manager and Team Leader at The Manchester College, UK and an independent counsellor in private practice.

Keith Tudor is professor of psychotherapy and head of the School of Public Health and Psychosocial Studies at Auckland University of Technology, Aotearoa New Zealand. He is the editor of Psychotherapy and Politics International, a fellow of the Critical Institute, an honorary senior research fellow at the University of Roehampton, London, and a visiting associate professor at the University of Primorska, Slovenia.

Siebrecht Vanhooren is an associate professor at the University of Leuven (KU Leuven, Belgium), where he teaches person-centred and experiential-existential psychotherapy to graduate and postgraduate students. He works as a therapist at CGG Prisma and PraxisP (Belgium). He is particularly interested in meaning, existential themes and post-traumatic growth in psychotherapy.

Fyodor E. Vasilyuk (1953–2017) was Chairman of Association for co-experiencing psychotherapy (CEP, Russia), psychotherapist, trainer and supervisor in CEP training programmes. Doctor of Psychology, Professor, Head of the Department of Individual and Group Psychotherapy of Counselling and Clinical Psychology Faculty in Moscow State University of Psychology & Education. He also worked as the Leading Researcher in the Psychological Institute of Russian Academy of Education, Laboratory of counselling psychology and psychotherapy (Moscow). He authored several books, including: *The Psychology of Experiencing, Experiencing and Prayer, Methodological Problems of Psychology* and numerous papers on the problems of experiencing, theory and method of CEP.

Emanuel Meireles Vieira is a professor of person-centred approach at the Psychology College in the Universidade Federal do Pará (Brazil) and is a Doctor in Psychology at the Universidade Federal de Minas Gerais (Brazil). His interests are on the relation between ethics, alterity, and psychology, mainly regarding the person-centred approach.

Julie Webb After working as an independent philosophical practitioner, Julie trained at Chester University in humanistic counselling, and has since worked for a number of years in private practice in Shrewsbury. She also worked as a counselling lecturer at Shrewsbury College of Arts and Technology, facilitating training for therapists, and CPD events. She has relocated her counselling and supervision practice to Cambridge. She is co-editor of *Therapy and the Counter-tradition: The Edge of Philosophy* (Routledge, 2016).

Sarton Weinraub is a licensed Clinical Psychologist in private practice in New York City specializing in the practice of humanistic (specifically person-centred) psychotherapy with an additional emphasis on alternative psychiatry, alternative diagnostics, and alternative views of the medical model being applied to the practice of mental health treatment. He is the Director of the New York Person-Centered Resource Center (nypcrc.org), a humanistic mental health treatment centre in New York City. Dr. Weinraub received his Doctorate and Master's degrees in clinical psychology from Saybrook University in San Francisco, California. Dr. Weinraub received his undergraduate degree from Goddard College in Vermont. He has also received training in the person-centred approach from the Independent Consultation Center in New York City and in psychodynamic-psychotherapy from the New York University Psychoanalytic Institute, as well as a great deal of individualized psychotherapeutic training from well-regarded psychotherapeutic practitioners from the United States and abroad.

Pavlos Zarogiannis lives in Athens, Greece, where he works as a psychotherapist, trainer and supervisor. He studied psychology, German literature and linguistics in Germany during the 1980s and has been trained in person-centred counselling/ psychotherapy and in focusing. In 2002 he became a Focusing Certified Coordinator for Greece and he founded – together with Anna Karali – the *Hellenic Focusing Center*. In the following years, they created their own training programmes in person-centred and focusing-oriented counselling/psychotherapy, in focusing and in supervision, which they teach in Athens, in Thessaloniki and in Cyprus. Pavlos was president of the former Hellenic Person-Centred Association from 1998–2003 and he is a founding member of the National Organization for Psychotherapy in Greece (NOPG) and of the new Hellenic Association for Person-centred and Experiential Approach (HAPCEA). Since 2015 he has also been editor of the Greek journal *Εποχή/Epoché – Psychotherapy, Phenomenology, Hermeneutics*.

INTRODUCTION

Manu Bazzano

I.1

Is there a future for person-centred therapy (PCT)? Some of its critics will say that its radicalism is largely assumed and thoroughly undeserved; that it is plagued by tribal dogmatism and a servile aspiration to please the Powers; that its humanistic ethos is now overrun by a geeky fascination with measuring what can't be measured; that its once quietly revolutionary stance morphed into the friendly face of neoliberal psychology; that in its copious borrowing from Christian morality and theology and from its own poor man's versions of Buber, Tillich and Levinas, it has misrepresented all the above while covering up its congenital inability for deep thought through second-hand philosophical varnish; that in its undigested use of attachment theory, neuroscience and object relations theory, it has become indistinguishable from other therapies; that its emphasis on love ignores the complexities and contradictions implicit in the human condition, betrays its deep-seated political naiveté while ushering in what psychotherapy has struggle so hard to overcome, namely Christianity's mystifying and life-denigrating hold on experiencing.

I know all of the above forms of critique by heart, for the simple reason that I agree with each one of them. But there are surprises in store.

The beautiful surprise this book presented me with was that while there is more than a grain of truth in all of the objections raised above, a new exciting path ahead can be forged by allowing proliferations and associations with some of the most progressive developments in philosophy, politics and spirituality while capitalizing on aspects of the approach that are recalcitrant to blind obeisance to the demands of neopositivism and neoliberalism.

The answer to the above question about a future for PCT that emerges from this book is a resounding, richly ambivalent and exigent *yes*.

Introduction **xvii**

There are so many novel contributions here from across the globe (beyond the usual suspects and household names), all of them committed to bring a gust of wild wind to an approach that has recently acquiesced to sleep placidly on rented, evidence-based laurels.

I.2

What keeps a tradition – any tradition – alive? For some, zealous preservation in aspic, its prophet frozen in time, duly embalmed and routinely celebrated. But can a static faith be truly *alive*? Rigid upholding of the alleged purity and orthodoxy of a doctrine invariably breeds ugly practices: exclusion, excommunication, and the explicit/implicit self-appointed investiture of authority by a selected group of knowledgeable experts. This stance is often characterized by fear of contamination from outside forces and influences; it replicates the wider political malaise that in various parts of the world gives rise as we speak to the alarming resurgence of nativism and a hatred of the foreign that is both vitriolic and uninformed.

For others, a tradition can be kept, if not exactly alive, at least afloat, by stretching its corpus of tenets and practices so that it roughly aligns with the rules of the leading creed and the style of the dominant trends in a particular society. This stance is as awkward as the first; particularly when the doctrine in question is avowedly progressive and its tenets are then opportunistically bent in the service of ideologies of control, *or* if the doctrine in question solemnly professes alignment (a.k.a. *congruence*) to organismic experiencing, only to then become congruent with the dictates of the market and the political structures that sustain it. Given the urgency of the political context in which we operate, both deliberate contamination and cross-fertilization of the kind found in this book can make for truly effective antidotes.

The rich weaving of creative contaminations the reader will uncover in these pages can go a long way, I believe, towards enhancing and renewing person-centred theory and practice. They widen the scope of the approach without betraying the original spirit. They enlighten and provoke without stooping to either orthodoxy or the pressures of social conformity and political acquiescence. This is because the type of cultural contamination favoured by the contributors in this book is not random nor is it naively (or self-servingly) dazzled by the shiny artefacts currently in vogue in the psychotherapy and psychology industries. Despite the profound diversity of disciplines and discourses presented here, each of them is sharply at variance with the status quo and the vested interests of neoliberalism and its cultural/scientific appendix, neopositivism.

Broadly speaking, they do so by appealing to two overarching narratives. One is inspired by *spirituality* – variously and experientially understood as immanence, the ineffable, the organismic, the unknown – as well as the demanding and very tangible presence of otherness within the other and oneself. Another is an equally impassioned plea for *progressive politics* through a diversely articulated and consistently persuasive call for the urgent redressing of power that, inspired among other sources by the aboriginal cultures of South America, sees human wellbeing as good-living-with-others and mother Earth.

Both narratives are far-reaching and subversive in their implications. In relation to spirituality, some chapters openly speak of *Agape*, a form of love whose source is found in the Bible and one that gestures towards a difficult, deeply empathic practice of 'no strings attached', of radical passivity as well as of potential bypassing of the power imbalance intrinsic in the therapeutic encounter. PCT has shared with Christianity the latter's revolutionary affirmation of love as well as – it must be said – its penchant for universalizing platitudes that end up embellishing the status quo while leaving it supremely unscathed. Others, perhaps more subtly and indirectly, refer to an *outside* that, while profoundly immanent and not independent of the usual venerable icons found in the Antique Shop of Salvation, effectively disrupts our tendency for self-boundedness and tempts us towards more expansive, compassionate and daring ways of being in the world. They do so in different ways: via links to *radical alterity* or otherness; via the articulation of notions of *plurality* and *multitude* that are not reducible to either facile subjectivism or blanket universal relatedness; via a reframing of *experiencing* that sits at the opposite pole of the dominant managerialism that now dominates the world of psychotherapy and training. Some chapters bring the challenge to the very heart of *logos* or discourse, to how we express (and often fail to express) the vibrancy of experiencing through a language that is simply unable to tune into a qualitative, affect-driven, perceptive domain of experience and becoming. Personally, I have found these chapters a delight to read; the weaving of poetry, drama, autobiography and imaginative thinking is a welcome antidote to the dreariness of most academic writing and editing.

I.3

It has been heartening for me over the last few years to discover, through dialogues that took place at the margins of person-centred orthodoxy, that my own growing sense of unease and dissatisfaction about the approach was echoed, encouraged and corroborated by many practitioners across the globe. They too, I soon found out, are similarly inspired by the broad legacy of Carl Rogers and its equally broad ramifications in personal, spiritual and political dimensions. This book is partly the result of these dialogues, pointing as it does towards new avenues of inquiry and experimentation within and without PCT. It presents imaginative and concrete ways out of a seeming impasse by eliciting and provoking novel ways of thinking about person-centredness. It encourages *heterodoxy*, heretical thought and a way of conceiving practice that is aligned to insights that derive from a kaleidoscopic variety of sources. This richness and variety provide, I believe, hearty nourishment and heady spirits for an approach that for decades now has starved, perched uneasily on the fence between pre-modern defence of the human and neoliberal fascination with the gadgetry of an accelerated cyber-world. In other words, I personally see current person-centred theory and practice as Frankenstein's famous Creature *in reverse*, i.e. conceived in the womb of deep human longings for meaning, autonomy, empathy and connectedness and then clutching the dangerous horns of the sacred cow, science, and filling its sensitive soul with techno-dreams of data, facts and quantitative measurements.

And yet, despite what I see as the obstacles posed by more institutionalized ways of learning and practising PCT, despite the difficulty of articulating a person-centred practice and ethos outside well-trodden and often stale paths, I find that the aspiration to keep alive a tradition we deeply care about is worth pursuing. Are there alternatives to the conventional and tired ways in which PCT is practised today? Reading the chapters in this book; reading within, above and between the lines, being receptive to contributions that are in turn playful, erudite, experimental, competent, fierce, committed, provocative and compassionate, the attentive reader will find that the answer is, again, *yes*.

I.4

It has been said that in order to properly envision the traits of a culture and dynamically enliven its presence and purpose in the world, one thing is needed above all: *the perspective of the foreign*. It is from amid the waves on the high sea that, looking back at the distant shore, we can begin to get a sense of the terra firma. What is striking about the contributions in this book is that many come from areas in the world outside the Anglo-American and European traditional strongholds. Several of these contributors are unknown to practitioners and trainees in Europe, UK and the US. Coming from Russia, Greece, New Zealand and notably Central and South America – Mexico, Argentina, Brazil – these original and thought-provoking ideas not only deserve to be known, studied and assimilated. They are *vital* to PCT's renewal.

I feel elated and inspired by this gust of fresh air. I remember all too vividly the dismay I felt only a short while ago, when my proposal to the person-centred department of a training institution to widen the scope and the ethos of our work was met with indifference and contempt. Admittedly, I've always been on the verge of 'ditching' the approach because of what I perceive as its close-minded tribalism and unwillingness to welcome the alleged threat of the new among its more or less official ranks. But equally I have been eager to sketch different allegiances between the person-centred approach (PCA) and other progressive strands. For instance, in my proposal I had suggested ways to include in the syllabus links to the following cultural strands:

- *Neurodiversity* and the neurodiversity movement that effectively redresses some of PCT's uncritical acceptance of mainstream neuroscience, of essentialism and a generalized neurotypical bias.
- The *affective turn* that took place in the humanities in the 1990s – whose occurrence had been barely registered in the world of therapy, let alone person-centred therapy – in order to redress the current person-centred bias towards the relational, its dependence on psychoanalytic intersubjectivity and

badly digested notions borrowed from Buber and Levinas, and above all to provide person-centred practice with an ethos and a theoretical articulation entirely independent of cognitivism and quantitative perspectives.

- Clearer links to a critical evaluation of existential/humanistic approaches that *misread affect* in onto-theological (Heidegger's *Stimmung* or 'mood') rather than in a naturalistic and organismic key (Whitehead, Jameson, Massumi, and others, including one Carl Rogers).
- The development of a person-centred perspective on '*mindfulness*', able to decouple the latter from the current reductivist grip and open it up to a knowledge/praxis of contemplative approaches that is organismic and phenomenological in outlook rather than prescriptive and religious.
- Links between person-centred theory and practice and *post-existentialist* and *contemporary empiricism* that help reformulate the PCA and refresh it through the use of stimulating new metaphors, i.e. the *rhizome* and the existential unconscious. Given that some of these developments are linked to the work of Deleuze and Guattari (1982), a concentrated study and research in this area may help reframe PCT as a valid critique/adjunct to the Laingian strand of critical psychopathology and corroborate current emphasis in the syllabus on the latter.

In my enthusiasm, I had joined an institution that prides itself in having a long-standing and successful person-centred department. I had thought that, particularly at MSc level of study, it would welcome critical thinking and links to other disciplines that are vital to the renewal of the PCA. But I had overlooked that, at the critical juncture when an institution is eager to gain university status, critical thinking is sidelined in favour of handed-down knowledge, marketing and the safe repetition of stale formulas. This is particularly true at a time when, thanks to the neoliberal takeover, universities are no longer places of culture and open debate but corporate schools of conformity.

PCT may not have a manifesto, but it has a clear ethos. Despite the diversity within the approach, there are ways to know if I veer away from a person-centred stance – for example, when the need to mollify policy makers overrides my aspiration to respond to the real need of my clients. Or when the simpler task of merely recycling and preserving a body of knowledge overrides the more difficult task of facilitating nothing less than human autonomy and human encounter, as well as the urgent requisite to write theory anew: by re-visioning, re-describing and re-expressing the approach in the crucible of practice and encounter.

I.5

The chapters that follow are widely different in their ingenious ramifications, but they all seem to share a fundamental starting point, one that I find paradoxically difficult to express *because* of its disarming simplicity. I will try to convey it by borrowing from a different tradition, one that, founded in the thirteenth century by 'mystical realist' Dōgen (Kim, 1975), is still alive and kicking as we speak. For Dōgen, all it takes for a tradition to come alive is that a splinter of it somehow touches the heart of even just *one* ordinary person like you and me. Blossoming within the heart of that person, the living teachings and practices of that particular tradition (in his case, Soto Zen) then come alive and are potentially *transmitted* to others – very much like a language, or an idiom, or, dare I say it, a *virus*.

But if that fails to happen, all the temples and rituals in the world are of no use. If that fails to happen, the churning out of papers, books, academic journals, seminars, the establishing of counselling, psychotherapy and supervision courses all proudly bearing the prophet's name and the logo of the tradition are utterly *pointless*.

When he travelled from his native India to China, the legendary monk and mythic founder of Zen Buddhism, Bodhidharma, met the emperor Wu, who had done a tremendous amount of work in spreading Buddhist teachings. The Emperor asked Bodhidharma: 'I have built hundreds of temples and promoted Buddhist monastic training and help widen the reach of the Dharma all over the land. What is my merit?' Bodhidharma replied: 'No merit whatsoever'.

Some practitioners revel in the fact that so many integrative counselling trainings begin with PCT and the 'core-conditions', while others get enthusiastic about finding new ways to *measure* those very same conditions. Others are happy to bend the person-centred ethos to the catechisms of the double-headed deity of neopositivism and neoliberalism. Perceiving the latter as the only game in town, they are concerned about the survival of our 'brand', forgetting that PCT is not a brand in the first place. To use a well-known image dear to the historical Buddha, a raft is useful in crossing the river. But there is no point in preserving and even enshrining the raft once it has done its job.

Others still are found boldly claiming PCT's paternity or supposedly natural allegiance to a host of arguably normative and, in some instances coercive and downright (arguably) backward-looking practices that include positive psychology, sectors of essentialist attachment theory, classic psychiatry and considerable sectors of neuroscience.

In some instances PCT has given birth, like hippy parents to an ultra-square progeny, to a new breed of neo-conservatives – writers and practitioners who whilst formally upholding person-centred principles, show unambiguous signs of having, in a perverse Foucauldian twist, fallen prey to the entrapments of power. It is not difficult to spot them. They will eulogize RCTs, revamp psychopathology, and colonize any space left for real debate at conferences and meetings with streams of data and blanket use of PowerPoint. The assumption behind these words and deeds appears to be that progress can be measured by how often state, government and governing bodies adopt a person-centred lingo. What is truly mind-boggling is that some of its most vociferous exponents claim to be inspired and having theoretical affinities with that 'true person of no status' (to borrow a phrase from the Zen tradition) that was Carl Rogers.

'Isn't it great', I remember reading a few years back, 'that the European Council had adopted the word "person-centred" in one of its statements?' I have witnessed a parallel of this with the mindfulness movement. I remember reading an interview

xxii Manu Bazzano

in a Buddhist magazine with people in the Pentagon. Wasn't it amazing, the journalist mused, that these people practise meditation? But surely one of the positive effects of intelligent meditation practice (as opposed to mere solipsistic concentration and relaxation) is that the person meditating is slowly beginning to question the very notion of war, the raison d'être of the military and of a department of defence, rather than, say, learning how to drop bombs 'mindfully'?

I.6

This book aims to launch – each chapter in its own distinctive way – a philosophically astute, spiritually minded and politically engaged vision for PCT and the PCA. This new vision does not waste time in recognizing the alleged friendliness of facts but questions instead the very notion of 'facts' – of data-driven, literally-minded, target-oriented, evidence-based 'facts'.

There is a world of difference between culture and acculturation. The former keeps a tradition alive by re-describing, challenging and revisiting its key principles. The latter is effectively a form of indoctrination: it simply recycles the tenets of the approach as if they were dogmas which are then passed on from one generation to the next.

When a therapeutic/philosophical approach is comprised of a set of stale notions, it will most likely be demoted from the rank of living *culture* to that of *acculturation*: what was once a vibrant doctrine becomes indoctrination. Perhaps one can find inspiration from considering a key notion that comes from the phenomenology of Merleau-Ponty (1989). A central method of enquiry, later applied to the psychotherapeutic endeavour, is that of *description*. The counsellor helps the client describe his experience, and is herself engaged in describing phenomena as they emerge in the therapy room. Description aids clarification, exploration, insight. But at times description is effectively re-description: this is particularly true when a familiar belief or response in the client's way of being-in-the-world is for the first time perceived in a new light. Similarly with culture (science, art – even religion): every epoch either discards or describes *anew* a particular tenet. In this sense then a paradigm shift is partly an act of re-description.

Re-vision is also *re-expression*, i.e. 'simultaneously a matter of refusing to transcend what is given and refusing to accept it' (Barber, 2014, p. 70).

I.7

PCT has been described as political naive and all-too-ready to embrace whichever view is dominant in science at any given time. This often means that PCT's compassionate engagement in practice fails to translate in the field of theory.

Can PCT embody a coherent alternative to the sweeping neoliberal, neopositivist take-over of the humanities? What would it take to revive at various levels (e.g. between trainers and trainees, clients and therapists, or in the production of person-centred literature itself) a more congruent and uncompromising stance that reinstates a therapeutic philosophy and a way of being that *refuses to mimic* dominant narratives? How can we reaffirm counter-traditional values in person-centred psychotherapy and counselling? These were some of the urgent questions I had in mind at the beginning of this project, and when I posed them to potential contributors in my invitation, the response was not only overwhelmingly positive, but also painstakingly precise in its articulation. The result is a collection of essays that may open a new path for contemporary PCT, pointing out ways to assimilate recent progressive developments *and* renewing vital links to its radical roots.

This assemblage of clinical studies and vignettes, of personal reflections, of in-depth discussions on aspects of theory and of crucial links to philosophy, spirituality and contemporary culture is shot through with passion, innovation and commitment to progressive practice.

I warmly invite readers to partake of this knowledge and share the enthusiasm for the practice of person-centred therapy. I invite you to help expand and deepen the existing body of theory and encourage others to participate in the joys and challenges of contemporary person-centred practice.

References

Barber, D.C. (2014) *Deleuze and the Naming of God: Post-Secularism and the Future of Immanence*. Edinburgh: Edinburgh University Press.

Deleuze, G. & Guattari, F. (1982) *Anti-Oedipus: Capitalism and Schizophrenia*, trans. by R. Hurley, M. Seem, and H. R. Lane. Minneapolis, MN: University of Minnesota Press. First published in 1972.

Kim, H.-J. (1975). *Eihei Dōgen – Mystical Realist*. Tucson: University of Arizona Press.

Merleau-Ponty, M. (1989) *Phenomenology of Perception*. London: Routledge. First published in 1945.

FYODOR E. VASILYUK

28 September 1953–17 September 2017

Tatiana Karyagina and Fedor Shankov

> The age of a dandelion is short, but the day is long.
> The blossom dissolved, but the light endures.
> A lightweight sky. Preparing for flight with no fuss.
> The soul is weightless. Awaits for an ongoing breeze.
> *Fyodor E. Vasilyuk*

Fyodor E. Vasilyuk, Doctor of Psychological Sciences, Professor, leading researcher at the laboratory of counseling psychology and psychotherapy of the Psychological Institute of Russian Academy of Education, head of the department of individual and group psychotherapy at Moscow State University of Psychology and Education, president of the Russian Association for Co-experiencing Psychotherapy, passed away on 17 September 2017 after several years of fight with cancer, leaving behind his wife, three children, five grandchildren, thankful and grieving clients, students and colleagues.

Fyodor was born in a family of geologists in 1953 in Donetsk. His father was a World War II veteran. Experience of conquering mountain peaks with his father in childhood clearly grew into the courage to tackle academic peaks. Fyodor Vasilyuk was a pioneer in many ways. He is a founder of Russia's first department for psychological counseling and psychotherapy, the initiator and first editor of the first Russian counseling and psychotherapy journal – formerly *Moscow Psychotherapeutic Journal*, now *Counselling Psychology and Psychotherapy*. One of his last projects was a conceptual framework of an international psychological center in Russia, which is the first one to function on the basis of insurance companies. Now it has over 200,000 clients and represents an important step towards the recognition of the necessity and importance of a properly regulated comprehensive system of psychological help in Russia at the state level.

He is an author of an original psychotherapeutic approach – *Co-experiencing Psychotherapy*, which he characterized as a result of grafting Carl Rogers' person-centred approach onto a tree of Russian cultural-activity tradition in psychology.

Vasilyuk was a direct student of some among the best of Russian psychologists: A.R. Luria, B.F. Zeigarnik, A.N. Leontiev, M.K. Mamardashvili, V.P. Zinchenko and others. From his postgraduate thesis emerged the book *Psychology of Experiencing* (1984). Until now, it is one of the most highly cited in the post-Soviet psychology literature. Purely theoretical, this book was written when psychological practice as such did not exist in the Soviet Union. But it foresaw this practice, and with the opening of the opportunity for its appearance, this book became an important source for its growing and development. In 1991, the book was translated into English and published in the UK (Vasilyuk, 1991a). In a letter to Gendlin, where he invites him to participate in a Co-experiencing conference, Vasilyuk modestly writes:

> It so happened, that I learned about your book *Experiencing and Creation of Meaning* only after I had already written my book [...] I have to confess it was a joyful delay: had I read your book earlier, there would be no point in writing another one on the same topic.
>
> *(personal communication)*

Fyodor was also the author of the first translation of Gendlin's paper – on sub-verbal communication - in Russia. His wife Olga Filippovskaya wrote a wonderful preface to the translation of Gendlin's *Focusing-oriented Psychotherapy*.

Meeting with Carl Rogers in Moscow in 1986 grew into finding a purpose in his life (see a broader description of his experience in his chapter in this book). By the way, Rogers himself mentioned him in his article about a trip to USSR:

> There was strong feeling that some should be thrown out [of the group], especially one man who had brought a melon as a peace offering, indicating that he knew he was not on the list but wanted to be anyway…
>
> *(Rogers, 1987, p. 52)*

Well, he did bring a watermelon to the group from the Crimea, where he worked then, in a small psychiatric clinic, where he had much more freedom and opportunities to fulfill his ideas than in Moscow. He went to Moscow to see Rogers' group without being in the list, but feeling absolutely sure, that he *had* to be there. That day was his 33rd birthday.

In his book *Experiencing and Prayer*, Vasilyuk (2005) says: 'not only the truth of one's personal falling can be "horrifying", but, for example, the truth of realizing your calling, which can be also frightening, having no apparent fulfillment' (p. 135).

He started to fulfill his calling that he felt during an encounter with Rogers by developing his own approach, which grew on the basis of the theory of experiencing and within the methodological paradigm of psychotechnics, which was developed by Vygotsky. This methodology is aimed to overcome the schism between academic psychology and psychological practice and could be a concrete answer to questions such as: 'What is the kind of science psychology should be so as to be able to extract knowledge from practice, to reflect the experience of practice, to generalize and make use of it – for the goals of its own development, and in order to improve the quality of psychotherapeutic education?' Or: 'How can the practice be organized so as to communicate with science, receive concepts from it and be a source of knowledge?' And: 'What is the role of philosophy, art and religion in understanding and substantiating of psychological practice?'

From this approach grew several new concepts and procedures: models of consciousness; structure of the psychotherapeutic situation; levels of co-experiencing; polyphonic supervision, that included experts from different professions to gain depth in understanding a psychotherapeutic case (philosophers, priests, artists, etc.), and so on (Vasilyuk, 2015). Students of Vasilyuk's workshops are notable for their sophisticated understanding of psychotherapeutic thinking and for a quality of reflection in their practice. In many other ways Fyodor stayed a consistent and loyal student both to Vygotsky's methodological clarity and Rogers' values and teachings in relation to counseling and psychotherapy.

More than a hundred articles, authored by Fyodor Vasilyuk, reflect the unique gift of addressing a Word – living, sensitive and poetic. He was able to see and name the subtle and intangible phenomena of experiencing and co-experiencing, uncovering their essence in a truly astonishing way.

In addition to these merits, each of the hundreds of his students, clients, colleagues – everyone who had ever experienced his involvement, faith, creative genius – was inspired by his simultaneous humility and strength, his glow and his sense of humour …

Besides academic challenges and his brilliant psychotherapeutic work, he carried out many deeds. He was truly a Person – in the sense of one who gave his life to what he believed in. Here are a few examples.

In 2016, when the war in his native Donetsk unfolded, his mother's museum, where she held her life collections of precious stones and minerals, was bombed. She fell with a stroke. Without saying anything to anyone, Vasilyuk took a month off during the academic year and went right into the epicenter of a war zone in order to take care of her.

He initiated the gathering of a group of Moscow psychologists in order to help the citizens after the devastating Armenian earthquake in 1988.

The chapter in the current book is his last one (Karyagina & Vasilyuk, 2018). He edited it despite going through two courses of chemotherapy, when he was not able to talk but only write for an hour a day.

Many things become apparent only now. After his death, several hundred people gathered to share how generously he supported them with advice, money and personal involvement. It is known that he had a thick list of names of the dead and the living for an everyday prayer. Let us hope, that we will capitalize on his lessons on how to be alive and to live genuinely, fearlessly facing all the challenges with courage, and to also practise what we believe in.

In an article about experiencing sorrow, arguing with Freud, Vasilyuk wrote:

> Human grief is not destructive (forgetting, breaking away, distancing), but constructive; its job is not to scatter, but to gather, not to destroy, but to create — create a memory
>
> *(Vasilyuk, 1991b, p. 232)*

References

Karyagina, T. & Vasilyuk, F. (2018) Dialectics of person and experiencing, in Bazzano, M. (Ed.), *Re-visioning Person-centred Therapy: Theory and Practice of a Radical Paradigm*. Abingdon: Routledge (in English).

Rogers, C.R. (1987) Inside the world of the Soviet professional. *Counseling and Values*, 32: 47–66. doi:10.1002/j.2161-007X.1987.tb00690.x (in English).

Vasilyuk, F.E. (1991a) *The Psychology of Experiencing*. London: Harvester Wheatsheaf (in English).

Vasilyuk, F.E. (1991b) Perezhit' gore (Experiencing grief) // O chelovecheskom v cheloveke (On humane in human) / Draft. E.V. Filippova; Edit. I. T. Frolova. – Moscow: Politizdat. Pp. 230–247 (in Russian).

Vasilyuk, F.E. (2005) *Perezhivaniye i molitva. Opyt obshchepsikhologicheskogo issledovaniya* (Experiencing and Prayer. From the point of view of general psychology). Moscow: Smysl (in Russian).

Vasilyuk, F.E. (2015) Coexperiencing psychotherapy as a psychotechnical system. *Journal of Russian & East European Psychology*, 52(1), 1–58, doi:10.1080/10610405.2015.1064721 (in English).

PART I
Some kinds of love: person-centred therapy and the relational dimension

Part I

1

THERAPY AS AN ACCIDENT WAITING TO HAPPEN

Julie Webb

Old tradition – new wave

>Accidental therapy – a
>Poesis that beckons
>The uncomfortable
>Precarious and fragile
>Becoming.
>Unconvinced of the
>Shamanic pretence of
>Pseudo-science
>The accidental therapist
>Can only practise
>Her faith in the
>Old tradition that
>De facto travels permanently
>On the crest of a
>New wave.

From: Samantha Coldman
To: Julie Webb
Subject: Re: Hello

Hi Julie,

It was so good to be back in touch and I was fascinated to hear that you are now a psychotherapist! I think that is so fantastic and really worthwhile, giving something back eh. I bet you hear some stories. Was Freud right – is it all about sex? Hahaha ☺
Sam

From: Julie Webb
To: Samantha Coldman
Subject: Re: Hello

Hi Sam,

I am enjoying being back in contact with you too, and feel so glad that we met up after all these years. As for being a therapist, I don't know that it is about 'giving back' for me. I have no altruistic motive, of that I am certain. I have to make a living so that I can house myself, feed and clothe myself. I want to do that in a way that makes me feel alive, that gives me time and space to think, to write, to walk, to breathe. I've done plenty of mind numbing jobs in my life-time so far, as you probably remember. I feel I know the difference between feeling alive in my work and feeling dead it in. I know the difference between feeling alive and dead in my life *per se*. Anyhow, it seemed natural that I would find myself on this path for a while.

I notice I wince after typing that :-/. I think I am supposed to be doing it for altruistic reasons. I think that is why my profession is expected to do so much free work or low paid work, we are supposed to be members of a sainthood – in more ways than one! As for it all being about sex, I am not a Freudian psychotherapist, I am a person-centred one, so I don't approach the client from that frame to begin with ☺.
Julie

From: Samantha Coldman
To: Julie Webb
Subject: Re: Hello

I think I know what you mean. I have been really bored in jobs, same old same old – that's why I gave up. I'm disappointed it's not all about sex otherwise I might have re-trained ☺. So, what is a person-centred therapist then? Or am I being a bit thick – is the clue in the title?
Sam

From: Julie Webb
To: Samantha Coldman
Subject: Re: Hello

Sam, I don't remember there ever being anything thick about you. You'd think the clue would be in the title wouldn't you, but I feel the title doesn't actually do it justice now. Back in the day (1950s) when the term client-centred was coined by its founder Carl Rogers, it was in reaction to Freudian psychoanalysis and pre-scriptive technique – you know, kind of knowing everything upfront and then making your client fit into the knowing – a kind of set theory. I would say I am more engaged with description than prescription and set theories. That is not to discredit Freud, his work was, and still is, very valuable – he was a pioneer after all, especially where ideas of unconscious process are concerned. Although you

wouldn't believe that talking to some therapists. I work with unconscious process (I would call it an actualizing tendency) in so far as I wait for it to reveal itself and its meaning for the client, not me. I mean, how could I possibly know someone else's unconscious process when I cannot know my own – that is why we call it unconscious isn't it?! Don't get me started …
Julie.

From: Samantha Coldman
To: Julie Webb
Subject: Re: Hello

So you don't have a set theory? What do you mean? And aren't you supposed to be able to know what's going on with a person? Isn't that the point of going to see a therapist? I have been close to seeing one myself, God knows I need one at the moment, life is so blah. I know I was upbeat when we first got back in touch but well, it's not easy for me, and Tom's always away, the kids have gone off doing their own thing and well, you probably deal with this stuff all the time but I am soooo bored and weepy ALL the time, and now you've got me doubting going to see a therapist that I thought could sort me out!
S.

From: Julie Webb
To: Samantha Coldman
Subject: Re: Hello

I'm sorry to hear that life feels blah for you Sam. Feeling bored and weepy sounds draining, and with Tom away and the kids off doing their thing I can imagine your boredom and weepiness. I am wondering how boredom and weepiness may be linked for you or not? It is not my wish to put you off seeking help. I am curious as to what it is that I have said that may have put you off, but perhaps the clue is in the questions that you have asked. I will try and answer them …

Set theory: I do work with a theory of sorts; a person-centred (PC) theory, but I feel it is more to do with concepts, backdrops, and attitudes than anything written in stone as a method or formula – despite how it is often so reductively taught. Concepts, backdrops and attitudes are a bit of a problem in the current culture of evaluation, statistics, and having to show at every breath I take that my breathing is of benefit to the client and by extension the organization's feel-good stats and targets. Of course, I want to be of aid. I feel better taking my fee when I feel that I am actually aiding the person who is paying for my time, but I can't afford to be too invested in that feeling either. The PC approach is grounded in a concept about the conditions required for optimizing that aid and that is grounded in what is fast becoming a radical ethics. It is my job to meet the client empathically (you know, can I put myself in the client's shoes? Of course, not fully or else I would lose sight of myself – though sometimes it might be advantageous for me to lose sight of me for a while); an attitude of non-judgement, an attempt to not judge the person adversely (though apparently it is OK for me to prize and encourage autonomy, how I do that without judging is beyond me); it is helpful apparently if I can be myself and not pretend to be an expert about the client's life or predicament (this is sometimes challenging as all too often I do not know myself – how can I possibly?). I am trying not to be too theoretical or else I could end up writing you an essay!

Knowing: This is a tricky one to answer as clients mostly arrive thinking I know stuff. I mean why would you cough up £60 an hour to someone you think *doesn't* know stuff?! I think though, it is more about my aspiration for an unconditional openness towards the client (and myself), than my knowing anything. Of course, I have spent many years training and being educated for the work. As you know, one of my backdrops is philosophy and that still underpins not just my work, but my very being in the world full stop. I guess then, I have a particular understanding and world view that necessarily impacts my work, because in a way, *I am my work*. I don't really have anything more tangible to offer than *me*. ☺.

Anyhow, I hope that helps clarify a little for you Sam. I would hate for you to be put off seeking help from a therapist just because of a misunderstanding created by me.
J.

From: Samantha Coldman
To: Julie Webb
Subject: Re: Hello

Crikey, that was more than I expected, but thanks for the explanation – I think! It sounds simple on the one hand and yet complicated on the other. You don't want to judge but find that you do. You aim to be yourself but don't always know what that is, and you want to understand from the client's point of view but have to keep yourself separate somehow or else you get 'lost' but getting lost might be helpful? Plus, there is not really a method or formula, it's all about concepts and backdrops, you have to understand stuff but not necessarily know stuff, and philosophy underpins your work although you are it – the work.

What little I know about therapy is that it's a space where I can come and talk and not be judged whilst I fathom stuff out. I mean it's the worst thing being judged eh. So, if you were sitting there listening to me talking about all my secrets, and thinking I was a dippy mare, or not very kind, or deceitful or something – would you say it? Because that would just make me feel like shit – although I would probably know by the look on your face without you saying it – either way – rubbish.

Don't you have to know how my brain works and why I think the way I do so that I can stop it?

I pondered on your question as to whether my boredom linked with my weepiness. It made me cry just thinking about it. I just feel a bit lost, kind of empty. I can be sitting there and just start crying for no reason and then I get irritated when Tom comes home, and he's been all busy and just wants to chill out. I know I should get a hobby or a job, just do something but I don't know what. Well, actually, I

do go to a book club on Wednesday mornings. I don't cry those days, mainly because the lovely Chris does such a good job of uplifting my spirits with knowledge and wit. Actually, emailing you lifts me a little too, even though the question you asked made me cry. It just all felt a bit hopeless in that moment. Maybe that's why I cry, I feel hopeless or life feels hopeless or something like that. What's it all for? I bet you're thinking I am dippy mare now ☺.
Sx

From: Julie Webb
To: Samantha Coldman
Subject: Re: Hello

Hi Sam,

It sounds like it really matters what I think of you. For the record, I have never felt you to be 'dippy'. Is that maybe how you see yourself? What if you are dippy Sam, what then? Wednesday book club looks important to you and Chris seems to make an uplifting impact on you and your day.

I am really enjoying you making me question what it is that I do as a therapist. Clients do it when they get angry with me for not fixing them or feeling undervalued by me somehow. I thrive on these moments in the work as they are sometimes the site for great movement. I mean, who cares what I think? Who am I in the scheme of things? Actually, there is a part of me that thinks it a real audacity to sell oneself as a therapist. I do spend most of the time disabusing clients of thinking I know better how to be a human than they do. In fact, I would say that is a prime factor in the work. Anyway, my current thinking is more an urge towards embracing the animal than the human. Our animality is more honest I feel, but that's another story. Therapy isn't about me knowing something clients don't. I think you are absolutely right – of course you will know if I am judging you. You are not stupid and neither are any of the clients that I have worked with: traumatized and troubled they might be, stupid they are not. Therapy is about movement. For sure, validation or soothing may be part of the dance, but it seems that when a client arrives feeling something has changed or moved then it seems therapy happened. I also think that by and large therapy happens outside of the therapy room in between sessions, so I don't always get to witness the moment. I usually hear the reporting of it, or observe the change. Sometimes the movement is in me too – how could it not be? I find that my work can be like reading a novel in the very moment and process of it being written. We have numerous drafts, and are constantly spell checking, with a thesaurus always at hand to find the right word to create the best description of the moment that shows us something in a new light. You know better than me, that the best writing always *shows* us something, rather than *tells* us something explicitly. It seems to me that the showing and the seeing can lead to subtle or great movement of the senses. I am back to movement again: a chance and a dance between the senses.

As for aiming to be myself but not always knowing myself, that is really about being willing to be open to the surprise. I mean, I might find in the moment that I have prejudices I didn't know I had, new feelings about past situations I thought had been dealt with, desires I didn't know were there. In fact, come to think of it, I sincerely hope that the truth is I can never know myself, otherwise I have no surprises left in life, and what a tragedy that would be. Thinking I really, really, know myself upfront in all my glory is likely to come crashing down in disappointing horror – and it has done so many times. Every person and situation that I encounter in life is going to bring up feelings that I didn't know I had, and that has to be wonderful!

You don't really want to get me started on the brain, or rather I don't want you to get me started on the brain. It seems to me that the latest neuroscientific findings have been hijacked by pop-psychology and meditation apps re-describing our existence as though we are just a brain on a pillow: a constant conflating of mind being IN the brain and not in my big toe too; no need of a body, anyone else, or chocolate cake – and what would I do without chocolate cake I ask?

I was wondering what you were reading at book club at the moment? I remember our uni days... ☺

Jx

From: Samantha Coldman
To: Julie Webb
Subject: Re: Hello

Well, you are never going to believe it, but I am reading *Room with a View* – haha good old Forster. Oh, do you remember our uni days? The laughter, and me having a crush on every tutor I encountered. I mean bloody hell, I married one – what was all that about? I feel like a completely different person now. I have no interests, no energy, and I can't remember the last time I had a really good laugh. Well, I say that but I have a good laugh on Wednesdays, and I do really look forward to going and being with the group. Chris creates a really happy and light-hearted vibe and I feel full of energy afterwards.

Sx

From: Julie Webb
To: Samantha Coldman
Subject: Re: Hello

Ahh Lucy must have a view! The right kind of view though. I never really reconciled within myself whether Lucy chose her own view. We as readers were supposed to find Miss Bartlett's constricted and constrained view for Lucy as a metaphor for the stuffy bourgeoisie. We were then called upon to accept George as some kind of Hades stealing his woman for a life underground, and of course after great struggle Lucy as Persephone succumbs. I would have much preferred Lucy to be not so genteel and create her own view and *beg* George to drag her away by her hair, into his underground cave.

I do remember your tutor cravings. There is a real energy in having a crush and you always seemed to be a bundle of energy in those days. I notice I feel a little sad that you feel you don't laugh much and have no interests. Except for your Wednesdays of course. Is Chris one of the members or is he the group leader or something?

Jx

From: Samantha Coldman
To: Julie Webb
Subject: Re: Hello

OMG! There was always something violent about your view of the world and isn't that a bit of a backward step for us women – being dragged by our hair into the man cave ☺? And don't be too hard on Forster, he was writing in a particular time and place. He is writing about freedom and love and unrestricted passion, and with such colour. The imagery is just delicious.

I think I was sounding a bit depressed in my other emails eh? I am sorry about that. I will try and be more upbeat from now on.

As for Chris, SHE is a tutor from the college and runs this book club. I just love her energy and there is something about her and the way she gets us to look at texts. She is a bit edgy too, comes out with stuff and makes connections I hadn't seen or thought of. I feel like I expand somehow when I am with her. Of course, then I come home and within half an hour I have dropped down again. Tell ya what … I wouldn't mind Chris dragging me by my hair into her cave ;-).

Sx

From: Julie Webb
To: Samantha Coldman
Subject: Re: Hello

I have never thought of my view as violent before and really appreciate that observation. And I think you are right in a way: maybe I am ferocious. Ferociously alive. Except when I am not. I feel that I witness violence with a small 'v' all of the time, as I watch people surreptitiously try and constrain and control others. I witness it in myself too: that twist in my gut when things aren't going my way. It seems we humans want to control everyone and everything: our feelings, our thoughts, our actions, the future, the present … we can be a self-righteous pack. There is a trend in therapy to diagnose a breath, breathed in a different way, as some kind of disorder or problem to be solved, by a professional fixer. Well, I am not interested in being a fixer-up-er or a magician with a bag of tricks that I got from the secret club of therapists that people in trouble don't seem to have access to. And it is confusing because there are some areas of therapy that advocate they do have the secret – do this, do that. I often find myself just sitting in silence with a client, but that can be treated as some kind of not doing whereas in fact, often there is a great deal going on.

I have found that it can be really alarming for people when they realize they have all the power in their very own hands.

A backward step, really is that what you think it would be for women? I feel a backward step is wanting to be dragged into the cave, asking to be dragged into the cave and then feeling guilty about it and afterwards accusing others of some injustice, becoming a victim, and somehow abdicating responsibility for the feelings that they actually had.

Apologies about assuming Chris was male. My stereotypical thinking thwarts me sometimes! I can really hear how energized and expansive you feel around her and I notice I felt a thud in my body when you described an energy drop when you are at home. I felt the energy rise again at the thought of you being dragged into a cave by her. I haven't experienced you being depressed in your emails and wondered why you use that term and why you would feel you have to be upbeat?
Jx

From: Samantha Coldman
To: Julie Webb
Subject: Re: Hello

Hold on a minute. If you haven't got any 'tricks' as you call them, what is it that you do exactly? And what is the problem with diagnosis? What if I am depressed and that is causing me to feel bored and makes me cry a lot? What if it can be treated? As for you mistaking Chris for a man, I suppose that is understandable, after all I did go out with half the lecturers at uni and none of them were women. It is strange finding myself so attracted to her, but I think about her all the time, wondering what she is doing, where she lives, what she eats, what music she likes. Do you think I have another crush? Haha – that would be mad eh, and bad, very bad.
Sx
PS: what is the point of being down? Surely it is better that I try and be upbeat?

From: Julie Webb
To: Samantha Coldman
Subject: Re: Hello

Why 'mad, and bad, very bad'? You find yourself in a strange place being attracted to Chris and I hear all the questions about what she likes. I am curious about what you imagine the answers to be. I have no idea whether you have a crush or even what a crush is for you – how could I possibly?

I couldn't quite tell from your email whether you are exasperated with me for not having any tricks. I get exasperated sometimes, I wish I did have a trick or a magic wand that just took all dilemmas and troublesome feelings away, but then isn't that the wonder of travelling through this short life that we have? Hitting a wall of dilemma decorated with graffiti-like desires and imaginings of possibility. Isn't the anxiety of dilemma, choice and possibility wonderful because it is full of life and tells us something matters, something is afoot? Could anxiety really be a creative energy for us to play with – a deep inner experience of something pure at work? I notice I am feeling really energized by our conversation Sam, and I remember all those years ago the conversations we would have into the wee small hours about Shakespeare and Forster and then Ballard and Roth. I always felt energized around you.

I am sorry if you feel I have dismissed any idea that you might be depressed and that something may be wrong with you. If you feel that something is physically wrong perhaps a trip to your doctor may be helpful to you. As for your PS: maybe there is no *point* to feeling down, or feeling upbeat. Maybe feeling down or upbeat is informing you of something and the experience is valuable in itself.
Jx

From: Samantha Coldman
To: Julie Webb
Subject: Re: Hello

Well if I wasn't exasperated, I am now. What do you mean, 'what would be bad' about me having a crush on Chris? I am married with two kids. Can you imagine the damage it would cause to everyone if I had an affair with her? Can you? No, you can't because you never commit to anyone do you? Still single all these years, what's that about Julie? And as for anxiety being the site of 'creative energy' – give me a break. My anxiety is bloody awful – I haven't slept in weeks for all these thoughts looping in my mind – which I've got to tell you feel like they ARE in my head – well except for when I feel sick. But anyway, it seems reasonable to go and see my doctor for a pill to help me sleep or stop my anxiety or something. Clearly no point in going to see a therapist to just go around in circles talking about it. I need something to happen. Yes, thank you, I do remember our conversations about Shakey and Roth & co., but you always managed to throw a spanner in the works by being a smart arse and bringing in soddin' Wittgenstein or Nietzsche or some other bloody philosopher that turned everything on its head and here you are doing it again. I am not twenty anymore, I have responsibilities and my family matter to me. Aaaarrrgh....

From: Julie Webb
To: Samantha Coldman
Subject: Re: Hello

Hi Sam,

My response to your last message seems to have really upset you. I was a little shocked and clearly hadn't realized that your crush has led to sleepless nights and thoughts of damage that may be done by having an affair with Chris. I can really hear your distress feeling anxious and sick. It wasn't my intention to diminish your experience by offering my own thoughts about what anxiety can be. Whilst I can hear the panic it seems to have caused you, and I can absolutely hear how important your family are, I make no apologies for my take on anxiety and for what it can offer me in terms of affirming my own lived experience.

It may be crass to say, and it may exasperate you even further, but I have to say I really enjoyed the energy you brought to our conversation in that last email. And you may be right: sometimes I am a smart arse. I can hear my mother now 'answer for everything', although she would always add 'just like your father'. She had always attributed freedom of speech to men and not women, which was really about her not feeling that she had the power to speak out at my father. A catty remark to me though is doable – good for her I say.

I was saddened to know that my speaking about philosophy felt like a 'spanner in the works'. You described the wonderful energy that Chris brings to your discussions by making connections, well, that is what philosophy does for me – it brings an energy and connection; a clarity that therapeutic writings often do not.

As for being single now, I can only imagine what state you were in to make such wounding remarks about my personal commitments.

I hope our conversations continue Sam, I really do, and I am sorry if what I have said is adding to your distress and dilemma at this time. I hope to hear from you soon.

Jx

From: Samantha Coldman
To: Julie Webb
Subject: Re: Hello

Julie,

I have pondered on your message for a week now. My head was spinning and yes, I was in a state, in fact, I didn't go to reading group. I have booked an appointment to see my doctor next week. I don't want to lose touch with you again but you are right – you are a smart arse, or at least that is how it feels for me sometimes, and I do feel diminished by you. So anyway, I decided to go over our emails and critique them. I have several questions that perhaps you could kindly say more about because at the time, I'll be honest, I kind of skipped over them. Partly because I didn't understand the point you were trying to make, and partly because they made me angry. So, to keep our conversation going, despite being as mad as I was, I do like our conversations and don't want to lose contact again, can you say what you mean about these quotes:

1. 'radical ethics'
2. 'a real audacity to sell oneself as a therapist'
3. 'our animality is more honest'
4. 'shows rather than tells'
5. 'they all have power in their own hands'.

Best,
Sam.

From: Julie Webb
To: Samantha Coldman
Subject: Re: Hello

Hello Sam,

It was so good to receive your message. I noticed that the back of my throat caught and tears welled, and I was really pleased to read that you wanted to keep contact. I shall do my best to explain my thoughts behind the statements that you have selected, although time has passed since I first wrote them, but anyway, here goes:

1 Radical ethics

The PC approach to therapy has been diluted so much in order to fit in with other therapeutic approaches (even those completely at odds ethically) that now it feels fitting to call the approach radical. Much literature and training describes PC in the context of therapy being all about creating the relationship and gives a simple nod to some very complex human aspirations such as empathy, unconditional positive regard and congruence (I described those earlier but not in those words). Apparently, if we can establish this relationship, which may take a session or two, it can be dispensed with or re-engaged if the relationship feels to be going awry. Then we can move on to doing a bit of CBT or two chair-work, or bringing out a bag of tricks in order to make therapy happen without any sense of the ethical importance that the PC approach to human distress brings. I want to say PC is not about establishing a relationship at all, and certainly not in the strange and often all too pleasing way it is taught and spoken about. It is about ethics par excellence.

Why ethics? Because the approach recognizes the value in our separation and our relatedness. Not relationship. I think they are two very different things.

Sometimes my client and I are completely at odds. I may not like him. I may not agree with him. I may not be able to accept his views. But here's the thing – it is not my place to accept or not, to agree or not, to like or not – they will be situations that we find ourselves in and we will, for sure, experience those differences. The ethics at play are not just about me taking some high and mighty stance about accepting another human being, but about both the client *and* me, finding a way to accommodate one another and our differences. Can we share the space that we find ourselves in? Will we be able to bear the atmosphere that we have created between us? It is not about me having the power to make a person be an accomplice in creating some agreeable, cosy, little friendship that actually I will forget about in my daily life or at least, most certainly after therapy is over. All I can do is aspire to be hospitable to the *other*, notice my experience as we engage, share that if I feel it could help, which is a delicate move sometimes as you have experienced with me Sam.

It is radical because it seems to be the only approach left that has patience enough to let whatever stirrings are being experienced come fully to the fore, in their own time, and be explored, without me saying whether or not it is right to do so. It is radical because all I am really interested in is the moment to moment experiencing and working with that, without trying to attribute sly little explanations of 'maybe you feel like that because dad took your toy train away when you were five years old'. Of course, it is easy to slip into that mode of thinking after years of training and working in this field because we can recognize some patterns, but every script is different for every person.

It is radical because the PC approach asks: Can I open myself to the possibility and probability of change within myself? Can I sit with anguish and anxiety that client work sometimes brings up in me? Can I open myself to the *other* and to the *other* in myself that I have not yet met? This idea has deep philosophical roots that is greatly lacking in the field of therapy as we err more and more towards creating a bag of tools to carve out our knowing with.

2 A real audacity …

Sometimes I am provocative. But let's think about this for a moment. What am I offering a person for £60 per hour? Me. And who the devil am I? No one. I know no more about being human than anyone else. I don't work to scripts. I have no formula to get my client through the day. I have no magic wand to wave their troubles away. I have conversation, a critical ear, a room detached from all other areas of mine and the client's daily life – a space we can call our own for accommodating one another in our encounter. Sometimes we may not have a room, sometimes we may go for a walk. Could the client get what he needs from anyone? – yes – but for some reason that seems unapparent, or unavailable and so he chooses to pay for therapy.

3 …animality is more honest

I find myself beginning to doubt the importance of the human. The human seems to attribute to herself great knowledge, reasoning and rationality as some kind of omnipotence, and a way to justify owning the world. Yet what I experience both within myself and from my encounter with others is that we flounder. Largely I feel because we have forgotten to pay attention to that tiny stirring deep within the belly that grows and erupts. That part of us that is animal. We are driven by want, and so is the animal and we want to separate ourselves from the animal as though it is something base, unattractive and unknowing. Well the animal knows something pure, and the purity may be base, unattractive and unknowing. How can I develop my ability to notice, pay attention, explore, enquire and perhaps embrace that part of me? And how can I accommodate the *other* when he needs to explore that in therapy? I aspire to be more animal and less the all-knowing human being sat in my therapist's chair.

4 Showing rather than telling …

I feel this to be fairly self-explanatory, particularly given your background in literature, but in the context of therapy, I try to refrain from telling a client what they should do, or what the state of affairs is for them. If I can just stay alongside them whilst they speak their narrative, then maybe they will hear their own story and choose to write anew. In that they we will see for themselves how they wish to lead their lives and possibilities and options for how they may do that.

5 ... power in their hands ...

When I go to therapy, it is usually because I have lost the power to see myself clearly enough to see my choices in life; to see that every step is my own; to take responsibility for my choosing even if my steps cause great upheaval. Equally to accept that I may not choose to cause great upheaval, and that equally is my power. For example, I do not have to choose the party-line or the status quo and when my anxiety stirs in my body therapy aids my ability to sit still and look at it and decide for myself what to do with it.

I hope all that is helpful somehow Sam. If it isn't, then it isn't, and I notice how tired I feel writing all that explanation to you. Perhaps I should have just given you a reading list, but I suspect maybe it isn't about you needing to know anything.

J x

From: Samantha Coldman
To: Julie Webb
Subject: Re: Hello

Hi Julie,

Sorry for the delay, it has taken me a while to digest all that and my feelings. I think you are right. I didn't need to know all that, though it has helped a bit. I think I needed to lash out and test you somehow; show you, or prove to myself that I am not stupid. I am very grateful for the attention you gave to answering my questions. I still haven't been back to my reading group. Something you said earlier in our conversation about you feeling energized by my upset struck a chord with me. I was pretty energized too (even though it made me really angry). There was action somehow. I took a pen and critiqued our emails and demanded you answer questions. I felt shaky but I liked it. I don't know what the infatuation with Chris is all about, and I still want to go there, but I'd like to understand my motives a little more. I am aware I want some action, some movement, and I want to feel alive, not bored and weepy. I have begun researching therapists. Am I right, did you mean that you have therapy? I still want somebody to tell me what is the best thing to do, but I do heed your words. I will keep you posted. I am sorry I tired you out and brought tears, and I was surprised that you responded to me. I am so glad that you did. Clearly you have seen the light in a way that I haven't – yet ☺
Take care,
Sam x

From: Julie Webb
To: Samantha Coldman
Subject: Re: Hello

Hi Sam,

It is good to hear from you. Good luck in your search for a therapist – and yes I do engage in therapy myself. It feels like we have both been on a bit of a journey as we get to know one another again and explore where we find ourselves in life at the moment.

Fortunately, I have never seen the light. I feel that is for *other-worldly* beings. I value not being other-worldly and only wish to be grounded in this moment, even if the ground falls away. I find that being a therapist is mostly a bitter-sweet agony.

I have sold fruit and veg, and chandeliers. I have administered and managed. I have taught and graded. But, engaging with another human being *without selling stuff*; engaging in the tender exploration of our very being as it is born, feels like the only practice worth engaging in to me. Yes, I feel that it is a practice, and a political one at that. I never know upfront how the practice will unfold, what the road is going to look like, and where the devil we will end up; and, make no mistake, it is always a *we*, even if the end results in two separate singularities housing their multiplicities and walking away in opposite directions. We are always affected by the *other*.

Take good care Sam, I hope we meet up again soon.
Love, Julie x

2

THE PSYCHOTHERAPEUTIC ENCOUNTER AS A POLITICAL ACT OF MICRO MULTITUDE

Claudio Rud

Introduction

This chapter outlines some of the developments I have been working on, based on findings made in clinical practice and the latter's connection to an alternative political project at variance with the one currently prevailing in the world, at least in the West and especially in my country, Argentina. From these premises, I will then try to develop an understanding of subjectivity which links person-centred therapy as a political practice that spills over onto the social field with a democratic political project that contains a similar philosophical basis of shared power, acceptance of differences, and the search for the common good that Spinoza (Negri, 2004; Deleuze, 2001) defines as *multitude*.

I understand the psychotherapeutic encounter as an instance of *micro multitude*, where the increase of common power does not imply the effacement of each singular power. The constitution of this event involves the questioning of the identity of the participants as fixed and neatly-defined entities, and promotes presence as a creative act, as well as the understanding that such relationship is what determines who we are at that moment.

Political considerations

Here are two everyday neoliberal statements heard in conversation in Argentina: 'Let's not talk about politics, let's talk about personal projects.' 'The motto of our time is peace, dialogue and democratic commitment' (never mind exorbitant increases in the price of public utilities and in the midst of police repression, legislative outrage, crushing of social achievements, violation of the law and so forth).

This new form of late capitalism, inherited from savage capitalism and defined as *neoliberalism*, has consequences that are translated into daily life and that affect us as subjects submitted to the imperative of the system, manipulated by the mass media of the global corporate power generating what is now defined as the 'post-truth', a word that entered the Oxford dictionary in 2016. We bear this condition in our countries, in our groups, in our families, inside the therapy room, and perhaps even more importantly inside each of us, something that manifests as effacement of the subjective dimension, as an accentuation of selfishness and competition, as a loss of the capacity to empathize as well as loss of joy. As it happens, neoliberal capitalist totalitarianism has been disguised as democracy and its result is the social catastrophe that we suffer in our country.

An Italian writer, Franco Berardi (2017, p. 12, author's translation), known as 'Bifo', author of many books on neoliberal politics, while visiting Argentina commented on the way we live in the form of social detachment:

> Dis-eroticization is the worst disaster that humanity can know because the foundation of ethics is not in the universal norms of practical reason but in the perception of the body of the other as a sensible continuation of my body. This is what Buddhists call the great compassion: the awareness of the fact that your pleasure is my pleasure and that your suffering is my suffering. This is precisely what we read every day in the newspapers: pity is dead because we are not capable of empathy, that is, of an erotic comprehension of the other.

This model leads us to experience and believe that life is like an *inclined plane* so that there is a mark that guides us where to move towards. So, there are those who come down, and those who go up, the climbers, those who have reached very high, and this is how culture builds the metaphor of *pretension*, which means to *tend* towards, or in a sense to be *tense* in relation to what will come. This obeys the strange logic of action that is geared towards the prevention of a fall. And so many young and not so young clients show up urged without knowing too clearly why or for whom, but living the imminence of a fall and animated by this permanent effort, their back weighed down by the burden of 'climbing'. In phrases such as 'you go up'; 'he or she is a high-up person'; 'he has low instincts'; 'those above'; 'those below'; etc., there is no doubt where the preference lies: in these narratives, up is better than down. Because of this, the subject begins this unbridled race to avoid 'being left out' and starts on a path of excessive consumption, the amount and the characteristics of which will depend on the degree of stress.

Byung-Chul, a philosopher of Korean origin, residing now in Germany for many years, contemplates this phenomenon with great lucidity: 'the motivation, the project, the competence, the organization and the initiative are inherent to the technique of psycho-political domination of the neoliberal regime' (Byung-Chul, 2017, p. 12).

Capital is no longer made up of objects, but of accumulation of signs – immaterial goods that act on the collective mind, preying upon our attention, imagination and social psyche through widespread use of media and information technology. This implies two important consequences: that the laws of the economy end up influencing the affective domain and the psychic equilibrium of society and, on the other hand, that the psychic and affective balance spreading in society ends up acting in turn on the economy.

Berardi (2007, p. 12) writes:

> The assertion of an ideology of neoliberal type has socially imposed the idea that we should all consider ourselves entrepreneurs. No one is allowed to conceive his/her own life according to more relaxed and equal criteria. Whoever relaxes is in danger of ending up in the street, or in a hospice, or in prison.

I've been experiencing the latter in my own life in moments of greater serenity and joy when I enjoy each experience in my work as in my private life – the urgencies of *having to produce* fill me with anxiety and discomfort. On this particular occasion, as a result of writing this chapter, these urgencies express themselves in a very sensitive and complex way, the joy that comes from the act of transmitting my ideas and the need for success, fame, prestige and efficiency – all of the above wrestling within me.

The kind of politics I am describing here promotes meritocracy, individualism (i.e. being a business person whose business is oneself) and the 'selfie' image. It presents itself as reality and truth, fracturing social bonds, insinuating itself among us in everyday life as a novel form of submission. With the emergence of a pacifying and democratic speech, we happily swallow the new drink *Neo-Liber* that transforms reality and ethics into 'post-truth' or 'alternative reality'. The drink spills over onto our culture in the form of psychological suffering that requires in turn a 'selfie' psychotherapy that reproduces the logic of giver (therapist) and taker (client) and that finally reinstalls the formula of the possessor and the dispossessed.

The above formula adopts the semblance of benevolence, but as a matter of fact installs the supremacy of the 'generous' possessor who does not appreciate the value of what he receives. In the case of psychotherapy, the client often has the courage to entrust his or her pain, suffering and vulnerability, while often the therapist does not adequately value what has been given. The same argument arises in economics, and it is the Chilean priest Hurtado (2013, author's translation) who makes this explicit with regards to working relations:

> There are those who delight in overwhelming their inferiors with their kindness, but deny them the most elemental justice. And then, they are astonished that their employees do not appreciate all that their kind employer does for them, that despite all their efforts are ungrateful and discontented. Although paradoxical, it is easier to be benevolent than fair, but benevolence without justice will not save the abyss between the employer and the worker, between the teacher and the student, between husband and wife. Such benevolence founded upon injustice will foster deep resentment. The one who feels superior is flattered, taking a paternal attitude because it gives him a delicious

feeling of control. Simple justice destroys that feeling and it places him on an equal footing with those esteemed by him as inferiors.

Politics and psychotherapy

Already in 1977, Rogers spoke of client-centred practice as a political practice. There are two passages from that period that for me evidence a strong re-reading of psychotherapy in relation to the balance of power in therapy which represented a significant step away from the medical model (where the relationship is deeply asymmetric), in regard to knowledge and therefore to power.

> The politics of the client-centered approach is a conscious resignation and avoidance, by the therapist, of all control over, or decision making, for the client.
>
> *(The Carl Rogers Reader, Rogers et al., 1990, p. 381)*

> As Gertrude Stein said of Paris, 'It is not what Paris gives you; it is what she does not take away'. This can be paraphrased to become a definition of the person-centered approach, the value-laden concept [that is] central [here]: 'It is not that this approach gives power to the person; it never takes it away'.
>
> *(Rogers, 1977, p. 8)*

Although the above statements made by Rogers marked a significant step forward in redefining the politics of the helping relationships, I find it equally necessary to mark two inherent discrepancies: first, the therapeutic relationship can indeed *give* power – a power given simultaneously to both therapist and client; this is effectively the creation of a common power. Secondly, I have frequently observed among colleagues that in their eagerness to help they are prone to giving recommendations, advice, and opinions that, ultimately, although seeming to be empowering clients on the surface, end up taking the power away from them.

A person-centred therapist told me a few days ago about what she came to understand as an instance of deep learning received from a client to whom, in her eagerness to help, she had suggested alternatives for relieving his pain. At some point in the session, the client interrupted her and said, softly but firmly: 'It sounds as if I cannot be really sad here'.

In this globalized world, there is a predominance of a particular aesthetic and production of meaning that responds to the laws of the market, and there are psychotherapeutic practices that accompany this model and propose fixed categories and a hierarchy of knowledge and power. This neoliberal model has been imposed not only in the political, social and economic spheres, but has also been introduced in the heart of subjectivity and even in the processes of subjectification. It filters into the practice of psychotherapy by promoting values, intentions and purposes that establish an efficient-*ist* and 'successful' model that places the relationship into political terms dictated by a scenario of possessor-dispossessed.

Assuming that the reality in its multiple nature operates with the logic of the rules of the game rather than with the laws that suppose a unique reality, I would briefly refer to the game that we are playing as a culture: ours is the game of dualisms, zapping, oppositions, diagnoses, discriminations, exclusions, a world in which both therapists and clients live the impossibility of *remaining with what is happening between them*. It is a game based on rules that affirm the validity of the submitter over the submitted; this game is supported by the metaphor of the survival of the strongest, the principle of competition ushered in by social Darwinism. There are alternatives to Darwinian theory, however: the biologist Brian Goodwin (2007) emphasizes the crucial importance in biological processes of the *relational order* among the components so that emerging qualities predominate over quantities. For him, we are cooperative *and* competitive, selfless and selfish, creative and playful as well as destructive and uncreative.

Crucial to these two different views is that one affirms the need to understand the therapeutic event as a political fact, a cooperative occurrence, and, as the feminist movement argued, that the personal is also political.

In political philosophy there are two different positions in relation to natural law. In Hobbes we find the notion of *people*, currently in force, which corroborates the neoliberal strategy. Here subjects are reduced to a passive unit of bodies and wills manipulated from the hierarchies of power. In Spinoza (1994), the notion of Multitude represents instead a plurality that persists as such, without ever converging into *One* or a unity, with a common expressive power that, nevertheless, respects the singular multiplicity. The Spinozist 'multitude' is democratic in a double sense: on one hand, as a designation of a popular power, an inalienable and non-transferable power, a right in act constitutive of the social reality; on the other hand, democratic multitude means preservation of the differences that constitute it by nature, resistance to uniformity; multiplicity without centre that never admits to be reduced to unity.

A multitude is a fabric of relationships, which allows us to think of the singular as an effect, as a knot of a moving weave of relationships, from which the notion of an individuality cut off from its surroundings is meaningless. Inspired by this process of intertwining between the human and the world, and from human to human, the building of community becomes the heart of the psychotherapeutic endeavour. In a sense, this means *turning the practice of psychotherapy back to the world from which it emerges*.

In accordance with the more general definition of multitude, I propose an understanding of the psychotherapeutic encounter as a *micro multitude* where the increase of common power does not imply the effacement of each singular power. When we affirm that we are but interwoven, expressive knots in constant movement and transformation, we also affirm that when we face another in the therapy room, we are being mutually constituted; there is an essential, reciprocal, inevitable mutuality in the encounter which I define as *radical reciprocity*. We are there, being other in front of another, mutually constituting one another in that moment. This effectively means displacing the 'internal statistic' from the viewpoint of the therapist who believes he or she knows whom he or she is going to meet. This applies to the other as well, and in this sense there is a mutual venturing out towards the encounter without intention to control, coming instead from the deep desire of meeting with another and with oneself.

In his book *The Time of the Multitude*, Morfino (2014) presents us with a new hypothesis: *the primacy of the encounter above the form*, a concept that runs throughout his book. In his conclusions, he ends with what could be called a politics of the encounter. The politics of the encounter is a proposal of political action that understands that fighting for the common freedom supposes that we relinquish our stories and abandon our dominant myths – the Subject, History, Unity, Simplicity – accepting instead the shared complexity and mystery of every single encounter.

Interestingly, he quotes Simondon's thesis, which affirms that the group – collective experience and group life – is not, as it is usually believed, the area in which the outstanding features of the singular individual are tempered or diminished but on the contrary it is the sphere of a *new individuation*, even more radical and creative.

All our power, that is to say all that we are capable of in the here and now, *is expressed there in communion with the power of the other*. Intersubjectivity and intercorporeality, in unison, build that full and intense common territory where psychotherapy and all inter-human encounters take place – something that bears decisive consequences for politics. As the individual is a *unio corporum* and *conexio idearum*, and as Nature is a huge complex individual, the *corporum* unions and the *idearum* connections can, by common action, constitute a new complex individual: the *multitude* which, in both Baruch Spinoza's *Theological Political Treatise* and his *Political Treatise* (Spinoza, 1994), constitutes the *political subject*. So in the field of psychotherapy we could speak of a compound subject, a *therapeutic subject* who is born as an expression of that *micro multitude*. According to Spinoza (1994, 1996), if two or more individuals are together in the same action at the same time, they are in a sense one singular thing. The central concept here is that *the relationship itself founds its terms*. In the encounter between two persons, when therapy occurs, the identity of each participant is configured at the starting point of that meeting. This, in turn, refers to concepts derived from this notion. The first one has to do with the *revision of the notion of identity* as fixed and immovable structure. If we understand that the identity is given by the circumstantial encounter, we see that the identity is a moving structure and in permanent modification. We are knots of a weave that is permanently knotted and unknotted.

The second concept derived from the above is *radical reciprocity*. There is an inevitable reciprocity in the therapeutic task that goes beyond the consciousness that both of us can have of what is happening. That is to say that the contact between at least two persons, devoid of all attribution to any of the parts, released of all meaning, exempt from all finality, is *deeply egalitarian*. Of course, with the burden of attribution, meaning, purpose, identity or better, identification and 'hierarchies', such contact may become asymmetric and because of these additions, therapists can attribute to themselves the 'power to touch' and to the patient the 'power to be touched'. The above scenario effectively gives a free rein to differences of powers, with authority bestowed on whoever has the power to touch.

We touch with the body, with words, with silences, with objects and from there, a winding path is traced that can range from healing and care to slavery, submission, torture and death. Not only is reciprocity originary, but also who I am in this relationship is given to me by the presence of the other and what the other is in this relationship is given to him or her by my presence. This leads me to incorporate the concept of *full presence*, by which I mean that presence is full when we can experience that who I am here is given to me from that particular relationship. For me the traditional three basic attitudes (Unconditional Acceptance, Empathy and Congruence) are included in therapeutic presence, emerging as the *expression of a single attitude*, by my paying attention to what I am experiencing as I am new even to myself. Congruence, then, is to be in the presence of that new one that I am, and to offer that new me at the time of the meeting. Therapeutic presence is not something that the therapist *does* but something that happens within that mutual involvement, within that expressive weaving that is the therapeutic encounter. Therefore, *we are not talking about two presences that add up but one that is expressed*.

This requires more of an attitude than a technique, more of an experiential commitment than an intellectual automatism, and it would be good to admit that to be able to place oneself in that *fullness of presence*, most of us have a long way to go, crossing a long trail of prejudices, labels and *furor curandis*, which I would less elegantly call the panic of not knowing what to do, or how to be in silence, in the vacuum of uncertainty. Nothing is more difficult than to understand and accept the spontaneity of biological and human phenomena in a culture like the current one oriented to explain away and present us with final formulas about everything pertaining to life.

I often observe in these difficult times that the main concern is to reach a safe harbour, and in many opportunities the journey matters little. Sometimes, I even doubt such a harbour exists; I frequently see this phenomenon in certain psychotherapeutic modalities that seek usefulness without considering the encounter, and even among those who claim to belong to the person-centred model. I firmly believe that the value of psychotherapy passes through the act of sharing and celebrating one with the other or others, the joy of the excursion into the encounter, into that shared intimacy.

In a previous article I asked myself a rhetorical question: 'Why does the rain exist?' as a way to reflect on the purpose, utility and outcome of some phenomenon or event. It is clear, at least to me, that the answer to that question can be made from two possible stances – both of them relating to the *purpose* of the phenomenon. These are answers to the question 'what for?' One answer, from the human perspective, could be: to irrigate the fields, to nourish the fields, to increase the flow of the rivers, to maintain ecological balance, to provoke floods, etc. This means there is a purpose that extends beyond the phenomenon itself, which transcends it. The power of rain from the human gaze lies in its consequences, in considering whether they are 'good' or 'bad'. Another possible answer, from a more encompassing view, would be that rain only exists in order to rain, that is to say that the phenomenon occurs as a pure affirmation of its occurrence, that it is *immanent*. From the human perspective, we think of rain with a criterion of utility rather than from the perspective of the whole nature. But rain happens for no other purpose than raining. In this case, the power of rain is that *it can rain*. We can also understand the interhuman encounter from one's own glance, from that of another or from both glances; we call the first one intentional purpose and the other, desiring purpose. For those of us practising person-centred psychotherapy, the absence of judgements of value about what is good or bad in relation to what our client is experiencing is crucial. And although the exercise of suspending judgement is possible only to some extent, there is a very subtle judgement that is filtered in the intentional purpose: that the conquest of that purpose is good and the deviation or the absence is bad. Just as with the rain, we can ask ourselves about the power of the encounter. Either what the encounter can be is in terms of its result, that is to say, *beyond the event* or the power of the encounter is in the encounter itself – the latter defined as desiring purpose. As a therapist, I offer place, time, openness, attention, desire (as the action of desiring), respect and a way of considering the encounter as a manifestation of my radical hospitality (Derrida & Dufourmantelle, 2000). What is truly therapeutic therapy? For me, this is akin to what Argentinean poet Roberto Juarroz evokes when he speaks of having no other goal than our open hands, without correcting them or guiding them. Finding our path, combining impossible dreams, that will lead us to a harbour.

At the heart of psychotherapy is the ability of the therapist to bring his/her experience into the encounter. In order to fully inhabit that experience of being in the encounter with the other, it is necessary to learn some things and unlearn others. It is important to understand that nothing happens outside a relationship, since we are expressions of relation and everything that happens is mutually constituted, so that such presence is also an event born of mutual involvement and radical reciprocity.

From this point of view, therapeutic presence is a relational event, emerging and at the same time weaving a mode of relationship, which is located in an interstitial space called 'in between'. Such presence has entity only in the relational space that is created with another. Therefore, we can say that we are not in relation, but that *we are relation*.

My effort here is to create an itinerary that would lead us to understand ourselves and to begin to see that what exists is itself the expression of infinite relationships; that what is happening here between the text and its readers is a maze of relationships with varying intensities. I consider psychotherapy to be a political practice, a practice that is *inevitably* political, that accounts for the human bond to the cosmos, one that affirms his *conatus* that is his effort to persevere in being, as defined by Spinoza, or his transformative tendency, as per Rogers' saying.

Both these authors founded a politics of human relations based on an autonomous, self-generating understanding of relationship(s), on the creative character of each encounter, on appearance as novelty, on experience as multiplicity, on time as duration, as interval, on the acceptance of passions, on freedom rather than vigilance and control. This is the path of the silent revolution, the fabric of solidarity networks that are fraternal, and weaving a pattern of life-affirming, of joyful passions and freedoms. This way of proposing the therapeutic bond is not limited to therapy. In transcending inevitably the everyday life of the person who comes to us, as well as his family and social relations, this proposal becomes deeply political, gesturing towards what Spinoza calls *a community of friends*. For Spinoza, if two people join forces, they will have greater power than each of them will ever have separately. They will also have greater right. And the larger the commonality of powers is, the greater their right will be.

At this juncture, a crucial question arises: 'What to do at this strange crossroads, at this place where the forceful exercise of neoliberal power and the demand of the "inclined plane" have led us?'

We need, I feel, to make room for chaos in psychotherapy and in our relationship with the other. It is the place of mystery, of renunciation of knowledge, of entrusted surrender to creativity and nature and its multiple manifestations. This implies creating space for the play of resonances – to trust that the other and I can together move forward in the direction of mutual transformation. It is to honour the complexity of the human, to approach this encounter with open hands, open mind and open heart. It is to recognize in this approach a genuine human level – to accept its complexity remembering that our contribution is no more nor less than contributing by presence to that sacred moment that constitutes each genuine encounter with someone. To make room for chaos is to give up an analysis that splinters and crumbles, it is to leave the computer behind, to stop being an agent of order and to be instead an agent of transformation, with the quiet assurance in our heart that this will touch both the other and us.

It is to pay attention to the multiple variations of experiences and affections, of the moving selves that we are, rather than trying to modify them, but simply making them visible and allowing their richness to emerge. It is to authorize and give oneself permission to be present, to affirm through presence our multiplicity of existing rather than settle for a limited sense of ourselves.

It is nothing more than continuing to walk this path that we have begun, by not letting ourselves be caught by the fear imposed by the logic of 'inside and outside', recovering the joy of the encounter itself, creating networks, reinforcing our militancy, our vocation for the power that connects us to the Earth, to the other species and to our brothers and sisters of all colours, creeds, and conditions. Because they are us.

At the beginning of this chapter I referred to the difficulty I had in writing, worried about the 'harbour', so I turned to a medium that I found comfortable as well as amiable, poetry, which resulted in the following synthesis of the chapter:

> To open ourselves inside
> the times,
> the memoirs,
> the memories,

the costumes,
the outlines of the body,
to join the eyes,
the ears
the primitive voices,
the chemical snail of the ancestors,
to leave behind the flow of electrons
and protons.
To throw ourselves
into the abyss of the encounter,
the intangible sound of
the sea that is hidden,
inside the pain,
to the cavern of dreams,
To fracture ourselves,
to break without fear,
in pieces,
fragments of
a shy colour
and another arrogant
and other
and other
and other
until
Understanding:
the commitment,
the shared caress,
the assemblage that
we are
we were,
that we will be.

References

Berardi, F. (2007). Entrevista Verónica Gago'. *Diario*, 12 November.
Byung-Chul, H., (2017) *Psychopolitics: Neoliberalism and new Techniques of Power*. London and New York: Verso.
Deleuze, G. (2001) *Spinoza: Practical Philosophy*. San Francisco, CA: City Lights.
Derrida, J. & Dufourmantelle, A. (2000) *Of Hospitality*. Stanford, CA: Stanford University Press.
Goodwin, B. (2007) *Nature's Due: Healing our Fragmented Culture*. Edinburgh: Floris.
Hurtado, S.A. (2013) *Humanismo Social*. Santiago de Chile: Ediciones Universidad, Kindle edition.
Morfino, V. (2014) *El Tiempo de la Multitud*. Madrid: Tierradenadie Ediciones.
Negri, A. (2004) *Subversive Spinoza*. Manchester: Manchester University Press.

Rogers, C. (1977) *On Personal Power: Inner Strength and its Revolutionary Impact*. London: Robinson.
Rogers, C.R., Kirschenbaum, H., & Henderson, V.L. (1990) *The Carl Rogers Reader*. London: Robinson.
Spinoza, B. (1994) *A Spinoza Reader*. Princeton, NJ: Princeton University Press.
Spinoza, B. (1996) *Ethics*. London: Penguin.

3

BEAUTY AND THE CYBORG

Manu Bazzano

Introduction

From its inception as client-centred therapy, PCT has been affected by the *beautiful soul syndrome* and an unspoken sense of moral superiority over other orientations. Like Jiminy Cricket in *Pinocchio*, we person-centred therapists can be relied upon to give voice to the conscience of the profession and – also like Jiminy Cricket – for producing little effect other than the comfort of hearing noble-sounding words spoken with conviction and a pleasant rhetorical flourish. Among the various noble words gaining currency in person-centred literature, *love* is becoming dominant. It shows up in person-centred literature in secular garb and in full theological regalia. Talking about love will illustrate some of the traits of the beautiful soul syndrome that afflicts the PCA.

The eagerness of some person-centred practitioners to see the approach accepted by the Powers prompted them to adopt wholesale the language, modality and worldview. This is when Beauty turns into the *Cyborg* – in science fiction, a creature that is part human, part machine. Patent examples of this phenomenon can be observed in sectors of academia, from psychology journals to the teaching of PCT in universities and therapy institutes to the style and content of presentations of person-centred-related ideas at international conferences and symposia. Within these scenarios, very little distinguishes PCT from other branches of academic psychology except for its humane vocabulary that cheeringly reminds us, as in a nature documentary watched on a computer screen, of the existence of trees in a real forest.

I believe both stances have value: Beauty and the Cyborg have something important to tell us about our current predicament as person-centred therapists navigating the complexity of a neoliberal landscape. Hence, rather than straightforward disapproval of either the naivety of Beauty or the frostiness of the Cyborg, this chapter maps out a *third route* that capitalizes on both while appealing to the key principle of the *organism* (Goldstein, 1995; Rogers, 1961). PCT, understood as an *organismic psychology* (Tudor & Worrall, 2006; Tudor, 2010), has a great deal to contribute to current debate, provided it can *expand* on the notion of the organism and include the non-human – both within and without the human.

Person-centred, human-centred, self-centred

PCT is stuck. Not only is it trapped within its vague notion of *person*, hence oblivious to new *emergent phenomena* (Moreira, 2012, 2016) that renew existence and re-establish exhilarating complicities with a dynamic world of becoming outside the narrow confines of personhood. It is also stuck with its notion of *presence*, (mis)understood metaphysically as the attribute of a spiritually-gifted therapist rather than, as Rud (2016) has been at pains to explain for some time, as 'mutually constituted' (p. 5), as belonging, I would add, to the neutral dimension of *affect* (Massumi, 2000; Jameson, 2014). Above all, PCT is stuck within its own incurable anthropomorphism – not only applied to animals but, crucially, to ourselves as humans, and which results in lofty denial of our human existence *in a continuum with animals*. Despite its emphasis on the organism, PCT has failed to question, alongside the majority of therapeutic philosophies, what Massumi calls 'our image of ourselves as humanly standing apart from other animals; our inveterate vanity regarding our assumed species identity, based on the specious grounds of our sole proprietorship of language, thought, and creativity' (Massumi, 2014, p. 3).

The vanity of anthropocentrism (a.k.a. human-centredness) and human *exceptionalism* is at the heart of PCT, and seriously hinders the development of its potential as a progressive and credible alternative to the spiritual poverty of neoliberal and neopositivist psychology that is all the rage today. But in order to let go of its tight grip on anthropocentrism, PCT would need to either think *outside* the frame of Christian theology and morality, or find new ways to re-vision these.

How can PCT be free of human-centredness, given that its roots are partly found in Christian theology, i.e. in a worldview that sees man and woman as the 'crown' of 'creation'? Interwoven with human-centredness are our own inveterate self-centredness and the sense of identity gained from substantiating a dynamic cluster of beliefs and practices collected over the years as precious stones. If for instance I happen to be a reputable person-centred practitioner, writer and tutor who has built over years a sense of personal and professional identity on the foundation of a handful of principles; if I have managed, thanks to my personal qualities of friendliness and political shrewdness to construct a solid alliance with a group of equally reputable PCT practitioners; if we have together succeeded in influencing what publications are to be acquired by the next batch of trainees, who will deliver the keynote address to the next conference and so forth, then, bingo! we have established a tradition that from that point on we endeavour to *preserve* and *defend* against perceivable threats. It *has* to be preserved, i.e. kept *static*, despite the fact that the philosophy we profess speaks of the *self* – let alone the approach – as 'a fluid process, not a fixed static entity, a flowing river of change, not a block of solid material; a continually changing constellation of potentialities, not a fixed quantity of traits' (Rogers, 1961, p. 122).

The tradition has to be defended because it constitutes my/our article of faith; to challenge it would be blasphemous. And even though the philosophy I profess has *encounter* at its core (Rogers, 1970), even though I pay lip service to open dialogue and honest conflict, the truth is it really frightens me when my beliefs are questioned.

Contemporary ethics and philosophy as well as various strands within therapy practices inspired by phenomenology and post-phenomenology tell us that a different perspective is possible. This view presupposes a movement towards *infinity* rather than *totality* (Levinas, 1999); it is *rhizomatic* rather than *arboreal* (Deleuze & Guattari, 1987; Deleuze, 1995). This view is counter-traditional (Bazzano & Webb, 2016); it points towards an *outside* that is transformative *and* thoroughly immanent (i.e. *remaining within* this world), rather than transcendent (i.e. *climbing out of* it).

What would it mean to adapt some of the above ideas to PCT? It would help it shed some of *its inherent positivism* – already present in Rogers. What does 'positivism' mean here? It is a way of thought that recognizes only what can be measured and verified. Applied to psychology, this means relying on a theory that recognizes only the presumed objectivity of science and the reliability of facts. Even more crucially: positivism champions the *reduction of experiencing to the self*, the geometric or shorthand translation of what is unknown and ineffable to the conscious and the quantifiable.

The link Deleuze makes (Deleuze & Parnet, 2002) between the *diagram*, i.e. the 'fixed set of relations that determine the world' (Barber, 2014, p. 47) and the *outside* (i.e. what is within the world but forever expanding beyond our reach) echoes the one made by Rogers (1951) between *self-concept* and *organism*. With a crucial difference: while for Deleuze (2008) 'the diagram stems from the outside but the outside does not merge with any diagram, and continues instead to *draw new ones*' (p. 89, emphasis added), Rogers, and person-centred therapists after him, truly believe that psychotherapy itself is 'a process whereby man *becomes* his organism – without self deception, without distortion' (Rogers, 1961, p. 111, emphasis added). This is a thoroughly positivist statement.

It is not my intention to berate the *positivity* of positivism. There are, however, political implications that need to be examined, for the updated version of positivism, namely neopositivism, is now the ideology of neoliberalism. What is neoliberalism? Blind obedience to the market; in the therapy world, the commodification of (human) experiencing by a host of strategies: New Public Management, evidence-based practice, managed care, randomized control trials and the generalized 'managerialism'. It is a concerted effort to turn therapy – a living practice dealing with living subjects – into a *commodity*, to destroy its raison d'être, limit its creativity and bring about a 'quasi-colonization of the therapy experience' (House, 2016, p. 251).

A comic faith

It is crucial to reflect as to whether we wish to align PCT to the forces of neoliberalism or rekindle instead its emancipatory flame. The first port of call for some PCT practitioners at this juncture is to appeal to religion, spirituality, or narratives that similarly champion the ineffable and the immeasurable. But this move too tends to bypass experiencing – this time in the service of transcendence rather than in the name of a Logos subservient to the market and corporate power. Both positivism and transcendent spiritualism violate experiencing and seize control over the psyche. Whether secular or religious, both share what Donna Haraway calls 'a comic faith in techno-fixes', the silly idea that technology 'will somehow come to the rescue of its naughty but very clever children, or what amounts to the same thing, God will come to the rescue of his disobedient but ever hopeful children' (Haraway, 2016a, p. 3).

In this spirit, a re-visioning of organismic psychology will have to outwit the customary traps of religion, of Christian morality, as well as the dangers inherent within a secularized, mechanized, market-driven view of psychotherapy. This is because both transcendent spiritualism and rational materialism share metaphysical views of experiencing instead of an attitude of *re-spect* (i.e., looking again, taking a second, attentive glance). But the latter can only be done through *suspending* religious/theological beliefs and by equally *forswearing* (Merleau-Ponty, 1964) scientific assumptions.

There is a wealth of inspiration and encouragement found within the *counter-tradition* and its wide array of emancipatory and transformative narratives. These are dynamically alive within contemporary philosophical, ethico-political and psychological practices but have strangely failed to reach the seemingly conservative, globally parochial world of PCT. The influence the above practices can exert on PCT would be akin to a tidal wave of progressive innovation that, if allowed, could bring PCT to the forefront of contemporary spiritual and politically emancipatory discourse, let alone at the cutting edge of mental health.

To be fair, a handful of person-centred writers have consistently alluded over the years to this counter-traditional trove of perspectives and innovative methodologies, endeavouring, to little or no avail, to open up the discussion within the person-centred international community (e.g. Rud, 2009, 2016; Moreira, 2012, 2016; Tudor & Worrall, 2006; Clark, 2016; Ellingham, 2016; Lee, 2017; Bazzano, 2013a, 2013b, 2014, among others). The lack of response may be due in part to the fact that innovative, substantial and far-reaching ideas (unlike, say, academic formulas routinely cooked up in psychology departments) take a long time to be understood and absorbed, particularly when they happen to belong to the counter-tradition. Unlike tonal variations on long-established themes within the Canon, counter-traditional ideas upset the status quo and are for that reason often met with strong resistance and even hostility.

The beautiful soul

A systematic definition of the beautiful soul (*die schöne Seele*) is found in Hegel (1807/1977) who was keen, in his *Phenomenology of Spirit*, to assess a stance he saw as typical of Romanticism, and best epitomized by Schiller. For Hegel, the beautiful soul:

> lacks force to externalize itself and endure existence. It does not want to stain the radiance of its pure consciousness by deciding to do anything particular. It keeps its heart pure by fleeing from contact with actuality and preserving its impotence. Its activity consists in yearning, and it is like a shapeless vapour fading into nothingness.
>
> *(Hegel, 1977, pp. 575–576)*

Critique of the beautiful soul syndrome has been used after Hegel as a way to justify lack of moral compass or ethical commitment. Despite this criticism, this notion is valuable for two reasons: (a) it describes a familiar stance within liberal, progressive and, one could say, post-Romantic thought; (b) it can help us reflect on the recent rise of bigotry, racism and nativism on a global scale. Not many had predicted Donald Trump's victory, or Brexit, or the success of the far right in Europe and elsewhere. Could those who were shocked by these events and meekly trusting in the benign unfolding of the formative tendency bear some of the traits of Hegel's beautiful soul? I certainly noticed these in myself. For instance, I presented a reading of hospitality (Bazzano, 2012) inspired by radical ethics, which strenuously defends the idea of *open borders* in relation to the influx of migrants and refugees. I still hold this position wholeheartedly – at its core, a critique of identity and of the violence it engenders; I've also been aware more recently of how easy it is to adopt a noble-sounding stance without confronting the social and political realities first-hand. I similarly advocated the notion of therapy as *unconditional hospitality* (Bazzano, 2015), aware of the insurmountable difficulties of upholding it. But it is one thing to have an aspiration (in this case, to be a good enough host and momentarily bracket my own self-centred agenda). It is quite another to say that positive change in the client happens *because of* my wonderful qualities of presence and love. Too many times I find myself marking case studies where the entire emphasis is self-congratulation, i.e. the ability of the person-centred counsellor-in-training to radiate love and presence and be the primary *cause* of positive change in the client. This is not due to a misunderstanding of person-centred theory in one or two trainees, but the faithful and consistent outcome of the culture of self-congratulation we have created in current person-centred trainings. If this comes as a surprise to some readers, they might not have noticed that this very same stance is rife among person-centred tutors. Here is an example.

I once heard a colleague address a class of trainee counsellors on the subject of deep relatedness in therapy. The heart of his argument was that good therapy is all about establishing deep relational links. Partly to demonstrate his point, he proceeded to read a poem a client had written to him to express how much the sessions had benefited her. The participants nodded and sighed in expressive agreement and, during the more lyrical passages, you could almost hear them hum and purr in unison. Part of me was eager to join the feel-good wave that by this point enveloped the room but I found to my disappointment that I couldn't. Maybe I had got out the wrong side of bed that morning, or plain and simple disbelief had the best of me. Soon it began to dawn on me: the client's poem was punctuated by the frequent use of the pronoun *you*. Addressed to the therapist, the poem was above all else *a glorification of the therapist himself*. How great, how skilful, how sensitive he had been in working with her and facilitating such depth of relating! As soon as I realized this, I wanted to throw up, cry out in disbelief or noisily and self-righteously disrupt what, to my cynical gaze, now looked like a deplorable charade. Mercifully, I did none of the above but managed to maintain a dignified bearing until the end. The afore-mentioned scenario is perplexing. It would not merit consideration if not for the fact that the above stance, promoted and uncritically accepted, has become mainstream within PCT trainings and practice. The uncritical way in which this formulaic 'depth' of relating has fast become an expedient staple in some PCT training courses could give us pause for thought. Among other things, this perspective is problematic because almost entirely embedded (as in the above example) within a narcissistic frame. This charge seems unfounded and counter-intuitive at first. How could an emphasis on love and relating be entrenched within the confines of narcissism? Surely, a shift of attention towards a depth of relating must represent a welcome shift from the Cartesian self, from Freud's psychic apparatus, from the individualistic notion of the human self that myopically disregarded basic patterns of early attachment and of human relating, let alone the truth of our being-in-the-world.

What's more, the luminous examples of Buber, Levinas and others gave impetus to an ethics that centred on the fundamental notion of human encounter and provided inspiration to the specificity of the therapeutic encounter. How can the Philosophy of the Meeting put forward by these thinkers be deemed narcissistic? And yet, the first thinker to fully articulate a similar argument – namely, that *I-Thou encounter is inscribed within a narcissistic frame* – was Levinas, one of the leading lights of the philosophy of the meeting. He took great pains to distance himself from Buber's thought and, in the 1980s, wondered whether clothing the naked and feeding the hungry would bring one closer to the other than the rarefied relatedness promoted by Buber (Levinas, 2008/1987). This was long before Buber's *I-Thou* (Buber, 2008) morphed into the Sentimental Doctrine whose recitation is now mandatory in person-centred trainings. This once inspiring memento of the formidable challenges inherent in human encounter, poised as it was against its *functional* counterpart (*I-it*), has now become in my view an insipid formula, a given – a gimmick. It is assumed that I-Thou modes of being can be fabricated with a little effort, goodwill and the mastering of a handful of skills; that behind its formulation lies the all-encompassing and comforting worldview of universal relatedness; and that various half-baked, duly measured and routinely if superficially researched formulas made in its wake are coherently aligned with it. But is it really so? Isn't Buber's 'I-Thou' instead a rare occurrence – an *accident* rather than the outcome of the noble effort made by therapists affected by the beautiful soul syndrome?

What is forgotten when we hurriedly summon a thinker such as Levinas to decorate an ideology of love and relatedness is that his is a *philosophy of separation* where there is great respect for Descartes' formal structures. There are many good reasons for pointing the finger at Descartes as initiator of the body/mind divide, but fashionable *tout court* dismissal neglects a crucial element, clarified by Levinas: the notion of separation is crucial in generating, in the third Cartesian meditation, a relation between the *res cogitans* (the mind, the 'thinking thing') and the infinity of God, thought beyond thought, thought as inextinguishable longing (Descartes, 1996). Levinas utilizes the formal categories of Descartes which alone allow the self to dare the thought of infinity through *desire*, which is the name Levinas gives to the thought that dares to think infinity. Not need, which speaks of hope of satisfaction; *not love, which wants union*. It is instead the desire of what the subject does not need – or, the realized love of desire which has remained desire.

Some kinds of love

> Love … is *the equivocal* par excellence
> *(Levinas, 1999, p. 255, emphasis in the original)*

A clear way in which the beautiful soul syndrome manifests within PCT is through the championing of the notion of love. Several person-centred practitioners openly speak of the important role love plays in therapy (Thorne, 2005; Schmid, 2016; Keys, 2017). In some cases, the championing of love comes with a welcome call for socio-political activism among customary allusions to theology. There have been attempts to build a 'theory of love' (Keys, 2017, p. 35) as well as a 'framework for love in therapy' (p. 37) that catalogues and classifies several dimensions of loving. Taking a step that boldly embraces the difficulties of accepting love in therapy, Keys writes:

> Maybe the strength of our feelings frightens us off talking about love, or maybe we don't want to enter into the unknown in the relationship, where we feel vulnerable and not in control. Maybe there are now so many counterfeit forms of love that it is too difficult to talk about it without misunderstanding. However, *avoiding love won't make counselling safer* … [but] can lead to unethical and unprofessional practice. It is time to reclaim love as central to the counselling encounter.
> *(Keys, 2017, p. 35, emphasis added)*

We cannot avoid this important dimension of experiencing and relating, and the above passage conveys in no uncertain terms the heart within the more 'clinical' notion of UPR. It also presents us with a stance emblematic of the beautiful soul, but one that is *updated*. The person-centred practitioner affected by the beautiful soul syndrome is not the ineffectual and poetic soul of Romantic lore, dissipating his/her life's energies in drowsy pre-Raphaelite semi-slumber. No. The post-Romantic beautiful soul is not happy pining away for the triumph of love in a world that elects white supremacists, bigots and racists as its leaders. The more active, socially-engaged beautiful soul wants love to be acknowledged in a world that only recognizes what can be measured and quantified. So it rolls up its sleeves, measuring and quantifying the dimensions of love, building a 'taxonomy of loving in therapy … based on Rogers's conditions for therapeutic change' (Keys, 2017, p. 35). As we shall see, this is where the Cyborg steps in.

Central to this taxonomy of love, equipped with its own obligatory grid, is the Biblical notion of *Agape*, or divine love, defined by Gillian Rose as 'transcendental in the medieval sense: it precedes the division of being into categories; while Eros is within categorical thinking' or, in other words, 'all speaking of God will slip inevitably but illegitimately into *anthropomorphic* and *anthropocentric* terms' (Rose, 1992, p. 168, emphasis added).

Discussing the Swedish theologian Andres Nygren, Rose makes an irreconcilable distinction between Agape and Eros. Person-centred writers (Schmid, 2016; Keys, 2017) present Agape as part of a taxonomy that smoothly includes Eros alongside other manifestations of love such as Storge and Philia. However, unlike Eros, Agape (divine love) is *beyond representation*. To represent it 'would be to confer on it the spurious status and authority of Eros' (Rose, 1992, p. 168). The central element in Agape is *faith*; it is not 'a question of working one's way up but of something offered which comes down' (ibid.). The fundamental difference here is that: '*Eros starts with the assumption of the Divine origin and worth of the soul; Agape, on the other end, starts with the conviction of one's own lack of worth*' (Rose, 1992, p. 168, italics in the original).

Eros is, in Plato's sense, *acquisitive* – in contemporary parlance: relational, desirous of self-actualizing and at all times wanting an *object* which can be either elevated or less so. Because of these characteristics, the fitting tutelary numen of the therapeutic encounter is Eros. Agape, on the other hand (as John's and Paul's Gospels present it), is unstructured and free, unbound by any object and/or objective, including objects such as therapeutic healing, self-acceptance or objectives such as positive change. It appears *ex nihilo*, i.e., out of the blue. It does not need or care for right conditions, be they core or hardcore. It is *creative*, and, I suggest, self-generative and probably allied with the notion of *grace*; most of all, 'Agape is the initiator of the fellowship with God' (Nygren, 1982, p. 80).

In the 1930s, Nygren (1982) drew a stark and convincing distinction between Eros and Agape, presenting them as incongruous and irreconcilable to one another and as such, difficult to marshal into an all-encompassing and neatly drawn taxonomy. In their effort to bring Agape within the therapeutic frame, some person-centred writers reproduce the same positivist craving discussed earlier in relation, namely the notion, rife in PCT, that the human self can, one fine day, with the help of a fine, loving therapist, become wholly aligned to, or congruent with the organism. They also conveniently evade the thorny dimension normally addressed by work on transference and counter-transference. It is, in short, a case of *spiritual bypass*.

Another problem that arises with presenting Eros and Agape as *compatible* (alongside Storge and Philia, which I will not discuss here) is that we neglect the centrality of Agape as divine love and make the latter pliable to a therapeutic articulation that conveniently forgets its source. This is a familiar move in the history of person-centred literature: Kierkegaard, Buber, Levinas have 'inspired' PCT but only in neutered form. Either their powerful religious messages have been duly secularized, or the more controversial elements suitably taken out. For instance: suspension of the ethical and anti-conformist celebration of individuation in Kierkegaard; I-Thou as pure accident rather than endeavour in Buber; primacy of separation over relatedness in Levinas.

Why are our person-centred champions of love not giving it to us straight? What could the implications be of stating more frankly that they see divine love as central in therapy? It would mean to align it to the Christianity of John's and Paul's Gospels, to the Augustinian theology of Luther. It would mean to own the fact that one aligns with a politically dominant Christian frame; it would mean accepting Christianity's claims as universal rather than culturally specific; it would mean reading other mytho-religious or secularist narratives that challenge the Judaeo-Christian worldview entirely within the frame of the latter. But it is precisely from this source, a selected, culturally dominant Judaeo-Christian frame that Keys (2017) weaves in psychological, transpersonal, physical and political intersections.

Here is an example: at the (so-called) 'transpersonal' level, Christian Agape manifests, Keys says, as 'Buddha nature' or as the person's 'divinity within' (p. 35). Alas, Buddha-nature is neither transpersonal nor does it represent our divinity within. It can be seen as such only if one *ignores the sheer otherness* of the Buddha's teachings in relation to Judaeo-Christian perspectives and inscribes them entirely within a more familiar and comfortable Judaeo-Christian frame of reference. In this way, aspects collected inside Keys' taxonomy are made to fit the presumed universality of Christianity. What began as an appealing emancipatory stance ushers in a dominant narrative that engulfs and neuters a rich plurality of other mythic and secularist accounts. I'm thinking not only of Dharma teachings but also of the myriad heretical positions *within* Christianity that are bypassed by the universalizing centrality of Agape, particularly when the latter is conceived reductively.

This particular move – wanting the ineffable and the transcendental to become quantified and measurable is the positivist move *par excellence*. In PCT, it also represents the shift from Beauty to the Cyborg: the overriding need to quantify, measure, catalogue and fit into a geometrical grid what is ineffable.

Love and 'the Powers'

To be clear: I'm championing the *primacy of Eros* in the therapeutic endeavour. This also implies giving primacy to *subversion*, an aspect of love that is glossed over by a more pious emphasis on Agape. In traditions such as Sufism (Attar, 2017), love is 'a profoundly irrational and asocial – even antisocial – force' (Creswell, 2017, p. 26). Even when inspired by the divine, it gestures towards the shedding of outward shows of piety in favour of an appreciation of the deeper mysteries of existence. No taxonomy is found here, but great, inspiring and moving poetry. What a pity that when speaking about something so subtle and elusive such as love, person-centred therapists feel compelled to use grids and frameworks instead of art and poetry.

In the retelling of Koranic tales found in the Persian poet Farid ud-Din Attar's *Conference of Birds* (Attar, 2017) poetry is found aplenty, alongside wonderfully subversive interpretations of religious tales. Here is a famous example, summarized by Robyn Creswell:

> Satan's refusal to bow before Adam as the rest of the angels do, a story that appears in several passages of the Koran, is not evidence of Satan's pride, as it is understood in traditional interpretations, but rather of his overpowering love for God, which did not permit him to bow to anyone else ... Attar goes further, saying that God's curse of Satan is to be prized, since any form of divine attention, even in the form of a curse, must be counted a blessing.
> *(Creswell, 2017, pp. 25–26)*

Within Christian theology too, there are subversive readings of love that are at variance with current person-centred championing of divine love. I'm referring in particular to John Howard Yoder (1994) and his convincing case for *immanent theology*. In expounding a way of thinking that thrillingly reminds me of Benjamin, Debord, Deleuze and Agamben, he affirms the fundamental fact that there are *no predetermined rules of possibility*. This is a radical political stance that breaks with what he variously calls the *given*, the *structure* and the *Powers*. For Yoder (1994), the Powers have their own method of consistency or self-maintenance. Their main reason for existing is self-preservation and they allege 'patterns or regularities that transcend or precede or condition the individual phenomena we can immediately perceive' (p. 38). Institutions, whether religious or psychotherapeutic, are geared above all towards their own self-protection *at the expense* of individuals and of the dynamic reality around them. They do so by establishing rules. The latter, however, are not 'separate from individuals', Yoder writes. 'The Powers, by providing social, political and economic structure, also produce individuals that are capable of responding to them, that are *complicit* with the possibilities they express' (Yoder, 1994, p. 68, emphasis added).

The task, when faced with this situation, is to actively *challenge* the Powers in order to renew the stagnant waters and create anew the conditions for actualization. *This* is an example of (subversive) love. This act comes from the *outside* of the Powers. It is a revolt against the status quo and those careful built identities and professional careers within the structures and the Powers, and as such it is met with resistance. For Yoder, the name Jesus gives to this revolt is *love*, but it is a love that comes down from the universal throne of Agape and adopts a *minority* position, in the sense of Deleuze's *minoritarian ethics* (Deleuze & Guattari, 1987). This position is not dutiful or sanctimonious; it does not seek the approval of governments and corporations or any of the dominant half-baked ideologies that serve them, but declares its autonomy and opposition. This act of peaceful revolt is a radical act of love, an act 'with no promise of effectiveness' (Yoder, cited in Barber, 2014, p. 124). '[With Jesus] effectiveness and success were sacrificed for the sake of love [and] this sacrifice was turned by God into a victory which vindicated to the upmost the apparent impotence of love' (Yoder, 2003, pp. 56–57).

The Powers deal with *majoritarian* consensus; majority 'implies a constant … serving as a standard measure by which to evaluate it … [It] assumes a state of power and domination, not the other way around. It assumes the standard measure' (Deleuze & Guattari, 1987, p. 105). Within PCT, the majoritarian position is not that of the greatest number but the one assumed by a handful of practitioners who yearn for the Powers' approval and are keen to align themselves with the Establishment's illusory claims of universality. Yoder again: '"Establishment" does not mean the [numerical] majority; it means the [numerical] minority who are in dominant social roles and claim the authority to speak for everyone' (Yoder, 1997, p. 3).

Technofixes

I am no Luddite. I am excited by the science of the late 20th century and its challenge of boundaries: between humans and animals; between humans, animals and machines; between the physical and the non-physical. There is an undeniable step forward constituted by symbiogenesis, co-evolution, bioethics and biopolitics (Haraway, 2016b). This is not fanciful 'post-modern' thinking but something corroborated by genetics tests on plants, animals and bacteria. It is becoming increasingly clear that different species crossbreed more than it was once thought, that genes are not only being passed down individual branches of the tree of life, but also transmitted between species on different paths of evolution. For evolutionary biologist Michael Rose, 'the tree of life is being politely buried' but 'what's less accepted is that our whole fundamental view of biology needs to change … biology is vastly more complex than we thought' (ScienceAndReligion.com, 2012).

Similarly, for biologist Michael Syvanen (ScienceAndReligion.com, 2012) the tree of life 'is not a tree any more, it's a different topology entirely. It is clear that the Darwinian tree is no longer an adequate description of how evolution in general works'.

I believe this rich contamination is to be wholeheartedly welcomed. It substantiates the counter-traditional view of an entangled, self-generating web of life constantly engendering new assemblages, new concepts and new emancipatory possibilities.

'Emancipatory' remains the key word here. It is not a matter of whether one defends the divine, the human or the machine or whether any of the above is preferable to the other. The question is *evaluative*: we need to establish whether the assemblages found in a particular cluster are animated by *active* or *reactive* forces, whether they favour greater freedom and solidarity, foster a deeper sense of justice, wisdom and compassion, *or* whether they continue to serve the old masters in new corporate garb. As I see it, the type of technoscience currently embraced by mainstream PCT does not open new frontiers, nor does it move past human exceptionalism or foster creative entanglement between the human, the animal and the machine. It is, instead, of the more reactive kind. It serves static forces of (self) preservation. It is part of a conservative project within PCT that is keen to use the master's tool in the foolish hope of dismantling the master's house. I have discussed elsewhere (Bazzano, 2016) how this fundamentally reactive project obeys the dictates of neoliberalism and strives to align the approach to the most conservative trends within philosophy of science and politics, and how it has uncritically embraced highly questionable stances such as positive psychology and psychopathology.

The above represents the least interesting and more crushingly dull aspect of the PCT Cyborg, and perhaps a sign that the latter, despite its tremendous potential, is been at present occupied by reactive forces.

I witnessed some of this first-hand in my four-year plus stint as editor of a person-centred international journal which, like a lot of other literature in the humanities, is driven by software programs such as ScholarOne providing 'comprehensive workflow management' (https://clarivate.com/products/scholarone) and representing one of the signs among others of the triumph of managerialism. Of course, a program like ScholarOne can be extremely useful in 'lowering infrastructure costs' (ibid.). Owing to the managerial turn in therapy and thanks to impressive levels of automation and customization that software such as this offers, it is also possible nowadays to be an editor of a person-centred journal with very little human input such as thinking critically and thoroughly. Overawed by gadgetry, data and the obsession to measure and quantify, the whole managerial computerization of therapy is at present geared towards greater control of experiencing and human experiencing in particular. This is because *control* – in person-centred terms, perpetuated by a narrow self-concept over a dynamically changing organism – is one of the main preoccupations of the neoliberal project. More specifically, this is about predicting the behaviour, controlling the acquiring choices of a regiment of customers. I like to believe that it is possible to direct the Cyborg in the direction of liberation, solidarity and compassion instead of manipulation, although this has not happened yet in mainstream PCT.

Empathic manipulators

Historically, the behavioural sciences have been at the forefront of the subtle and not-so-subtle work of manipulation perfected by neoliberalism, designed, according to the moral philosopher Tamsin Shaw, to 'determine the news we read, the products we buy, the cultural and intellectual spheres we inhabit, and the human networks, online and in real life, of which we are a part' (Shaw, 2017, p. 62). She goes on to say:

> Aspects of human societies that were formerly guided by habit and tradition, or spontaneity and whim, are now increasingly the intended or unintended

consequences of decisions made on the basis of scientific theories of the human mind and human well-being.

(Shaw, 2017, p. 62)

Governments and private corporations use the behavioural sciences not in order to convince us consciously by appealing to reason. Instead, they effectively 'change behavior by appealing to our nonrational motivations, our emotional triggers and unconscious biases' (Shaw, 2017, p. 62). Great effort has been employed in recent years by psychologists to construct a methodical understanding of our nonrational motivations. The reason for doing this is that in this way 'they would have the power to influence the smallest aspects of our lives and the largest aspects of our societies' (ibid.). The pioneering work of Daniel Kahneman and Amos Tversky is one of the most consistent examples of this, having provided the basis for this new kind of behavioural science and recently been made available to the layperson (Kahneman, 2012). The behavioural sciences are still the favourite top tool of manipulation utilized by neoliberalism as these present a dependable pedigree. Kahneman had divided the functions of the human mind into two: System One, 'which is fast and automatic' and includes 'instincts, emotions, innate skills shared with animals, as well as learned associations and skills'; and System Two, which is 'slow and deliberative and allows us to correct for the errors made by System One' (Shaw, 2017, p. 62).

In 1955, when he was only twenty-one years old, Kahneman devised personality tests for the Israeli army. Anticipating by some fifty years methodologies employed in the CIA's torture programmes and devised by Positive Psychology (a great favourite among some person-centred practitioners), Kahneman discovered that

> optimal accuracy could be attained by devising tests that removed, as far as possible, the gut feelings of the tester. The testers were employing 'System One' intuitions that skewed their judgment and could be avoided if tests were devised and implemented in ways that disallowed any role for individual judgment and bias.

(Shaw, 2017, p. 62)

Because of the thorny political implications that this summons, any move from Beauty to the Cyborg in PCT is fraught with serious difficulties. There are worrying signs that aspects of PCT can be used in support of a more empathic and even loving manipulation of consumers and the fostering of narratives of violence and aggression such as the one deployed overtly and covertly by Positive Psychology. The embracing of Positive Psychology by PCT practitioners who see a continuum between the two approaches (e.g. Joseph, 2015 among others) is a case in point. Several other examples can be found elsewhere (Bazzano, 2016), but the crucial point here is that in our effort to make PCT more relevant to our contemporary world we should not abandon fundamental ethical and political priorities, and should decide what ends the approach should serve – solidarity and emancipation or coercion and manipulation.

Necessarily insufficient

Were one to look for them, antidotes to neoliberalism and its cultural hegemony are found at the dawn of PCT. In June 1936, Rogers attended a three-day workshop conducted by Otto Rank on his "new post-Freudian form of psychotherapy" (Kramer, 1995, p. 263). Unfortunately there is no transcript of this workshop, but in all probability it drew on Rank's *Will Therapy* (Rank, 1978) which was first published in English in July of that same year. Encountering Rank 'contributed decisively to what Rogers came to call client-centered therapy. "I became infected with Rankian ideas", Rogers said' (Kramer, 1995, p. 263).

Rank exerted a pivotal influence on the work of Rogers; some of Rank's central notions present rich and inspiring connections to PCT. Above all, Rank's view of scientific psychology as *necessarily insufficient* (Rank, 1932) in explaining and dealing with human experience provides a powerful counterpoint to neopositivism. The latter is only the late manifestation of a tendency that has plagued the therapy world from its inception. Rank wrote: 'The main trouble with the scientific approach to human nature is not so much that it has to neglect the personal, so-called subjective element, but that it has to *deny* it in order to maintain the scientific attitude' (Rank, 1996, p. 221).

Psychoanalysis itself, despite its early championing of the unconscious (albeit in a reified form), had stooped to the coercive demand for scientific proof: 'In interpreting the human element scientifically, psychoanalysis had to deny it and so defeated its own scientific ideal, becoming unscientific by denying the most essential aspect of the personality' (ibid., pp. 221–22). That very same tendency is found within PCT. All one needs to do is to substitute 'unconscious' for 'organismic experiencing'.

It is my view that a *battle* needs to be fought in order to retrieve the soul of PCT, a battle between *incompatible* worldviews. One assumes that psychology can measure, check and control human experience; the other recognizes that psychology and psychotherapy are *necessarily insufficient* in comprehending human experience. Both Beauty and the Cyborg in their own very different ways espouse the first stance, despite Beauty's talk of love or maybe *because* of it. Rather than an impasse, the recognition explicit in the second stance is a fertile ground for creativity in our practice. This battle has been going on for a long time within the world of therapy, as Rank testifies:

> So the battle is really on – not between different schools of psychoanalysis but between two worldviews, which have been in conflict with one another since the dawn of science with the early Greeks ... This conflict will not be lessened until we admit that science has proved to be a complete failure in the field of psychology, i.e., in the betterment of human nature and in the achievement of human happiness towards which all mental hygiene is ultimately striving. The result of scientific psychology can be summed up today as the recognition that it is necessarily insufficient to explain human nature, far less to make the

individual happier. The error lies in the scientific glorification of consciousness, of intellectual knowledge, which even psychoanalysis worships as its highest god – although it calls itself a psychology of the *unconscious*. But this means only an attempt to rationalize the unconscious and to intellectualize it scientifically.

(Rank, 1932, p. 222)

In the same book Rank argues that, in therapy, '… we find ourselves directly face to face with experience, which is neither scientifically nor technically controllable, indeed hardly comprehensible while it is being enacted' (Rank, 1932, p. 242).

Alongside Ferenczi, Rank understood experience (*Erlebnis*) as the 'strange consciousness of living' (Kramer, 1995, p. 224n), as something one can live and breathe but not understand, let alone compute (Ferenczi and Rank, 1924). What this means is that the living moment, the present of our incarnate existence, is fundamentally *unknowable* and strange. For some of us, having to live with this strangeness is intolerable, the possibility of responding creatively to the challenge posed by our existence may feel remote, thus we may react with *neurosis* (in Rank's language) or *incongruence* (in Rogers' language). Rank wrote:

> My extensive experience and study (both theoretical and therapeutic) have led me to the conviction that the scientific side to human behavior and personality problems is not only insufficient but leaves out the most essential part: namely, *the human side* – the characteristic of which is just that it can't be measured and checked and controlled.
>
> *(Rank, 1996, p. 221)*

Beastly love

In one of Angela Carter's terse and stylish rewritings of fairy tales and legends (Carter, 1979), she twice reworks *Beauty and the Beast*, this famous story of redemption through love. In the original story, as in its countless conventional versions, the Beast is transfigured into a beautiful prince because of the tears of love Beauty sheds over his wounded body.

One of Carter's two versions, titled *The Tiger's Bride*, ends very differently. The ending comes as a revelation and a shock on the very last words of the tale, when the tiger embraces her and she is delighted to find that when her skin is licked off she sees a beautiful fur underneath. Rather than the organism being incorporated into the self-concept or the unconscious into the conscious, this represents the opposite movement: *where it is, I shall be*. No longer enclosed within her own preciousness and worthiness, the beautiful soul opens itself to the fullness of organismic experiencing, an immanent domain of more expansive, unruly and thoroughly unquantifiable experiencing. For the first time, the ineffectual beautiful soul is capable to attend to *presence* – incarnate and alive, more akin to Caravaggio's men and women than the spiritless, moralizing benevolence of theologians.

References

Attar, F. (2017) *The Conference of the Birds*, Trans. Shole Wolpé. New York: W.W. Norton & Co.

Barber, D.C. (2014) *Deleuze and the Naming of God: Post-Secularism and the Future of Immanence*. Edinburgh: Edinburgh University Press.

Bazzano, M. (2012) *Spectre of the Stranger: Towards a Phenomenology of Hospitality*. Eastbourne: Sussex Academic Press.

Bazzano, M. (2015) 'Therapy as unconditional hospitality', *Psychotherapy and Politics International* 13(1): 4–13.

Bazzano, M. (2013a) 'Togetherness: Intersubjectivity revisited', *Person-Centered & Experiential Psychotherapies*, DOI: doi:10.1080/14779757.2013.852613.

Bazzano, M. (2013b) 'One more step: from person-centered to eco-centered therapy', *Person-Centered & Experiential Psychotherapies*, 12(4): 344–354, DOI: doi:10.1080/14779757.2013.856810.

Bazzano, M. (2014) 'On becoming no one: Phenomenological and empiricist contributions to the person-centered approach', *Person-Centered & Experiential Psychotherapies*, DOI: doi:10.1080/14779757.2013.804649.

Bazzano, M. (2016) 'The conservative turn in person-centered therapy', *Person-Centered & Experiential Psychotherapies*, DOI: doi:10.1080/14779757.2016.1228540.

Bazzano, M., & Webb, J. (Eds.). (2016). *Therapy and the Counter-tradition: The Edge of Philosophy*. Abingdon: Routledge.

Buber, M. (2008) *I and Thou*. London: Continuum.

Carter, A. (1979) *The Bloody Chamber*. London: Vintage

Clark, D. (2016) 'Thinking about the other: conversations and context' in C. Lago & D. Charura (Eds) *The Person-centred Counselling and Psychotherapy Handbook*. Maidenhead: Open University Press, pp. 277–287.

Creswell, R. (2017) 'The seal of the poets', *New York Review of Books*, LXIV(16): 24–27.

Deleuze, G. (1995) *Negotiations*. Translated by M. Joughin. New York: Columbia University Press.

Deleuze, G. (2008) *Foucault*. London: Continuum.

Deleuze, G., & Guattari, F. (1987) *A Thousand Plateaus: Capitalism and Schizophrenia*. Minneapolis, MN: University of Minneapolis Press.

Deleuze, G. & Parnet, C. (2002) *Dialogues II*. London: Continuum.

Descartes, R. (1996) *Meditations of First Philosophy*. Cambridge: Cambridge University Press.

Ellingham, I. (2016) 'A person-centred, process-related conceptual frame'. Presentation, PCE SymposiumLausanne, 15–17 April.

Ferenczi, S. & Rank, O. (1924) *The Development of Psychoanalysis*. New York: Dover.

Goldstein, K. (1995). *The Organism*. New York: Urzone.

Haraway, D. (2016a) *Staying with the Trouble: Making Kin in the Chthulucene*. Durham, NC: Duke University Press.

Haraway, D. (2016b) *Manifestly Haraway: 'A Cyborg Manifesto', 'The Companion Species Manifesto', Companions in Conversation (with Cary Wolfe)*. Minneapolis: Minnesota University Press.

Hegel, G. W. F. (1977). *Phenomenology of Spirit*. Originally published in 1807; trans. A. V. Miller. Oxford: Oxford University Press.

House, R. (2016). 'Beyond the measureable. Alternatives to managed care in research and practice', in J. Lees (Ed.), *The Future of Psychological Therapy*. Abingdon: Routledge (pp. 146–164).

Jameson, F. (2014). *The Antinomies of Realism*. London: Verso.
Joseph, S. (2015). *Positive Therapy: Building Bridges between Positive Psychology and Person-centred Psychotherapy*. Hove: Routledge.
Kahneman, D. (2012) *Thinking, Fast and Slow*. London: Penguin.
Keys, S. (2017) 'Where is the love in counselling?' *Therapy Today*, December, pp. 34–37.
Kramer, R. (1995) 'The birth of client-centered therapy: Carl Rogers, Otto Rank, and beyond', *Journal of Humanistic Psychology* 35(4): 54–110.
Lee, D. (2017) 'A person-centred political critique of current discourses in post-traumatic stress disorder and post-traumatic growth', *Psychotherapy and Politics International*, 15(2): e1411.
Levinas, E. (1999) *Totality and Infinity: an Essay on Exteriority*. Pittsburgh, PA: Duquesne University Press.
Levinas, E. (2008) *Outside the Subject*. London: Continuum.
Massumi, B. (2000) 'The autonomy of affect'. In W. Rasch & C. Wolfe (Eds.), *Observing Complexities: Systems Theory and Post-modernity Cultural Critique*. Minneapolis: University of Minnesota Press (pp. 83–109, 273–298).
Massumi, B. (2014) *What Animals Teach us about Politics*. Durham, NC and London: Duke University Press.
Merleau-Ponty, M. (1964) *Sense and Non-sense*. Evanston: Northwestern University Press
Moreira, V. (2012). 'From person-centered to humanistic-phenomenological psychotherapy: The contribution of Merleau-Ponty to Carl Rogers's thought', *Person-Centered and Experiential Psychotherapies*, 11(1): 48–63.
Moreira, V. (2016). Keynote presentation. WAPCEP Conference, 22 July, New York City.
Nygren, A. (1982) *Agape and Eros*. Chicago: University of Chicago Press.
Rank, O. (1932) *Modern Education*. New York: Knopf.
Rank, O. (1978) *Will Therapy: An Analysis of the Therapeutic Process in Terms of Relationship*. Tr. J. Taft. New York: W.W. Norton.
Rank, O. (1996) *A Psychology of Difference: the American Lectures*. Selected, edited and introduced by R. Kramer.Princeton, NJ: Princeton University Press.
Rogers, C. (1951) *Client-centered Therapy: Its Current Practice, Implications and Theory*. London: Constable.
Rogers, C.R. (1961) *On Becoming a Person*. Boston, MA: Houghton Mifflin.
Rogers, C.R. (1970) *Carl Rogers on Encounter Groups*. New York, NY: Harper and Row.
Rose, G. (1992) *The Broken Middle: Out of our Ancient Society*. Oxford: Blackwell.
Rud, C. (2009). Revision of the notion of identity and its implications in PCA clinical practice. *Person-Centered and Experiential Psychotherapies*, 8(1), 33–43.
Rud, C. (2016). 'The philosophy practice of Spinoza and the person-centered paradigm'. WAPCEP Conference, 23 July, New York City.
Schmid, P. (2016) 'All you need is love? Is psychotherapy healing through love?' Presentation, PCE Symposium, Lausanne, 15–17 April.
ScienceAndReligion.com (2012) 'The illusion of a crumbling worldview', https://iaincarstairs.wordpress.com/2012/04/17/the-illusion-of-a-crumbling-worldview (accessed 26 Dec. 2017).
Shaw, T. (2017) 'Invisible manipulators of your mind', *New York Review of Books*, LXIV(7): 62–65.
Thorne, B. (2005) *Love's Embrace: the Autobiography of a Person-centred Therapist*. Ross-on-Wye: PCCS Books.
Tudor, K., & Worrall, M. (2006) *Person-centred Therapy: A Clinical Philosophy*. London: Routledge.

Tudor, K. (2010) 'Person-centered relational therapy: An organismic perspective', *Person-Centered and Experiential Psychotherapies*, 1(9): 52–68.
Yoder, J.H. (1994) *The Politics of Jesus: Vicit Agnus Noster*. Grand Rapids: Eerdmans.
Yoder, J.H. (1997) *For the Nations: Essays Evangelical and Public*. Grand Rapids: Eerdmans.
Yoder, J.H. (2003) *The Original Revolution: Essays on Christian Pacifism*. Scottdale, PA: Herald.

4

WALKING BACKWARDS TOWARDS THE FUTURE

Reclaiming the radical roots – and future – of person-centred therapy

Keith Tudor

Looking back

What is now known as person-centred therapy has its roots in various traditions: Christianity, empiricism, humanism, phenomenology and existentialism (see Tudor & Worrall, 2006). As far as the therapeutic relationship is concerned, person-centred therapy has been heavily influenced by Rankian therapy, founded by Otto Rank and developed by Jessie Taft, Frederick Allen and Virginia Robinson at the School of Social Work at the University of Philadelphia, USA. Rogers had been introduced to Rank's work through a former member of staff at the Child Study Department in Rochester, New York, where Rogers and some colleagues invited Rank to conduct a seminar which took place in June 1936. Whilst there is some debate about the extent to which Rogers was "transformed" by his brief and limited contact with Rank (see Kramer, 1995), he hardly referred to Rank in his own work, though he did credit Jessie Taft and Frederick Allen (and, later, another social worker, Elizabeth Davis, whom he had employed in Rochester) for their influence on his work.

Three major influences on Rogers' thinking about and development of the therapeutic relationship may be traced through these colleagues back to Rank's ideas:

1. The emphasis on the patient's positive will as the source of growth in therapy. In his book on *Will Therapy* (Rank, 1978, which first appeared in German in 1931, and was translated by Taft and published in English in 1936), Rank advanced the idea that humans are directed by their own will and not internal or external forces. Thus therapy becomes the process of freeing the client to assume responsibility for her or his choices and direction. This is akin to Rogers' non-directive therapy (Rogers, 1939), based on a person's tendency

to actualise (see Rogers, 1963). Writing about Taft's *Relationship Therapy* – which, in 1937, Rogers had referred to as "a small masterpiece of writing and thinking" (Rogers in Rogers & Hart, 1937, p. 515), Rogers (1939) commented: "its major value may be ... the fresh viewpoint of non-interference and reliance upon the individual's own tendency towards growth which it has emphasized" (p. 200).

2. The focus on understanding rather than interpretation.
Rank himself was critical of the techniques of interpretation and began to move away from the use of interpretation (at least of the past) and towards a focus on the therapist's *understanding* of the patient. His followers took this a step further in emphasising the importance of the client's own understanding of her or himself, through self-insight and self-acceptance within the therapeutic relationship – and, thus, the therapeutic relationship became the vehicle and focus of the therapy (Taft, 1933).

3. The emphasis on the present.
According to Rank, all emotional life is grounded in the present, and, indeed, he was the first to use the phrase "here-and-now" in psychotherapeutic literature: "Freud made the repression historical, that is, misplaced it into the childhood of the individual and then wanted to release it from there, while as a matter of fact the same tendency is working here and now" (Rank, 1978, p. 39). Instead of the word *Verdrängung* (repression), which laid stress on unconscious repression of the past, Rank preferred to use *Verleugnung* (denial), which refers to the emotional will to remain ill in the present – a term that Rogers was later to use as one of the defences he identified in client-centred personality theory (Rogers, 1951). As Rank put it:

> The neurotic lives too much in the past [and] to that extent he actually does not live. He suffers ... because he clings to [the past], wants to cling to it, in order to protect himself from experience [*Erlebnis*], the emotional surrender to the present.
>
> *(Rank, 1978, p. 27)*

Elsewhere, and influenced by the work of Daniel Stern on the present moment (Stern, 2004), I have made the point that person-centred therapy could equally be referred to as "present-centred therapy" (Tudor, 2010a).

Referring to this kind of therapy as "relationship therapy", as Taft did in 1933, was the original "relational turn" – away from both one-person psychoanalysis and one-person behaviour therapy – and predates the more recent relational turn in psychoanalysis by some 50 years. In 1942, Rogers adopted this term from Taft, using it to describe his "newer psychotherapy", the basic aspects of which he identified as characterised by: warmth and responsiveness; permissiveness in regard to the expression of feeling; certain therapeutic limits, e.g., about time; freedom from pressure and coercion; and the client having an increased ability to respond genuinely – aspects which prefigured his later theory of therapeutic conditions (Rogers, 1957a, 1959) and of process (Rogers, 1967a).

One of the original radical aspects of person-centred therapy is, precisely, its focus or centredness on the client. I argue that this is radical in that it returns to the root of therapy in focusing on the person at the centre of the healing, i.e., the client. Thus, in 1951, Rogers wrote a chapter on therapy or the therapeutic relationship *as experienced by the client*, in which he identified six elements of such experience: that of responsibility, exploration, (the discovery) of denied attitudes, of reorganising the self, of progress, and of ending. Rogers' next and, arguably, most famous development was his formulations of the necessary and sufficient conditions of therapy (Rogers, 1957b, 1959), in which he described, in effect, the qualities of the therapeutic relationship by means of certain necessary – and sufficient – attitudes. He identified these as a result of research which, nowadays, would be considered a form of grounded theory (see Strauss, 1987), whereby theory is constructed from the ground of the client's experiencing. Significantly, Rogers identified qualities not only of the therapist, i.e., to be in psychological contact, congruent (genuine or authentic in the relationship), unconditional in her or his positive regard, and empathic in her or his understanding, but also those of the client. These were also to be in psychological contact, to be incongruent (by virtue of being vulnerable or anxious) and to experience or perceive the therapist's regard and empathy. Commenting on this further, Rogers (1967a) referred to the sixth condition, the client's experience and/or perception, as the central or "assumed condition" (p. 130), a statement that clearly places the assessment of the efficacy and, ultimately, the outcome of therapy in the experience/perception of the client.

Rogers' theory of conditions – and relationship – describes a person-to-person relationship, which, in their major article on the therapeutic relationship, Gelso (2010) referred to as the "real relationship", as distinct from the "unreal" transferential/countertransferential relationship. While I don't agree that transference phenomena and what Rogers referred to as "attitudes" are unreal, I agree with his critique that the artificial fostering of transference in order to maintain a long-term psychotherapeutic relationship – with the implication that psychotherapy is, by definition, long-term – may suit the practitioner more than the client. Shlien (1984) went further, stating that "'*transference' is a fiction, invented and maintained by the therapist to protect himself from the consequences of his own behaviour*" (p. 153). Shlien built his case for a counter-theory of transference in part by identifying what he viewed as "the illogical assumption that any response that duplicates a prior similar response is necessarily replicating it. ... In the first instance, the original love of the child for the parent is not transferred [as] ... there was no earlier instance" (p. 174). He went on to argue that understanding and misunderstanding roles and behaviours in the present "*should be the first hypothesis* [and] account for the major affects of love and hate" (p. 174). Shlien's article was so stimulating and provocative that, three years later, a whole issue of the *Person-Centered Review* was devoted to the theme of transference, reproducing his article and publishing various commentaries on it. In one, Maddi (1987) supported Shlien's position and further argued that transference is "logically implausible" and, moreover, dangerous: "If you cannot trust your reactions to things in the present, then you have no decision-making grounds to stand on. You also have no basis for taking the present seriously" (p. 179). Maddi laid the origins of this problem squarely with what he referred to as "This major thrust of psychoanalytic theory [which] is toward skepticism, self-preoccupation, inertia, nihilism and finally, meaninglessness" (p. 179). I appreciate both Shlien's and Maddi's critique of the excesses of psychoanalytic thinking and its implications for a rarefied, interminable, expensive and, therefore, elitist practice. Nevertheless, I think it is important to acknowledge the usefulness of the phenomenon in therapeutic practice and everyday life. Given the importance of mutuality in person-centred theory, I suggest that it is more useful and consistent to (re)claim the *mutual* possibility of transference in a therapeutic relationship and, therefore, that the therapist may transfer projections onto the client, and that this is not always *counter*transference, and that this is best represented by the term "co-transference". Originally coined by self psychologists, this term acknowledges the responsibility of the therapist for their part in the relationship and its dynamics, and does not carry the same sense of blame inherent in the term "countertransference". As Sapriel (1998, p. 42) put it, co-transference:

> better reflects the reality that meaning is being co-created by both subjectivities ... with neither person holding a more objectively "true" version of reality than the other. It reflects an appreciation of the inevitable, moment-by-moment participation of the therapist's subjective organisation of experience in a system of mutual influence.

Other developments in thinking about the therapeutic relationship in person-centred psychology include: the development of the concept and practice of "working at relational depth" (Mearns, 1996; Mearns & Cooper, 2005); the development of relationship as the art of encounter (Schmid, 1998), and that this represents a "togetherness" (Bazzano, 2014); relationship as contact (Krietemeyer & Prouty, 2003); the acknowledgement of the influence of community and wider systems on relationships (Barrett-Lennard, 2005), and of the planet (Neville, 2012); a reclaiming of the therapeutic relationship as dialogic (Schmid, 2006), and as founded in organismic psychology and, hence, *relating* (Tudor & Worrall, 2006; Tudor, 2010b).

Finally, it is important to note that Rogers viewed the therapeutic relationship as (but) one instance of all relationships and that the same "lawfulness" – of genuine acceptance, understanding and a communication of that understanding – governs *all* relationships (Rogers & Dymond, 1978).

Looking under

Having looked back at the history of some of the understanding of the therapeutic relationship in person-centred therapy, I now turn to what lies beneath this understanding, i.e., what is under our standing as person-centred therapists. It is not enough simply to claim that person-centred therapy is radical or even revolutionary, as, for instance, Bozarth (1998) does, or that it is a paradigm, as, for instance, Hutterer et al. (1996) do. The word "radical" derives from the Latin word *radix* meaning root and, more broadly, a sense of going to the original, as represented by the first part of the chapter. The political sense of radical as meaning reformist or Left dates back to the early 19th century (Common Era) and its application to a section of the British Liberal Party. Thus, in order to assess the radical or reformist nature of person-centred therapy, let alone its potential, it is necessary to define our terms and to understand them in the context of some organising principle(s) or framework(s); and, as this book names person-centred therapy as a radical paradigm, I consider this enquiry in terms of paradigms. Such an approach is entirely consistent with Rogers' view of the importance of theory – and, in effect, meta-theory; as he himself put it: "One cannot engage in psychotherapy without giving operational evidence of an underlying value orientation and view of human nature. It is definitely preferable, in my estimation, that such underlying views be open and explicit, rather than covert and implicit" (Rogers, 1957a, p. 199).

Paradigms and paradigm analysis

In his treatise on *The Structure of Scientific Revolutions*, Thomas Kuhn (1996/1962) reflected on the history and practice of modern scientific inquiry, and argued that, in order to be effective, scientific inquiry should be based on paradigms. Paradigms are constructs that identify and encompass broad relationships between two or more general categories, and are defined by basic assumptions underlying the nature of the subject. Burrell and Morgan (1979) identified four sets of assumptions by which they conceptualised and elaborated the nature of social science: (a) ontological assumptions, that is, about the essence of things; (b) epistemological assumptions, that is, about the nature of knowledge; (c) assumptions about human nature; (d) methodological assumptions – which I have used to frame my analysis of transactional analysis (see Tudor, 1996). Thus, in themselves, paradigms are not theories but, rather, bundles of theories that offer a way of conceptualising, organising and structuring "intellectual curiosity" and research (see Janos, 1986), as well as a focus for scientific disciplines. They also offer a map whereby we may trace our "ancestors of the mind" (Traue, 2001) and see where they have moved across or shifted paradigms. Furthermore, paradigms are social conventions which represent and reflect a consensus in a particular field or discipline, conventions and consensus which are established and maintained by "experts" – or, indeed, practitioners and researchers – in that field. As Kuhn (1962/1996) put it: "a paradigm is an accepted model or pattern" and, moreover, "Paradigms gain their status because they are more successful than their competitors in solving a few problems that the group of practitioners has come to recognize as acute" (p. 23).

In their work on organisational analysis, Gibson Burrell and Gareth Morgan (1979) brought a sociological perspective to Kuhn's paradigm analysis. They argued that "assumptions about the nature of science can be thought of in terms of ... the subjective–objective dimension, and assumptions about the nature of society in terms of a regulation–radical change dimension" (Burrell and Morgan, 1979, p. 21). Burrell and Morgan discussed the relationship between their two dimensions, and juxtaposed them as axes by which they defined four distinct sociological paradigms which they labelled broadly as functionalist, interpretative, radical humanist, and radical structuralist, and within which they identify a number of intellectual traditions thus, in the functionalist paradigm, integrative theory and social systems theory; in the interpretive paradigm, phenomenology and hermeneutics; in the radical humanist paradigm, critical theory and French existentialism; and in the radical structuralist paradigm, conflict theory and contemporary Mediterranean Marxism.

Burrell and Morgan made a number of points about the nature and use of paradigm analysis:

1. That, although each paradigm contains a variety of viewpoints, there is essential unity within the paradigm, defined by its external boundaries.
   In their original diagram, Burrell and Morgan (1979) represented each of the four paradigms as four enclosed squares. For instance, the "essential unity" of definitions and concepts of therapy within the radical humanist paradigm is defined by "its concern to develop a *sociology* [and psychology] *of radical change* from a *subjectivist* standpoint" (p. 32). Whilst I agree with Burrell and Morgan about the unity of a paradigm, I am now less convinced that there are fixed, rigid external boundaries.

2. That "social theorists can be located within the context of these four paradigms according to the meta-theoretical assumptions reflected in their work" (Burrell & Morgan, 1979, p. 24).
   Thus, when Rogers (1957a) refers to "man" as having "characteristics which seem inherent in his species ... [and which are] positive, forward-moving, constructive, realistic, [and] trustworthy" (p. 200), he is describing a voluntaristic view of human nature which represents a subjectivist approach to social and psychological science. This, together with his belief that "to be a human being is to enter into the complex process of being one of the most widely sensitive, responsive, creative, and adaptive creatures on the planet" (ibid., p. 201), places him squarely in the radical humanist paradigm. Significantly (with regard to our current interest), the article in which Rogers described human beings in this way, "A note on 'The nature of man'", was written in response to a commentator (Walker, 1956) who had suggested that, while Freud inherited the tradition of St Augustine, Rogers was the successor of the 18th century Swiss philosopher, Jean-Jacques Rousseau. Rogers' (1957a) response and his reference to the importance of the underlying value orientation and "philosophical substratum" (p. 199) reflects his own interest in meta-theory.

3. That, by definition, the four paradigms are mutually exclusive.
   Kuhn (1962/1996) argued that rival paradigms are incommensurable; Burrell and Morgan (1979) maintained this view, stating that "a synthesis [of them] is not possible" (p. 25). This is one of the reasons why paradigm analysis is

useful; it reveals and describes the conceptual and theoretical assumptions underpinning differences, which lead to and are often demonstrated in differences in practice and action. A number of practitioners and theorists view the person-centred approach, principles and skills as a good, (if only) basic grounding, but that to work effectively as a psychotherapist, a person needs further training – in another theoretical orientation or modality. Such a person might go on to train in, say, psychodynamic psychotherapy. The problem here is that, as the underlying assumptions of the two approaches are mutually exclusive, the practice that is the operational evidence of those different assumptions is also mutually exclusive. Thus, if you have a view of the state of nature as "solitary, poor, nasty, brutish and short" (as did Thomas Hobbes, 2010), then you would find person-centred education/training (based on assumptions derived from Rousseau) somewhat difficult. Making underlying views open and explicit and having sharp differences is not the problem; having and leaving assumptions covert and implicit is, in this context, problematic.

Person-centred therapy: A radical humanism

So, is person-centred therapy radical? In their description of the radical humanist paradigm, Burrell and Morgan suggested that its frame of reference is "committed to a view of society which emphasises the importance of over-throwing or transcending the limitations of existing social arrangements", and that what underlies this is the view that "the consciousness of man is dominated by the ideological superstructures with which he interacts, and that these drive a cognitive wedge between himself and his true consciousness" (Burrell & Morgan, 1979, p. 32). They also traced the intellectual foundations of the paradigm to the German idealist tradition (of Kant, Hegel and the young Marx) and an "infusion" of phenomenology (dating from Husserl). Here, drawing on Burrell and Morgan's summary of the radical humanist paradigm, I note aspects of person-centred theory that reflect these points.

Alienation and false consciousness, and the inhibition of true human fulfilment. This is reflected in person-centred theory (PCT) in the concept of "distorted perception" (Rogers, 1951); the elaboration of alienation as the basis of psychopathology (Tudor & Worrall, 2006); and the understanding of the inhibition of fulfilment through "conditions of worth" (Rogers, 1959), initially from the external environment, and then internalised. As Bozarth (1998) put it: "Conditionality is the bedrock of Rogers' theory of pathology" (p. 83). In a rare reference to alienation, Rogers himself described one of the profound consequences of empathy: "empathy dissolves alienation" (Rogers, 1980a, p. 151).

Release from the constraints which existing social arrangements place on human development. PCT posits the actualising tendency as the sole motivation for human development (Rogers, 1963) that supports the client's inherent direction in terms of a contactful, acceptant (non-judgemental), caring, and empathic relationship (see also Brodley, 1999). Writing about empathy as a healing agent, Rogers (1986) suggested that "it brings even the most frightened client into the human race. If a person can be understood, he or she belongs" (p. 129).

Critique of the status quo. This is found in PCT in its critique of the status quo in the therapeutic field, for example, with regard to diagnosis, transference, and the expert clinician/therapist (Rogers, 1951); to education (Rogers, 1969); and to the helping professions (Rogers, 1973), for a contemporary reflection on which, see Tudor (2014).

Society as anti-human. In his description of the qualities of "the person of tomorrow", Rogers (1980b) included having a scepticism regarding science and technology, being anti-institutional, and being indifferent to material things.

Articulation of ways in human beings can transcend spiritual bonds and realise their full potential. This is represented in PCT in the concepts of the actualising tendency (Rogers, 1963), the fully functioning person (Rogers, 1959), and personal power (Rogers, 1978)

Central emphasis on human consciousness. This is reflected in the focus in person-centred practice on awareness (which Rogers viewed as synonymous with consciousness), and reflective consciousness (see also Wijngaarden, 1990; Neville, 1996).

Looking forward

"Ka mura, ka muri" is a Māori *whakatauki* or proverb that is generally interpreted as "walking backwards towards the future", a psychological and social posture that informs this chapter. Looking back from what is now generally referred to as the person-centred approach, with its different "tribes" (Sanders, 2004) to "person-centred therapy" (from Rogers, 1967b), "client-centred therapy" (Rogers, 1951), "relationship therapy" (Rogers, 1951), and "newer ... psychotherapy" (Rogers, 1939), to "non-directive therapy" (Rogers, 1939), we can see that it was heavily influenced by Rankian therapy. Ellingham (2011) proposes that early Rogerian therapy "was nothing other than a re-espousal of Rankian relationship therapy" (p. 185). This perspective has led to a certain reclaiming of relationship, relationality and relating as being at the heart of therapeutic encounters between people – and between people and the environment.

In a number of publications and especially those written towards the end of his life, Rogers looked both back and forwards. In the interviews that David Russell conducted with him in 1985 and 1986 (the last less than two months before Rogers' death in February 1987), Rogers commented positively about the person-centred approach (PCA) with regard to research; its theoretical development (he referred specifically to Shlien's countertheory of transference); its application (he referred to the example of supervision); its development in a number of countries; the fact that its theoretical formulations were – and are – drawn from practice and have continued to be tested; its contribution to humanistic psychology; and that what he referred to as this "point of view" "started from individual therapy [and] is now becoming significant in international and interracial situations" (in Rogers & Russell, 2002, p. 306).

54 Keith Tudor

TABLE 4.1 Historical development of paradigms with regard to health and applied to person-centred therapy

Paradigm development, and the progress of science	Pre-paradigm period, pre-science	Conventional paradigm, i.e. "normal science"	Post-paradigm period, revolutionary science
Approach to health	Holistic	Dualistic	Holistic/integrated
Focus	The person	Illness	Illness and health, the whole person
Integration/ differentiation (of mind and body)	Mind and body undifferentiated	Mind and body differentiated and split	Mind and body inseparable, integrated
Identification of problems/ symptoms	Self-report	Diagnosis (medical/ psychiatric)	Diagnosis, and self-diagnosis
Conceptualisation of health	Subjective categories, e.g. humours	Objective categories based on clusters of symptoms	Changing categories
Treatment	Natural remedies	Allopathic medicine	Allopathic, homeopathic and complementary/ alternative medicine
Respondents	Healers	Qualified doctors	Qualified doctors and complementary/ alternative health practitioners

In his work on paradigms, Kuhn (1996/1962) made a second point about the historical development of disciplines and paradigms, and the change or "shift" between paradigms. Taking examples from physics and, specifically, from physical optics, Kuhn observed that, in the 18th century, physics taught that light was material corpuscles (Newton) and, later (in the early 19th century), that it was transverse wave motion (from Young and Fresnel); and that both these and, before them, various other competing schools of physics represent one variant of Epicurean, Aristotelian or Platonic theory. The characterisation of light as *photons*, i.e. quantum-mechanical entities which exhibit some characteristics of waves and some characteristics of particles (Plank, Einstein and others), however, represents a transformation of the previous paradigm of physical optics theory. Table 4.1 represents Kuhn's historical/developmental perspective on paradigms applied to the field of health, following which I apply it specifically to person-centred therapy.

Here I apply Kuhn's perspective on paradigms to person-centred therapy.

- *Its approach to health.* This is, theoretically, holistic/integrated (see Rogers, 1957a, 1967b; Sanders, 2000; Tudor & Worrall, 2006), though there is little use or development of the language of holism in person-centred literature and, indeed, in some quarters, an undue focus on parts or configurations of the self. Also, in my experience, many person-centred practitioners actually subscribe to a bio-medical model of health and illness.

- *Its focus.* This is on the person, and as a whole person (Rogers, 1957a, 1967b), although, I would say that, in practice, its proponents tend to privilege health over illness, and, I suggest, could develop more of a dialogue and dialectic between health and illness and the meaning of illness. Also, and especially in an era of ecopsychology and post-humanism, I think we need to revisit the usefulness of the metaphor of the person. Echoing Martin Buber's phrase "I-Thou" with regard to relationship, Rank (1978/1931) wrote that "the ego needs the Thou in order to become a Self" (p. 290) and some within the person-centred and experiential nation, notably Peter Schmid, do suggest a greater focus on the "Thou" (e.g., Schmid, 2006). I suggest that we need to extend this to include the "thou" of other beings and, indeed, the environment and the planet. As the Māori proverb referring to the mighty Whanganui river suggests: *Ko au te awa, ko te awa ko au* (I am the river and the river is me), a perspective that, earlier this year, was enshrined in New Zealand law by the *Te Awa Tupua (Whanganui River Claims Settlement) Act* which conferred a legal personality on this river.
- *Its integration/differentiation.* Person-centred psychology is based on mind and body integration (see Rogers, 1967a; Brown, 1990), and the term "person-centred" is now used in other spheres such as medicine and nursing to reflect both this sense of integration as well as a centredness on the person. Within person-centred therapy, I don't see so much attention given to the body or the somatic aspect of the person and, therefore, to such integration. With regard to differentiation, there are different views about the desirability of what Swildens (2004) referred to as "process differentiation" (see Takens & Lietaer, 2004).
- *Its identification of problem/symptom.* Typically, person-centred therapists do not focus on this, a stance that is also found in Taft (1933), who reported that she aimed "to ignore content", preferring "to go through to the fundamental attitude and emotions behind it" (p. 108). In his critique of diagnosis, Rogers (1951) asserted that, "In a very meaningful and accurate sense, therapy is diagnosis, and this diagnosis is a process which goes on in the experience of the client, rather than the intellect of the clinician" (p. 224). I think that this is a particularly radical perspective which, unfortunately, too few person-centred practitioners maintain or promote in the face of the powerful medical paradigm and establishment, and government funding of therapies based on diagnosis by experts.
- *Its conceptualisation of health.* The person-centred approach to health is framed in terms of fully functioning (Rogers, 1959), on the person being in process, and on fluidity, which Rogers (1967a) viewed as a social value, but which is rarely discussed in the person-centred literature.
- *Its treatment.* As the term "treatment" is more associated with the medical model and represents a one-person psychology (Stark, 1999), it is generally not used in person-centred psychology. Its therapy or healing is based on contact, listening, love and understanding and, crucially, a dialogic relating with the

client. It is arguable as to whether person-centred therapy is more homeopathic than allopathic (see Townsend, 2006), and most of its practitioners and their employers would see it as complementary to medicine and other therapeutic approaches. However, its practitioners rarely position themselves as "alternative" and in that sense radical, for instance, as against the medical model, the psychiatric system, and oppressive forms and systems of diagnosis.

- *Its respondents.* Person-centred therapists are generally lay professionals, i.e., not medically qualified practitioners, although many are somewhat conservative and uncritical, especially of the increasing professionalisation of therapy. Rogers was both quite radical and somewhat prescient in this respect: his paper on "Some new challenges", delivered to the annual meeting of the American Psychological Association in 1972 and published the following year (Rogers, 1973) – with its challenge to being whole persons, acknowledging plural realities, developing human science, doing away with professionalism, and embracing design – anticipated and still addresses contemporary challenges (Tudor, 2014).

From this, I suggest that, while aspects of person-centred therapy (and, more broadly, the person-centred approach) can be located in the post-paradigm period, there are others that still represent a more conventional paradigm that is based on and subscribes to "normal" or traditional, modernist science. Nevertheless, reclaiming the spirit of Rogers' original work (walking backwards), I suggest that person-centred therapy can have a radical future if it dares to move beyond a focus on the self (Self) and even the person to one that embodies an eco-psychotherapy that, even when working with individuals, encompasses a wider vision of relationality and sustainability.

References

Barrett-Lennard, G. T. (2005). *Relationship at the centre: Healing in a troubled world*. London, UK: Whurr.

Bazzano, M. (2014). Togetherness: Intersubjectivity revisited. *Person-Centered & Experiential Psychotherapies*, 13(3), 203–216.

Bozarth, J. (1998). *Person-centered therapy: A revolutionary paradigm*. Ross-on-Wye, UK: PCCS Books.

Brodley, B. T. (1999). About the nondirective attitude. *Person-Centred Practice*, 7(2), 79–82.

Brown, M. (1990). *The healing touch: An introduction to organismic psychotherapy*. Mendocino, CA: Liferhythm.

Burrell, G., & Morgan, G. (1979). *Sociological paradigms and organisational analysis*. London, UK: Heinemann.

Ellingham, I. (2011). Carl Rogers' fateful wrong move in the development of Rogerian relational therapy: Retitling "relationship therapy" "non-directive therapy". *Person-Centered & Experiential Psychotherapies*, 10(3), 181–197.

Gelso, C.J. (2010). *The real relationship in psychotherapy: The hidden foundation of chance*. Washington, DC: APA.

Hobbes, T. (2010). *Leviathan: Or, the matter, forme, and power a common-wealth ecclesiastical and civil* (I. Shapiro, Ed.). New Haven, CT: Yale University Press. (Original work published 1651.)

Hutterer, R., Pawlowsky, G., Schmid, P.F., & Stipsits, R. (Eds.). (1996). *Client-centered and experiential psychotherapy: A paradigm in motion.* Frankfurt am Main, Germany: Peter Lang.

Janos, A. (1986). *Politics and paradigms: Changing theories of change in social science.* Redwood City, CA: Stanford University Press.

Kramer, R. (1995). The birth of client-centered therapy: Carl Rogers, Otto Rank, and "the beyond". *Journal of Humanistic Psychology*, 35(4), 54–110.

Krietemeyer, B., & Prouty, G. (2003). The art of psychological contact: The psychotherapy of a mentally retarded psychotic client. *Person-Centred & Experiential Psychotherapies*, 2(3), 151–161.

Kuhn, T. (1996). *The Structure of Scientific Revolutions.* Chicago, IL: Chicago University Press. Originally published in 1962.

Maddi, S. R. (1987). On the importance of the present: Reactions to John Shlien's article. *Person-Centered Review*, 2(2), 171–181.

Mearns, D. (1996). Working at relational depth with clients in person-centred therapy. *Counselling*, 7(4), 306–311.

Mearns, D., & Cooper, M. (2005). *Working at relational depth.* London, UK: Sage.

Neville, B. (1996). Five kinds of empathy. In R. Hutterer, G. Pawlowsky, P.F. Schmid & R. Stipsits (Eds.), *Client-centered and experiential psychotherapy: A paradigm in motion* (pp. 439–453). Frankfurt am Main, Germany: Peter Lang.

Neville, B. (2012). *The life of things: Therapy and the soul of the world.* Ross-on-Wye, UK: PCCS Books.

Rank, O. (1978). *Will therapy* (J. Taft, Trans.). New York, NY: W.W. Norton (Original work published 1931).

Rogers, C. R. (1939). *The clinical treatment of the problem child.* Boston, MA: Houghton Mifflin.

Rogers, C.R. (1951). *Client-centered therapy.* London, UK: Constable.

Rogers, C.R. (1957a). A note on the "Nature of Man". *Journal of Counseling Psychology*, 4(3), 199–203.

Rogers, C. R. (1957b). The necessary and sufficient conditions of therapeutic personality change. *Journal of Consulting Psychology*, 21, 95–103.

Rogers, C.R. (1959). A theory of therapy, personality and interpersonal relationships, as developed in the client-centred framework. In S. Koch (Ed.), *Psychology: A study of science, Vol. 3: Formulation of the person and the social context* (pp. 184–256). New York, NY: McGraw-Hill.

Rogers, C. R. (1963). The actualizing tendency in relation to "motive" and to consciousness. In M. Jones (Ed.), *Nebraska symposium on motivation* (pp. 1–24). Lincoln, NE: University of Nebraska Press.

Rogers, C.R. (1967a) A process conception of psychotherapy. In *On becoming a person* (pp. 125–159). London, UK: Constable (Original work published in 1958).

Rogers, C. R. (1967b). *On becoming a person.* London, UK: Constable (Original work published 1961).

Rogers, C. R. (1969). *Freedom to learn.* Columbus, OH: Charles E. Merrill.

Rogers, C. R. (1973). Some new challenges to the helping professions. *American Psychologist*, 28(5), 379–387.

Rogers, C. R. (1978). *Carl Rogers on personal power.* London, UK: Constable.

Rogers, C. R. (1980a). Empathic: An unappreciated way of being. In *A way of being* (pp. 137–163). Boston, MA: Houghton Mifflin (Original work published 1975).

Rogers, C. R. (1980b). The world of tomorrow and the person of tomorrow. In *A way of being* (pp. 339–356). Boston, MA: Houghton Mifflin.

Rogers, C. R. (1986). Rogers, Kohut, and Erickson: A personal perspective on some similarities and differences. *Person-Centred Review*, 1(2), 125–140.

Rogers, C. R., & Hart, J. (1937). Looking back and ahead: A conversation with Carl Rogers. In J. T. Hart & T. M. Tomlinson (Eds.), *New directions in client-centered therapy* (pp. 502–534). Boston, MA: Houghton Mifflin.

Rogers, C. R., & Russell, D. E. (2002). *Carl Rogers the quiet revolutionary: An oral history*. Roseville, CA: Penmarin Books.

Rogers, C. R., & Dymond, R. F. (1978). *Psychotherapy and personality change*. Chicago, IL: University of Chicago Press. Originally published in 1954.

Sanders, P. (2000). Mapping person-centred approaches to counselling and psychotherapy. *Person-Centred Practice*, 8(2), 62–74.

Sanders, P. (2004). *The tribes of the person-centred nation: A guide to the schools of therapy associated with the person-centred approach*. Ross-on-Wye, UK: PCCS Books.

Sapriel, L. (1998). Can gestalt therapy, self-psychology and intersubjectivity theory be integrated? *The British Gestalt Journal*, 7(1), 33–44.

Schmid, P. (1998). "Face to face": The art of encounter. In B. Thorne & E. Lambers (Eds.), *Person-centred therapy: A European perspective* (pp. 74–90). London, UK: Sage.

Schmid, P. (2006). The challenge of the Other: Towards dialogical person-centered psychotherapy. *Person-Centered & Experiential Psychotherapies*, 5(4), 240–254.

Shlien, J. (1984). A countertheory of transference. In R. Levant & J. Shlien (Eds.), *Client-centered therapy and the person-centered approach: New directions in theory, research and practice* (pp. 153–181). New York, NY: Praeger.

Stark, M. (1999). *Modes of therapeutic action: Enhancement of knowledge, provision of experience, engagement in relationship*. Northvale, NJ: Jason Aronson.

Stern, D. N. (2004). *The present moment: In psychotherapy and everyday life*. New York, NY: W.W. Norton.

Strauss, A. L. (1987). *Qualitative analysis for social scientists*. New York, NY: Cambridge University Press.

Swildens, H. (2004) Self-pathology and postmodern humanity: Challenges for person-centered psychotherapy. *Person-Centered & Experiential Psychotherapies*, 3(1), 4–18.

Taft, J. (1933). *The dynamics of therapy in a controlled relationship*. New York, NY: Macmillan.

Takens, R. J., & Lietaer, G. (2004). Process-differentiation and person-centeredness: A contradiction? *Person-Centered & Experiential Psychotherapies*, 3(2), 77–87.

Townsend, I. (2006). Almost nothing to do: Supervision and the person-centred approach in homeopathy. In K. Tudor & M. Worrall (Eds.), *Freedom to practise: Person-centred approaches to supervision* (pp. 225–246). Ross-on-Wye, UK: PCCS Books.

Traue, J. E. (2001). Ancestors of the mind: A Pakeha whakapapa. In R. Brown (Ed.), *The great New Zealand argument: Ideas about ourselves* (pp. 137–147), Auckland, Aotearoa New Zealand: Activity Press (Original work published 1990).

Tudor, K. (1996). Transactional analysis intragration: A metatheoretical analysis for practice. *Transactional Analysis Journal*, 26(4), 329–340.

Tudor, K. (1999). "I'm OK, You're OK – and They're OK": Therapeutic relationships in transactional analysis. In C. Feltham (Ed.), *Understanding the counselling relationship* (pp. 90–119). London, UK: Sage.

Tudor, K. (2009). We cannot imagine without the other: Contact and difference in psychotherapeutic relating. *Forum* [The Journal of the New Zealand Association of Psychotherapists], 14, 46–61.

Tudor, K. (2010a). "A lifetime burning in every moment": Strangeness and complication in neopsychic functioning. Paper given at the Annual Conference of the New Zealand Association of Psychotherapists, Dunedin, Aotearoa New Zealand, 18–21 March, 2010.

Tudor, K. (2010b). The fight for health: A heuristic enquiry into psychological well-being (Unpublished context statement for PhD in Mental Health Promotion by Public (Published) Works). School of Health and Social Sciences, Middlesex University, London, UK.

Tudor, K. (2010c). Person-centred relational therapy: An organismic perspective. *Person-Centered & Experiential Psychotherapies*, 9(1), 52–68.

Tudor, K. (2014). Back to the future: Carl Rogers' "new challenge" reviewed and renewed. *Self & Society: An International Journal for Humanistic Psychology*, 41(2), 17–24.

Tudor, K., & Widdowson, M. (2008). From client process to therapeutic relating: A critique of the process model and personality adaptations. *Transactional Analysis Journal*, 38(3), 218–232.

Tudor, K., & Worrall, M. (2006). *Person-centred therapy: A clinical philosophy*. London, UK: Routledge.

Walker, D. E. (1956). Letter to the editor. *Journal of Counseling Psychology*, 3, 229–230.

Wijngaarden, H.R. (1990). Carl Rogers, Carl Jung and client-centered therapy. In G. Lietaer, J. Rombauts & R. Van Balen (Eds.), *Client-centered and experiential psychotherapy in the nineties* (pp. 469–479). Leuven, Belgium: Leuven University Press.

5

ETHICS AND THE PERSON-CENTERED APPROACH

A dialogue with radical alterity

Emanuel Meireles Vieira and Francisco Pablo Huascar Aragão Pinheiro

Introduction

The subject of ethics is often bypassed in the psychologist's training. At times, technical learning, necessary for professional integration, overrides the discipline's fundamental discussions. It is rare for psychologists to debate the ethics that constitute their practices. At most, they speak of the deontic codes that govern the profession.

This work aims to reflect on the relationship between ethics and the person-centered approach (PCA). It discusses the ideas of authors who question the perspective established by Carl Rogers, itself based on Emmanuel Levinas' Ethics of Radical Alterity. The ideas of this French-Lithuanian philosopher show that addressing the Other is accepting the radically different, which, in both the necessity of its exteriority and in its anteriority to ontology itself, constitutes subjectivity. Some of the positions presented here make strong qualifications concerning theories and practices in the psychological field, particularly concerning the PCA. There are also those who recognize the limits of Rogers' thought but seek to discover potentialities and create alternative positions through an extemporaneous dialogue between Rogers and Levinas.

Figueiredo and philosophy of science

Initially, we will use philosophy of science, essential to the thinking of Luiz Cláudio Figueiredo, a professor at the University of São Paulo (Universidade de São Paulo) and an important Brazilian scholar of the epistemology of psychology, who sees a tension in the relationship between psychology and epistemology. Figueiredo argues that the systematic study of private experience, an object of investigation in different psychological theories, was not a discovery but rather an invention enabled by the failure of the modern epistemological project (Figueiredo, 1992,

1996). These reflections are important because he does not see the history of psychology as a chronological sequence of theories but instead conceives of them as different rooms of an abode (*ethos*) for human experience. This implies that it is ethics, rather than epistemology, that will more clearly demonstrate the distinctions between psychological theories.

According to Figueiredo (1996), from the 17th century until the middle of the last century, Western culture has been deeply engaged with determining which forms of knowledge would be valid and capable of producing true statements. This engagement has led to discussions in epistemological and methodological fields, greatly influenced by Cartesian rationalism and the empiricism of Francis Bacon.

In general, these philosophical perspectives assume a subject that is capable of knowing the world through rationality and thereby using systematic ways to understand and explain reality. On the one hand, there is the knowing subject; on the other hand, there is the object to be known and apprehended according to the method used by reason.

Thus, ideas of freedom and of the individual are essential to reason for it to legitimize itself as a suitable form of knowing the world. This statement becomes more robust when one considers that, in Christian thought, hegemonic in 16th-century Europe, nature should be contemplated rather than unveiled by the human eye. Man was seen as just one more being among the divine creations; he had no individuality (or even uniqueness) within the social context. To reach the secure foundations of a scientific knowledge, where the knowing subject sets itself apart from the entities to be known, it was necessary to conceive a privatized subjectivity from which it was possible to root out any phenomenon that clouded his vision of a reality to be represented.

Also according to Figueiredo (1996), the self-centered individual postulated by Modernity began to be questioned in the second half of the 19th century. Until then,

> the "psychological" was not an object, or, at least, was not primarily an object of investigation. To become so, it was necessary, alongside the strengthening of privacy, for it to enter into crisis and turn into an object of suspicion and special care.
>
> *(Figueiredo, 1992, p. 129)*

If this individual flung himself into the natural world with ideas about prediction and control that guide the hard sciences, his humanity and the tribulations resulting therefrom – such as finitude – remained a great mystery to himself.

A gap was then created in the possibilities of an epistemic subject, an unexpected emptiness in the modern promises of progress and a full knowledge of oneself and the world. It is this gap that created the conditions for questioning established by Modernity, from what Figueiredo (1992) calls the territory of ignorance, which we shall discuss below. This implies that the psychological subject finds possibilities for existing when the epistemic subject fails and its limits are noted.

Figueiredo (1996) subsequently states that "the field of psychology itself, from the epistemological point of view, would be a *defecation* of the purge operated by the method in the process of constituting the purified subject" (p. 23). In other words, that which hinders the functioning of the method and stains the image of the almost-omnipotent rational individual is labeled "psychological."

For Figueiredo, the territory of ignorance comprises axiological poles that alternate between moving closer and moving farther apart, forming a triangle whose vertices maintain a relationship of tension. Different psychologies can be identified according to their greater or lesser proximity to each of the vertices, without ever being fixed on only one side of the triangle. The meeting points between the lines that form this triangle are the liberal, the romantic, and the disciplinary. In the liberal, we have "the reign of the sovereign 'I' with clearly defined, self-contained, self-styled, and self-known identities" (Figueiredo, 1992, p. 150). Thus, liberalism is concerned with an assumption of autonomy, of an "I" capable of self-control and self-knowledge.

Romanticism values "the power of nature's impulses and forces much more than consciousness or man as a whole. The valorization of nature is opposed, as something more original and true, to civilization with its rules, methods, and etiquette" (Figueiredo & Santi, 2005, pp. 36–37). Romanticism thus gives emphasis to intuitiveness, to a wisdom present in nature that precedes reason:

> The pole of discipline holds new technologies of power, both those that can be exerted over recognizable and manipulable identities according to the principle of calculating, functional, and administrative reason, and those that affect weakly structured identities open to manipulation through the calculated evocation of suprapersonal forces embodied in charismatic figures or figures projected in nostalgic or revolutionary legends and myths.
>
> *(Figueiredo, 1992, pp. 150–151)*

According to this quotation, subjectivity, in the disciplinary pole, becomes an object to be manipulated using previously defined objectives. Therefore, it uses science and its ability to make probabilistic calculations as a reference figure to be followed by the collective.

In the movements toward or away from each of these poles, each psychological theory can be understood as "a device capable of *providing, configuring, training, and constituting* both men and their worlds ... they are, in other words, *human facilities*" (Figueiredo, 1996, p. 26). For Figueiredo, each of these human facilities would constitute an *ethos*, that is, they would constitute an abode and a destination for man to cope with what modern ideology rejects in their constitution.

Therefore, for Figueiredo, before discussing the epistemologies of psychologies or judging them according to a knowledge model to be followed, it is essential to understand the abodes that they constitute for the human. As stated above, the psychological phenomenon can only be conceived in that which epistemology lacks; that is, in that which escapes its control.

As discussed thus far, before considering the epistemological foundations of psychologies, one must ask about the abodes they represent for the human, in particular where modern knowledge is recognized as ignorant, or, as Figueiredo (1992) says, in the territory of ignorance.

Possible abodes for the PCA in the territory of ignorance

We need to situate the ethical debate in the context of the Rogerian oeuvre. Given the urgent need to provide an abode for the human within psychologies, what ethos can be recognized in Rogers' production?

In the Rogerian oeuvre, there is no explicit discussion of ethics. However, there are notes that take into account the values implied by the PCA, particularly in regard to the distinction between techniques and attitudes. Another point where the ethical question may be inferred is in the debate between humanism and behaviorism present in American psychology in the 1950s.

In defining the facilitative attitudes around which the entire model of the PCA relationship was structured, Rogers makes it clear that they are not only techniques to be employed outside a context of values. It seems then that, for this theoretical approach, values precede techniques. According to Kinget (1977), these values relate to a positive and liberal concept of man and human relations – concepts very close, in fact, to what Figueiredo (1996) defines as the romantic and liberal poles that comprise the territory of ignorance. The positive concept appears in the boundless confidence that the therapist places in the client and the therapeutic relationship. The liberal conception, in turn, is noted in the idea of a man who is free and capable of choosing without any environmental determination, despite the contingencies inherent to this reality.

Amatuzzi (2010) analyzes the PCA as more than a technique. For him, Rogers not only defines new ways of doing but also of being with the other based on the following values: "the person, inter-human communion, and honesty about differences" (p. 24). Thus, Amatuzzi leads the discussion on therapist attitudes into the realm of ethics, of a way of being that guides relations with the other.

When Rogers' theory is defined using the idea of attitudes, it emerges that, unless the therapist claims the values that underlie his techniques for himself, they would not be effective. It is in this sense that Rogers (1976) states: "I suspect that each of us would be equally effective if we held quite different theories, providing we believe them" (p. 218).

Another point where we can situate the ethical question in Rogers is his debate with Skinner. For Rogers (1974), his disagreement with Skinner is philosophical. The Rogerian definition, however, is vague and does not clearly explain the ethical aspect involved in this debate. In the symposium that shows the differences between them, it is very clear, for us, that what is at stake is a question of commitment to the ethos of their respective knowledges. For Skinner (Rogers & Skinner, 1956), it is necessary to overcome the concepts of choice, responsibility, and justice to create conditions for a scientific study of human behavior. Thus, instead of mind, soul, or any other concept that refers to an internal entity commanding human action, radical behaviorism elects to study behavior, understood as an organism's interactions with the environment.

Assuming that, in fact, control is inherent to behavior, the scientist, according to Skinner (2005), can contribute to government planning, seeking the welfare of the governed. According to the founding figure of radical behaviorism,

> if a science of behavior can discover those conditions of life which make for the ultimate strength of men, it may provide a set of "moral values" which, because they are independent of the history and culture of any one group, may be generally accepted.
> *(Skinner, 2005, p. 445)*

As observed, Skinner recognizes that science has the ability to discriminate the good, in addition to historical and cultural aspects. The value that would guide the control exerted by this science would be the long-term strengthening of the species, such that "control is ethical if it is exerted for the sake of the controlled" (Skinner, 1988, p. 175). Skinner (2005) himself recognizes, however, that there are no guarantees as to the purposes for which this knowledge would be developed.

Rogers, in turn, states that the human being is essentially free and separate from other beings precisely because of her capacity for choice and self-determination. For him, the objective of someone seeking psychotherapy is to become what he or she is (Rogers, 1961). For the founder of the PCA, science, as a human invention, is made by people and thus always implies a choice of values (Vieira, 2009). For this reason, Rogers does not share Skinner's optimism and asks value questions regarding behavioral control: "Who will be controlled? Who will exercise control? What type of control will be exercised? Most important of all, toward what end or what purpose, or in the pursuit of what value, will control be exercised?" (Rogers & Skinner, 1956, p. 1060). This is the philosophical distinction Rogers (1974) refers to when he compares his thinking to that of a behaviour analyst. Despite all the ingenuity of Rogerian humanism (Moreira, 2007), his ethical criticism of Skinner points to an interesting fact: science does not exist as an entity detached from a historical process of interests. If ethics, for Skinner, is defined as control exercised for the good of the controlled, for Rogers, the definition of what is good in this context is of fundamental importance because there are always choices made by scientists.

Therefore, the ethos of Rogers' theory is a humanism close to the romantic and liberal poles defined by Figueiredo (1996), with all the conflicts and approximations that such an alliance can cause. There are even moments when we can identify a disciplinary stance in Rogers: for example, when he establishes the ideal of a fully functioning person (Rogers, 1963) as something to be reached at the end of the therapeutic process. In addition, in an early period of his work, Rogers (1951) expresses a deep belief in reaching a type of equation of the therapeutic relationship, in a model then prized by the hard sciences. Rogers' humanism, by the very assumption of autonomy to which Amatuzzi (2010) refers, is deeply committed to the image of a self-centered and conscious man who is able to be determined from his choices – as is postulated by Modernity. The human facility identified in him suffers at times from elements that recognize aspects escaping from this image and de-centering this self-determined subject (Williams & Gantt, 1998).

The following is a relevant question: is there space for the dissonant, the absolutely strange? What commitments does this form of acceptance assume? Thus, we wonder what possibilities for opening to difference can be visualized in the PCA through a dialogue with Levinas' Ethics of Radical Alterity

The ethics of Levinas

Levinas is considered a dense and unconventional thinker. Often treated as hermetic, this French-Lithuanian Jew from the Hasidic tradition affirms ethics' precedence to ontology. According to Freire (2002), instead of thinking about the question of being, Levinas puts being into question. According to Pivatto (2000) and Poirié (2007), even if Levinas cannot be reduced to being merely a Jewish thinker, World War II left deep marks on the constitution of his thought. Levinas was a prisoner of war, intimately living the horrors arising therefrom; thus, he was part of a series of authors who questioned everything that created the conditions that allowed that conflict to occur – that is, the fundamentals of Modernity.

Modernity had been established before the two great wars of the 20th century, making reason and the concept of a free individual into guarantees that man would no longer be subject to tyrannies, such as those that occurred during the medieval period in Europe (Figueiredo, 1992). According to Poirié (2007), however, the beginning of the last century is marked by a profound interrogation of Modernity and its promises, in particular the notion of a free and full subject, knowledgeable about himself. Levinasian thought lies at the foundation of these questions. It is a philosophy that rigorously and prudently affirms the radicalism of ethics in the human constitution. For Levinas, affirming that the human is based on ontology could mean the violence of the definition, the closing of this being's meaning, because philosophy's first concern would be with what it is. According to Goodman, Dueck, and Langdal (2010), Levinasian philosophy critiques the cult of the narcissistic and heroic self that is present in Western society and so often shown in psychological concerns and theories.

For Levinas (2007), the plane of immanence in phenomenology, based on the idea of an intentional consciousness that captures objects from the world by attributing meaning to them, resembles violence. In this sense, the Other, for Levinas, is not an object of knowledge, does not offer the possession of consciousness, and therefore cannot be unveiled (Vieira & Freire, 2006). Capturing it for knowledge would mean killing its difference. All Levinasian philosophy is structured by an affirmation of the impossibility of the Other's assimilation by the Same; that is, something that always escapes the totalization operated by knowledge.

With respect to Heidegger, it is possible to identify severe criticism of his thinking in Levinas, for neglecting ethics and emphasizing Being. Levinas attempts to move away from interiority to go toward the Other, facing a non-transferable responsibility.

Despite the Levinasian critiques of Husserl and Heidegger, Levinas does not reject the notion of Being; he instead bases it on other foundations. In *Totality and Infinity*, Levinas (1961) addresses the birth of the Subject from the tension between interiority and exteriority. If modernity establishes a self-referential and self-centered subject, Levinas (1961) affirms that this interiority is only possible from a relationship with the absolutely Other. That is why his thinking can be called an Ethics of Radical Alterity, as it is the relationship with alterity that establishes us as subjects. It should be noted that Levinas does not simply treat the Other as someone different from me but as someone else, that is, all and any Other, the absolutely and radically different.

Because it is based on this relationship with difference, the Self is subjected to it and not its own master, a troubled interiority assailed by an exteriority over which it has no control. For Poirié (2007), "the Subject – or subjectivity – is born from the *there is* (*il y a*), there opposing [him] and there refusing [him]" (p. 16). The *il y a* postulated by Levinas is an impersonal being, a "*murmuring* silence, which is heard as the deaf and invisible presence of an undefined being, a being that excludes humanity, that challenges existence" (Poirié, 2007, p. 17). It is the relationship of subjection to this impersonal being that creates conditions for the Subject in Levinas, which is responsible for the Other in a passive relationship (Levinas, 1982).

For Levinas, the responsibility for the Other is not a choice. As Freire (2000) rightly says, it is an uncondition; that is, it cannot be otherwise because it is this relationship that characterizes the human. The Subject's abode, then, is ceded, with doors and windows open to visits from the foreign, which calls it to responsibility from an infinite height.

We thus come to another important characteristic of Levinasian thought: the insurmountable verticality of the relationship between the Self and the Other. Unlike Buber (1970), for example, Levinas does not describe the relationship with difference as horizontal and mutual. Although he recognizes the immense value of the Buberian oeuvre and the ethical proposition it contains, Levinas (1987) identifies in it the danger of possession that the condition of equality assumed in a mutual relationship may suggest. Thus, there is no synthesis in this necessarily unequal relationship because the only possible answer to the Other is "here I am," because it is for and by Him (Levinas, 1982).

Alterity, for Levinas, is always something that escapes, that is unattainable in its totality, and that leads us, therefore, to the idea of Infinity revealed by the Face, which is not phenomenological because it could otherwise be easily captured by an image. In the Ethics of Radical Alterity, the Face of the Other comes to me through language rather than image (Freire, 2000; Vieira & Freire, 2006). According to Bauman (2011), "awakening to the Face ... is such an overwhelming shock that it makes all those rational considerations that rest in the arrogance of the world of conventions and contractual obligations ridiculously insignificant" (pp. 87–88). It is a Face, therefore, that requires the Self to give an answer to the Other. Due to its non-phenomenological characterization, the Face cannot be destroyed because, even if the physical death of the Other can be effected, I am vulnerable and passive when faced with the terror of its irreducible difference. Therefore, the Other, unlike the Heideggerian *Dasein*, is a being-beyond-its-death (Freire, 2002).

The language through which I arrive at the Face is a *saying*, rather than a *said* (Levinas, 1961); that is, language that is a *"turning to another* ... Language is not an experience nor a means of knowing another, but the place of an Encounter with the Other, with what is foreign and unknown from the Other" (Poirié, 2007, p. 22). The *said* is the discourse that is not open to transformation, while the *saying* inaugurates new possibilities, openness, and exposure to the response required by the Other (Levinas, 1982).

The Saying that comes from the Other opens the subject to a dimension of Desire, in this context taken from the idea of Infinity. Thus, Desire in Levinas is not characterized by lack but by excess. In other words, rather than referring the subject to what it is lacking, the desiring dimension of subjectivity's ethical constitution refers it to that which exceeds it and which is prior to itself; it is a hunger that feeds on hunger (Freire, 2000). According to Freire (2002), the desire for the Other is always something that "... escapes me and haunts me" (p. 57). It is therefore a diachronic relationship, which makes the encounter with a purported wholeness impossible.

This impossibility is why Levinas insists on the idea of a "bad conscience of" (Freire, 2000, 2001, 2002; Levinas, 2007). The ontological tradition of philosophy ignores and is sometimes allergic to the excess that accompanies the idea of Desire. For the French-Lithuanian author, "consciousness implies presence, positing-before-oneself, in other words, 'worldliness', the fact-of-being-given. It means being exposed to capture, to taking, to comprehension, to appropriation" (Levinas, 2007, pp. 140–141). As observed, consciousness for Levinas necessarily refers to apprehension and, therefore, the attempt to capture the Other's difference.

Levinas wonders what escapes the apprehension of consciousness and, thus, affirms the possibility of thinking about difference, of seeing it not according to what it lacks or what it still is not, but considering its alterity as such. He thus affirms the positivity of a dis-interested consciousness (Freire, 2000), responsible for deconstructing the human, turning it inside out. His ethics breaks with a tradition that recognizes the human according to a consciousness that captures and mathematizes the world.

Places for strangeness in the person-centered approach

Having presented the general principles of the Ethics of Radical Alterity, we can now return to the questions raised earlier in this text regarding possible abodes for the disruptive in the PCA. Therefore, we will explain the different productions that take Levinasian ethics as a possible boundary for defining a new ethos for the human in the approach in question.

Two clarifications must be made, however, before we proceed. The first is that, as seen above, Rogers has clearly defined an affiliation with the romantic and liberal poles that underlie the psychological field. However, according to Figueiredo (1992), we can argue that no psychological theory is attached to any of these poles because it contains characteristics relevant only to this in the totality of its elements. Thus, the reflections that follow point to other possibilities for a relationship with alterity in Rogerian discourse because, like all the discourses of psychological theories that therefore inhabit the "territory of ignorance," it may present different facets – including that of sheltering the foreign, which we discuss here.

The second point that deserves clarification concerns the fact that, although therapeutic work takes places in a relationship that involves paying for a professional service, it can also be understood, according to Levinas, as based on ethics rather than only the technical and mechanical execution of a common task. According to Williams and Gantt (1998), the word "therapeutic" is of Greek origin and denotes service or attendance, which means that, from a Levinasian perspective, a relationship is therapeutic to the extent that it takes the need to recognize the ethical obligation to the Other as a fundamental task.

Goodman et al. (2010) corroborate the above argument when they state that the psychologist can assist his client with opening to alterity, such that "therapy, instead of being a means of restoring persons to cultural status quo … might be better understood as a process wherein persons redefine their personal freedom" (p. 679). The redefinition of freedom referred to by Goodman et al. touches precisely at the point of the insurmountable responsibility for the Other.

Thus, in the Rogerian framework, the debate on the feasibility of a therapeutic relationship built on ethical foundations has its origins in 1957, when Rogers and Buber waged an intense discussion about mutuality in the therapeutic relationship (Anderson & Cissna, 1997). Rogers and Buber disagreed on the subject because, according to Buber, the therapist–client relationship cannot be an I–Thou relationship because it is unequal. Also, according to Buber in that debate, this inequality occurs because the therapist provides a professional service, which situates him in a different place from that of the client to the point that the client cannot ask the therapist for details about his personal life. The therapist, on the other hand, is given this right.

Rogers, however, disagrees with Buber. For him, the consideration of the other as a person, according to the ideas of empathy and unconditional positive regard as values experienced in the relationship and underlying this same relationship, gives the therapist–client relationship an ethical foundation that precedes any technical work. For Rogers, however, if there is no authenticity to the consideration of the other as a person, the relationship will not be effective. This means that, although it is technical work for which the therapist receives financial compensation, it is ethics, understood as the way of responding to the other's call, which supports the psychotherapist's work.

In this sense, the position of Schmid (2007) is interesting. He defends the therapeutic relationship, in the theoretical framework of client-centered therapy, as an I–Thou relationship. According to Schmid (2007), the therapeutic relationship is fundamentally a response to the call made by the Other in his or her misery and suffering, "thus all psychotherapy takes its origin at the Other. It sees him or her as a call and a provocation" (p. 42). This provocation should be answered with attitudes of not-knowing and acceptance for the strange that makes it such that the Other, before anything else, is a priority. Thus, according to Schmid (2007), "psychotherapy must be regarded as an ethical phenomenon and enterprise" (p. 42). Schmid further clarifies that "ethics means the philosophy of the challenge of living in terms of how to respond, to live responsibly, to live one's responsibility" (p. 42). In short, it is precisely the ability to respond to the Other's call, rather than the technical or financial aspect itself, which characterizes a relationship as therapeutic, such that it either has this as a value that can be operationalized in the relationship, or it does not. The following paragraphs will therefore analyze this subject in the person-centered therapeutic relationship.

Gantt (2000), for example, uses Levinasian ethics to propose a psychotherapy model in which the therapist responds to the ethical obligation to "suffer" the vicissitudes of the client's experiences with him. This author states that current forms of psychotherapy were founded according to the medical model, such that mental disorders are characterized similarly to any organic condition. According to this perspective, human suffering is just another symptom within a framework in which the other loses its uniqueness.

Larner (2011), in turn, uses Derrida and Levinas to propose an integration between therapy models derived from modern science and postmodern proposals. The former values techniques based on scientific evidence whose effectiveness has been proven, and the latter understands the human being as relational and immersed in culture. This integration would be called paramodern. Using Derrida, the author proves that, to deconstruct modern paradigms, it is necessary to make use of their contributions, such that the proposed therapy derived from the paramodern approach gives "equal priority to science and relational or dialogic encounter with the other" (Larner, 2011, p. 831). Moreover, considering Levinasian philosophy, ethical concerns would highlight epistemological questions, such that the obligation to respond to the other's suffering would authorize the integration of techniques from different models, even though they contradict each other.

Williams and Gantt (1998) understand that Rogers, as well as Maslow and other humanistic psychologists, are attached to an individualistic conception of the self, such that the inner self is extremely relevant in their theories. This attachment means that "others are important as mirrors to one's own feelings, and, thus, as means to one's own fulfillment" (p. 258). According to the authors cited, and unlike Levinas, humanistic psychology would therefore take the other as a means, not an end, which would characterize an ethical violence by the third force in psychology.

Freire (2000), in turn, is critical of the relationship between alterity and the PCA. Among other aspects, his criticisms are directed to the symmetry that Rogers acknowledges in the relationship with the other. This assumption would not be consistent with the ethics of Levinas for which the Other, from an insurmountable height, demands a response. The possibility of empathetically understanding the other, of entering into its universe of meanings and trying to communicate the understandings obtained, is also questioned because it is based on a sense of interiority that must be overcome. For Levinas, as noted above, the Other's exterior constitution of itself would be important. On the other hand, there is the very impossibility of encounter, which would make empathy impossible. The Other leaves only traces of its passage; upon arriving, there is only an empty place.

Based on the questions of Freire (2000), Vieira and Freire (2006) move forward in an attempt to rethink the PCA in such a way that this psychological approach would open up space in its concepts for strangeness and the radical difference that demands the absolutely Other, but they clarify that they do not intend to produce an approach with a Levinasian foundation. In discussing the conditions that facilitate the therapeutic process (unconditional positive regard, authenticity, and empathetic understanding), the authors note some possibilities for opening to alterity that can be explored. To this end, they propose that, to accept the radical difference defended by Levinas, ex-centricity, in the sense of de-centering, should be present in the stances adopted by the therapist.

Also according to Vieira and Freire (2006), unconditional positive regard can be a door to alterity by allowing therapist and client to be surprised by the unpredictable that they both bring, such that what is unusual in the human condition is heard and accepted without the predisposition to refute this difference due to prejudices. From another perspective, this way of looking at discourse and experience is also defined as a "non-possessive love," which would imply not reifying the person making use of prior categories, such as psychopathological categories. With regard to authenticity, Vieira and Freire (2006) use the notion of "authentic speech" (Amatuzzi, 1989) to show that there is an unstoppable movement, external to the subject, which expresses a flow that triggers new meanings when faced with crystallized experience. There would be no access there to a person's essentiality but rather the revelation of a creative attitude that is not reduced to a cognitive apprehension of one's own totality. For Vieira and Freire (2006), empathy, conceived in terms of ex-centricity, can be seen as an attempt to listen to the strange that speaks in front of the therapist, the difference that erupts, averse to any control. Putting oneself into the place of the other would therefore not imply imprisoning it in a universe of one's own meaning and imposing this understanding upon that which demands its previously usurped space.

Schmid (2008), in turn, takes the idea of a person, in Rogers, to discuss psychotherapy as an ethical discipline and profession. According to Schmid, we can define a person from an individualistic perspective, equating person to individual, as Rogers does, or from a relational perspective, in which "a person is anyone who became himself or herself precisely through others, which implies interdependence, solidarity and responsibility" (p. 3). As maintained by Schmid, the presence of the therapist as a person in both these dimensions consists in being affirmed with the Other and simultaneously being placed against it, establishing a clear recognition and affirmation of these differences in the relationship. The idea is to arrive at a "mutual recognition as people rather than knowledge about the other" (p. 7), which means an openness to the Other's difference, which proves to be a mystery beyond what we can perceive through our theories and techniques. Schmid, inspired by Levinas, compares the relationship with the other's difference to the therapist's relationship with his client. According to Schmid, the relationship with alterity is "a request and a provocation and the relationship with it is, in principle, asymmetric. The person who needs represents a demand" (p. 7). This demand means that the therapist is faced with an ethical imperative to respond to the Other (responsibility, or ability to respond) and recognize him or her as a person.

Even in the wake of his reflections on a relationship based in personhood, Schmid states that empathetic understanding would mean letting oneself be touched by the other's reality and touching it at the same time. While acknowledging the impossibility of fully understanding the Other's difference, Schmid (2008) states that "being empathetic means building a bridge toward an unknown land" (p. 8), unlike that postulated by Freire (2000). This openness to the unexpected would be an epistemological foundation for person-centered therapy because it implies a position in relation to the Other that privileges the recognition of its difference rather than the knowledge of its totality. For Schmid (2008), knowledge is based on judgment, while recognition takes place through trust, expressed in psychotherapy as unconditional positive regard, or even as love or Agape, a type of non-possessive love that does not require anything from the Other but is merely put at its service (Rogers, 1976). This type of love, which is present in unconditional positive regard, also as per Schmid (2008), would imply a reversal of the usual order of communication: I–Thou would become a Thou–I relationship, such that the reference and priority would be found in the Thou. For Schmid, this reversal would be the meaning of responding authentically and would be "the" ethical challenge of the relationship.

Also from a Levinasian perspective, Vieira and Pinheiro (2013) use a rereading of a Rogerian clinical case to attempt to envision the therapeutic process as an accepting environment for Alterity. For these authors, therapeutic change would not seek a greater integration of one's own experience. The process of recreating oneself in therapy would be mediated by the assumption of estrangement brought by the exteriority constituting the person.

According to Rogers (1963), a successful therapeutic process would lead the person to his or her full functioning, which is characterized by the following: the possibility of opening to his or her own experience; an increase in his or her confidence to use the body as a screen to evaluate actions; and continuously living in the here-and-now. With regard to personality, there would be greater integration and, therefore, appeasement of the permanent tension between culture, the self, and the body. Culture, through meaningful people, requires the subject to adapt to its rules of belonging and become worthy of love and consideration. The body, in a radical way, demands that its needs be met, leaving the self straining to maintain a consistent self-concept when confronted with these two conflicting interests.

Vieira & Pinheiro (2013) problematize the therapeutic process model postulated by Rogers, stating that it "ignores a dimension of strangeness in the constitution of the psyche and seeks to reduce it to what can be recognized by the self" (p. 235). Nonetheless, the authors argue that it is not unusual to come across reports of therapists and clients in situations in which estrangement manifests and surprises them. Rogers, however, would treat such manifestations for an identity bias because he would not understand the very feelings brought by difference but rather would seek to integrate it into the previously known dynamics, making the subject responsible for the effort to recognize the foreign as also a part of himself.

More generally, with the exception of studies by Freire (2000, 2001) that declare Rogers' allergy to Alterity and the impossibility of accepting the strange in the PCA, all the authors discussed here have sought to reposition the PCA, to see gaps where the acceptance of radical difference can be thought. They start from the basic assumption that, even though Rogers never acknowledges Alterity as such, it would be possible to redesign concepts and attitudes so that this aspect, essential to the constitution of subjectivity, can be thought.

It is necessary, however, to go further: not only to recognize the Other in theory but also to put this new ethical position to the test in practice. It is essential to carry out empirical research, assuming that psychologists will genuinely attempt to accept the alterity that, regardless of their desire, will reclaim its usurped place.

Conclusion

Obviously, the discourse of alterity, as conceived in this text, was not present in the work of Rogers, which makes no reference to Levinas' thinking. The discussion with other philosophers, including existentialists, pragmatists, and philosophers of science, was recorded in numerous texts by the founder of the PCA. There were debates, even if extemporaneous, with thinkers such as Kierkegaard, Buber, Tillich, Dewey, Capra, and Polanyi, among others, but Levinas was never on this list. However, this absence does not diminish the PCA. Rogers, in his own way, and limited by the historical and cultural conditions that were distinctive to him, revolutionized psychological thought in such a way that his work already deserved reverence.

However, two aspects cannot be ignored. A first point: Rogers might not have recognized Radical Alterity in his theoretical formulations; he may even have tried to supplant it, but that does not mean he has not come across it in his practice. With regard to clinical practice, Vieira and Pinheiro (2013) give evidence to corroborate this argument. The second aspect is that the PCA's own concepts are not necessarily completely averse to Alterity. It is necessary, however, with a certain Deleuzian inspiration, to make the author, with his own words, say what he never said.

In the threads of alterity that Rogers' work bears, small lines of escape can be pulled out from between the lines, which may expand the power of a revolutionary thinking. This task, for example, is what Vieira and Freire (2006) attempt when they paste the adjective ex-centric onto facilitating conditions, as well as when Schmid (2008) revises the concept of a person. Vieira and Pinheiro (2013) make advances in the attempt to observe the marks left by alterity through the concept of body.

Finally, it should be strongly emphasized, although it has already been noted in this work's introduction, that we do not agree with the creation of a Levinasian PCA. It is philosophy's role to problematize, to ask questions, to bring thought towards the seemingly weightless, but not to supplant psychological concepts.

Psychology and philosophy are distinct fields of knowledge production, despite the possible construction of communication channels between them. On this point, psychology's role is to revise its formulations based on the concerns produced by philosophy, but, fundamentally, agreeing with Rogers (1951), the main propellant for reconstructing theoretical convictions must come from daily practice, which, in psychotherapy, is revealed by electing experience as the supreme authority. The formulations should be taken to previously unthought fields, thus enabling alterity to aerate thought and reconstruct it.

The everyday encounters and disencounters with people and with lived situations are the best propulsion mechanisms for thinking about a practice in which alterity can be accepted. It is not expected to be an unthinking practice but rather the very overcoming of the separation between theory and practice. In this sense, it is not the discourse on alterity but rather addressing the radical difference that is imposed upon the Rogerian psychologist every day that will most strongly affect the PCA. Thinking this way, we do not move away from the PCA but instead become increasingly Rogerian, in what was perhaps one of the greatest and most important teachings of its founder: "the facts are friendly."

Note

A version of this chapter was first published in *Theory & Psychology* by SAGE. Permission to include it here has been granted, for which we are grateful.

References

Amatuzzi, M. M. (1989). *O resgate da fala autênticas: Filosofia da psicoterapia e da educação* [Rescuing authentic speech: A philosophy for psychotherapy and education]. Campinas, Brazil: Papirus.

Amatuzzi, M. M. (2010). *Rogers: Ética humanista e psicoterapia* [Rogers: Humanist ethics and psychotherapy]. Campinas, Brazil: Alínea.

Anderson, R., & Cissna, K. (1997). *The Martin Buber–Carl Rogers dialogue: A new transcript with commentary*. New York: State University of New York Press.

Bauman, Z. (2011). *Vida em fragmentos: Sobre a ética pós-moderna* [Life in fragments: On post-modern ethics] (Werneck, A., Trans.). Rio de Janeiro, Brazil: Zahar.

Buber, M. (1970). *I and thou* (Kaufmann, W., Trans.). New York, NY: Charles Scribners's Sons.
Figueiredo, L. C. M. (1992). *A invenção do psicológico: Quatro séculos de subjetivação – 1500–1900* [The invention of psychology: Four centuries of subjectivity – 1500–1900]. São Paulo, Brazil: Escuta.
Figueiredo, L. C. M. (1996). *Revisitando as psicologias: Da epistemologia à ética das práticas e discursos psicológicos* [Revisiting psychologies: From epistemology to the ethics of psychological practices and discourses]. Petrópolis, Brazil: Vozes.
Figueiredo, L. C. M., & Santi, P. L. R. (2005). *Psicologia: Uma (nova) introdução* [Psychology: A (new) introduction]. São Paulo, Brazil: Educ.
Freire, J. C. (2000). As psicologias na modernidade tardia: O lugar vacante do Outro [Psychologies in late modernity: The vacant place of the Other] (Unpublished doctoral thesis). São Paulo, Brazil: Universidade de São Paulo.
Freire, J. C. (2001). As psicologias na modernidade tardia: O lugar vacante do Outro [Psychologies in late modernity: The vacant place of the Other]. *Psicologia USP*, 12(2), 73–93.
Freire, J. C. (2002). *O lugar do Outro na modernidade tardia* [The place of the Other in late modernity]. São Paulo/Fortaleza, Brazil: Anna Blume/Secult.
Gantt, E. E. (2000). Levinas, psychotherapy, and the ethics of suffering. *Journal of Humanistic Psychology*, 40(3), 9–28.
Goodman, D. M., Dueck, A., & Langdal, J. P. (2010). The "Heroic I": A Levinasian critique of Western narcissism. *Theory & Psychology*, 20, 667–685. doi: doi:10.1177/0959354310370238.
Kinget, G. M. (1977). Além das técnicas [Beyond the techniques]. In Rogers, C. R., Kinget, G. M. (Eds.), *Psicoterapia e relações humanas: teoria e prática da terapia não-diretiva*. Vol. 2 [Psychotherapy and human relationships: Vol. 2] (pp. 9–18). Belo Horizonte, Brazil: Interlivros.
Larner, G. (2011). Deconstructing theory: Towards an ethical therapy. *Theory & Psychology*, 21, 821–839. doi: doi:10.1177/0959354310395061.
Levinas, E. (1961). *Totality and infinity: Essay on exteriority*. The Hague, the Netherlands: M. Nijhoff.
Levinas, E. (1982). *Éthique et infini: Dialogues avec Philippe Nemo* [Ethics and infinity: Dialogues with Philippe Nemo]. Paris, France: Librairie Arthème Fayard et Radio-France.
Levinas, E. (1987). *Hors Sujet* [Outside of the subject]. Paris, France: Fata Morgana.
Levinas, E. (2007). A consciência não-intencional [Unintentional consciousness]. In Poirié, F. (Ed.), *Levinas: ensaios e entrevistas* [Levinas: Essays and interviews] (pp. 135–147). São Paulo, Brazil: Perspectiva.
Moreira, V. (2007). *De Carl Rogers a Merleau-Ponty: A pessoa mundana em psicoterapia* [From Carl Rogers to Merleau-Ponty: The worldly person in psychotherapy]. São Paulo, Brazil: Anna Blume.
Pivatto, S. (2000). Ética da alteridade [Ethics of alterity]. In Oliveira, M. (Ed.), *Correntes fundamentais da ética contemporânea* [Fundamental approaches from contemporary ethics] (pp. 79–99). Petrópolis, Brazil: Vozes.
Poirié, F. (2007). *Emmanuel Lévinas: ensaios e entrevistas* [Emmanuel Levinas: Essays and interviews]. São Paulo, Brazil: Perspectiva.
Rogers, C. R. (1951). *Client-centered therapy: Its current practice, implications, and theory*. Boston, MA: Houghton-Mifflin.
Rogers, C. R. (1961). *On becoming a person: A therapist's view of psychotherapy*. Boston, MA: Houghton-Mifflin.
Rogers, C. R. (1963). The concept of the fully functioning person. *Psychotherapy: Theory, Research, and Practice*, 1(1), 17–26.
Rogers, C. R. (1974). In retrospect: Forty-six years. *American Psychologist*, 29(2), 115–123. doi: doi:10.1037/h0035840.

Rogers, C. R. (1976). Algumas lições de um estudo de psicoterapia com esquizofrênicos [Some learnings from a study of psychotherapy with schizophrenics]. In Rogers, C. R., & Stevens, B. (Eds.). *De pessoa para pessoa: o problema de ser humano* [Person to person: The problem being human] (pp. 211–224). São Paulo, Brazil: Pioneira.

Rogers, C. R., & Skinner, B. F. (1956). Some issues concerning the control of human behavior: A symposium. *Science*, 124(3231), 1057–1066.

Schmid, P. (2007). The anthropological and ethical foundations of person-centered therapy. In Cooper, M., O'Hara, M., Schmid, P., & Wyatt, G. (Eds.), *The handbook of person-centered psychotherapy and counseling* (pp. 30–46). New York, NY: Palgrave Macmillan.

Schmid, P. (2008). Conocimiento o reconocimiento? La psicoterapia como "el arte de no saber": Perspectivas de más desarrollos de un paradigma radicalmente nuevo [Knowledge or acknowledgement? Psychotherapy as "the art of not-knowing": Perspectives of more developments of a radically new paradigm]. Retrieved from http://members.kabsi.at/pfs0/paper-pcep1-span.pdf.

Skinner, B. F. (1988). The operant side of behavior therapy. *Journal of Behavior Therapy and Experimental Psychiatry*, 19(3), 171–179.

Skinner, B. F. (2005). Science and human behavior. Retrieved from http://www.bfskinner.org/newtestsite/wp-content/uploads/2014/02/ScienceHumanBehavior.pdf

Vieira, E. M. (2009). Sobre a proposta de conhecimento presente na teoria Rogeriana, ou da sabedoria residente na ignorância [On the proposal for knowledge present in Rogerian theory, or the wisdom residing in ignorance]. *Revista do NUFEN*, 1(2), 4–19.

Vieira, E. M., & Freire, J. C. (2006). Alteridade e psicologia humanista: Uma leitura ética da abordagem centrada na pessoa [Alterity and humanist psychology: An ethical lecture on the person-centered approach]. *Estudos de Psicologia* (Campinas), 23(4), 425–432.

Vieira, E. M., & Pinheiro, F. P. H. A. (2013). Person centered psychotherapy: An encounter with oneself or a confrontation with the other? *Estudos de Psicologia* (Campinas), 30(2), 231–238.

Williams, R. N., & Gantt, E. E. (1998). Intimacy and heteronomy: On grounding psychology in the ethical. *Theory & Psychology*, 8(2), 253–267. doi: doi:10.1177/0959354398082010.

PART II
The politics of experience

6

DIALECTICS OF PERSON AND EXPERIENCING*

Tatiana Karyagina and Fyodor E. Vasilyuk

Tatiana Karyagina We decided to talk about dialectic in the form of a dialogue – quite an appropriate genre for this topic, I think.

Personality and experiencing are two key categories for the person-centred and the experiential approaches. Let's start with the question of what problem we see here. By saying "we", I mean not only you and me, but also all of us, the psychotherapeutic school of co-experiencing psychotherapy (CEP). Being a purely Russian approach, the CEP Association is a member of the World Association for Person Centred and Experiential Psychotherapy and Counselling (WAPCEPC), and the European Associations for Person-Centred and Experiential Psychotherapy and Counselling (PCE-Europe).

As an experiential approach, CEP is based on the theory of experiencing. However, this theory has developed in the context of cultural-historical psychology or, as it is sometimes called, cultural-historical activity psychology founded by L.S. Vygotsky and his students and peers, A.N. Leontiev and A.R. Luria (Yamagata-Lynch, 2010). When speaking about the psychotherapeutic approach itself, you always note that CEP is like engrafting the person-centred therapy of Rogers into the prolific tree of the cultural-historical theory (Vasilyuk, 2015).

I know well what our "experientiality" means both in theory and in practice. Experiencing is our key reliance, the healing factor, the inner work of the client that results in the effects of the therapy. The whole CEP process is aimed at maintaining this inner work of experiencing. But how "person-centredness" and "experientiality" are correlated is an open question.

I understand that this question is not only about our school. WAPCEPC and PCE-Europe were founded in 1997–98, while we joined them only in 2016–17 and still do not quite understand their "political" history, i.e. what was the integration process of the person-centred and the experiential schools into one family (PCE). But, as we know, person-centred therapists still raise questions about experiential therapists – to what extent are they "our folks" (Kirschenbaum, 2012)? Nevertheless, the association has existed for 20 years already.

Therefore, my first question will be the following: the name of the association has two parts linked by the conjunction – person-centred *and* experiential. What does this "and" mean? How are these two categories, on which the whole life of the family is centred, "person" and "experiencing" correlated?

Fyodor Vasilyuk Indeed, this "and" causes some ambiguity. Unfortunately, we have scarce knowledge about the contemporary history of the person-centred approach (PCA). It may be assumed, that when, by the late 1990s, the authority of Eugene Gendlin almost reached the level of Carl Rogers, and experiential approaches became the most well-formed, well-organized direction of development and innovation in PCA, the integration of its two branches under a single association was virtually a political event.

T.K. Experiential approaches became too specific to remain under the auspices of PCA, but at the same time, they were too close to split off.

F.V. The alternative to integration might have been sad: the classic therapy of Rogers and the focusing-oriented therapy of Gendlin, and the growing emotion-focused therapy (EFT) would have developed in parallel, inevitably moving away from each other.

But the core of the problem seems to pertain not to the authority of these two therapeutic geniuses or the equality between them. While paying great honour to Eugene Gendlin and his contribution to the PCA, it would be fair to say that the authority of these two figures is of different historical scale. Rogers created a new therapeutic world, while Gendlin invented a new psychological theory (of experiencing) and a new therapeutic method (focusing).

If it is not the equality of authority that matters, why have the person-centred and the experiential approaches formed the name of the new association on a parity basis? It may be assumed that the intuitive or quite conscious rationale for such a name was not a political, but an essential one, because the integration reflects the conceptual integrity of the family.

This gave rise to a conceptual diarchy, with a natural tendency to focus on one of the categories, to proclaim it dominant, and make theory and practice dance to its tune.

T.K. I would like to note one more aspect of the problem that makes this topic important for us. It seems to be also related to difficulties faced by our approaches. I mean anthropological problems of personality and experiencing; because psychotherapy is the child of its era and the answer to questions raised in this era.

We are talking about total virtualization of life and the resulting depersonalization and dilution of personality. At the same time, experience is for sale, turned into a product or a mechanism of manipulation, for example in advertising. Philosophers write about "experience society", "experience economy", "emotional capitalism"

(Schulze, 1992; Illouz, 2007). As a result of this selling, experiencing becomes impersonal, clichéd, orchestrated. You are in the process of a divorce – read *Eat, Pray, Love* (Gilbert, 2007), and the hole in your experiencing will be patched. Dozens of talk shows in different countries are strangely similar, transmitting the same scenarios of experiencing a "trauma", pushing the same proven buttons. "Trauma" has almost turned into a cliché. One day at supervision session we discussed whether Anna Karenina had a "trauma" to get away from both therapist's and client's cliché.

F.V. We indeed observe that experiencing is no longer a local concept, but renewed as a cultural category important for understanding the ongoing anthropological shifts as it was when it was originating in the end of the 19th century (Gadamer, 2006). Such transformation unveiled problems in the category itself. And one of them is the possibility to detach experiencing from a person, and turn it into a separate reality.

At the time, John Stuart Mill wrote about an intricate strategy of happiness: to be happy, the individual has to set a goal. The process of achieving the goal makes the individual feel happy, ignoring happiness itself (Mill, 2009/1879). It is not all that easy, but we see how a sort of addiction evolves when the individual strives for experiencing, not life. If we see experience as a subjective reality that is subject to its own laws, that attests itself whilst ignoring objective reality, then it distorts reality in the end.

Another pole of the alienation of experiencing and personality is the opposite tendency to cultivate the non-experiencing person, or "managerialism": the rationalistic construction of successful destiny by given patterns without listening to the mystery of being that unfolds from deep experiencing.

T.K. A non-experiencing person is much easier to control (Bazzano, 2016). Meanwhile, we lay responsibility for what we do on, for example, the brain. It controls us, for better or worse. I'm waiting for someone to recognize the brain as a person.

F.V. Indeed, these are global anthropological challenges to which psychotherapy, as an anthropology practice, has to respond. In my opinion, PCE therapy has that potential, because personality and experiencing are not only central but also interrelated categories.

T.K. But how can we think about this interrelation having in mind the possibility to detach experiencing from the person as we can see in reality outside psychotherapy?

F.V. Let's give the situation a logical test. I suggest removing this "and" conjunction in psychotherapy. Now there is no link between personality and experiencing. Can we think of some approach or episode in the therapy, where the person category dominates, while the experiencing category is being ignored? In theory, yes. Technically, this may look like that. For example, a woman tells about her dramatic relationship with her teenage daughter. With great respect to her daughter as a person, she is not able to experience her mothering in full, being continuously blamed for the "lack of mother's care", and desperately escaping, for example to long business trips.

If in response to her complaints we said: "Ok, what are you going to do as a person?", would this be an obvious appeal to personality, a personal challenge? Yes. Rogers used other methods, but here we have a straightforward realization of the personality-oriented, not the experiential approach. When, instead of experience that can be expressed or empathized with, we have "this", we cannot express our empathy with "this" – we just appeal to personality.

I used to witness some brutal existential versions of group therapy within a whisker of provocation. Members of the group are put into conflictual existential situations, often involving moral choice – for example, when they have to leave the group that is of great value for them, or commit treachery – in short, the situation of a clear moral conflict. The therapist doesn't support or empathize. In contrast, he/she does everything to lock the individual in this unbearable situation, providing an opportunity to reach a sort of existential "dao" of purely personal nature. He/she waits for the person to be revealed in the individual, and to solve the problem in some unusual way.

This is one side of the coin. Let's look at the other pole. Can we imagine experiential psychotherapy that completely ignores the person? Yes, we can. Sometimes during the work of the members of our family, we observe a clear dominance of this pole, the experiential one. Such sessions are full of tears and emotions from both the therapist and the client, of sentimentality, extreme emotional states. Feedback from clients shows that this work can be of great value. But, in my opinion, in such cases, there is no room for a person to reveal him or herself.

Finally, if we consider the situation, where there is neither person nor experiencing, then we can recall orthodox behavioural therapy. The main mechanism, on which this therapy relies, is conditioning mechanism.

This simple typology allows us to review the question in the following way. If we drop one of the poles, we get the approach that does not correspond to the spirit of the Rogerian tradition.

T.K. When I asked several psychotherapists how they would define their identity, they answered: "I am a person-centred experiential psychotherapist". The person-centredness, as I understood it, is seen as an ideological value of the approach that determines the strategy: acknowledgement of human individuality or uniqueness, its ability to be actualized and the primary importance of therapeutic relations for this. And the word "experiential" is more about the method.

F.V. At least in the above-mentioned cases such differentiation is drawn intuitively and looks like that: I identify myself in a dual way, but with two different levels of the approach. One is the value level, and here I am a person-centred therapist. But methodologically I am an experiential therapist. Can we conclude that it is allowed not to be an experiential therapist by method?

T.K. At the WAPCEPC conference in 2016 Germain Lietaer raised the same question in his presentation: Was Rogers' work experiential? And the answer was: Yes, it was, his main method is the reflection of feelings (Lietaer, 2016).

F.V. If I had to answer this question, I wouldn't focus on the empathy method. I suggest the following formula: Rogers is not an experiential therapist because he uses reflection of feelings. He is a person-centred therapist and thus he is an experiential therapist.

To illustrate this formula, let me give you an example from my own experience. On 28 September 1986, I was lucky to become a member of the Rogers group in Moscow. On the second day, Rogers gave a short, 20-minute demonstration session with me. After five minutes, I felt that there was no need to have someone interpret for me. My English was not very good, but at the moment I understood not only the general idea, but some of the finest linguistic and semantic nuances. These were 15 minutes in my life when I knew English like a native. It's a pity that I couldn't preserve that gift.

However, I received another much larger gift. Coming back home in the evening glory of Moscow streets, I distinctly felt that something important was entering into my life. Emotionally, it was manifested as complete, absolute, comprehensive, guaranteed happiness. Strong, physical joy overwhelmed me. There was no exaltation, outburst, euphoria, or "subjectivity" in that feeling – it was solid and steady like October in the Mediterranean. It was not just feeling. It was a powerful experiencing process unfolding and acting inside me. The feelings didn't come one after another, I was not looking for an exact word to express that feeling; to a certain extent it was an objective, self-developing process, to which I had access both through my mind and my will. It contained optimistic and sensible understanding of the way I was going and determination to follow it (after 30 years I may confirm that it was not self-deception). Now I was ready to attempt to heal an absolutely dead-locked relationship. The important feature of this deep personal experiencing was its inner directedness at other people. I wanted not just to share this gift, but also to give it away so that they could experience what I experienced.

Coming back to the question. Was it experiential therapy? Yes. But not because Rogers took me through focusing on my experiencing, expressing it and going ever deeper into the layers. I may testify another feature of the process. Carl Rogers' personality was piercing through all these layers instead of consistently progressing from one to another, seeking for my personality. And then there was the Encounter (maybe it coincided with my acquisition of the language). The most amazing thing is that my personality found by him in this Encounter was not a usual shabby gentleman. It was someone inside me (no – it was me) – brand-new, in all his glory, determined to live a true life, but, despite all this novelty, he was someone very familiar and close to me, as if we knew each other from childhood.

Of course, it was only one of thousands of Rogers' sessions, but it seemed to reveal in relief the spirit and the strategy of his work: look for a person in the first place, and experiencing will follow.

T.K. After your story all I want now is to sit in silence and try to imagine how it was and to find something similar in my life. I was then a second-year student, and couldn't even get to the lecture by Carl Rogers in Moscow State University – the hall was overcrowded. It is difficult to come back to reality, but let's try to think over both your experience and an alternative one.

So, we have the method used by Rogers himself, his way of being in therapy. As I understood you, "experientiality" in Rogers' sense, as you felt it when being his client, means that personal contact initiated an experiencing process and this experiencing work became the healing factor. Moreover, as you stressed, the experiencing process was not the same as emotions and feelings. It was something powerful and strong that engaged mind, will, body and senses in the process, and also productive as it transformed intentions, habits, renewed your Self, and turned you to the Other. Indeed, it was experiencing *work*, but you participated in that work.

Hence, as you see it, we have to talk about experiencing not as an application of the method of reflection of feelings, but as something that does work in the therapy process.

F.V. Yes, we may put it like this. In classic work by Rogers the person was present in such full form and acceptance as may have never been before. At the same time, it was present not as a pure existential function, but as the experiencing person going deeper in his/her experience together with the therapist, contacting, thinking over and working with this experience.

Now this "and" between the "person" and the "experience" is not about the combination of two things of the same rank or of different levels; this is an active, creative combination of the author and the work, of *who* (experiences) and *what* (is being experienced).

Playing a symphony

T.K. I wonder if we can say that Rogers' work combined the categories of person and experiencing in the following manner: Rogers appealed to the client's personality, although not behind or beyond experiencing, but *through* experiencing itself. *He was not looking for the person behind the experiencing layers*, as you called them, and he was not analysing these experiencing layers separately from the person but looked for the author of these layers.

This can be done without special technique. Although if we analysed the transcript of your session with Rogers, we would find the same reflection of feelings. This has led us to a "being-doing" differentiation.

F.V. Yes, when speaking about the differentiation between doing–being or technique–relations approaches, it may sound like a reproach or warning from traditional person-centred therapists against too much use of techniques, as a kind of finger-pointing at Gendlin (Kirschenbaum, 2012). Many good therapists can't simply stay with being and the way of being. They need technique. It could well be though, that the maestro himself, Rogers, didn't recognize his technique. He was told: "What a good passage, how did you strike this chord?" He answered: "C'mon, guys, I was playing a symphony! It doesn't matter all that much. Do you think you may learn chords and play a symphony? Of course, there will be no symphony without chords, but the symphony is not about chords".

T.K. But what is this reliance on technique? This reliance on goal-setting, a special activity that can be described, quantified, verified, measured. Also, technique is about something concrete, "physical" to which certain efforts may be applied. But the person is an elusive phenomenon. By definition, technique cannot be applied to it. While experiencing, although not material either, is a real, alive tissue of consciousness, and its relation to specific behaviour is easily recorded. We may to a certain extent touch it and do something with it. Therefore, "experientiality" is being talked about as a characteristic of the method.

I realized that while we were discussing the notion of person and personality, I imagined it as a small human being, or homunculus, moving his/her hands. There he or she has experiencing and tries to do something with it. This is, of course, the question of language and the way of thinking, I mean, how we used to think about person or experiencing, etc. May be it's the right time to discuss what is a person?

F.V. This is an important topic. I absolutely agree that this conversation has led us to some questions that may seem naïve: what is a human being? What is a person? What is experience? Not in general, but in this context. How do you think we can problematize this topic – the concept of person in the context of experiencing? What meta-categories do we see as the most appropriate for thinking about the notion of person as well as adequate to the spirit of person-centred psychotherapy? What categories are not adequate? From the moment you said you saw a homunculus, it sounded as if you were trying to give up seeing it.

T.K. Indeed, I did it unwittingly. This is a habit of our mind, our consciousness, to think about the person, personality as about some substance or to put it inside a human being as a homunculus that controls us, our brain, our body, our soul, etc. To think about personality as about some core that can be depicted in the form of a container filled with personality content, and this content brims out from time to time, catalysing the ongoing psychological processes – which obviously is not our method.

The main category is the process. The person is the experiencing process. The main concepts in experiential philosophy and Gendlin's practice are "moving forward", "felt shift", i.e. *any movement is better than stagnation*. It is important that we have moved from the original form of "experience" to "experiencing" to underline the process (Gendlin, 1973).

I would also single out as relevant categories the existence–essence opposition and the question of what is of primary importance. For Gendlin, essence is of secondary importance to existence. In this context, Gendlin is the follower of the branch of existentialism where existence precedes essence, and essence is created during concrete steps of experiencing.

Rogers states that the actualizing tendency is the primary essence which, when allowed to be properly manifested and to function, will bring the result (Rogers, 1989). All that is needed is to create the appropriate conditions. Predetermination of the procedural result, namely a positive result, which has been and is being strongly criticized, for example, by existential psychotherapists, is postulated. They call it young American naïve optimism of "self-made" people at odds with the ways of old and wise Europe (for example, Spinelli, 2005).

F.V. Now I would introduce the concept of a position taken by a thinker or a therapist towards the notion of person. When we talk about the actualizing tendency as the process unfolding in certain conditions, what do we mean? What position does the subject take?

When you said you imagined a homunculus, this was an everyday objectifying setting, an objectifying position from the outside. The person was an object, in whom something was unfolding. But there seems to be nothing close to that in Rogers' practice. He takes the position *inside* the dyad, inside the encounter or dialogue. His statements about the need to create the conditions for a person to unfold and/or manifest himself/herself are not the subject of a scientific claim, not a hypothesis or a theory. This is the basic, the fundamental personal intuition. It is strongly criticized, it triggers violent criticism: "How one can be so naïve in the 20th century with all its horrors?"

If it was so easy – all people are good, you just need to create the conditions – it wouldn't stand up to criticism. But he doesn't take the position from the outside, he says: this is You, and this is Me who believes in you. I believe in you with my whole Self. This is the subject of inner belief and corresponding inner activity, not external scientific belief that if you do this, will actualize that. And if someone is capable of this, the other individual will respond and open himself/herself to him. And who is not capable, or when someone is not capable of this, they try to achieve such a state through techniques.

T.K. Again we have this being–doing opposition. But I don't want to oppose these two things. I think about how Rogers and Gendlin, experiencing and person complement each other. Gendlin came to Rogers with the idea of experiencing (Gendlin, 2000). And I guess this kind of idea had to appear in Rogers' theoretical system – what else could he use to appeal to a human being of integrity?

Gendlin talks about the experiencing process as a flow, and the individual gets access to it through different focusing activities by following instructions or without them. The client develops it like a film and expresses, symbolizes. Meanwhile experiencing changes, he/she again expresses the felt sense and moves forward giving experiencing an opportunity to symbolize itself: a special focusing instruction – "let the words come by themselves". But this is also a sort of external position as person, of looking at the interior process from outside. As Barbara Brodley quite sceptically wrote, focusing gives me a feeling that the client is watching the movie and retelling the therapist all he/she sees in detail (Brodley, 1990).

Thus, if we were to logically sharpen this position, the experiencing is conceived as a natural, spontaneous process that the individual finds in its finished form. Yes, it is partly vague, felt by the "silent" body that someone needs to get talking. Experiencing develops through clarification of what is not clear now, what is at the edge. This process inside oneself can be very active, but speaking only about the process bears the risk of seeing it as a separate reality outside the person.

F.V. I agree with you that the concept of experiencing should have inevitably been reflected somehow in Rogers' theory. Person and personality always need to be considered in the context, first, of life in the universe and, second, in the context of the Other – communication, dialogue. The danger of thinking about a person or personality naturalistically, as a reality defined from itself and in itself and living inside by its own laws is the danger of essentialism.

We say that person is unthinkable inside itself and thinkable as a correlate in the system and in relation. In relation to what? To *life in the world*. When Rogers has a session with a client, they talk about his/her family structure, etc. They discuss what worries the client in terms of his/her living world, as we would call it. Without this, there is no personality as such, no cut-off essence. Then, theoretically, we can also say that a person or personality has to be thought about inside this life relation – a person and the world, not inside a human being.

The second reason why we cannot take an objectifying position towards personality is that if we want to encounter the real person, we have to enter into personal relationship with this person for this person to manifest itself. This is what differentiates therapy from a laboratory experiment. All this has brought us to the idea of anti-naturalism, anti-essentialism. This concerns precisely theoretical questions, conceptualizations rather than practice if we talk about Rogers and the tendency in his theory towards essentialism.

T.K. Gendlin joins the existentialists in their denial of predetermined essence. Within some areas of existentialism, there is great sensitivity for the freedom of the person, to the point that it is seen as absolute. The person can't be reduced to any definitions, laws, or rules. However, if we are talking about how essence is born in experiencing, from the perspective of the cultural-historical activity theory (CHAT) our vision can't be limited to the interpretation of experiencing as the process. From our point of view, experiencing is an activity,[1] not just the process. It exists at different levels, including the level of immediate experience that largely flows in Gendlin mode, so to speak. But there are also other levels where the subject of experiencing is active (Vasilyuk, 2016). Therefore, we are talking about the work, the inner activity of experiencing and about the person as the subject, the "actor" of such activity.

F.V. To discuss the question of person and experiencing from our position, we may recall the concept of higher mental (or psychic) function by L. S. Vygotsky (Van der Veer and Valsiner, 1994) and relate it to experiencing. Whose function are we talking about? That of the person. It develops inside a dialogue, within joint activities. Why is it called higher? It maintains natural content, but is mediated by cultural means as well as dialogue.

I have a metaphor of an English garden. It's all natural, but the gardener helped it to grow to its full potential and beauty, to manifest itself, to talk itself out. He was attentive to its relief, level differences, its flora, and created something more natural than just a weed-covered field. The same with the person: after good therapy, it becomes more natural. Natural, but not wild. That's why I have the metaphor of the English garden, not just a garden for what happens in psychotherapy.

T.K. We take on Rogers' floral metaphors. But gardener aside, can we say that the person is the master of experiencing? That experiencing belongs to person?

F.V. "Master" is one variant; it can be the author or the victim of experiencing. I think it's rather the *author*, the subject of experiencing. What kind of subject? Saying it's just the subject of experiencing is not enough. It is the *subject that enters into a relationship with its experiencing*. And person-centred therapy is the therapy that helps her/him to enter into such a relationship – to enter bravely because the individual fears his/her experiencing; to enter creatively because the individual stagnates in relationship with his/her experiencing; to enter actively because the individual sometimes surrenders to his/her experiencing; to enter in the state of freedom, not slavery. These oppositions may continue. It is enough to have even these three afore-mentioned oppositions to put a problem for therapy. Even the coordinates system consisting of these three oppositions presents a problem for the therapy – theoretical, methodological and supervisory. What relationship between person and experiencing do we support in person-centred and experiential therapy?

The client as a person has a certain attitude towards his/her experiencing. It ranges from personal connivance with his/her experiencing to slavery, when experiencing gets the individual under control in the form of a blind passion, strong affect. On the opposite side of the range is another danger: an attempt to control one's experiencing constructively.

T.K. This resembles what we discussed in the context of anthropological problems.

F.V. Yes, and the difficulty is that this is also the problem of scientific thinking. Indeed, academic psychology often presents experiencing as a self-acting process unfolding inside the person, and all the person needs is to speak about it, to describe it. Anyway, personality joins the game when experiencing has already taken place.

However, therapeutic and life practice make one aware of the entirely different attitude of the person towards experiencing. The person tries to influence experiencing, participate in it. Sometimes this bears fruit, sometimes not. Anyway, there is a fundamental fact: the person *participates* in his/her experiencing.

There is one interesting example. Nikolenka, the character of Leo Tolstoy's novel, *Childhood, Boyhood and Youth*, attempts to influence his experiencing of being in love. The young man, a first-year student of Moscow University, pays a visit to his childhood friend Sonetchka, whom he hasn't seen for many years. On his way he refreshes his memory of how passionately he was in love with her as a child, fuelling his feelings. A new setting of being in love forms. It is not a spontaneous self-acting process, but a targeted inner activity. What is it motivated by?

First, by the romantic image. Nikolenka knew that Sonetchka, while travelling abroad, cut her face with pieces of a carriage's window glass.

> Since I had read somewhere of a lover who remained true to his adored one in spite of her disfigurement with smallpox, strove to imagine that I was in love with Sonetchka, for the purpose of priding myself on holding to my troth in spite of her scars.
>
> *(Tolstoy, 1917, p. 214)*

The second motive is of the social norm. Nikolenka envies his friends who are in love already, he is *supposed* to be in love; he follows the behaviour of his besotted peers.

This inner work on planting the seed of love was effective. The characters started to chat in a free and easy manner, but while she had been speaking,

> I had been thinking over my position at the present moment, and had come to the conclusion that I was in love with her. The instant, however, that I arrived at that result my careless, happy mood vanished, a mist seemed to arise before me which concealed even her eyes and smile, and, blushing hotly, I became tongue-tied and ill-at-ease.
>
> *(Tolstoy, 1917, p. 216)*

Here we have the direct result of one's inner work on experiencing: wanted to be in love – now I am in love. But, of course, the reader understands the artificial nature of this self-made feeling, which is confirmed by the episode taking place the previous day. Having visited his friend in the countryside, Nikolenka enjoyed the reading of his friend's sister Varenka. She had a pleasant, rich voice. "How I wish that I wasn't in love already!" (Tolstoy, 1917, p. 242).

T.K. A good example for the conclusion! Yes, the person is active, while also dialogic. If we come back to the dilemma between technology and relations, it is possible to say that it is not the "doing or being" opposition, but "both doing and being" statement.

F.V. Sometimes there is an objective controversy between therapeutic goals: providing support to personality focused on being and assistance in a specific situation of symptom manifestation. The processes of symptomatic and personal changes do not always go in parallel. For example, important personal work may be done without significant symptomatic changes. I had a client who didn't manage to get rid of a symptom, but in the end of the therapy she said: "I came to you being the symptom and now leave you with the symptom." It was important for her to feel that she could live with the symptom, have a certain attitude, tolerate it, struggle with it, etc.

Now we come back to the idea that we want freedom of the person and freedom of experiencing. We want such personal attitude and participation in experiencing when the person is respectful of experiencing, can be in dialogue with it, sometimes in conflict; sometimes the person fears experiencing and may try to do something with it. Experiencing should be creative, full of cultural means, poetic in this sense; it should be open, full of courage, and brave. It can be painful, heavy, and difficult. To be open for it, the individual needs to have the Other who confirms it at the moment, otherwise he/she wouldn't manage. Together with the client, we build our relationship, in which freedom of experiencing is born, but he/she also builds a relationship with his/her experiencing.

T.K. Our co-experiencing is also thought as a multi-layer activity of the therapist in support of these processes, as personal participation in personal experiencing of the other (Vasilyuk, 2015; 2016) and his/her activity, work of experiencing – plus the therapist and his/her activity of co-experiencing form the integrity of the therapeutic "we".

A single ellipse with two focuses

F.V. Tatiana, I think our discussion has raised more questions than it answered. Can we try to formulate our main idea more clearly? I suggest expressing it as a geometric metaphor. When we say "person-centred" or "experiencing-centred", our mind uses its habits and draws a picture of a single centre with a circled area around it. And if we follow this imagination pattern, we will have a geometric picture consisted of two circles, each with its own centre. And there is "and" between them. If we assume it as a starting point of our thinking in this topic, then we can't believe that these two circles will ever become one organism. Unity will never be saved however you interpret the "and" link. Our main idea about the dialectic unity of personality and experiencing needs to get the updated version of the original thought.

Do you remember how at maths classes the teacher fixed two pegs to the school-board, bound a rope to them and a pupil pulling on the rope with a chalk drew a perfect oval? If not, you certainly will find the video how to do it on the internet. Only after the drawing, the teacher gave the definition: "An ellipse is a geometric locus of points, for which the sum of distances to two given points F1 and F2, called focuses, is constant and exceeds the distance between two focuses."

Now, not two circles, but *a single ellipse with two focuses* – person and experiencing – is the model that, in my opinion, expresses in a graphic form our intuition of indissoluble unity of person and experiencing. This unity is dialectic and dynamic. The therapeutic process, moving along the orbit, may come as close as possible to one pole, while moving away from another, and vice versa. But the integrity of the person-experiential therapy is maintained thanks to the efforts of the therapist who, like that pupil, should not let the rope hang loose and should keep it strained to bind two poles – person and experiencing.

T.K. This is indeed a good illustration! I watched the video how to draw an ellipse. There are a lot of them on the internet with many views. I was excited to see that in the era of computer graphics people still enjoy such an easy, uncomplicated manual activity to create simple and clear beauty. This is so close to my perception of the person-experiential therapy. Thank you, Fyodor!

F.V. Thank you, Tatiana!

Notes

* This chapter is an edited version of a paper published in Russian in the Journal *Konsul'-tativnaya psikhologiya i psikhoterapiya* [Counselling Psychology and Psychotherapy], 2017. Vol. 25, no. 3, pp. 11–32. doi:10.17759/cpp.2017250302.
1 In CHAT "activity" is a meta-category that expresses the meaning of "a molar and nonadditive unit of subject's life" and is aimed at overcoming Cartesian differentiation between subject and object, a man and the world. In psychological analysis, activity is seen as a structure of actions organized as a whole. Such structure is organized, on the one hand, by motives, goals, meanings, and, on the other hand, by means of action. The activity structure has many levels including also unconscious, automatic and involuntary actions and operations. (See Yamagata-Lynch, 2010.)

References

Bazzano, M. (2016). The conservative turn in person-centered therapy, *Person-Centered & Experiential Psychotherapies*, doi:10.1080/14779757.2016.1228540.
Brodly, B.T. (1990). Client-centered and experiential: two different therapies. In G. Lietaer, J. Rombauts and R. Balen (Eds), *Client-centered and experiential psychotherapy in the nineties* (pp. 87–108). Leuven: Leuven University Press.
Gadamer, H.-G. (2006). The aesthetics of genius and the concept of experience (Erlebnis). In *Truth and method* (pp. 49–69). 2nd revised ed. London; New York: Continuum.
Gendlin, E.T. (1973). Experiential psychotherapy. In R. Corsini (Ed.), *Current psychotherapies* (pp. 317–352). Itasca, IL: Peacock. http://www.focusing.org/gendlin/docs/gol_2029.html.
Gendlin, E.T. (2000). Foreword. In C. R. Rogers and D. E. Russell, *Carl Rogers: the quiet revolutionary, an oral history*. Roseville, CA: Penmarin Books. http://www.focusing.org/gendlin_foreword_to_cr.html.
Gilbert, E. (2007). *Eat, pray, love*. London: Bloomsbury.
Illouz, E. (2007). *Cold intimacies: The making of emotional capitalism*. Cambridge: Polity Press.
Kirschenbaum, H. (2012). "What is "person-centered"? A posthumous conversation with Carl Rogers on the development of the person-centered approach. *Person-Centered & Experiential Psychotherapies*, 11(1), 14–30, doi:10.1080/14779757.2012.656406.

Lietaer, G. (2016). His master's voice: Carl Rogers' response modes in therapy and demonstration sessions throughout his career. A quantitative analysis and some qualitative-clinical comments. In *Integrity. Interdisciplinarity. Innovation.* WAPCEPC 2016 conference. Program. Part B. p. 64. http://www.nypcrc.org/pce2016.

Mill, J.S. (2009/1879). *Utilitarianism.* London: The Floating Press.

Rogers, C. (1989). *On becoming a person: A therapist's view of psychotherapy.* Boston: Houghton Mifflin.

Schulze, G. (1992). *Die Erlebnisgesellschaft: Kultursoziologie der Gegenwart.* Frankfurt a.M.: Campus.

Spinelli, E. (2005). *The interpreted world: an introduction to phenomenological psychology.* London: SAGE.

Tolstoy, L. (1917). *Childhood, boyhood and youth.* London & Toronto: J.M. Dent & Sons.

Vasilyuk, F.E. (2015). Coexperiencing psychotherapy as a psychotechnical system. *Journal of Russian & East European Psychology*, 52(1), 1–58, doi:10.1080/10610405.2015.1064721.

Vasilyuk, F.E. (2016). Semiotics and the technique of empathy, *Journal of Russian & East European Psychology*, 53(2), 56–79, doi:10.1080/10610405.2016.1230994.

Van der Veer, R. and Valsiner, J. (eds.) (1994). *The Vygotsky reader.* Oxford, UK; Cambridge, USA: Blackwell.

Yamagata-Lynch, L.C. (2010). *Activity systems analysis methods: Understanding complex learning environments.* New York: Springer Science+Business Media, LLC.

7

ACTUALIZING TENDENCY, ORGANISMIC WISDOM AND UNDERSTANDING THE WORLD

Salvador Moreno-López

Introduction

In this chapter, I present reflections on my psychotherapeutic practice from a person-centered perspective and propose to extend and make explicit some aspects of the actualizing tendency and organismic wisdom proposed by Carl R. Rogers. I will argue that the understanding of the world is a fundamental, inseparable, dimension to understand and promote the functioning of both the actualizing tendency and the organismic wisdom.

One of the theoretical pillars of the person-centered approach is the notion of an actualizing tendency as the common basis for all human motivation. In Rogers' (1980) words:

> The person-centred approach rests on a basic trust in human beings, and in all organisms ... We can say that there is in every organism, at whatever level, an underlying flow of movement toward constructive fulfillment of its inherent possibilities. In human beings, too, there is a natural tendency towards a more complex and complete development.
>
> *(pp. 117–118)*

His basic trust in the organism and in the human being led him to locate psychotherapy clients as protagonists of their personal development and therapists as companions. Rogers was astonished by this tendency. In one of his examples he describes how a potato, despite poor environmental conditions, can generate sprouts to grow and seek the light. He says:

> The sprouts were, in their bizarre, futile growth, a sort of desperate expression of the directional tendency I have been describing. They would never become

plants, never mature, never fulfill their real potential. But under the most adverse circumstances, they were striving to become. Life would not give up, even if it could not flourish.

(p. 118)

Directional and interactional

At some point later in the same passage, he comments that some people who go to therapy have lived in such unfavorable conditions that their lives seem abnormal and inhumane. And although their behaviors may seem strange, inadequate and useless, they nevertheless do the best they can to take care of themselves and promote their survival and development. From this perspective, Rogers' proposal emphasizes what I will call the *directional* (optimistic) facet of the actualizing tendency. In this chapter, I emphasize another facet, which I call *interactional*, and it refers to the consideration that a person's life and his/her living are an ongoing interaction with other human beings in a concrete world. Although this interactional aspect requires one to attend to the necessary conditions for the development of the directional and optimistic facet of the actualizing tendency in such a way that it may be expressed with greater richness and complexity (Rogers, 1957, 1959), it is also important that the conditions for a proper functioning of the interactional facet of the actualizing tendency are made explicit.

Rogers (1980) thought that an organism ordinarily does not develop negative capacities. It does not

> actualize its potentiality for self-destruction, nor its ability to bear pain. Only under unusual or perverse circumstances do these potentialities become actualized. It is clear that the actualizing tendency is selective and directional – a constructive tendency, if you will.
>
> (p. 121)

However, when we realize that these perverse circumstances are not as unusual as we would like, we face a major problem. Let's see some examples: malnutrition, lack of hygiene and an unstable household during the first years of life – among other factors – play a decisive role in the developmental possibilities of a child. Deficiencies in these areas can leave negative outcomes, which can in turn become insurmountable in later years. And certainly, children who grow up in these conditions have great disadvantages compared to children who grow well nourished, cared for and with a warm and stable family. Something similar can be said about the importance of the relationship with the parental figures in that stage of life. The same applies to the impact that the absence of loving parents, relatively stable and safe, with enough time and willingness to play with their children, has in the socio-affective development. Children are affected by the socio-affective, economic, cultural and political conditions experienced by their parents, as well as by their anguish of not knowing if they will have something to eat every day, if there will be water, or medicines if they become ill, etc. Although it must be acknowledged that the absence of parents and the lack of a close and warm relationship with their children can occur both in situations of extreme poverty and in situations of extreme wealth, other conditions too can make great differences in the development of children. What I emphasize here is the need to take into account the influence of socio-economic, cultural, political, religious and environmental conditions on human development, along with interpersonal relationships.

"Buen Con-Vivir"

It has concerned me that by emphasizing the directional facet of the actualizing tendency, we could forget how important it is to understand and transform the sociocultural and political conditions in which we live, in a way that they may support and promote the *Buen Con-Vivir* [1] (good-living-with-others); i.e. good living of all human beings, taking care of the earth as the household in which we live (Boff, 2002, 2009; Rodríguez, 2016). While recognizing how valuable and surprising this tendency to life, differentiation and complexity is, I have also asked myself: will it not be equally important to identify ecological, economic, social, political, cultural, religious and interpersonal conditions that best support everybody's human development from the actualizing tendency?

Max-Neef's (1998) saying has particular resonance here: "But poverty is not only poverty. It is much more than that. Every poverty generates pathologies, when it exceeds critical limits of intensity and duration" (Max-Neef, 1998, p. 43). And these pathologies are no longer just individual, but *social*. Therefore, the existence of such collective pathologies requires different treatments than hitherto used, since "it does not make sense to heal an individual and then to return him/her to a sick environment" (p. 48). That is, proposing an individualistic understanding of clients, without taking into account the world in which they live, can be misleading and can lead us onto paths that stray away from an ethical point of view, a necessary emphasis on justice.

As a psychotherapist, I ask myself how to deal with and respond to the problems of insufficient salary, unemployment, violence, insecurity, lack of protection, marginalization, discrimination, exile and forced immigration, injustice, illegality, corruption, extortion, kidnapping, and murder experienced by many who come to therapy. These inhumane social, economic, political, cultural and religious conditions are now everyday problems for *millions* of human beings. Even we, as psychotherapists and human beings, are affected to a greater or lesser extent by these circumstances. Can we ignore them and address only the directional aspect of the actualizing tendency? ... I do not think so.

In my own professional practice of more than 40 years, and in that of many of my colleagues, when an adult comes to psychotherapy s/he usually feels overwhelmed by pain, frustrated, discouraged, anxious, sad, disconcerted, fearful, and insecure. S/he recognizes that her/his daily living is painful, difficult, unsatisfactory and afflicted. Often, s/he also relates all sorts of physical symptoms. What hampers his/her well-being is somewhat incomprehensible because his/her attempts to resolve the suffering have been useless. In addition to telling how s/he feels and showing some of the emotions that hurt him/her, this person also alludes to several circumstances of his/her life: to relationships and interactions with family, friends, bosses and co-workers, neighbors, etc. It also includes the conditions of work or unemployment, the characteristics of the neighborhood and the house or department in which s/he lives, the means of transportation, access to health care services, and the quality of care s/he receives. In addition, s/he makes some references to the role s/he plays in his/her family, to the responsibilities that this entails, and to the satisfactions and frustrations that s/he finds in his/her daily living-with-others. It is clear then, that this person is an *embodied human being* who lives in interaction with other human beings, in *concrete* socio-cultural, economic, political, religious and ecological contexts.

From the above observations and reflections, I have come to think that emotional problems do not occur only as individual, psychological, internal phenomena. Rather, they are experiences that occur *in the interaction* with other people, in a particular world and need to be considered from these various aspects.

To find and generate ways to *Buen Con-Vivir* (good-living-with-others), a person needs to attend to and understand him/herself as much as s/he needs to understand others with whom s/he shares his/her daily life and the world in which others live. So, we can say that there are three inseparable and indispensable dimensions of daily living: (1) to understand oneself, (2) to understand others and (3) to understand the world in which all live together.

From this perspective, what I said before implies that a person does not have in him/herself everything s/he requires to understand him/herself in his/her daily life, to learn how to have a *Buen Con-Vivir* and his/her environment, or to change what hinders his/her development or make him/her suffer emotionally. A client needs to *interact* with others and their circumstances, under certain conditions, to encourage changes and different ways of relating. Then, if the psychotherapist understands how other people and the world become present in his/her client's life, s/he will be able to understand him/her better and will have more precise clues than if s/he does not have that knowledge and understanding.

Rogers (1951/1965) certainly attended, on the whole, to the client's lived world. For him, "every individual exists in a continually changing world of experience of which he is the center" (p. 483); therefore, "the best vantage point for understanding behavior is from the internal frame of reference of the individual himself" (p. 494). However, here I propose to extend the horizon to include also the understanding that I as human being and as psychotherapist can have of the client's world, with the collaboration of different scientific disciplines and other valid sources of knowledge and understanding (Freire, 1993). For example, if the client feels unprotected economically or legally in some circumstances, how are we to differentiate if his feeling unprotected is related to the lack of accessible support for his problems or to his ignorance about helping agencies in his town or to his difficulty in understanding the socio-political conditions in which he lives, or maybe a little of each of these aspects (Moreno and Casillas, 2015)? Of course, it may also happen that the person, because of other experiences in his life, feels insecure, vulnerable, distressed, helpless, all at the same time. This emotional dimension has to be also understood, taken into account and hopefully transformed. My cautionary point is this: let us not reduce the lived world to something that is "inside" the person, in a way that we can disengage from what is "outside". In addition, I think it is necessary to create new conceptual models and metaphors, referred to as *new cartographies* by Najmanovich (2009), in order to understand how we conceptualize inside/outside and subjective/objective, as others have done (e.g., Gendlin, 1984, 1997, Max-Neef, 1998; Najmanovich, 2001).

My personal relationship with Carl Rogers and my reading of his texts (Rogers, 1951/1965, 1957, 1959, 1961, 1969, 1975, 1980) awakened in me the curiosity to observe and identify patterns in my professional work, thus expanding my educational and psychotherapeutic practices (Blanco and Moreno, 1985). Also, I was invited to reflect on these observations to try to explain and understand them, using some theoretical and philosophical references. I value that Rogers has exposed his ideas, theories and research results always in relation to some data, either from clinical practice or formal research, and reminded us that they are knowledge, reflections, results and provisional theories, in an ongoing process and transformation (Rogers, 1959, 1961). At the same time, I learned from Paulo Freire (1972, 1993) the importance and value of praxis, that continuous movement and interaction between action and reflection. Although they start from different epistemologies, some apparent similarities between Rogers and Freire in seeking an interaction between practice and theory, between action, reflection and research, have been meaningful to me. With Freire (1972, 1993), I also began to become aware of the World; that concrete world in which we human beings live, in relationships with other people, influenced and bounded by economic, social, political and ecological conditions that historically we are finding and building. This world, so marked by inequalities and injustices, some of them structural, was somewhat diluted in Rogers' ideas and theories. It is from this expanded context that I now return to my reflections and proposals.

Reflections and learning from the practice of psychotherapy

Let's start with Susana's case. She is a 43-year-old teacher. She works in a university where she carries out academic and administrative activities. Susana works as a coordinator and is responsible for organizing and evaluating school programs conducted by other teachers. For years, she has worked hard to improve her department, both at the level of procedures and results. At the same time, she has sought to grow as a teacher. To do this, she studied a master's program that would help her have a clearer vision of her educational work and to improve her ways of interacting with the students.

She has good reasons to be satisfied and appreciates her success. She considers herself a responsible person, and values her job. She is satisfied with the improvements made in her department and would certainly like to have the dean's and her colleagues' recognition for the way she has worked and for the results obtained.

She is currently in difficult circumstances. She feels very worried and disconcerted because for some months she noticed that four colleagues have been doing activities that hinder her in fulfilling her duties and make her look bad to other colleagues and the rector of the university. When she thinks about this, she feels sad, discouraged, angry, bewildered, and sometimes guilty. She begins to wonder what she has done wrong or what she needs to do better, or if she has the necessary skills to do the job or if it is time to retire or go to another institution. When she has talked about this situation with the rector, she has not found the support she was looking for. He seems to disregard her colleagues' actions and tells her not to worry. Because of that, Susana feels uncertain and vulnerable, frightened and insecure, recognizing that some colleagues do not appreciate what she does, and also take actions to, as she says, "make her stumble" or they "gossip" about her. They prevent her from carrying out some of her activities, ignore her authority and make programs without requesting her authorization, and even complain about her with the rector. For her part, Susana tries to do her job well and presents her reports as requested.

Reflecting on what her colleagues do and how little support she feels from the rector, and feeling somewhat ignored and vulnerable, Susana wonders if she is doing her job well, and if it is time to leave and go to another institution.

In a situation like this, we can also find that the client's assessment of herself is somewhat impaired by several experiences in her history, and that she has a strong need for recognition, perhaps related to affective deficiencies in the relationship with her parents. It is possible to assume that these and other emotional wounds come into play in the perception of her situation in the university and in what she identifies as alternatives for action. In fact, by the way she expresses herself, it seems to me that the focus of attention is basically on her, seeking there the cause of her discomfort and the alternatives to solve it. Susana wonders what is wrong, if she has the skills to perform her job well, if her training is insufficient, if it is time to leave that position and look for another job. In doing so, she invests a lot of time and energy. What she hardly does is reflect on the circumstances of the institution.

When I realized what she was feeling and doing, I wondered if it would be important and pertinent to invite her to expand her sense and feeling, along with her reflective gaze, to include other aspects of the situation. This meant to look at issues such as: workplaces, salaries, promotions, prestige and power within the institution, the union's role, and the current economic and political conditions of higher education institutions in the country, among others (Moreno and Casillas, 2015).

I also wondered if instead I would have to wait and see whether at any moment she would think about these and other aspects – perhaps after leaving that university and finding similar problems (or worse) elsewhere. How can one help a person realize that she has the capacities and resources to understand herself well and change what she needs in the direction of her well-being and development? Is it not pertinent or appropriate that a person-centered psychotherapist suggests talking about issues like these, even if they are important aspects of the client's existential situation and the cause for her suffering?

Eventually, I chose to bring up these issues in the sessions, little by little, starting with one or two questions, then following the conversation from what she expressed. Some of the questions I had in mind, and that I thought might be useful, were: who are these colleagues who bother you? What are they looking for in the institution and in the union? In what way does what you do and the position you hold at the university relate to what these colleagues want? How are the workers of the institution grouped? How does the rector relate to each of the groups? What support does the rector need from these groups to stay in his position? I asked the questions at different times, seeking to invite without imposing and waiting so that she did what she wanted to do with them.

At the beginning, Susan looked surprised and her puzzled look seemed to be saying "What does this have to do with what happens to me and how I feel?" I reflected to her that she did seem surprised and puzzled about my questions. She said: yes. We paused for a moment so that she had time to *sentipensar*[2] *(sense-feel-think)* each question. I kept expressing my understanding of her expressions and sayings. And from there, if pertinent, I asked a new question. Little by little, her facial expression was changing. It seemed to me a mixture of reflection, surprise, bewilderment and identification of new understandings. "Maybe not everything is up to me. Maybe it's not that I'm wrong or that I'm not good in my job anymore. It may be that I have not noticed the power struggles in the institution for positions and privileges. And there I am in the middle of it, even if I don't want to be. I interfere with some of them and I am useful to others by the way I do my job. So, they value what I do at their convenience," she says at the end of a session. I accompany Susana in her reflections and attempts to broaden her understanding of circumstances. I reflect, I resonate, I am silent, letting myself feel her experiencing and my experiencing in relation to our interaction.

Being-Interacting-in-the-World involves attending to such interaction with a stance that pays attention to wholeness and movement. In other words, I cannot understand my client apart from her interactions with her world. And she cannot understand herself outside of such interactions either. Moreover, if what she is looking for is change, in order to live better with others in the concrete circumstances of her life, then she requires knowing, understanding and sometimes explaining those circumstances.

Susana could benefit from understanding the economic, legal, political, sociocultural and psychosocial dimensions of her workplace and from identifying the "rules of the game" at the university, both the explicit and the implicit ones. I think that understanding the situation would help her identify her position in that context and what she can do as a worker and to find out what she needs to pay attention to in order to avoid a written warning or even a dismissal; and to clarify what to do so that neither her colleagues nor the dean hinder her professional development in the institution.

I think it would also help her to find out about the current employment conditions in her country and city when considering the alternatives of staying or quitting her job.

In this context, it seems to me that a psychotherapeutic process is not only intended to help her find ways of being at peace with herself and with those she lives with, but also to identify ways of interaction that allow her to be in the best possible way in that job, if she chooses. Or, failing that, to have the strength and ingenuity to find a job with better conditions (Moreno, 2009, Moreno and Casillas, 2015).

A person-centered psychotherapy should consider this condition of *being-in-the-world* as a *basic referent* that guides interactions in the process. To look at the person first as an individual and then in relation to others implies the risk of ignoring the understanding and transformation of the world as indispensable actions to achieve the changes sought in psychotherapy.

Because of the above, some of Moreira's (2001) reflections regarding the capitalist notion of the person and the confusion they generate between person and individual are relevant to me. She says, for example, that the capitalist notion of person, "at the same time that it postulates individual freedom, conveys the idea of the person as being for work, an idea that favors capital's accumulation. The free person is the person who has a vocation for work" (p. 170). And then, referring to the notion of person in Carl Rogers' writings, she comments: "The Rogerian notion of person is the fruit of a dichotomous vision of the world. Subjectivity is exalted, while importance, weight and effectiveness are subtracted from objective reality" (p. 182).

For person-centered therapy, the goal is to develop a full, free and responsible person. Then, a new question arises: What kind of freedom and responsibility are we talking about? Moreira points out: "According to Rogers, his theory identifies an essential and intrinsic freedom, which bases the idea of a person as free subjectivity, with important political consequences" (p. 183). It seems that Rogers speaks about an individual freedom in the way this is conceived and understood by economic liberalism.

The question is, what freedom and responsibility does the current capitalist economic system promote? As Smith (Max-Neef & Smith, 2011) points out:

> We could look with innocent eyes at how the world works and say that it is up to our societies to decide what they want. Do we want to exclude the weak, the different, or do we want the inclusion of all of us in the community? Vox Populi must decide. But that would be naive. Unfortunately, at this historic stage such a decision has been captured by the powerful.
>
> (p. 56)

It seems then that at this level we are not all free to decide. In a context of high unemployment and low wages, what is the freedom that each person has in choosing his/her job? And then, although it is true that, as Frankl (1950) pointed out, we always have freedom of attitude in the face of adverse circumstances, we also should be very careful to avoid justifying them, saying that in the end, all that matters is that we can survive.

What freedom does Susana have, I wonder, to quit her job and look for another, when the probability of a better alternative is very low?

As with Susana, in psychotherapy I have found many people living in situations that have challenged my understanding and assumptions about my work as a psychotherapist. Their stories have led me to rethink ways to understand the actualizing tendency and the organismic wisdom in relation to a *sentipensada* understanding of the world.

Body wisdom and understanding of the world

> I have myself stressed the idea that man is wiser than his intellect, and that well-functioning persons come to trust their experiencing as an appropriate guide to their behavior.
>
> *(Rogers, 1977, p. 246)*

> White men must be crazy: they believe that thinking occurs in the head.
> *(Anonymous South American Indigenous (cited by Najmanovich, 2001, p. 2)*

It has taken me a long time to understand that organismic wisdom includes both ways of processing information at a given moment in my life and the contents of that information. As a process, it is an inclusive, complex, intuitive, non-verbal, at least partly a non-conscious way of orienting my interactions in the world. In relation to content, this wisdom is nourished by what has been lived and learned throughout life. Therefore, it is a more reliable guide in those circumstances and contexts in which a person has experiences and experiential knowledge than in those where s/he does not. In addition, it must be remembered that relying on experience is also something learned in interactions with culture and the environment, and not just an innate/biological characteristic. Rogers (1977) himself believed "that individuals are culturally conditioned, rewarded, reinforced, for behaviors that are in fact perversions of the natural directions of the unitary actualizing tendency" (p. 247). And because of that, they may move organismically in one direction, and struggle in another in their conscious lives. I would add that it is important to remember that a human being is not a natural phenomenon – if we understand it as being without culture, society, economy, politics, religion and the environment. Therefore, we must also examine the socio-cultural, economic, political, religious and ecological conditions, as long as they promote or not an adequate recognition of the experiencing as a source of appreciation and guidance for daily living. This means that organismic wisdom must be looked at as an interactional and historically situated phenomenon.

Before giving some examples, I recall what Najmanovich (2001) has pointed out in relation to these issues. She says:

What we call human experience is something that occurs to us and that goes on in the social realm, that we tell others and ourselves in a language, something that happens to us in the space-time in which we live and that takes on meaning and value only in terms of our sociocultural history. The body is our site where we are affected and the territory from which we act. It is not only a physical body, nor merely a physiological machine; it is a living organism capable of giving meaning to the experience of itself.

(p. 2)

And for his part, Gendlin (1984) claims: "In humans the complex animal is always also elaborated by social forms. But as the organism lives these forms it can reject and further elaborate them in turn" (p. 154). As human beings, at the same time that we are shaped by socio-cultural forms, we can also modify them to some degree, according to our living conditions and if we do it with others.

In both authors, we can identify *recognition of interaction* as a fundamental characteristic of human living.

Some examples

I would now like to give an example of this organismic wisdom's interactional quality in relation to the understanding of the world. If I get lost in the mountains of Chiapas, a region and an environment unknown to me, it will be much more difficult to orient myself than if I get lost in Mexico City. In the same way, I have more resources to guide an interaction and a conversation with people in a city than with people from a small indigenous population in the sierra. I have always lived in a medium-sized or large city. In both situations, I will do my best; I will take advantage of my bodily wisdom resources. However, there will be differences in my interactions, according to my experiences. My organismic wisdom will be poorer and undifferentiated where I have less knowledge. And without enough valid understandings about the organization and social, cultural, economic, political, ecological and religious functioning of the world in which I live, my life can be more difficult, erratic and painful. This is also found in some cases in psychotherapy, so let's look at some examples in this area.

Rubén, a 40-year-old resident of the Purhembe region around Lake Zirahuén in Mexico, comes to the clinic because he feels anxious, moody and has difficulty sleeping. He feels guilty about not being patient with his wife and daughters and being always worried. He lives in a small town so he needs to travel to other places to sell his handicrafts. On some days he makes the products, and on others he goes out to sell them. Going to sell *bateas* (wooden dishes for multiple uses) implies transport expenses and the uncertainty of how much he will earn. Sometimes, he gets only the bus ticket, and often the income is not enough to obtain the most basic food. Currently, he sometimes buys anxiety pills prescribed by a physician. This means an additional and, given his income, considerable expense. He told me part of his life story, a history full of affective and economic deficiencies, of sadness and tenacity, surviving in the forests where he cuts the wood to make his crafts.

I believe that some of his childhood experiences, in the relationship with his parents and relatives, are partial explanations of his current state of mind and his modes of interaction. There are also other experiences that probably had a traumatic effect on him, such as the time he was wounded with a knife by a thief. However, there are also other aspects. Therefore, when expanding the horizon of understanding, among the many aspects of his life, I highlight those related to his work and the sale of his crafts. I ask myself: how is it for this man to live in constant uncertainty, not knowing how much he will sell and how much money he will get to pay the expenses of food, house, transport and health? How would it be for him to go to the city to offer his *bateas* and to negotiate with each potential client – most of them *mestizos* [3] – Rubén being indigenous – the best possible price, that never seems to come close to a fair price for his work and production costs? How to address his feeling ashamed for not earning enough to give his family better food and living conditions? How may I understand his feeling incapable and guilty about his shortcomings, and his feeling fearful and insecure in the city? How to deal with these aspects of his living in psychotherapy?

Recently, I found an article by Gendlin (1984) that corroborated my reflections. He says:

> People in so called minority groups gain a lot of strength from discovering that such subjective difficulties are not their individual traits, but are systematically generated by the experiences the social structure assigns them. Recognizing this, an individual becomes stronger.
>
> *(p. 155)*

I cannot but smile when I read the *so called minority groups*. In Mexico and in many other countries these groups are unfortunately a *big majority*. So, we have a very different view. I also find it challenging to recognize that, in cases such as that of Rubén, these lived difficulties are particular (not individual) and at the same time embedded within the social structure. In psychotherapy, we can work towards recognizing the presence of the actualizing tendency and organismic wisdom in him, and taking advantage of all his experiences, knowledge and understandings of the world. At the same time, it is necessary to extend the vital horizon to identify constraints, restrictions and possibilities arising from the socio-economic structure, and the cultural, political, religious and environmental conditions in which each person lives. How to do it? We need to generate new answers.

For the time being, I integrate as contents of the psychotherapeutic dialogue the actions he takes to sell his products and the way he buys his medicine. In the first case, we look for alternatives to improve his income. In the second, we talk about how he can get them cheaper, and about activities that he can do to be calm, without medicine; for example, paying attention to his breathing and sensations.

Esther's example

Esther, a 35-year-old woman, has two children and a very bad relationship with her husband. He beats her and does not give her enough money to support her children. Legally, these are punishable behaviors. Esther has asked for divorce, and he has told her that he will not grant it. Besides, he has threatened her by saying that, if she leaves, he will take her children away and prevent her from seeing them. She feels very frightened and distressed, does not sleep well, gets angry easily and scolds her children a lot. "I want to be more patient with them, but I cannot," she says. "If he gave me the divorce and we live separately, that would be the best. I'm afraid of reporting his threats to the police. I don't want him to take my children away." I wonder what is and what will be the impact and consequences for these children living in that family environment, where they will hardly feel loved, respected, understood and cared for. I also wonder what alternatives this woman has in facing the situation and which of these she would consider taking. It is clear to me that she feels unprotected and defenceless, fearful and insecure, threatened and cornered.

In psychotherapy, it is necessary to attend to the client's feelings and her modes of relationship with other people, and also to seek that in the process she feels better, with confidence in herself, with enough clarity to generate alternatives that allow her to leave that painful situation. Esther feels sad, desperate, frustrated, frightened and vulnerable. Her nuclear family does not support her. Her mother says: "This is your cross, you have to bear it". And although she rebels, she also feels unprotected. Thinking about the possibility of losing her children makes her anxious. Besides that, she feels unable to defend herself, trapped, with no way out. I wonder then: in psychotherapy, in addition to attending to how Esther feels, should we also look at the circumstances in which she lives to understand them and identify possible means of support as well as alternatives? Is it pertinent to talk about the legal conditions that can protect her (or not) in relation to her husband, divorce and the threat of taking away the children? Should she ask for legal advice to know the details of the case from that perspective? Is it necessary to comment on alternatives available for her in case she had to leave and go somewhere else? Is it a good idea to identify a safe house for violated women, for example?

The words of José Ortega y Gasset (1914/2004) come to me insistently: "I am myself and my circumstances, and if I do not save them I do not save myself either" (p. 757). They remind me that I cannot understand myself apart from my circumstances that are constituted by other human beings as well as an ecological, social, economic, political, cultural and religious environment. So I listen to Esther's motivation that comes from the actualizing tendency; I listen to her ambivalent quest to feel and be in a better situation with her children. I attend to what she wants to do, recognizing the different aspects and contradictions that she finds in that search. Furthermore, I think it is important that she finds a support group, since her family doesn't accept her, and insists that Esther must endure her situation. With this attitude, they effectively encourage her indecisiveness and her guilt about wanting to change. I think it would then be useful for her to extend her understanding of the world in which she lives. In this way, she might identify other action alternatives.

As Gendlin (1984) says:

> Humans are social. Therefore, it is difficult for one person alone to have a complete conviction that the society's message is wrong. You need other people ... Of course, you may know a social pattern to be wrong ... But this knowing might not make a bodily sureness, alone.
>
> *(p. 155)*

This implies that it is necessary, among other things, to recognize oneself as belonging to a politically oppressed group to be more likely to *sentipensar* critically against the dominant ideology (Gendlin, 1984). As long as Esther stays in her family's worldview, it will be almost impossible for her to act in order to change her circumstances. She needs a different, broader understanding of the sociocultural world in which she lives, to be able to identify and generate new alternatives in her daily living.

Rita's example

Rita is 27 years old. She finished university three years ago and has been working as an architect. She came to the office because she lacked enthusiasm and had difficulties in establishing close and lasting relationships. She complains that she has no friends, and that she hardly enjoys her job. She lives with her parents and feels treated like a 15-year-old girl. That makes her angry with herself and, at the same time, makes her wonder what she is doing there, living with her parents. In many parts of Mexico, in some social groups, this is a frequent condition, that of young adults living in the parents' home and not marrying. They rebel against the rules that their parents put on them and, at the same time, expect the benefits of having a place to live, eat and some additional supports, if possible.

In this context, for Rita to live with her parents is not unusual but uncomfortable. On the other hand, as a professional, she is in charge of building houses, in the company where she works. She has to hire, coordinate and supervise construction workers. In a session, Rita expressed her dissatisfaction and concern about workers' salaries, especially those of lower rank. They seem insufficient and unjust to her. She wonders if she can do something about it and after some reflection concludes that she cannot. She does not assign wages. The company does. And they are paid the same as most construction workers in the area where they live. Sometimes she feels sad and even somewhat guilty about these working conditions. But what can she do? Additionally, she complains about her own salary. She says that she is paid less than her male colleagues, doing the same job. That also seems unfair to her. She has protested with her bosses, but she did not get a pay rise. Months later, Rita leaves the company, joins a colleague and starts her own business. They began by making repairs and modifications in some buildings and then started to build one or two houses. The issue of wages reappears. She asks herself again if she could pay more. She analyses the economic situation and concludes that it is not possible. She does not quite understand what is happening and feels frustrated and discouraged. Maybe we need to understand how this economic system works in relation to wages, I thought. This could give us clues to know which changes depend on us and which do not and, in any case, clarify how to proceed with those that we can promote.

Gendlin (1984) says:

> Today many millions have lost their jobs. Most of them are helpless and ashamed. They blame themselves, although they have no say in how economy is run. Such super-ego attacks make it noticeable. We all work in the work-forms that are given, and we don't control the conditions.
>
> *(pp. 153–154)*

I have already mentioned Gendlin's point about the difficulty of individually facing the messages and slogans endorsed by the dominant society and culture. We need others, we need to do it collectively. For this reason, it seems pertinent to include in some session reflection on this aspect of the functioning of the economy and of society. And to be able to do that, as a therapist, I need to learn, understand and reflect on the subject too.

The richness and complexity of organismic wisdom

In my search, I find Max-Neef and Smith (2011). They say that, to begin with, "we can only try to understand what has become our part; that understanding is the result of integration, whereas knowledge has been the result of separation" (p. 21). This gives us some clues about alternatives on how to approach the knowledge and understanding of the world. Later, they point out: "economics play a role in society that is parallel, and complementary, to that of the law: that of a bastion of a class structure" (p. 25). I identify in these thoughts some directions on how to keep working. Thus, from these experiences, observations and reflections, plus some dialogues with colleagues and texts of different authors, this is what I deduce: *organismic wisdom requires that I understand experientially other people and the World, so that it can express all its richness and complexity*. That is to say, I need to construct and appropriate embodied understanding, which allows me to understand and explain phenomena and situations with and in which I live, in the different circumstances and contexts of my life. And of course, I also need to review what are the understandings and knowledge that I appropriate and use, from an ethical horizon of *Buen Con-Vivir* (good-living-with-Others) (Boff, 2002, Freire, 1993, Max-Neef & Smith, 2011, Rodríguez, 2016).

I think that the great and serious problems we experience today as humanity and as concrete individuals in different countries are a sign that the ways of interaction between one and other, and the forms of social, economic, political and religious organization have not been appropriate. They do not promote favorable conditions for sustainable, just, and fair development for all. And they do not generate socio-economic and political conditions that make it possible for people to live in decent conditions, with sufficient and fair wages, access to health services and learning, with jobs that recognize their contributions to the production of goods, services and wealth that benefit others.

In reflecting on these examples and others from professional practice, it is clear to me that we need to recognize the understanding of the world in which we live as a fundamental ingredient for the proper functioning of the organismic wisdom. At the same time, for those of us who work as psychotherapists, important questions arise in relation to this scenario: how do we contribute with our work to maintain or change the social conditions? What do we contribute to people's *conscientização* [4] (loosely translatable as awareness) processes (Freire, 1972, 1993, 1970/2005) or how do we contribute to their taming? How do we promote our own *conscientização* and in what way are we alienated by the dominant social practices? To think collectively about the theories from the new socio-historical situations that we live in now is one of several important tasks to realize. In this text I have reflected, in dialogue with colleagues and different authors, as well as with those clients whom I have accompanied in psychotherapy or consulting. Certainly, the circle of my dialogue is much broader than can be thought by the cited cases and references. I have given just a few examples. Moreover, one of my purposes in writing this text has been to invite a dialogue to those who find in it directions that resonate significantly with their living and their work as psychotherapists.

In short

The actualizing tendency remains a central reference for understanding the energy and direction in which human beings move in our daily interactions. At the same time, this can be understood not only as a biological dimension but also considering two facets: the directional and the interactional. This differentiation is only conceptual. Finally, human biology is inseparable from social, cultural, economic, political, religious and environmental dimensions. The problem is that we need new cartographies to speak, think and act on these dimensions and facets in more humane ways.

I recognize the value of organismic wisdom (Rogers 1959, 1977, 1980) or body wisdom (Gendlin 1984, 2007). It is a concept that aims at recognizing a peculiar way of "processing" all the information we receive, moment by moment, considering the experiences of our personal history. This wisdom is also an assessment process on which we can depend to guide us in our daily interactions. At the same time, I emphasize the need to expand and enrich our understanding and knowledge of the world we live in, with the complexity of its several interrelated and moving dimensions and aspects.

Finally, I point to the understanding of the world in which we live as a process. This is necessary and indispensable when we attend to the actualizing tendency and the organismic wisdom. This understanding involves a diversity of ways of knowing, all connected from the experiential dimension. Here, I return to the aspect of meaning that Rogers (1961) speaks about in relation to learning, in the sense of searching embodied knowledge, including theories, that we feel to be valuable, and help us to live better. In addition, mine is an invitation to attend to the ethical and social dimensions to discern which of our understandings contribute to the construction of a Human World with justice and fairness for all (Blanco and Moreno, 1985, Freire, 1972, 1993, Max-Neef and Smith, 2011, Moreno, 1983).

Inspired by Octavio Paz (1957), I *sentipienso (feel-think)* that:

> We are life / we become with each other / sharing the bread and the air / polluting the water and ravaging the jungles / being supportive and extending the hand / receiving the one who is like us and expelling the different / we become with others / in our daily actions and omissions / others and I / we do not exist without each other / although sometimes we feel that we are alone among many people.

Notes

1 A Spanish expression that refers to a good-living-with-others and the *Pachamama*, the mother Earth. It is related to a cosmic vision of some aboriginal cultures of South America.
2 *Sentipensar*: I use a Spanish neologism that means to experience sensations, feelings and thoughts in one integrated process (Galeano, 1990, Moreno, 2009).
3 *Mestizo*: In a generic sense, I mean people who are not Indigenous. This implies that they have some European roots mixed with Indigenous, African, etc.
4 I use Freire's word in Portuguese, as is used in the English version. It "refers to learning to perceive social, political and economic contradictions, and to take action against the oppressive elements of reality" (Freire, 1970/2005, p. 36).

References

Blanco, R. & Moreno, S. (1985). Grupo terapéutico o educativo. *Revista DIDAC*, No. 6, 2–7.
Boff, L. (2002). *El cuidado esencial. Ética de lo humano, compasión por la tierra*. Madrid: Trotta.
Boff, L. (2009). ¿Vivir mejor o el buen vivir? *América Latina en movimiento*. online: http://www.alainet.org/es/active/29839.
Frankl, V. (1950). *Psicoanálisis y existencialismo*. México: Fondo de Cultura Económica.
Freire, P. (1972). *Pedagogía del oprimido*. Buenos Aires: Siglo XXI Argentina Editores.
Freire, P. (1993). *Pedagogía de la esperanza*. México: Siglo Veintiuno Editores, S.A. de C.V.
Freire, P. (1970/2005). *Pedagogy of the oppressed* (30th anniversary edition). New York: Continuum. Online: http://www.msu.ac.zw/elearning/material/1335344125freire_pedagogy_of_the_oppresed.pdf.
Galeano, E. (1990). *El libro de los abrazos* (3rd ed.). México: Siglo Veintiuno Editores, S.A. de C.V.
Gendlin, E. T. (1984). The political critique of "awareness." *The Focusing Folio*, 3(4), 139–157. From http://www.focusing.org/gendlin/docs/gol_2133.html.
Gendlin, E. T. (1997). *A process model*. New York: The Focusing Institute.
Gendlin, E. T. (2007). New patterns of relating to the new town. *The Focusing Folio*, 20(1), 165–171.

Max-Neef, M. (1998). *Desarrollo a escala humana* (2nd ed.). Montevideo: Nordan-Comunidad.
Max-Neef, M. & Smith, P. (2011). *La economía desenmascarada. Del poder y la codicia a la compasión y el bien común*. Barcelona: Icaria.
Moreira, V. (2001). *Más allá de la persona. Hacia una psicoterapia fenomenológica mundana*. Santiago: Universidad de Santiago.
Moreno, S. (1983). *La educación centrada en la persona* (2nd Ed.). México: El Manual Moderno.
Moreno, S. (2009). *Descubriendo mi sabiduría corporal. Focusing*. Guadalajara: Focusing México.
Moreno, S. & Casillas, E. (2015). Psicoterapia y bienestar en la vida cotidiana. In T. Zohn, E. Gómez & R. Enríquez (Eds.). *La psicoterapia frente al bienestar y el malestar* (pp. 167–199). Guadalajara: ITESO/UDG.
Najmanovich, D. (2001). Del cuerpo máquina al cuerpo entramado. *Campo Grupal*, 30, 2–4.
Najmanovich, D. (2009). El cuerpo del conocimiento, el conocimiento del cuerpo. *Cuadernos de campo*, 7, 6–13.
Ortega y Gasset, J. (1914/2004). *Obras completas*. Vol. 1. Madrid: Taurus/Fundación José Ortega y Gasset.
Paz, O. (1957). Piedra del Sol. Published in *Libertad bajo palabra*. México: Fondo de Cultura Económica. Online: http://homozapping.com.mx/wp-content/uploads/2014/03/piedra_de_sol.pdf.
Rodríguez, A. (2016). Teoría y práctica del buen vivir: Orígenes, debates conceptuales y conflictos sociales. El caso de Ecuador. Doctoral thesis. Universidad del País Vasco.
Rogers, C. R. (1951/1965). *Client-centred therapy*. Boston: Houghton Mifflin Company.
Rogers, C. R. (1957). The necessary and sufficient conditions of therapeutic personality change. *Journal of Consulting Psychology*, 21, 95–103.
Rogers, C. R. (1959). A theory of therapy, personality and interpersonal relationships as developed in the client-centred framework. In S. Koch (Ed.), *Psychology: A study of a science. Vol. 3: Formulations of the person and the social context*. New York: McGraw Hill.
Rogers, C. R. (1961). *On becoming a person*. Boston: Houghton Mifflin Company.
Rogers, C. R. (1969). *Freedom to learn*. Columbus: Charles E. Merrill Publishing Co.
Rogers, C. R. (1975). Empathic: An unappreciated way of being. *The Counseling Psychologist*, 5, 2–10.
Rogers, C. R. (1977). *Carl Rogers, on personal power*. New York: Delacorte Press.
Rogers, C. R. (1980). *A way of being*. Boston: Houghton Mifflin Company.

8

PERSON-CENTRED APPROACH AS DISCURSIVITY AND PERSON-CENTRED THERAPY AS HETEROTOPIC PRACTICE

Pavlos Zarogiannis

Introduction

At the time of its appearance, 1940–1960, the person-centred approach (PCA) was a new, genuine model in the psychotherapeutic world. It was considered to be quite radical because it proposed a different anthropological model and, accordingly, an alternative view for psychotherapy, person-centred therapy (PCT).

The radicalism of the PCA though, as with every radicalism and originality, isn't an intrinsic quality that lasts forever. The fate of radicalisms is usually either decay and eventually oblivion, or integration and normalization. What once were alternative, avant-garde movements, radical ideas and theories become gradually common practices and generally accepted regularities. An unfortunate progress which, according to some scholars, characterizes advanced capitalism, because, thus, it manages to renew, enhance, maintain and develop itself further.

The PCA is herein certainly not an exception, and if it wants to avoid the danger of giving in completely to the dominant neoliberal, neopositivist paradigm of our time and still remain radical, it needs revision and redefinition. However, a redefinition and revision only of its content, i.e. of its central terms, isn't enough and doesn't protect the PCA from decay, oblivion or the complete integration in a western-type social normativity.

What is primarily needed, is a revision and redefinition of the PCA as such. The PCA should re-invent itself.

Modernity and person-centred discourse

This is a man's world

Yes, of course, root metaphor(s). Probably, within modernity, two fundamental metaphors are at work. The one is a root metaphor indeed. The other is, though more popular, a derivative. The first one – *man* – functions rather in the background; the second – *machine* – is more obvious and quite innocent.

Could it be that the "machine" has been created upon the image, the archetype, of "man"? Is it just a coincidence that both possess similar features? Or, is "man" the main metaphor and "machine" a metonymy? But let's suppose that there are two metaphors.

As Ellingham (2001) accurately notes, the machine as root metaphor has certain fundamental features as the dualistic view between body and mind, the belief in the existence of units in all levels of life and the clear distinction between mind laws and physical laws. Similarly, man, as the other basic metaphor, cultivates implicitly a logocentric, anthropocentric, disembodied, rationalistic subjectivity.

The modernistic paradigm/worldview is supported and enhanced by three additional metaphors: that of the *container* (Kövecses, 2004), repression and representation (Freud, 2008; Rogers, 1951, 1957, 1959). These have for their part specific common features, e.g. vision (Arendt, 1998), space and analogy, the interaction of which makes imagery, two-dimensional pictures and, subsequently, these additional metaphors possible.

Consequently, in the modernist paradigm, our sense of reality is shaped and conceived in terms of vision/image, spatial-topography and analogical representation.

Specifically, Kövecses notes that the way we think of and talk about human beings and their organism (or their body), is as a container (Kövecses, 2004); a kind of box namely, in which we place (but we prefer to believe that it's already there) a certain content (substance): entity-like units, like thoughts, feelings, ideas, memories, wishes, information, knowledge, experiences; i.e. contents, already shaped and formed, that remain there till the time comes to be recognized and revealed.

The container metaphor is easily traceable in all major psychotherapeutic approaches: the behaviourist black box, the psychoanalytic human organism, the person-centred organism/envelope (Rogers, 1959). An interesting issue though is that major psychotherapies presuppose the existence of another container within the first one. This presupposition makes thus the repression/denial hypothesis possible. Parallel to the psychoanalytic unconscious-repressed/conscious model, the PCA creates its own incongruence/congruence model. According to this, accurately symbolized and distorted experiences enter the self, whereas experiences incongruent with the self-structure are denied/repressed, thus, are kept away from potential symbolization and awareness (Rogers, 1951).

Within this metaphorical image of the container-repression/denial nexus, symbolization is conceived as analogical representation, for which the axiom *aliquid stat pro aliquo* applies, i.e. something stands for something else in a 'one to one' analogy within a codified (sign) system. Words are regarded as signs (the signifier) which re/present something else (the signified), a feeling, a thought, a wish, an experience, etc. (Rogers 1951, 1959). The representational model presupposes a relatively stable relation between (representing) signifier and (represented) signified, and this lets us believe that the only way of understanding something really and completely is through language and linguistic symbolization.

Despite Hegel's and Lacan's notion that the word/symbol kills the thing. Despite – also – the idea that language is a virus (Laurie Anderson). A small dose of it is quite bearable. Too much of it makes sick and creates symptoms of linguistic fetishism.

The interaction, crossing and implicit functioning of the two root metaphors (man/machine) and their derivatives (container, entity-like content, repression/denial, linguistic representation) determine, of course, not only positive sciences, but all sciences, including humanistic sciences like sociology, psychology, etc., as well as modern social and symbolic structures like psychotherapy.

It's not surprising, then, to discover that core concepts within the PCA/PCT too are perceived and conceived in a modernistic way, i.e. logocentric, static, vertical/hierarchical, linear, spatio-topographical.

The person-centred discourse

But as long as the PCA remains within the modern paradigm, it must unavoidably bear all the consequences this particular paradigm induces. And the consequences are not limited only in the PCA's scientific potential and theoretical view of human nature; they affect the PCA itself. They render the PCA not just as a psychological/psychotherapeutic approach, but also as a discourse (Foucault, 1981).

> A discourse is not a language or a text but a historically, socially, and institutionally specific structure of statements, terms, categories, and beliefs … Discourse is thus contained or expressed in organizations and institutions as well as in words;
>
> *(Scott, 1988, p. 35)*

Or, in other words, discourse is: "a cultural order that allows all subjects socialized under its reign to talk with each other and to interact" (Frank, 1984, p. 105).

As with every society, modern society establishes, allows and/or imposes the production, occurrence, organization, selection and redistribution of certain discourses and discursive practices – with the support of the afore-mentioned metaphors/models, along with some other specific procedures. It does that in order to constitute, maintain, organize and manage its social network and its human potential, and in order to avoid unpredictable dangers. Among those discourses and discursive practices are psychology and psychotherapy, including the person-centred approach and psychotherapy. From a Foucauldian perspective, the PCA is not just another approach which dynamically entered the psychotherapeutic scene in the middle of the 20th century. It is also an institutionalized science/theory/practice, a social and symbolic structure – namely a discourse and a discursive practice, emerged in a concrete socio-political context, which actually made possible and allowed its very occurrence. This socio-political context imposed upon the person-centred discourse a set of features, a set of controlling procedures, which it has been carrying intrinsically ever since. A conscious effort is needed in order to recognize, moderate and eventually transform them.

More precisely, the person-centred discourse, as every discourse, experiences in its own body and, at the same time, imposes upon others, procedures of exclusion, like prohibition, division and rejection. There is the so-called "taboo of the object of speech, ... and the privileged or exclusive right of the speaking subject" (Foucault, 1981, p. 52). That means that person-centredness is exactly defined and determined; moreover, it is not anyone who can speak about person-centredness; only those that are seen as experts and are recognized/accepted as person-centred, those who can provide the necessary requirements (studies, training, etc.), as well as psychology and psychotherapy professionals.

Who writes actually here, in this book? And from what position? What are the necessary qualifications?

In addition, the opposition between reason and madness is reproduced within the person-centred discourse. This opposition refers to the person-centred speaking subject, i.e. the one who is recognized as person-centred therapist, scholar, expert cannot but be reasonable. His/her speech, either as a theoretician, or as a practitioner, in order to be socially accepted, cannot be totally free, mystic, paranoid, fragmented, delusional; it must have logical coherence, the right grammar, syntax, continuity ... And, of course, he/she cannot be false. At every single moment in his words and his actions the division between truth and falsity must be absolutely clear. Even more, he or she – who talks in the name of the PCA and of person-centredness – must have the intention of saying the truth, the truth of the PCA, the truth of psychology, of science; every truth. He/she must seek, confirm and ratify the truth, because he/she essentially and purely seeks just knowledge. The will to truth meets and crosses the will to knowing (and the will for/to power) also in the person-centred discourse. Every person-centred proposition is controlled and delimited.

These procedures of controlling and delimiting "operate in a sense from the exterior" (Foucault, 1981, p. 56). At the beginning, they are imposed onto the person-centred discourse. Subsequently, person-centred discourse enforces and establishes these controlling and delimiting procedures, along with some other internal procedures, in its own inner realm, to all those individuals who want to be person-centred and represent person-centredness. In these internal procedures – which "are nonetheless principles of constraint" (ibid., p. 61), despite their positivity and their multiplicatory role – the commentary, the author and discipline are included.

According to Foucault, the commentary, by creating a "hierarchy between primary and secondary text", allows, on the one hand, the creation of new propositions, and, on the other hand, "it is to say at last what was silently articulated 'beyond', in the text" (ibid., p. 58). In this sense, in the person-centred discourse Rogers' writings are of course the primary text and the whole person-centred bibliography (after his own) is nothing else but a commentary, a continuing, endless commentary to this primary text. "The open multiplicity, the element of chance, are transferred, by the principle of commentary, from what might risk being said, on the number, the form, the mask, and the circumstances of the repetition" (Foucault, 1981, p. 58).

What about this text? My text? This book? Commentaries, repetitions, returns, departures.
Complementary to the commentary, the principle of the author restricts the contingent outgrowth of the person-centred discourse through a personal identity, which "has the form of individuality and self" (ibid., p. 59), i.e. Rogers, Gendlin, Mearns, Bazzano, etc.
And me as the author of this text? Me?

> Here I'm playing an old literary trick, the trick of pretending I know [something] about many things in order to make the reader believe … . But I suppose other writers have other tricks, don't they? … Yes, everybody has his own trademark, or someone else's for that matter, since we seem to be plagiarizing all the time.
> (Di Giovanni et al., 1973, pp. 25, 26)

The name of the author, i.e. Rogers, guarantees the order and the coherence of the primary person-centred texts in intersection with a third principle of limitation, that of discipline. As discipline, the person-centred discourse protects and ensures the continuation of certain discursive characteristics by creating its own terminology, objects, methods, its own set of true propositions, rules, definitions and techniques, which all make possible the formulation of new propositions. That means that a text, a theory, a presentation, a research, in order to count as person-centred, must always and anew prove its person-centredness, which is already defined within the person-centred discipline.

Additionally, a third group of controlling procedures is necessary. To this group belong the ritual (i.e. all kinds of psychotherapeutic rituals including the person-centred ones), the so-called "societies of discourse" (i.e. the psychotherapeutic society/world), and the doctrines/dogmas (Foucault, 1981, pp. 61–64). They all aim to organize and control the speaking subjects, because discourses are not open to everyone. Certain requirements (i.e. studies, academic degrees, training, etc.) are needed if someone enters, for example, the order of the person-centred discourse.

Certainly, all the above-mentioned procedures affect the PCA and apply to it. Moreover, the PCA as discourse, as a psychotherapeutic discourse, appropriates them – some of them more, while other less of course – to the degree that it repeats in its interior all kinds of procedures of power and control, such as prohibitions, formulation of rules, principles, taboos, criteria for true-false propositions, hierarchical structures, distinctions, classification, criticism, rejections, eliminations, claims for authenticity, faithful descendants and unfaithful apostates, definition of an orthodox dogma as validity measure of true person-centredness, creation of friends and enemies, schools and sub-schools, directions, kinship, factions, tribes, etc.

Would it be too much to think of PCA, in this context, as a psychotherapeutic discourse, i.e. as another invention, another symptom of modernity?

Now, what is striking is the fact that someone could have drawn almost the same conclusions, if he had preferred to remain just in the context of the PCA and had applied the very terms of the PCA to the PCA itself.

In that case, he/she could have seen the whole PCA as an evolving organism with *its own* phenomenal and perceptual field, actualizing tendency, behaviour, internal frame of reference, organismic valuing process, locus of evaluation. He/she would have seen that the PCA has also created an identity, a kind of a self-concept/ self-structure with its very own conditions of worth (procedures of control and restriction), with its own symbolizations, distortions and denials.

An interesting issue would have been then, to see the PCA's self-concept more closely. How flexible and open or rigid and narrow (similar to the Foucauldian discourse) that self is; furthermore, to see if the PCA (nowadays, every time) is in a state of congruence or incongruence; if it follows its actualizing or its self-actualizing tendency; if it has created self-configurations and if yes, of what kind; if it has integrated, and to what extent, empathy, unconditional positive regard and congruency in relation to itself, but also in relation to other approaches, theories, sciences.

Could it be that the PCA, trying too hard to form its own identity, has forgotten its organismic quality and has been identified with just one version of itself, whereby this version has become also its dominant self-concept?

And would it be then too much to say that PCA, despite its original dynamics, freshness and progressiveness, couldn't resist its transformation from an alternative psychotherapeutic discourse to a mainstream, rigidly-structured institution?

Isn't then justified the assumption that PCA has really undergone a conservative turn and faces nowadays the danger of falling into the trap of scientism and neoliberalism (Bazzano, 2016)?

Modern self as 'internal discourse'

How would it actually be, if someone would apply the Foucauldian notion of discourse in PCT's personality theory?

A possible outcome could be then that *self* is a kind of internal discourse, a kind of modernistic "invention", and the *conditions of worth* some kind of introjected procedures of control, restriction and subjugation of a radical organismicality, which is implicit intricacy, and might actually be anarchistic materiality, undetermined potentiality, unpredictable situatedness.

Could that furthermore mean that the formation of the self and, consequently, the formation of a certain subjectivity, i.e. a form of life, is, not only, but also the transformation of life into bios (from the Greek word 'βίος') (Agamben, 1998)?

And if yes, could that also mean that bios – although inseparable from life in human beings – although necessary in order to give meaning to life and to the human existence – is, additionally, nothing else but a way of organizing, restricting, subjugating, controlling life and its intricacy?

However, based on this unavoidable differentiation between *life* (organism/private) and *bios* (self/public) – in spite of the danger of their clear and absolute distinction – according to Foucault and Agamben, modern society will manage to transform politics into bio-politics.

This is a notion that needs to be reconsidered and revised today, since bio-politics turns away from life and, under the conditions of advanced and global neoliberal capitalism, is moving towards death, becoming gradually thanato-politics, i.e. politics of death (Braidotti, 2013).

But if Foucault's and Agamben's notion is true, then the formation of self, of modern self, isn't merely an innocent, yet unavoidable, process of subjectification. Moreover, the formatted self isn't just a necessary frame of reference and orientation. The formation of a self would mean the creation of a controlling structure of life too; a controlling structure with concrete technology, organization and order which transcends the family scenario and worth-system, and contains always a social scenario, a socio-cultural worth-system.

Person-centred particularity/otherness

It may be that PCA couldn't avoid its institutionalization and normalization. Its potential, however, can transcend that. PCA is, can be, much more than that. The time of its occurrence as well as its theory could confirm it.

Of course, time cannot justify everything; however, it is an important factor. While psychoanalysis and behaviourism are genuine offspring of modernity, PCT arises at a time which signifies the passage from modernism to post-modernism. PCT is coming to life at a passage, at an edge, at an end point which is also a beginning. "Rogers straddled the divide between modern and postmodern" (Tudor & Worrall, 2006, p. 36).

Passage, limit, marginality is exactly what accompanies PCA, ascribing to it an intrinsic ambiguity. Neither fully modern, nor quite (post)modern, PCA certainly contains a multitude of modern features and carries, undoubtedly, a lot of modern ideology, but it also encloses important features of the post-modern, such as organism, wholeness, change, relation, process, flow; features that Gendlin will further develop, theorize and underpin.

Exactly. Neither fully modern, nor quite (post)modern. Being-at-the-limit, being-a-limit is the particularity or otherness of PCA, which is often rejected as lack, deficiency, flaw (Ellingham, 2001, p. 96); not mistakenly, as long as PCA chooses to identify itself with only one of its dimensions, that of modernism and discourse. Acting like this, PCA fails to recognize its other dimension, the whole of its potential, which could help to transform itself, to avoid sedimentation and freeze in a rigid, self-sufficient narcissistic self-image.

The marginality of PCA is neither crucial flaw, nor luck, nor deficiency, i.e. negativity; actually, it's asset, advantage, qualification, i.e. positivity.

(Post)modernity and person-centred discursivity

This is a ... woman's world (?)

It is positivity, because in virtue of this intrinsic marginality PCA can transcend modernism and the order of discourse. In order for this to happen, something more than the redefinition of central PCA terms is required. What is needed is a redefinition and revision of PCA itself, i.e. a change of how PCA perceives and understands itself.

Revision and redefinition means that PCA should be described with new terms, regardless of the fact that we call them terms of a new emerging paradigm, of second modernity, (post)modern, post-human, post-feminist, new materialistic. A new, an-other perspective is needed.

The word postmodern has many problematic connotations. I'll use it nevertheless, but I'll write 'post' in a parenthesis as (post)modern, and sometimes with a strikethrough line, ~~postmodern~~.

As it is already known, the new perspective replaces the root metaphor of the machine with the image of a *living organism*; it replaces the container metaphor with *the open system*, and representation with terms as *simulacrum, arbitrariness, presence, contingency, virtuality, performativity, effect*. Beside that, it emphasizes the dimension of *time* – cyclical, spiral, repetitive – inviting us, in this way, to think in terms of *movement, change, alterity*; space becomes concrete as *locality* and *situatedness*; and *materiality, process, interaction, togetherness/unity* are conceived as primary conditions.

And what would be the root metaphor of this new (postmodern) paradigm/era?

If we argue that the root metaphor is the living organism and take into consideration the features the new paradigm has (processual, open, holistic), could we again assume that the *living organism* is a metonymy and the root metaphor is something else? And what would be that? Could now the root metaphor be *woman*?

Woman as perceived by men (and in opposition to man) within the frame of a binary logic?

~~Postmodernity~~ *and beyond: Gendlin's process philosophy (of PCA)*

This exact kind of revision and redefinition of PCT is what E. Gendlin undertook, already, in the 1960s. Giving PCT the necessary philosophical background, especially within the frame of hermeneutics and phenomenology, he was able to radicalize it. At the same time he was able to reformulate basic hermeneutic and phenomenological terms.

His philosophy (*Philosophy of the Implicit*) is close to the newly-emerging, (post) modern paradigm but it goes further than this; it goes beyond the (post)modern paradigm and its dead-ends (Gendlin, 1997b, 1999, 2003; Levin, 1997).

It's a new approach to, and a reformulation of, basic hermeneutic terms, and also "a new approach to what phenomenologists call 'phenomena,' a deliberate way to *think* and *speak with* what is more than categories (concepts, theories, assumptions, distinctions …)" (Gendlin, 1991; 2004, p. 127; Levin, 1997, p. 42).

Life is process: a becoming.

Gendlin's philosophy, as a process philosophy actually (Gendlin, 1997a; 1997b), goes beyond all the assumptions of traditional phenomenology claiming that contents and structures of consciousness and experience are not primary givens, but derivates. They are generated by (a) process. Process has thus a primary status. As he writes, "Process generates structures: Structures alone don't generate process" (Gendlin, 2012). That means that *everything can be conceived in processual terms*; either as a process, i.e. as becoming, or as an effect of a process. Process "is the becoming of experience" says Whitehead (Whitehead, 1978, p. 166). Gendlin would say process is the becoming of *experiencing*.

Experiencing life.

As life-philosopher, he goes back to the most basic fact, *life*. Life as it lives itself; life as it lives itself in us and as it's lived by us is a process, i.e. movement, change, flow, action; ongoing, continuous, endless. Life – as it lives itself in us and as it's lived by us – we feel it, we experience it; we 'experiencing' it.

Experiencing is life.

But although life is lived/experienced as a whole, it appears in consciousness only partially, i.e. as partial experience (thought, imagery, judgement, idea, memory, emotion, wish). Life is namely always more than any partial manifestation of it (thought, theory, science, philosophy, etc.) can ever reveal. This points to a "whole-part" dynamic, already known as hermeneutic circle, which Gendlin renews and expands through the term experiencing – probably a "translation" of the German word *Erlebnis* (lived experience) (Mohanty, 1997).

Gendlin opposes experiencing to the purely psychological and static term experience (Ellingham, 2001; Ikemi, 2017), and considers, subsequently, experience an aspect of experiencing (Gendlin, 1959, 1961, 1962/1997, 1968, 1991, 2003).

Experiencing is the living process, life, which wants to live, express itself and move forward. Experiencing is probably close to the immanence (Deleuze, 2001) and sustainability of life (Braidotti 2005/2006).

Paraphrasing Vygotsky, experiencing:

> unlike speech, does not consist of separate units. When I wish to communicate [...] that today I saw a barefoot boy in a blue shirt running down the street, I do not see every item separately: the boy, the shirt, its blue color, his running, the absence of shoes. I conceive of all this in one [...], but I put it into separate words. A speaker often takes several minutes to disclose one [experiencing]. In his [body] the whole [experiencing] is present at once, but in speech it has to be developed successively. [Experiencing] may be compared to a cloud shedding a shower of words.
>
> *(Vygotsky, 1986, p. 251)*

"Cloud" (experiencing) means unseparated multiplicity (Gendlin, 1997b; 2003); "shedding a shower" is an explication and symbolization of this unseparated multiplicity conceived as an interaction, as a zigzag process between this unseparated multiplicity and any kind of symbol which explicates it. "Of words" could mean also images, sounds, gestures, behaviour, meaning, theories, etc.

Interaction is inter-action, intra-action (Barad, 2007), in-between-action that presupposes and points to an undifferentiated wholeness. Parts (units: thought, feeling, concept, meaning, experience, self, etc.) are temporary explications, effects, *unfoldings* of their interaction, i.e. concrete elements of an in-process inter-action; nothing, no part as unit, exists by itself, only in relation and in constant interaction with something else. Interaction precedes and transcends the interacting parts; parts are differentiated and created retrospectively in the context of a reflective conceptual classification and linguistic expression. In Gendlin's model, parts, units, monads don't have interactions; they are (their) interactions. The same is the case with us. We don't have interactions. We are our interactions.

Becoming is unfolding.

Unfolding should be clearly understood horizontally and in no case vertically/hierarchically.

In the unfolding process of experiencing, there aren't higher or lower levels, just instances, occurrences of the implicit. What every time occurs (formed and symbolized) depends on what is exactly needed in the concrete situation in order for the situation to change. Symbolization isn't representation, but reference, differentiation *and* carrying forward. The symbol/word is a reference to the living situation *and* a differentiation of the unseparated multiplicity of experiencing that carries experiencing and situation forward. The symbol is a result of an interaction, a zigzag process, a crossing between experiencing and language, between personal sense and social meaning.

Life, living, experiencing is a process, a becoming, an unfolding actualized constantly as an interaction between an implicit and an explicit dimension. Experiencing as characteristic of inner life has its own structure and continuity which always contains cognition/thought, affect and volition (Dilthey, 1894). That means that the (subjective-internal) experiencing contains thinking, feeling and wishing relative to an (objective-external) situation, while it always implies its expression (symbolization) and its understanding. *In experiencing there is actually no inner/outer,* no hidden/revealed dualism, but a oneness which operates simultaneously at two distinctive dimensions each with different order and with different levels of interacting.

The implicit dimension of experiencing is pre-reflective and pre-conceptual. Experiencing here refers to the so-called wholeness of the living process, to the potential of our existence, to the contingency of our life, to the immediacy of our being (Gendlin, 1973), which is unseparated multiplicity, intricate plurality, immanence, an en-folded oneness, a unity multiple in itself. Implicit experiencing is a concrete, present given that can be directly referred to. It has certain characteristics, it contains implicitly the needed next step and has a specific meaning. Its meaning results from the interaction that takes place between body and environment – actually in implicit experiencing *'body and environment' are one interaction*. Meaning here is implicit meaning, felt in the body and by the body. A felt meaning namely. A bodily felt meaning/sense.

The implicit part of experiencing has a responsive order and so the ability to *interact* with a variety of symbols and respond to them accordingly. It can be un-folded, take the form of units/monads, and become explicit. The explicit dimension of experiencing is reflective and conceptual. Through the interaction with symbols (language, culture, history) implicit experiencing can be explicated further in partial units within the context of a reflective activity; it can be symbolized; can become distinctive singularity (word, image, thought, concept, feeling, emotion, wish) and thus explicit meaning (Gendlin, 1973), which in turn can lead to *understanding*. Implicit experiencing can become explicit experience.

It should be noted here that implicit experiencing can never be replaced or entirely actualized, i.e. transformed by symbols, because it is always more than its *explication*. Nevertheless, every explication – while it carries forward implicit experiencing – changes this very implicit experiencing retrospectively. Implicit experiencing remains implicit, but every explication changes it.

Experiencing is a bodily process.

Experiencing has a certain locality: *body*. Probably due to the double nature of body, experiencing has a double nature too. Body in phenomenology is a double oneness. It has an objective/explicit (*Körper*) and a subjective/implicit (*Leib*) dimension. These "two" bodies can never replace each other; on the contrary, the one presupposes the other. This ambiguity and oneness implies always the body in Gendlin's philosophy.

The use of such words like objective and subjective may imply binary logic and dualistic thinking, but at the level of linguistic explication, description and communication, a different wording, now, seems impossible.

Gendlin holds on to this double being of (the) body, because the one without the other would lead either to mere anatomy, or to pure metaphysics. *Leib* needs mate(r)iality in order to become real, existent, singularity, to be present, immanence, and *Körper* needs mentality, in order to become absent, plural, abstraction, transcendence, language. Otherwise how can Word (Logos) become Flesh and Flesh Word? Body is one: Flesh and Logos.

So, when words are coming, they are coming bodily. "The 'coming' of words is bodily, like the coming of tears, sleep, orgasm, improvisation, ..." (Gendlin, 2004, p. 132), because the experiencing body knows (the) language/culture/history (ibid.). As Massumi and Manning (Massumi, 2011, p. ix) write, what moves as a body, returns as the movement of thought.

This body, Gendlin's body, is body in-process, is process, processes. Bodies are becomings.

The oneness *body* never exists by itself. The body is always *body and* ... (Gendlin, 1993). Body and *environment* is another unity, so that a body always presupposes, constitutes, refers to, *implies* an environment (situation), so much as an environment (situation) always presupposes, constitutes, refers to, *implies* a body. The one inhabits the other (Gendlin, 1997a).

"Body-environment" is one. We usually think that body and environment are two different units, which first exist by themselves and then interact with each other. It's not like that. They differentiate themselves and become units in the context of a dis-identifying reflective perspective. According to Gendlin, we live in bodies, environments, situations. We are our bodies, our environments, our situations

(Gendlin, 1993; 1997b). And since a body lives a situation in *a certain way*, the body always knows implicitly what a situation means and needs in order to move forward. The body has/is this exactly implicit knowing. It lives/senses/experiences it as felt meaning.

All these theoretical suggestions don't mean a lot, if they can't prove their validity in living situations, i.e. in therapy, but mostly and importantly in life; in plain, mundane life. For, as Gendlin believes, in a very phenomenological manner, every theory must be grounded in life and not life in theory.

Gendlin's psychotherapy: PCT as Focusing Oriented Therapy (FOT)

In Gendlin's work, the metaphor of the machine-container is replaced by the *reality and actuality (not the metaphor) of the living body*, the model of repression by the concepts of *unfolding, retrospectiveness* and *carrying forward* and finally, the model of representation by the concepts of *reference, differentiation, response* and *completion*. In this way Gendlin overcomes the limitations of the modern-postmodern paradigm and formulates his own version of psychotherapy which is at the same time a revision of PCT, finally termed Focusing-oriented Psychotherapy (FOT) (Gendlin, 1959, 1964/1973, 1968, 1969, 1973, 1984, 1996; Purton, 2004).

His view liberates PCT from the static, dualistic, modern paradigm of humanistic essentialism and its features: the denial/repression model and the binary, conceptual thinking (inner/outer, hidden/visible, past/future) and becomes holistic, interactive, processual due to the concept of experiencing.

In Gendlin's perspective:

- therapy is *one* continuous interaction that takes place simultaneously at different levels (between therapist and client, body and situation, implicit experiencing/responsive order and language/symbolic order, therapeutic hour and life);
- *every* therapeutic element is part of the interaction between client and therapist; part of their implicit relation/process/understanding; an unfolding/explication of their togetherness; even therapy itself and also (the very qualities) "client" and "therapist";
- within this interaction *everything* can be conceived as a process, a becoming: therapy, self, accurate symbolization, incongruence, distortion, denial, psychological maladjustment, empathy, unconditional positive regard, congruence, presence, psychological contact, meaning, understanding …;
- experiencing is *the* fundamental "principle" of this interaction/process.

So, that's person-centred and/as focusing-oriented therapy (PC-FOT):

- the *carrying forward* or the *reconstitution* of the relationship with one's own *experiencing*.

Accurate symbolization, distortion and denial are possible ways of *connecting/ disconnecting* with one's experiencing. Incongruence/psychological maladjustment is a manner of experiencing, a skipping, blockage, or stoppage, which has probably led to the creation of a frozen whole, or a structure-boundness which doesn't allow experiencing to be carried forward, since it can't unfold itself as the concrete situation would need it to. In such cases, the interaction with others (situation/ environment) *and* the interaction with symbols (words, events ...) has been either distorted, interrupted or even blocked from the very beginning (Gendlin, 1962/ 1997, pp. 242–244, 1964/1973, p. 22, 1984; Purton, 2004, pp. 56, 96, 125, 177).

This would further lead to new, more personal, symbolizations and subsequently to *new meaning* and *understanding*. Symbolization – every symbolization – is an explication process, a gradual unfolding/signification that takes place *only* in inter-action(s). It starts as a direct referent (bodily felt sense). Through different levels of interaction (between body and situation, therapist and client, implicit experiencing/ responsive order and language/symbolic order), it takes gradually an explicit form as a symbol (word, image, sound, movement, action, etc.).

If we also take into consideration that every symbolization doesn't just represent the client's experience (inner reality), but *carries* his/her experiencing (therapist/ situation/living) *forward*, then, by doing so, it changes it. And that's exactly the therapeutic in therapy. Symbolization changes experiencing and, in this sense, functions *retrospectively*, and creates a before and an after. In a certain way, it (re-)creates the so-called past, and also the future. What a client symbolizes contains the presence, the influence of, and the interaction with, their therapist.

If we recall now that *experiencing* is a unity of inner and outer reality/situation, then clients' experiencing and symbolization always contain implicitly and necessarily their therapist.

An explicit formulated empathic response that occurs in a specific moment, for example, expresses the therapist's experiencing with their client and with his or her own particular situation/life. But it's only a partial symbolization of the whole implicit intricacy of the therapeutic interaction, i.e. an instance of an ongoing implicit empathizing interaction between therapist and client. It's valid only in the context of this interaction, of course, and only retrospectively. Only if it helps the client to get in touch with his or her experiencing and only if it carries the client's (and therapist's) experiencing/living forward (Gendlin, 1968), does it become an empathic response. In this sense, there are no empathic, unconditional positive regard, congruent responses a priori (that would make them techniques), only a posteriori (that makes them qualities); they become empathic, unconditional positive regard, congruent responses in a concrete therapeutic interaction.

The parallel becoming of self: therapist's and client's.

All that has been said about the cloud of experiencing and its unfoldings applies to the PCA concept of self (Tudor & Worrall, 2006). In the cloud, there is no such entity as an already structured, formed, differentiated self. Self (-image/-structure/- concept) extracts itself in a reflecting, symbolizing, dis-identifying process of explication. There is no such thing as a self in the container of an en-closed organism waiting the "attentional viewing beam" (Gendlin, 2004, p. 143) in order to be perceived and acknowledged. The explicit self, the one who consciously perceives itself and the others, is also an effect, an un-fold, a facet of a process. What does pre-exist in the cloud of (the) experiencing (body) is a pre-reflective, pre-conceptual sense of "me", a felt self, a selfhood; the vague but distinct sense that this particular situation refers to me, addresses me. My response makes out of me an "I". Upon the sense of "me", the certainty of the "I" will always and anew form itself. Self/I are becomings too. I become.

In this sense, "clients" and "therapists" are instances of their interaction. They are becomings, as well – open possibilities, becomings and un-becomings, successes as well as failures.

Person-centred discursivity

Gendlin's theory shouldn't be limited only to central PCA concepts. It should also be applied to PCA as such. Then PCA could be described as a holistic organism in-process; in constant change, alterity and transformation; in-inter-action with its economic, political and social/cultural environment. Its identity could be conceived as an open, creative, changeable, processual, never final, never exactly determined tendency.

Gendlin's contribution would be, then, to give PCA back its radicalism. Thereupon, PCA wouldn't be just another discourse among all others, but it would be in the position to discover another quality, its discursivity, and allow its discursivity to unfold.

Foucault (1998) working on the topic of the author's function, writes that:

> there appeared in Europe another, more uncommon, kind of author, whom one should confuse with neither the "great" literary authors, nor the authors of religious texts, nor the founders of science. In a somewhat arbitrary way we shall call those who belong to this last group "founders of discursivity".
>
> *(p. 217)*

And he continues: "they are unique in that they are not just authors of their own works. They have produced something else: the possibilities and the rules for the formation of other texts" (ibid., p. 217).

According to Foucault, founders of discursivity (like Freud, Marx and others) don't just create a new discourse; they don't just create a whole new field of thinking, speaking, acting and behaving. By formulating their own theories and hypotheses they make possible the occurrence of similar and also different texts and theories which in turn guarantee the continuation, necessary transformation and endless reformulation of the originary discourse. In order to be conceived as new, all "new" discourses within a discursivity field need to return to the originary discourse, confront themselves with it and differentiate themselves from it.

In this sense, Rogers could be also seen as a founder of the person-centred discursivity which made possible all those directions/divergences that we usually call today – within the person-centred approach – schools, factions, tribes …

If the PCA could discover and accept its discursivity, i.e. its contingency, randomness, discontinuity, then it shouldn't need its homogeneous continuation, but its *heterogeneous dispersion*; it wouldn't need any kind of classification, but a cartography; various schools, tribes, directions, … they would be just necessities, necessary returns to the origin, to Rogers, and at the same time removals, departures. They wouldn't be threat or danger, but constitutive transformations of its very existence, necessary manifestations/actualizations of its further living in another form.

Then, we could overcome the concept of self as an inner discourse and replace it by a selfhood, an inner discursivity open to changes, transformations, creative transpositions, multiple subjectivities, even disruptions.

Person-centred heterotopia

If the PCA – as a broad theoretical body – could manage to discover and accept its implicit intricacy, discursivity, and marginality, then that could help PCT as FOT (being one possible discursive practice within the PCA discursivity field) to claim the status, the quality, of a *heterotopia*. That means PC-FOT would remain, of course, an ordinary discursive practice, as an institutionalized social and symbolic practice, i.e. as a therapeutic practice. But it could become, eventually, also a heterotopic practice (Zarogiannis, 2014), a practice which could transform the psychotherapeutic space to a heterotopia.

According to Foucault (1998), heterotopias have the property "to suspect, neutralize, or invert the set of relations" which happen "to designate, mirror, or reflect" (p. 3). Furthermore, they have a double functionality: they are producers of knowledge, as well as sites of resistance. "By juxtaposing and combining many spaces in one site, heterotopias problematize received knowledge by destabilizing the ground on which knowledge is built" (Topinka, 2010, p. 54).

As heterotopic practice, i.e. inside and also outside the social matrix, as a marginal practice, always at a limit, at an edge, PCT, by interrupting ordinary life (the repetition of the same/given), would create a necessary interstitial distance (Critchley, 2008; Topinka, 2010), and a space wherein usual ordinary life could be "suspended, contested, and inverted" (Zarogiannis, 2014, p. 45).

This is a possible way for PCT to avoid any trap of regularization, normalization and conservatism, because it could always be a step further, beyond, elsewhere; it could be something else. Furthermore, it could create the appropriate condition of helping people to discover, accept and bear their openness, contingency, peculiarity, their liberating *potentia* (Braidotti, 2011), the implicit intricacy of their life and its *narratability* (Cavarero, 2000) … but this is the beginning of another text, another story…

> [His] spoken English is unbelievably good, but when he writes English he becomes very stiff and formal. But then, isn't that a tendency we all have? …

Not too imposing words, no? ... We all have the pleasures of the reader, but the writer has also the pleasure and the task of writing. This is not only a strange but a rewarding experience.

(Di Giovanni, et al., 1973, pp. 107, 121, 165)

References

Arendt, H. (1998). *The human condition*. Introduction by Margaret Canovan. Chicago: University of Chicago Press (first edition 1958), 22–78.

Agamben, G. (1998). *Homo Sacer: Sovereign power and bare life*. Stanford, CA: Stanford University Press.

Barad, K. (2007). *Meeting the universe halfway: Quantum physics and the entanglement of matter and meaning*. Durham, NC: Duke University Press.

Bazzano, M. (2016). The conservative turn in person-centered therapy. *Person-Centered and Experiential Psychotherapies*, 15(4), 339–355.

Braidotti, R. (2005/2006). Affirming the affirmative: On nomadic affectivity. In: *Rhizomes*, 11/12.

Braidotti, R. (2011). *Nomadic subjects. Embodiment and sexual difference in contemporary feminist theory*. New York: Columbia University Press.

Braidotti, R. (2013). *The posthuman*. Cambridge: Polity Press.

Critchley, S. (2008). *Infinitely demanding: Ethics of commitment, politics of resistance*. London: Verso.

Cavarero, A. (2000). *Relating narratives: Storytelling and selfhood*. London and New York: Routledge.

Deleuze, G. (2001). Immanence: A life. In: *Pure immanence. Essays on a life*. New York: Zone Books, 25–33.

Di Giovanni, N. T., Halpern, D., & MacShane, F. (eds) (1973). *Borges on writing*. New York: E.P. Dutton & Co., Inc.

Dilthey, W. (1894). *Ideen über eine beschreibende und zergliedernde Psychologie*. Bd 2. Berlin: Verlag der Kφniglichen Akademie der Wissenschaften.

Ellingham, I. (2001). Carl Rogers' 'congruence' as an organismic, not a Freudian, concept. In: G. Wyatt (ed.), *Congruence*. Volume One of *Rogers' therapeutic conditions: Evolution, theory and practice*. Ross-on-Wye: PCCS Books, 96–115.

Foucault, M. (1981). The order of discourse. In: R. Young (ed.), *Untying the text. A post-Structuralist reader*. Boston, London, Henley: Routledge and Kegan Paul, 51–78.

Foucault, M. (1998). What is an Author? In: *Aesthetics, method, epistemology*. New York: The New Press, 205–222.

Frank, M. (1984). *What is neostructuralism?* Trans. Sabine Wilke & Richard Gray. Minneapolis: University of Minnesota Press.

Freud, S. (2008). *Five lectures on psycho-analysis*. La Vergne, TN: BN Publishing.

Gendlin, E.T. (1959). The concept of congruence reformulated in terms of experiencing. University of Chicago Counselling Center Discussion Paper, 5(12).

Gendlin, E.T. (1961). Experiencing: A variable in the process of therapeutic change. *American Journal of Psychotherapy*, 15(2), 233–245.

Gendlin, E.T. (1962/1997). *Experiencing and the creation of meaning*. Second edition. Evanston, Illinois: Northwestern University Press.

Gendlin, E.T. (1964/1973). A theory of personality change. In: A.R. Mahrer and L. Pearson (eds), *Creative developments in psychotherapy*. New York: Jason Aronson (1973). Originally published in P. Worchel and D. Byrne (eds) *Personality change*. New York: Wiley (1964), 439–489.

Gendlin, E.T. (1968). The experiential response. In E.F. Hammer (ed.), *Use of interpretation in treatment: Technique and art*. New York: Grune & Stratton, 208–227.
Gendlin, E.T. (1969). Focusing. *Psychotherapy: Theory, Research and Practice*, 6(1), 4–15.
Gendlin, E.T. (1973). Experiential psychotherapy. In R. Corsini (ed.) *Current psychotherapies*. Itasca, Illinois: F.E. Peacock, 317–352.
Gendlin, E.T. (1984). The client's client. In: R. Levant and J.M. Shlien (eds), *Client-centered therapy and the person-centered approach*. New York: Praeger, 76–107.
Gendlin, E.T. (1991). Thinking beyond patterns. In: B. den Ouden and M. Moen (eds) *The presence of feeling in thought*. New York: Peter Lang, 21–151.
Gendlin, E.T. (1993). Three assertions about the body. *The Folio* 12(1), 21–33.
Gendlin, E.T. (1996). *Focusing-oriented psychotherapy*. New York: Guilford Press.
Gendlin, E.T. (1997a). *A process model*. New York: Focusing Institute.
Gendlin, E.T. (1997b). How philosophy cannot appeal to experience, and how it can. In: D. M. Levin (ed.), *Language beyond postmodernity. Saying and thinking in Gendlin's philosophy*. Evaston: Northwestern University Press, 3–41.
Gendlin, E.T. (1999). Authenticity after postmodernism. *Changes: An Inter-national Journal of Psychology and Psychotherapy*, 17(3), 203–212.
Gendlin, E.T. (2003). Beyond postmodernism: From concepts through experiencing. In: R. Frie (ed.), *Understanding experience: Psychotherapy and postmodernism*. London: Routledge, 100–115.
Gendlin, E.T. (2004). The new phenomenology of carrying forward. *Continental Philosophy Review*, 37(1), 127–151.
Gendlin, E.T. (2012). Process generates structures: Structures alone don't generate process. *The Folio: A Journal for Focusing and Experiential Therapy*, 23(1), 3–13.
Ikemi, A. (2017). The radical impact of experiencing on psychotherapy theory: an examination of two kinds of crossings. *Person-Centered and Experiential Psychotherapies* 16(2), 159–172.
Kövecses, Z. (2004). *Metaphor and emotion. Language, culture, and body in human feeling*. Cambridge: Cambridge University Press.
Levin, D. M. (ed.) (1997). *Language beyond postmodernism. Saying and thinking in Gendlin's philosophy*. Evanston, Illinois: Northwestern University Press.
Massumi, B. (2011). *Semblance and event. Activist philosophy and the occurrent arts*. Cambridge, MA/London, England: The MIT Press.
Mohanty, J. N. (1997). Experience and meaning. In: D. M. Levin (ed.), *Language beyond postmodernity. Saying and thinking in Gendlin's philosophy*. Evanston: Northwestern University Press, 176–189.
Purton, C. (2004). *Person-centred therapy. The focusing-oriented approach*. London: Palgrave Macmillan.
Rogers, C.R. (1951). *Client-centered therapy*. London: Constable.
Rogers, C.R. (1957) The necessary and sufficient conditions of therapeutic personality change. *Journal of Consulting Psychology* 21, 95–103.
Rogers, C.R. (1959). A theory of therapy, personality and interpersonal relationships, as developed in the client-centered framework. In: S. Koch (ed.), *Psychology: A study of a science, 3. Formulations of the person and the social context*. New York: McGraw-Hill, 184–256.
Scott, J. W. (1988). Deconstructing equality-versus-difference: Or, the uses of poststructuralist theory for feminism. *Feminist Studies*, 14(1), 32–50.
Topinka, J. R. (2010). Foucault, Borges, heterotopia: Producing knowledge in other spaces. *Foucault Studies* 9(9), 54–70.
Tudor, K., & Worrall, M. (2006). *Person-centred therapy: A clinical philosophy*. London: Routledge.

Vygotsky, L. (1986). *Thought and language*. Cambridge, MA, London, England: The MIT Press.
Whitehead, A. N. (1978). *Process and reality: An essay in cosmology*. Corrected edition, D. R. Griffin & D. W. Sherburne (eds.). New York: Free Press. (1929).
Zarogiannis, P. (2014). What is therapeutic about therapy? Part II: FOT as heterotopia. In: G. Madison (ed.), *Focusing-oriented psychotherapy. Beyond the talking cure*. London and Philadelphia: Jessica Kingsley Publishers, 43–51.

9

CLIENT-CENTERED

An ethical therapy

Bert Rice and Kathryn A. Moon

A path not taken

People come to therapists. They might be hurting, confused, in conflict, wanting to understand themselves or others better, wanting to feel less alone, wanting to change or be changed, seeking guidance, or wanting to learn how to communicate in relationship. Perhaps they are forced to attend. We say they are coming "for therapy."

Before beginning to practice therapy, co-author Kathy thought about why her own therapy had not given her a sense of self-ownership. She realized that she had surrendered herself to her therapists, whom she perceived as authority figures. Going forward, she required a method for herself as therapist that would address the ethical issue of power in relationship. For co-author Bert this imperative happened, not in thinking about therapy, but in rebellion and political engagement.

We are client-centered therapists. However, the premise of our client-centeredness does not match the basis for the theory developed by that therapy's founder, Carl Rogers. Rogers defined client-centered therapy in axiomatic, scientific terms, asserting that six therapeutic conditions comprised therapy and effected constructive personality change (Rogers, 1959, p. 213). This interest or investment in effecting change within or upon another is something we wish to abandon here. We would replace it and emphasize instead a moral enunciation of respect for the person attending therapy, an acknowledgement of the full personhood of that individual.

In a sense, we are taking a road suggested but not taken by Rogers who saw humankind as subjectively free in a world that could be accounted for through science, that is, in a determined world. Rogers was aware of the "deep paradox" of this view of the person (Rogers, 1965, p. 152). Rogers' major theory statement noted that "The general orientation of philosophical phenomenology" would likely further influence the described approach (Rogers, 1959, p. 250). The path not taken was in the direction of "... find[ing] more room for the existing subjective person who is at the heart and base even of our system of science" (p. 251).

Therapy is defined, and its power relationship discussed

Some people define therapy in positive prescriptive terms, that is, as a helpful process, one in which a client benefits as the result of a relationship with a therapist. The benefit is seen as a form of healing, a change for the better, a relieving of tension, etc. For example, "psychotherapy is the releasing of an already existing capacity in a potentially competent individual" (Rogers, 1959, p. 221). There are many ways of doing therapy, and one of those approaches, client-centered therapy, is the subject of this inquiry.

Departing as we do from a scientific justification, we rely on an ethical frame for theory and practice. Specifically, we are perusing whether client-centered therapy, if done faithfully to its theory, is consistent with certain moral values and, therefore, ethical. The above definition of therapy, however, assumes that therapy is an efficacious activity, and, therefore, that definition is not useful to us. Our definition of "therapy" must cast it in more neutral descriptive terms. In this vein, the ancient Greek word "therapeia" ("Therapy," *Collins English Dictionary* (n.d.) online) had multiple meanings including "attendance." We define "therapy" as a relationship between or among two or more persons, at least one of whom is a "client," and at least one of whom is a "therapist," in which the focus of attention of all parties is upon the client and which exists for the client.[1] It differs from a friendship in that the focus of attention between friends, at any given moment, can be on either one or the other, and in that a friendship exists for both. In therapy, the therapist is welcoming, attendant upon, receiving of, and joining with the client, in the service of the client.

The focusing of attention away from the therapist and toward the client gives the therapist a certain power over the client. The client is gazed upon by the therapist and is vulnerable in a way that the therapist, who gazes, is not. To one degree or another, in entering into therapy, the client reveals herself.[2] It is the client's thoughts, feelings, intentions, losses and self-preoccupations that lie naked under a spotlight.

This "power over" (Proctor, 2002) is inherent in therapy. Although, in the outside world, a particular client may have status or power of personality superior to that of her therapist, the fundamental relational inequality between therapist and client is always present.

Client-centered therapy is described

Carl Rogers created client-centered therapy, and the definitive theoretical statement of it was published in 1959 (Rogers, 1959). In this section we present our understanding of that description of "client-centered therapy" in order to clarify the nature of the therapy approach at the center of our ethics investigation. In the

1959 theory statement Rogers instructs the client-centered therapist engaged in a session with a client to do exactly two things: experience an empathic understanding of the client's internal frame of reference and experience an unconditional positive regard for the client (Rogers, 1959, p. 213). Rogers' full theory statement contains six requirements for therapy; only those two, however, are tasks for the therapist.

Although Rogers (1959, pp. 210–213) used the terms "empathy" and "empathic understanding" interchangeably, a therapist's empathic understanding is not the same as a general feeling of empathy. It is, rather, an attempt to follow the client's lead and to understand, moment to moment, the fullness of what she is expressing from her perspective. The therapist adopts the client's frame of reference in preference to her own to prevent her ideas and feelings from distorting the client's meaning. This creates an opportunity for a more accurate understanding of what the client is expressing, thereby minimizing the possibility of the therapist missing the client.

"Unconditional positive regard" is centrally related to the respect we believe to be the basis for therapy. That term, though, can be misunderstood as saying that the therapist should always judge the client's self-expressions positively. We suggest that "unconditional positive regard" should be understood as *unconditional regard that is positive rather than as positive regard that is unconditional*. Unconditional regard means acceptance: the therapist accepts each client self-expression equally; none is privileged over another. Judgment is the opposite of unconditional regard, so the therapist does not judge any expression of the client. The therapist neither supports nor criticizes. "Positive" in the context of unconditional positive regard means that the unconditional regard is not only benign, it is warm. It comes from a place of caring, not one of indifference. Unconditional positive regard flowing from an empathic understanding, then, can be restated as an abiding warm acceptance.

Other aspects of Rogers' (1959, p. 213) client-centered theory include the congruence of the therapist in relationship to the client and the client's perception of the empathic understanding and unconditional positive regard of the therapist. These requirements for therapy might be misunderstood as part of the therapist's responsibilities. Unlike understanding and accepting, congruence is not something a therapist does. It relates to the genuineness of the therapist (p. 214). The therapist can be incongruent on purpose, by dissembling, or not on purpose, by not being accurately aware of her own internal reactions to situations as they arise. Dissembling is irrelevant to client-centered therapy because a therapist who is completely absorbed by her experiencing of empathic understanding and unconditional positive regard cannot be lying.[3] Unintentional incongruence is, of course, outside the awareness of the therapist, but to the extent that the therapist is incongruent in this way, her understanding is less accurate and her warm acceptance less complete.

Finally, within Rogers' description of client-centered therapy, the client must perceive, to some degree, the understanding and warm acceptance of the therapist. We agree with Rogers (1959, pp. 213–214) that making sure this happens is not a task of the therapist. The therapist needs to experience empathic understanding and unconditional positive regard; we believe that if a therapist takes on the additional task of intentionally communicating to the client that the therapist understands and warmly accepts her, the therapist will be distracted from experiencing empathic understanding and unconditional positive regard. The practice of client-centered therapy from the perspective of the therapist, then, consists of a person who experiences an empathic understanding and a warm acceptance of each expressed aspect of another's frame of reference and who does nothing more.

Freedom as ethical premise for practice

Earlier, we referred to "certain moral values" as the measuring stick for determining whether or not a particular approach to therapy is ethical. What values are involved?

We would say that the most basic human right is the right to life. In living as human beings we have thoughts and feelings, and we make choices. Our common meta-value, then, is freedom: freedom to think, to feel, to choose. The diminishment of freedom limits our ability to choose, to make connections, to live. In general we believe it is immoral to impose limits on the freedom of others. The limitation of freedom reduces our humanity.

The most basic human right, then, the right to life, can be restated as *a right to freedom*, a right to *self-direct*; that is, freedom to move, to think, to feel and to make choices. The existence of any "power over" relationship between or among persons threatens this right. As we have seen, the practice of therapy is predicated upon a "power over" relationship: the therapist has power over the client. Therapy, then, is inherently dangerous to this human right. For a therapy approach to be ethical, its practice must turn this danger on its head and actively strive to minimize it.

The medical-model concept of therapy rests on a different ethical premise

Many approaches to therapy are derived from a medical model. The client is analogous to a patient, someone in need of some sort of treatment (help) to cure an ailment (to solve a problem). The therapist is analogous to a doctor; she is the active agent in producing this cure.

In these approaches therapists share a common goal, to help the client. We can infer the ethical stance of these therapists; they take the view that whatever they can do to help the client is moral, and, furthermore, it is immoral to fail to act in the best interests of the client. The meta-value of these approaches is client welfare rather than our chosen meta-value, client freedom.

There is a strong emphasis in the literature of therapy on empirical evidence of the success of a particular approach, often in a particular context; the question often asked is whether or not an approach can be said to be "evidence-based" with respect to the treatment of a particular category of problem. Does the research indicate that clients are helped? This literature assumes client welfare to be the goal of therapy and has no relevance to any approach that puts client freedom above welfare, respect above help.

We believe there are serious problems with the methodologies employed in quantitative research that allegedly measures whether or not clients are helped, but our views on that research are of no importance to this inquiry. What is important is that, no matter how well research measures outcome, that research has no bearing on our ethical premise, respect for the freedom of each person to self-direct.

We reject Carl Rogers' actualizing tendency

While setting forth the theory of client-centered therapy in 1959, Rogers also delineated a theory of personality that included the description of an "actualizing tendency." The actualizing tendency "is the inherent tendency of the organism to develop all its capacities in ways which serve to maintain or enhance the organism" (Rogers, 1959, p. 196).[4] This concept has been said to be foundational to client-centered therapy (Rogers, 1980; Bozarth and Wang, 2008; Brodley, 2011c).

We believe that the majority of those who self-describe as client-centered therapists view the actualizing tendency as the basis for their trust that the practice of client-centered therapy is able to promote "positive therapeutic change" in clients. These therapists believe that if they and their clients truly engage in client-centered therapy, positive therapeutic change will occur. Whether or not this is a goal of theirs (as it is for those who practice one of the "medical-model" approaches) they accept it as justification for their practicing client-centered therapy.

Since we hold a person's right to self-direct as primary and freedom as our meta-value, this justification does not work for us. We also find:

> the use of the actualizing tendency hypothesis as foundation for practice tainted by a deterministic view, as well as reeking a bit of therapist expertise over a bug under glass. A scientific approach to client-centered therapy seems under-advanced, a vestige from a medical paradigm that potentially pollutes both thought and practice.
>
> *(Moon, 2008, pp. 204–205)*

Another reason for rejecting the actualizing tendency is its inconsistency with the idea of human freedom. The actualizing tendency, according to Rogers, is always present within the organism and, taken together with environmental factors that influence decisions, accounts for the behavior of the organism (Brodley, 2011c; Rogers, 1959). Since the actualizing tendency describes the organism as self-maintaining and self-enhancing, it follows that each choice made by a sentient being, including a human, is the best possible choice that she could make, given the environmental circumstances. If each choice made is always the best possible choice, then there is no alternative, no worse choice to be made. The "best" choice, then, is the only choice, and there is no freedom to choose.

Since our ethical premise pre-supposes a capacity for freedom within human beings, we reject the actualizing tendency.

The ethical therapist respects the client's right to direct her own life, including her time in therapy

What can a therapist do to abandon or, at least, neutralize, the power she has over a client? The relationship between client and therapist is complex. Either or both of them may speak about their own lives, about the lives of others, and about any subject imaginable, may ask questions about anything and answer questions, may be silent, and may use their bodies, including their faces, to be expressive without words. Each of these behaviors is a form of self-expression and, also, can be used as a form of attempted communication. We use "self-expression" and "attempted communication" to mean slightly different things. To self-express is simply to put something out there, to give "voice" to something, with or without words. To attempt to communicate is to intend that another receive a particular message.

Within the therapy hour, then, both the client and the therapist self-express, and each of them may attempt to communicate with the other. Since the focus of attention of each person is on the client, it is the client's self-expressions and attempts to communicate that are central to the therapeutic process, and the therapist's self-expressions and attempts to communicate may be thought of as responses to the client.

The client's special vulnerability and the therapist's consequent power over the client can be gleaned from this description of the therapy process. Since the therapist is not the focus of attention, there is little danger that her right to self-direct or her sense of self will be impinged upon in the course of therapy. Ordinarily, the client lacks the power to direct the therapist away from where the therapist wants to go. A client who feels diminished or thwarted by the therapist can feel her only recourse is to quit therapy.

The therapist's power over the client allows the therapist systematically to influence the client's direction. For a therapist to practice ethically, as defined by our premise, the therapist must not use this ability, must not exercise this power. Instead, the therapist must adopt an attitude of profound respect for the client, and the therapist's decisions about her behavior with this sovereign person must emerge from this attitude of respect.

For the ethical premise to be met, the therapist must hold this attitude of respect about every part of the client's life, including the time spent together in therapy. For us, the ethical therapist works with openness toward the client's feelings, perceptions, intentions and manner of self-presenting. The therapist does not try to influence in any particular direction the client's choices outside the therapy relationship nor choices inside that relationship.

Historically, this attitude of respect has been termed the "nondirective attitude" (Brodley, 2011a; Raskin, 2005). We prefer "attitude of respect" because, rather than foregrounding a lack of directive intent inside the therapist, it describes a positive presence of an active valuing of the client's lead.

Following the client's lead as witness or companion in the client's therapy is not always perfectly straightforward or unidirectional. It includes the possibility of bending or accommodating to the client's questions and requests. Not intending to direct can fold back on itself when, in response to a client's request for direction, the therapist complies. Nonetheless, "Systematic avoidance of clients' questions and their requests is, effectively, a form of control over the therapeutic process and over the client" (Brodley, 2011a, p. 56).

Whatever the client's form of expression, then, she takes the lead in therapy, and the therapist follows that lead as witness to and companion on the journey of another.

Our ethical premise does not require the client always to regard her therapy as nondirective

Before coining the term "client-centered therapy," Rogers sometimes referred to his work as "non-directive therapy" (Bozarth, 2000; Rogers, 1946). As we have said, for a therapy to be ethical according to our ethical premise, the therapist must have an "attitude of respect" for the client, that is, a nondirective attitude. Frequently the nondirective attitude is confused with being "nondirective" or "nondirectivity" (Levitt, 2005). Each of these terms differs from the nondirective attitude, since they refer to the impact on the client of therapist behaviors, whereas the nondirective attitude is an expression of an internal stance of the therapist (Moon, 2005).

What the therapist brings to therapy and what the client takes away may be two very different things. The therapist's attitude of respect informs everything she does in relating to the client. The therapist is aware she is having an influence on the client, but there is no intention to influence the client in any particular direction. This is just as true within the hour of therapy as it is when applied to the client's life outside.

The therapist's attitude of respect limits the freedom of the client as little as possible. Nevertheless, the client is free to regard any interaction with the therapist as nondirective or as directive. For the therapist to limit that freedom by trying to ensure that the client perceives the therapy as nondirective would not be consistent with our ethical premise. One situation in which a client may perceive or experience directivity is when a therapist checks her understanding of what the client has just expressed, and the client receives that checking as implicitly critical or (more likely) supportive. The client thus feels directed by the therapist one way or the other.

Another common situation occurs when the client explicitly or implicitly asks the therapist a question, directing the therapist to respond from the therapist's own frame of reference. If the therapist answers the question, the client might feel moved in the direction suggested by the therapist or in some other direction. If the therapist does not answer the question, the client can feel directed to stop asking questions at all or at least to stop expecting answers. Either way, the client is unlikely to experience the exchange as "nondirective," regardless of the attitude of the therapist.

The therapist cannot, however, attempt to alter client perceptions of directivity in the relationship without violating our ethical premise. There is a paradox at work here: no matter how respectful the attitude of the therapist is, the client must remain free to regard herself as having been directed. Our ethical premise requires the therapist to possess a nondirective attitude and to be un-invested in whether or not the client perceives the therapy as nondirective.

The practice of client-centered therapy, if faithful to its theory, is ethical

Given our ethical premise, for a therapy approach to be ethical, the approach must require the therapist, to the best of her ability, to abandon her power over the client. It demands that the therapist adopt an attitude of respect for the client's right to self-direct in all aspects of her own life, including the time she spends with the therapist. It insists that the therapist refrain from supplanting or thwarting the client's judgment.

In the practice of the approach labeled client-centered therapy, the therapist has exactly two tasks: to experience empathic understanding and to experience unconditional positive regard. Neither understanding a person nor warmly accepting her requires a therapist to exercise power over that person. Both are consistent with an attitude of respect within the therapist toward the person.

In fact, if a therapist has no goals other than to understand and warmly to accept the client, the therapist's attitude of respect is present. The therapist cannot have a disrespectful attitude, an attitude that the client should not be free, and simultaneously maintain consistent empathic understanding and unconditional positive regard toward the client while doing nothing else.

We conclude, therefore, that a therapist who practices client-centered therapy is engaged in an ethical practice, and that client-centered is an ethical therapy.

Notes

1 The same principle applies if either client or therapist or both of them is/are plural; we shall simplify our language by referring to each party in the singular.
2 In recognition that gender is not binary and with a desire to move away from dividing us by gender toward unifying us in personhood, we shall use traditionally feminine pronouns (she, her, herself) whenever singular pronouns are required.
3 The issue of a client-centered therapist experiencing a persistent judgmental feeling toward a client has been discussed elsewhere (Brodley, 2011b; Moon, 2005; Rogers, 1959, p. 214; Rogers & Truax, 1967, pp. 100–102).
4 An alternative description of an actualizing tendency, not addressed here, has been proposed (Bazzano, 2017).

References

Bazzano, M.(2017). A bid for freedom: the actualizing tendency updated. *Person-Centered & Experiential Psychotherapies*, doi:10.1080/14779757.2017.1361860.

Bozarth, J. D. (March 25, 2000). Non-directiveness in client-centered therapy: A vexed concept. Paper presentation at the Eastern Psychological Association, Baltimore, MD. Retrieved November 2, 2017 from http://personcentered.com/nondirect.html.

Bozarth, J. D., & Wang, C. (2008). The "unitary actualizing tendency" and congruence in client-centred therapy. In B. E. Levitt, (Ed.), *Reflections on human potential: Bridging the person-centred approach and positive psychology* (pp. 102–115). Ross-on-Wye, England: PCCS Books.

Brodley, B. T. (2011a). The nondirective attitude in client-centered therapy. In K. A. Moon, M. Witty, B. Grant, & B. Rice (Eds.), *Practicing client-centered therapy: Selected writings of Barbara Temaner Brodley* (pp. 47–62). Ross-on-Wye, UK: PCCS Books. (Reprinted from *The Person-Centered Journal*, 1997, 4(1), pp. 13–30.)

Brodley, B. T. (2011b). Congruence and its relation to communication in client-centered therapy. In K. A. Moon, M. Witty, B. Grant, & B. Rice (Eds.), *Practicing client-centered therapy: Selected writings of Barbara Temaner Brodley* (pp. 73–102). Ross-on-Wye, UK: PCCS. (Reprinted from *The Person-Centered Journal*, 1998, 5(2), pp. 83–116.)

Brodley, B. T. (2011c). The actualizing tendency concept in client-centered theory. In K. A. Moon, M. Witty, B. Grant, & B. Rice (Eds.), *Practicing client-centered therapy: Selected writings of Barbara Temaner Brodley* (pp. 153–170). Ross-on-Wye, UK: PCCS. (Reprinted from *The Person-Centered Journal*, 1999, 6(2), pp. 108–120.)

Collins English Dictionary (n.d.). Therapy. *Collins English Dictionary – Complete & Unabridged 10th Edition*. Retrieved August 12, 2017 from Dictionary.com website: http://www.dictionary.com/browse/therapy.

Levitt, B. E. (Ed.). (2005). *Embracing non-directivity: Reassessing person-centered theory and practice for the 21st century*. Ross-on-Wye, England: PCCS Books.

Moon, K. A. (2005). Non-directive therapist congruence in theory and practice. In B. E. Levitt (Ed.), *Embracing non-directivity: Reassessing person-centered theory and practice for the 21st century* (pp. 261–280). Ross-on-Wye, England: PCCS Books.

Moon, K. A. (2008). An essay on children, evil and the actualizing tendency. In B. E. Levitt (Ed.), *Reflections on human potential: Bridging the person-centred approach and positive psychology* (pp. 203–214). Ross on Wye, England: PCCS Books.

Proctor, G. (2002). *The dynamics of power in counselling and psychotherapy: Ethics, politics and practice*. Ross-on-Wye: PCCS Books.

Raskin, N. J. (2005). The nondirective attitude. *The Person-Centered Journal*, 12(1–2), 5–22. Also in B. Levitt (Ed.), *Embracing non-directivity: Reassessing person-centered theory and practice for the 21st century* (pp. 329–347). Ross-on-Wye: PCCS Books. (Original manuscript written in 1947.)

Rogers, C. R. (1946). Significant aspects of client-centered therapy. *American Psychologist*, 1, 415–422.

Rogers, C. R. (1959). A theory of therapy, personality, and interpersonal relationships as developed in the client-centered framework. In E. Koch (Ed.), *Psychology: A study of a science: Vol. 3. Formulations of the person and the social context* (pp. 184–256). New York: McGraw-Hill.

Rogers, C. R. (1965). Freedom and commitment. *Etc.*, 22(2), 133–152.

Rogers, C. R. (1980). The foundations of a person-centered approach. In *A way of being* (pp. 113–136). Boston: Houghton Mifflin.

Rogers, C. R., & Truax C. B. (1967). The therapeutic conditions antecedent to change: A theoretical view, in C. R. Rogers (Ed.), *The therapeutic relationship and its impact: A study of psychotherapy with schizophrenics* (pp. 97–108). Madison, WI: Univ. of Wisconsin Press.

10

EXPERIENCING AND THE PERSON-CENTRED APPROACH

Nikolaos Kypriotakis

Lying there

Waves

Lying there in a large oblong cardboard box, my entire torso, hands and head within the box, my legs outside, my knees bent, I had the whole sky with a big blazing blinding sun above me. In the paradise of my childhood years, in that time of concentration and expansion, that day … I was holding that book, Herbert Read's *A Concise History of Modern Painting* in my hands … and was often letting myself go blind, and, then, would press the book, open, upon my eyes, close my eyes … and give myself to the blinding midday … protected.

In that book, there, then, I was reading a poem by Wols. I was reading about his absolutely abstract type of expressionism, about these multi-expressive forms, biological forms, cellular and atomic structures, this unclearness or irregularity, as Herbert Read (1959, pp. 254–258) had written, referring also to György Kepes (1956) *The New Landscape in Art and Science*.

Now I am laughing: Art was discovering the structures of modern science, that science which was/is at the leading edge of science. Science was discovering the echo of the universe and organisms, leaving behind the absolute authority of quantities and measurements, of cause and effect relations, even of logic … Art and Science are still discovering them, structures and meta-structures … they are creating them; as much as our language, our old language, does.

Here, now, beside the sea, wearing my wide-brimmed hat, and holding in my hands another book – a book about phenomenology – I am watching, I am listening to the small waves of the gulf. I am watching them being repeated without being repeated, and I remember, I recall, I re-experience this sense from my childhood, the biological "forms" at this moment, this internal congruence.

The small waves in the harbour are being repeated without being repeated, the small waves are the same and yet not the same ... like the words ...

There is a hesitation here ... what is it with words? When are words adequately descriptive? And when are waves well described? When do words represent satisfactorily, when do they point sufficiently towards experience, towards a living process? And what could possibly mean here "represent", "satisfactorily", "sufficiently"? Words are repeated ... without being repeated (?).

Something with them, something about them, seems too little, insufficient ... as useful as they are ... words. And they are useful, and so is any kind of logical positivism or operationalism, and so are measurements and quantities, cause-and-effect relations, symbols, mathematics, every form of expression and symbolization. And yet ... How does one stand opposite these forms ... or in front of these biological forms? My body, the world, waves, pebbles, leaves on the trees ... fingers like branches, the writing hand, the look/gaze and the eyeball, the body ...

Something in/with words, something in their "method", something in my (our) "linguistic" attitude, seems static, overlaying, overlapping (rather than revealing), schematic, schematizing, restrictive ... intellectual, academic, abstract, dead, or at least dried out.

Empiricism

The scientificity of waves

With Galileo, science comes actually to encounter all this, the somatic world of matter, the world of the real and/or the "real", Universe, Nature. With experiment and experimental control, science exposes its concepts and processes, the very phenomenology of reality itself (this bottomless source of "reality" and "objectivity"), to the "Ocean" of reality, to a new type of empiricism, a scientific experimental empiricism.

Reversing, in a way, *Solaris* (Lem, 2003), we go on listening to this Ocean, we continue reading into this Ocean, narrating this Ocean to ourselves – and not vice versa. We read "reality" into/within "reality"; we overlay it with forms and structures of the "real".

Concepts and models in modern physics and science are founded and re-founded, under the authorship and normativity of "science", a "philosophy" of Nature and Reality, a structured expansive conjugated homogeneity, a well-elaborated body of knowledge and power. Physics constructs its own meta-physics, while science and technology have become ever more powerful, ever more threatening; a true globalized will to power, a true will to will, after the deconstruction and the crisis of meaning in our societies.

> [T]he prevailing scientific world view has generally been to suppose that, at bottom, everything is to be described in terms of the results of combinations of certain "particle" units, considered to be basic. This attitude is evidently in

accord with the prevailing tendency in the ordinary mode of language to treat words as "elementary units" which, one supposes, can be combined to express anything whatsoever that is capable of being said.

(Bohm, 2005, pp. 51–52)

However, despite this mechanistic order, in a living organism: "each part grows in the context of the whole, so that it does not exist independently, nor can it be said that it merely 'interacts' with the others, without itself being essentially affected in this relationship" (ibid., p. 219).

There is a method there – experimental empirical control. There is a *source* that constantly surprises us and disturbs or upsets our readings. In this text I want to talk about this source and its dynamic applications; crossing this incessant fragmentation, these problems, paradoxes, contradictions, self-deceptions – these historical remnants or limits of expressivity, these models, these dualities: "Thing" and "process", "thing" and "thought", context and content; soma and significance, soma and meaning; body as *Körper* and body as *Leib*; body and mind, matter and thought, material and mental, physical and psychic, the manifest and the subtle.

The meta-language in modern physics is both philosophical and psychological: the implicate order, the *enfolding/implicate* and *unfolding/explicate* universe and consciousness (Bohm 2005); soma-significant and signa-somatic processes (Bohm, 2003); the meaning of meaning as the implicate order; the way in which meaning is organized; the *implicit* order/character of experiencing and its relation to *explicit* symbolizations of its aspects; transformation, transition, communication and creation of meaning.

Relativity and quantum physics (may) stand in direct contradiction, but they both fundamentally point to undivided, unbroken wholeness of the totality of existence as an undivided flowing movement (Bohm, 2005). For Whitehead, "concrete human experience, in each of its concrete moments, is not an external relation between someone experiencing and something experienced". It is "an integral inclusive reality within which, as aspects of itself, there are differentiated, among others, the human organism from his or her environment, the human subjectivity from the human body, [...] more generally, the experiencing from the experienced" (Nobo, 2003, p. 224).

Whitehead (an "abstraction-dealer") – being a radical empiricist "in precisely [William] James's sense"– prevented himself from committing what he called "the fallacy of misplaced concreteness", the fallacy "of substituting the abstractions produced by our simplification and analysis of experience for the fullness of experience itself" (Auxier & Herstein, 2017, p. 42).

Similarly, Gendlin (an abstraction-dealer himself) rooted himself in a non-naïve empiricism, i.e. in the concrete bodily felt experiencing. He writes: "Theory is made by people and can never be such that people can be derived from it" (Gendlin, 1973a, p. 329). Also, "I love theory, but it does not ground life. Many people think everything is 'based on' theory. If that were so, what would theory be based on?" (Gendlin, 1986, p. 141).

Is Rogers too an abstraction-dealer? Or rather an empiricist as well as a traditional thinker? – traditional in his language, scientific explanations, in a dualistic, static worldview. Could this be the reason, why PCA/PCT should be revised and redefined? Did it come to a (post-modernist) dead-end? Is it integral and inclusive? Or does it contribute to the fragmentation of the different kinds of therapy?

Rogers places "experience" at the centre of his theory and practice. But he understands experience in a rather traditional manner, as something already constructed, as part of the phenomenal field, which lacks its accurate symbol/concept. Symbolization is more or less an intellectual endeavour. Rogers' PCA may imply *relational depth*, but misses *other* aspects of *experiential depth*.

Experienciality

Is "waves" the right word, concept?

> Most people encapsulate themselves, shut up like oysters, sometimes before they have stopped being undergraduates, and go through life barricaded against every idea, every fresh and unconceptualized perception. [We need …] methods for training people to pass at will from conceptualized perception to direct virgin perception. The exercise keeps the mind fresh and sensitive and teaches a wholesome understanding of the function of language and its dangers, when taken too seriously, in the way that all pedants, doctrinaires and dogmatists invariably do, with such catastrophic results.
>
> *(Huxley, 2000, pp. 28–29)*

Commenting on science's preoccupation with the universal laws of nature, Gendlin (1997a) states that Galileo's empirical testing did not import the concrete particular itself "into" science, but, rather, the empiricists added to logical science a *relationship* to concrete operations. He considers that this relationship could be made systematic (the systematic criteria of empirical testing). We must leave the logical and the empirical testing orders intact, but must add a *third dimension*: concepts that can refer to experiencing and, also, provide systematic methods to allow logical and objective concepts so they can profitably relate to the quite different experientially referring concepts.

This principle traverses Gendlin's whole work and effort, at least the way I understand it. He says he wants to show "a new approach to what phenomenologists call 'phenomena,' a deliberate way to *think* and *speak with* what is more than categories (concepts, theories, assumptions, distinctions…)" (Gendlin, 2004, p. 127).

He wants to go beyond the dead-end aspect of postmodernism, which "frees us from any privileged set of categories, but leaves us only with an aporia, still only on the level of concepts" (ibid., p. 127). Is this a new phenomenology? Or perhaps, an *Experiential Phenomenology* or *Phenomenology of Carrying Forward*.

In *Experiential Phenomenology*, the emphasis is on the concrete, lived, felt steps, while words and, eventually, theories (e.g. about therapy, like the PCA or *Focusing-oriented Therapy* (FOT)) are only tools for these steps. *Carrying forward* signifies a continuity-in-change characteristic of the body's process, to distinguish it from abrupt change and no change (Gendlin, 1973b, pp. 321, 325). This concept goes beyond the traditional logic regarding concepts of change and the postmodern deconstruction of this logic. It goes beyond the metaphysically saturated concepts of progressive development and beyond the teleological conception of potentiality (Levin, 1997, p. 42); like, for example, in Rogers' "seven stages of process" or the fully-functioning person.

Within the frame of his Experiential Phenomenology, Gendlin wants to find a way to come into contact with the experiential "Ocean", i.e. the experiential intricacy/multiplicity of all forms of life, just as Galileo once did within the scientific frame. How do we let "this" ocean speak and carry us forward? He writes: "Situations and bodily-implied speech and action are one system of carrying forward". He tries to develop a science "of the first person"; a science specializing in living bodies that sense themselves, and in processes in which our "I" senses itself (Gendlin, 1999).

In this way, philosophy, includes again practice; it *is* practice (how could it be otherwise?). In this way, philosophy and (philosophically informed) psychotherapy become "experimental" and experiential.

To this aim, he develops his own experiential practice (*Focusing*), psychotherapy (*FOT*), philosophy (*A Process Model*), theory construction (*TAE*) (Gendlin, 1981, 1986, 1996, 1999, 2000, 2004).

Taking *experiencing* as the starting point for his Experiential Phenomenology, Gendlin (1997a) analyses in detail, initially, the functional relationships between *experiencing* (felt sense/felt meaning) and *symbols* (symbol: being anything that may have a symbolizing role). He examines what he calls phenomenological transitions/relationships: "conceptual models in terms of which human phenomena can be considered by theory"; *parallel* (*direct reference, recognition, explication*) and *creative*, "specific", "nonparallel" (*metaphor, comprehension, relevance, circumlocution*), without seeing this differentiation as final or closed (ibid., pp. 90–137). These transitions/relations allow felt senses and symbols to acquire meaning. Felt senses are not mere senses; they are (bodily) felt, (bodily) experienced, lived/living meanings, necessary for symbols to have "meaning".

He then, explores the *characteristics* of the felt meaning as they function within/into the creation of new, further meanings and emphasizing the *basic principles* of his work. One is referred to as a *reversal of the usual philosophical order*, i.e. logical and conceptual relationships do not determine the creation of meanings but this – the creation of meanings – is determined by the function of concrete experiential/felt meanings, to which we refer directly.

His philosophy recognizes the priority of making experiential sense, rather than giving priority to some cognitive system and reading it into experience. Any occurred experiential making-sense can be explained in retrospect, by interpolating cognitive units (ibid., p. xviii). Thus, experiencing (as a *responsive order* more than any verbal or logical order) can respond differently to different assumptions, definitions, assertions, conditions, determinants of any kind, but with greater precision, intricacy and excessiveness than what could have arisen from what our usual, conceptual/logical approach to it could provide.

Gendlin (1997a) is interested in a new beginning, i.e. to look at the experiencing process and the propositions (its verbalizations and symbolizations) as they interact with each other, to free ourselves from the (dead-end) prospect/perspective that experiencing should be rendered without its rendering having an effect on that very experiencing. He is interested in a "solution", a successful phenomenological method, or "basis" (p. 288). That basis, he suggests, is the experienced – the living experiential process. He is interested in the "how" of this basis. *How* do we have and *how* do we use this basis? *How* is it that this is the basis of our claims and meanings? *How* is the result of this basis (and its use) "more than simply another imposed scheme" (ibid., p. 290)? For him,

> It is scandalous that current philosophy appeals to something beyond verbal schemes, and yet claims that its assertions are "merely" read off, or that they "merely" state this something. It is as if, having said that direct experience or knowing how is not a scheme, contemporary philosophers pretend that it shows its schematic organization on the very face of it.
>
> *(ibid.)*

These philosophers "fail to examine just what their basis is and how they use it", having left this "something other than schemes" – the (…) – "in this unexamined state of mere feeling" (ibid.).

The whisper of thought and language

The whisper and sound of waves

Here, now, beside the sea, the light gradually fades away (carrying our metaphors, reflecting them) and the sound and the overtone echo of this visible/invisible flow ever reaches the shore, one shore. Its sound is ever repeated without being repeated.

All words (concepts, theories, elaborate intellectual arguments) seem to me to ultimately refute each other, at least in time, or in the thickening of experience, or with the advent of … the end.

As they accumulate in memory, monuments themselves of discreteness and "clarity", of units and modules, of negation, and negation of negation, negating movement and, finally, potentially, life.

As new forms of Zeno's paradox, they are unable to follow our experiential flow or to describe satisfactorily our internal experiential movement, what is already here, still "unknown" and "vague" but perceptible, experienced, sensed, felt. They are paradoxical – word-paradoxes.

They are paradoxical if taken seriously. Can anyone take words or theories seriously? Every kind of reductionism, the words about essence, about Being(s) and not-Being(s), of Oneness and n-Oneness, thingness or no-thingness? All of these words are clothes that get old and narrow and worn out, all of them showing their limits by different weight, metaphorical, relative and referential, inductive. They are assembled as a multitude of voices, sound signals and signs, a multitude of tails and chains, one pulling the other, one sounding for the other, as if they were born all together for one another, in the untroubled space of the self, when the body is asleep, resting, when it calms, echoing in this room, a narrow or wider room, the special one word that holds together, implies, continues the "world", "life": echoing "I" … "me" … Otherwise, a cry (of pain or joy) would be enough.

Do they all end up not succumbing to this erosion? to the deadening of the end, to the wastage of time? and only the books, the tele-vision, the other (small and big), the talking lips, are investing or being invested in new brains, in new memories, drawing the limits of the world again, repeating without repeating the echoing of the situations of the past, in a new earth, demystifying and enchanting at the same time a new life.

And then, after the words of exactness, the exact sciences, those that do not speak but measure and test/control, or speak silently, at least, or whisper, and convince us, those that prove, those that define objectivity and measure its degree or scale, those that control predictability, control the predictable repeatability of the "waves" and conclusions, certainties or probabilities – of the potentialities of these certainties; those [sciences] that want to improve life (do they manage it?).

Light gradually fades (carrying our metaphors, reflecting them) and the echo of this visible/invisible flow ever reaches the shore, one shore. Its sound is ever repeated – without being repeated.

What do I want to say? That all things overlap? Body, environment, life and nature, situation? That, even language lies? That this falsity, this untruth, looks like part of the "truth"? I would like to describe who I am: … (silence) … and who I am not: … (silence) …

Agony, nothingness and being, empiricism, pragmatism, relativism, skepticism, agnosticism, humanism, body, death, pain (the whisper of thought and language).

Or: anything that exists is felt, feeling, experience; experience is the meaning, the important thing, the wall that strikes at your foot is the essence … and in this sense breathing, heartbeat, the vortex of the guts, something bright in the eyes, or the darkness of the night.

Experiencing

The corporeality of waves

"To 'exist' came to mean to appear to us. The very word for things became (and still is) 'phenomena'. This is the old subject-object puzzle: what exists can only be a known-by" (Gendlin, 2016, pp. 78–79).

Experiencing (or *Erlebnis*, lived experience, as they usually translate it), in Gendlin's sense, refers to directly given phenomena, or stream of feelings, to "concretely" felt, present, experienced or implicit, felt meaning. It refers to (bodily) felt, experienced occurrences and situations. An individual may refer to it in her own phenomenal field. Its conceptual content may be explicitly known or not; this explicit knowledge of content can occur in gradation, progressively and creatively (Gendlin, 1997a, p. 239). Experiencing is "existential", i.e. something in time and space, concrete (ibid., p. 240), while perceptions and concepts are "about" or "of" something existential, i.e. they have an object. Experiencing may be "*known, observed*" only "as it is 'symbolized' in *some* way", e.g. by being "directly referred" to, for example as a felt "this", where "symbols *refer to* and *differentiate* some experiencing, but do not *represent* it", as it happens to be in other kinds of symbolizations, like conceptualizations (ibid., p. 238). It is directly felt/observable (direct reference is an observable reference) by an individual and it is also indirectly observable by others, by the expressions of the individual. It is "something present, although ... chiefly felt rather than known" (ibid., p. 242). It has identifiable characteristics (modes and types) as empirical observation: intensity, richness, detail, multiplicity, degree of presence, quality, quantity, etc. It is implicitly full of meaning; it can have many explicit conceptualizations, without itself being part of explicit conceptual contents. We can refer to it directly, and it "is defined as the felt datum of an individual's inward direct reference in his phenomenal awareness" (ibid., pp. 243–244). More generally, the experiential organismic process (experiencing) refers to "perceiving", "thinking", rather than "perception", "concept", although the lively process/action of "perceiving", "thinking", can be itself the object of our attention reflectively. Experiencing is evaluative, purposive, focal (Gendlin, 1973b, p. 326). Experiencing is pre-conceptual, pre-reflective, and, as an adaptive, inter-modifying, inter-affecting integration, manifold and continuity, it implicitly contains a complex dynamic (mutually modifying) organization, continuously functioning (momentarily) in the present in an integrative way (Gendlin, 1959).

No (theoretical) scheme, or set of definitions and concepts, or set of units, can express or represent or be equal to experiencing or a fragment of experiencing – or existence (Gendlin, 1973b, p. 322). However, we can experientially check the validity of characterizing *bodily felt* experience – the compound of experiencing and its current symbolization/meaning/significance – as being "non-numerical" (we can directly refer to it and select our cognitive units, not predetermined, neither them nor their number), "multischematic" (we can apply any given conceptual schema), and "interschematizable" (we can apply any other experience and then schematize) (Gendlin, 1973a, p. 299).

The above descriptions are yet another scheme which is imposed upon and "read" into experiencing, although this schematization can be done in different ways, as Gendlin mentions; e.g. in a way that has as its basis *process, interaction, body, steps of experiential expression* as opposed to definitions.

But this phenomenological attitude and method offers more than that. It radically leads us back to experiencing and its unfolding/enfolding, so that different creative possibilities can occur; different self-directive, *self-narrating* capacities.

There is a shift from *what* is being said about something (content) to the *relationship* this content has with experiencing. Does all order, meaning, all rationality, *totally* derive from historical and cultural determinants or is it that "life and situations always make much more intricate sense than could follow from just the historical determinants" (Gendlin, 1997a, p. xvii)? Does not the same apply to any conceptualization, schema, or, even, ontological universality?

It is intriguing *how* in different schools of therapy the so-called-ontological and the so-called-ontic seem to be emerging into each other and *how* they are placed together, hierarchically or not. Up to a point they all develop some kind of interpretative "ontology" more or less restrictive upon the "ontic": *formative/actualizing tendency*, the so-called *existentialia*, *experiencing*, etc.

What is important is not schemas as such, but the *role* of the *directly referred to* experiencing; or any experiential *vehicle* to promote this process in an optimal, humane way, e.g. like *Focusing* or the *quality of the relationship* of the therapist and the client in PCT: empathic, authentic/genuine and accepting. Style, words, theory may vary – their experiential effect remains.

The ontological scheme could be *death*; or it could be *life*. Or, it could be *anything*; one, any, symbolization or any experience (any symbolization of an experiencing).

The role of experiencing

The waves are the ocean

The *role* of experiencing and its relationships with every symbolization and creation of meaning help Gendlin to re-articulate Rogers' concept of *congruency*; to show the prospects opened up in scientific research, in the context of psychology or psychotherapy; and to generally indicate the significance/necessity of *direct reference* both for the client and for the therapist, and for the therapist's responses ... Gendlin regards the therapist's direct reference to the client's experiencing as a principle that lies at the base of PCT. If the client does not refer the therapist's response to his own experiencing then "he is left with only the concepts of that response" (Gendlin, 1997a, p. 264).

The "discrepancies between self-concept and experience, awareness and experience, etc." (Rogers 1959, p. 250), the mis-match between self-concept and experience which arises through the introjection of conditions of worth (Purton, 2014b), as Rogers' central view upon psychological trouble and disturbance, give shape to Rogers' notion of incongruence. Subsequently, congruence between self and experience arises "[w]hen self-experiences are accurately symbolized, and are included in the self-concept in accurately symbolized form" (Rogers, 1959, p. 206).

Gendlin contrasts "experiencing" to (Rogerian) "experience". He sees Rogers' term "experience" as a construct which consists of "all that could be, but is not necessarily, in any sense in awareness" (Gendlin, 1997a, p. 242). Thus, it is "constituted of contents that are posited in the individual. These contents are the same in nature, whether they are in awareness or denied to awareness." Experience in awareness means, for Gendlin, "*explicit* contents of awareness". When denied to awareness, "these *same* contents are still posited in the person, as if they were *explicit* contents of some absent conceptualization" (ibid., p. 242).

Gendlin emphasizes three characteristics of experiencing: its *implicitly* meaningful character; its being in awareness, an implicit non-conceptual awareness in a process of feeling; its being "something other than any of its conceptualized aspects" (ibid., p. 243), which only form a small part of the implicitly contained meanings, whereby "their implicit weighing in feeling can occur in a present moment" (ibid., p. 257). He emphasizes the importance of enabling theory "to refer to experiencing as a direct datum, an observable dimension" (ibid., p. 244). He thinks that this "is made possible by the use of the term 'experiencing' not as a theoretical construct of any sort, but as a term that refers to a direct datum of any individual" (ibid., p. 244).

We see in Rogers' notion of "experience" – the part that refers to those experiences which can't have access to awareness – that there is an echo of "the unconscious". But, as Purton writes,

> If we stick to the phenomenological view of "experience" as that which is in one's awareness then "unconscious experiences" is a contradiction in terms. On the other hand if we allow that there are unconscious experiences then there must be ways of establishing when these experiences occur.
>
> *(Purton, 2004, p. 48)*

Gendlin replaces the talk of what is "unconscious" by the talk of what is *implicit*. "The process of therapy, for Gendlin, is not a matter of making conscious what was unconscious, but of making explicit what was implicit" (Purton, 2004, p. 48).

Thus, from this perspective, incongruence "is a matter of a person not adequately symbolizing their experiencing, where 'experiencing' (unlike Rogers' 'experience') refers to what is going on in that person's awareness" (ibid., p. 203).

What is "there" for Gendlin, or what was "there" when referring to the past, is a whole indefinitely implicit intricacy of life, whole intricate situations and implications of situations with a multitude of implicit meanings and aspects. There was nothing "hidden". What now may be seen as "hidden" "there" was (or, better, "was") just implied "there"; as an aspect/meaning of the intricate situation as a whole, the same way as eating is implied in a hunger situation, but is not yet there.

We can give to such intricate wholes our attention, as we do in *Focusing* and FOT, when we wholeheartedly give our sustained attention to our actual felt *responses* (to what we feel or how we find ourselves responding to situations – yet vague and unclear), articulating them, in a continual *zigzagging* between our response and the right way to articulate it, letting our *response* gradually inform our *view* of how things are, reaching a point where our stated view of things is an adequate articulation of our response, which now is an already changed response, a response changed through articulation, accurately formulated in direct reference to the felt response.

Attending to our situations *that way* is a changing in attitude, in how we are *living*. We find new words as new *deeds*, new *Äusserungen* (Wittgenstein's *spontaneous utterances*), new responses, and not merely (new) descriptions/reports of (new) (bodily) "feelings". Attending to our sensations like in a mindfulness "body scan" will not get us far (Purton, 2014a, p. 232).

These spontaneous, unrestricted (felt) responses are contrasted to fixed, over-familiar, conventional utterances/articulations, *structure-bound* inauthentic expressions, compulsive responses, which do *not* come "freshly from our current experiencing" (Purton, 2004, p. 205), which are *not* "socially undefined and thus unconceptualized meanings" (Gendlin, 1997a, p. 256), which are *not* informed of the intricate richness of our situations and our felt responses to their movements.

Similarly, in a (Gendlian) genuine/authentic way, "[t]he therapist needs to respond from their felt experiencing if the client is to be helped to do the same" (Purton, 2004, p. 206) and not only from "conceptualizations *of the client's experience*" (Gendlin, 1997a, p. 258).

This difference in how Rogers and Gendlin see congruence "is closely related to different philosophical perspectives on how language relates to the world" (Purton, 2004, p. 205). Gendlin (2016, p. 82) writes that he has been thinking and speaking *both from and about* the ongoing process of thinking and speaking. Thus, the words "say what they are doing", and they are doing what they say (from that very speaking). He tries to overcome the philosophical problem that no theory of language seems possible: i.e. theory cannot encompass language, because theory exists only within language; the actual working of language always exceeds theory and concepts. Thus, he devises a mode of language in which what he says about the process of meaning-formation also happens in the very sentences that tell about it. Concepts have a "nonrepresentational relationship" to that process, they do not pretend to represent what language does; where language is always a newly forming bodily interaction with others in situations (Levin, 1997, pp. 44–45). Language is implicit in the body (in environment, in situations), and, as Butler (2015, pp. 20–21) writes, body escapes both every possible linguistic effort of capture, and the subsequent effort to determine ontologically that very escape (although body depends on language so that it can be known).

Away from the traditional "picture" theory of language, where language represents the world and the structures of language represent structures in the world, "in Gendlin's thinking language is seen as creating meanings rather than as acquiring its meanings through 'corresponding to', 'reflecting' or 'being congruent with' a non-linguistic reality" (Purton, 2004, pp. 205–206). While we can observe what people say about themselves ("self-concept"), we can't observe their "experience". They too can't observe the elements of their experience that are not in consciousness, which are precisely "the ones that are of interest in connection with incongruence" (Purton, 2014b, p. 68).

Purton sees, in the congruence/incongruence picture presented by Rogers, the old (compelling) Cartesian philosophical picture of the "inner" and the "outer".

Epilogue

Wave-ing

Is Gendlin's experiential thinking a critique of (abstract, passive, non-gestural, non-re-enactive) thinking/speaking/relating and a commentary on the ontic-existential in relation to the ontological? Maybe it is; some philosophers shy away from physics for fear of reductionism; they also shun human experiencing for fear of psychologism. Anything "ontic" appears to be a threat to philosophical discourse (Gendlin, 1989).

Gendlin, by reformulating PCT's concept of "experience" and its most central hypothesis of "congruence-incongruence", and through his major philosophical assumptions (experiencing, process, interaction, body, etc.), offers not just a new emphasis on *experiential concreteness* and *felt-sensing*, not just a new basis, but also new theory. He also offers a new phenomenological, philosophical background to PCT; a new connection to science, a new scientific model and a new language. Isn't this also a revision, a *necessary* revision? (I wouldn't dare argue whether it is *sufficient*.)

In *A Process Model*, Gendlin (1997b) extensively develops his philosophy of the implicit and constructs a model for the "space" of behaviour formation and possibilities – of perception and consciousness, and of life process in general. In that work, interaction and the relational character of life and being is primary, e.g. interaction between body and environment, between ourselves and society – or therapist and client.

My aim here, though, was to elaborate on the creative, responsive, emergent, embodied, implicitly precise, more than logical, more than conceptual, order of *ideation* and *meaning creation*. Mainly, on the *tension* between felt-sensing (felt-responding) (whether spontaneously or not, whether authentically or not) and the creation of meaning, of (world/situational) views, or of articulating, of thinking, of symbolizing in general.

There, in that tension, of what is the meaning of meaning, I find "experiencing" (or just "existing", "living") to be quite useful, especially when informing and transforming our current "scientific" or "rational" style of doing education, science, or therapy, whether PCT, FOT or anything else; when informing and transforming educators, scientists and therapists themselves.

I seem to find in that tension a new procedural, more than logical, experiential (non-metaphysical) *edge* which I also find (intellectually) in the language of modern physics. More than that, what is being underlined t/here, is my concern about our *attitude towards language itself*. In that sense, what would complete this article is a reference, not only to the above mentioned "direct virgin perception", but also to what we usually call mystic/mystical experiences, or even to "states" of (extreme) pain and agony.

Notice

Inter-waves

This text is interrupted by another text, in a manner of an experiential "creative regress" (or "instance of itself") written in a direct way, which imprints my "spontaneous" inner "wave ripples", my "experiencing", regarding the writing of this article.

A "this", a wave, a "this"-wave, was an instance of (a) "such"-wave, of (a) wave-thisness, of (a) wave-ness. And not only. Also, a universal/category, "wave" (or wave-ness) was taken as an experiential "particular" from which new universals were generated (Gendlin, 1997a, p. xx) – my whole text. My first "sense", this "sense" of the waves, poetic and indefinite yet, however, felt and moving, the Wols' poem, inevitably bound up with my childhood years, seems to be the final one.

In the meantime, an inquiry and study process has occurred, practical/experiential phenomenological inquiry, based on my experiencing, my experiencing-as-returned-back-to-me. Thus, this sense, this meaning of the waves, seems to have been redefined, to have revealed some of its facets and aspects. I find that the one text reveals the other, as they work complementarily. That is why I keep both of them as one.

References

Auxier, R. E. & Herstein, G. L. (2017). *The Quantum of Explanation. Whitehead's Radical Empiricism.* London and New York: Routledge.

Bohm, D. (2003). Soma-significance and the activity of meaning. In Lee Nichol (Ed.), *The Essential David Bohm.* London and New York: Routledge (Taylor and Francis e-Library).

Bohm, D. (2005). *Wholeness and the Implicate Order.* London and New York: Routledge (Taylor and Francis e-Library).

Butler, J. (2015). *Senses of the Subject.* New York: Fordham University Press.

Gendlin, E. T. (1959). The concept of congruence reformulated in terms of experiencing. *Counseling Center Discussion Papers,* 5(12). Chicago: University of Chicago Library.

Gendlin, E. T. (1973a). Experiential phenomenology. In M. Natanson (Ed.), *Phenomenology and the Social Sciences.* Vol. I (pp. 281–319). Evanston: Northwestern University Press.

Gendlin, E. T. (1973b). Experiential psychotherapy. In R. Corsini (Ed.), *Current Psychotherapies* (pp. 317–352). Itasca, IL: Peacock.

Gendlin, E. T. (1981). *FOCUSING.* New York: Bantam Dell, Random House Inc.

Gendlin, E. T. (1986). *Let Your Body Interpret Your Dreams.* Illinois: Chiron Publications.

Gendlin, E. T. (1989). Autobiography – Phenomenology as non-logical steps. In E.F. Kaelin & C.O. Schrag (Eds.), *Analecta Husserliana.* Vol. XXVI. *American phenomenology. Origins and developments* (pp. 404–410). Dordrecht: Kluwer.

Gendlin, E. T. (1996). *Focusing-Oriented Psychotherapy: A Manual of the Experiential Method.* New York: Guilford Publications, Inc.

Gendlin, E. T. (1997a). *Experiencing and the Creation of Meaning, A Philosophical and Psychological Approach to the Subjective.* Evanston, Illinois: Northwestern University Press.

Gendlin, E. T. (1997b). *A Process Model.* New York: The Focusing Institute. From http://www.focusing.org/gendlin/docs/gol_2161.html Retrieved: 8 March 2009.

Gendlin, E. T. (1999). *A Philosophical Car for Focusers, 1999 Model.* New York: The Focusing Institute, http://www.focusing.org/gendlin/docs/gol_2186.html, retrieved 20 May 2017.

Gendlin, E. T. (2000). Introduction to 'Thinking At The Edge'. *The Folio: A Journal for Focusing and Experiential Therapy,* 19(1), 1–8.

Gendlin, E. T. (2004). The new phenomenology of carrying forward. *Continental Philosophy Review,* 37(1), 127–151.

Gendlin, E. T. (2016). A changed ground for precise cognition. In D. Schoeller & V. Saller (Eds.), *Thinking Thinking. Practicing Radical Reflection* (pp. 50–91). Freiburg/München: Verlag Karl Alber.

Huxley, L. A. (2000). *This Timeless Moment: A Personal View of Aldous Huxley*. Berkeley: Celestial Arts.

Kepes, G. (1956). *The New Landscape in Art and Science*. Chicago: Paul Theobald.

Lem, S. (2003). *Solaris*. London: Penguin. Originally published in 1961.

Levin, D. M. (1997). Gendlin's use of language: Historical connections, contemporary implications. In D. M. Levin (Ed.), *Language beyond Postmodernism. Saying and Thinking in Gendlin's Philosophy* (pp. 42–64). Evanston, Illinois: Northwestern University Press.

NoboJ. L. (2003). Whitehead and the quantum experience. In T. E. Eastman; H. Keeton (Eds.), *Physics and Whitehead: Quantum, Process, and Experience* (pp. 223–257). New York: State University of New York.

Purton, C. (2004). *Person-centred Therapy. The Focusing-oriented Approach*. London: Palgrave.

Purton, C. (2014a). The myth of the bodily felt sense. In G. Madison (Ed.), *The Theory and Practice of Focusing-Oriented Psychotherapy* (pp. 221–233). London: Jessica Kingsley.

Purton, C. (2014b). *The Trouble with Psychotherapy. Counselling and Common Sense*. London: Palgrave.

Read, E. H. (1959). *A Concise History of Modern Painting*. New York: Frederick A. Praeger.

Rogers, C. R. (1959). A theory of therapy, personality and interpersonal relationships, as developed in the client-centered framework. In S. Koch (ed.) *Psychology: A Study of a Science, 3. Formulations of the Person and the Social Context* (pp. 184–256). New York: McGraw-Hill.

11

EXPERIENTIAL–EXISTENTIAL PSYCHOTHERAPY

Deepening existence, engaging with life

Siebrecht Vanhooren

Introduction

> Therapy is of the essence of life, and is to be so understood.
>
> *(Rogers, 1951, p. x)*

With this introductory sentence in his book *Client-centred therapy*, Carl Rogers expresses his fascination for the unique life process of the client. He shares this view with other existential and humanistic pioneers such as Rollo May (1983). From May's point of view, at the heart of therapy lies his concern and care for the client's *being*. Clients do not only bring their problem but their whole existence into the consultation room. Therapy is about helping clients to experience their existence in a more profound way and to become oriented toward the fulfillment of their existence (May, 1983).

From his early work on, Rogers (1942) emphasizes how therapy can help clients regain their freedom to make authentic choices, find new ways to relate to others, and discover new directions in life. Therapy is originally characterized by the absence of techniques that would reduce the self-directive power of the client and by a well-defined therapeutic presence which expresses a sacred and empowering respect for the client's process (Rogers, 1942, 1951, 1980).

Rogers' introductory sentence also expresses his concern about the downside of theorizing the client's and therapist's experiences. Instead of supporting the uniqueness of every therapeutic encounter, theory could become a narrowing framework. Paradoxically, even a person-centered theory could serve as a constricting mindset which could prevent the therapist from meeting the client at the fullest. Gendlin (1990) expresses the same concern when he notices that *focusing* – the experiential method he developed in order to deeply connect with the client's existence – is sometimes used as a technique. In those cases, focusing does not support the life process of the client; it is used as a way to *do* something when meeting the client seems too challenging for the therapist. "The essence of working with another person is to be present as a living being," Gendlin (1990, p. 205) states. "Do not let focusing, or reflecting, or anything else get in between ... You can have at least as much courage as the client has" (Gendlin, 1990, p. 206).

The courage to be with the client's existence – and with one's own existence at the same time – might be an even bigger challenge for contemporary therapists compared to therapists in the past. First, due to the *zeitgeist*, therapists are encouraged to work in a more solution-oriented way. As they become specialists in micro-tasking and in the treatment of very specific client problems, the majority of therapists express that they don't feel equipped to meet the existential layer of the client's problems such as meaning in life (Hill, 2016). Although micro-level process-outcome research might have been successful when it comes to achieving contemporary evidence-based requirements for therapy (Angus et al., 2014), this might have been at the expense of the loss of the art of *not-knowing* and the capacity to fully resonate with the process of the client (Bazzano, 2016; Ikemi, 2017; Vanhooren, 2014). Although knowledge about micro-processes, markers, and tasks doesn't necessarily mean that therapists would not be able to resonate with the client's being, a framework that connects this contemporary micro-knowledge with a theory of *being* does not exist at the moment. As a result, therapists often feel lost when they discover that their clients actually bring their whole existence into the therapy room.

Second, contemporary western society is facing unseen challenges such as mass migration, an increasing older population, climate change, etc. Existential themes such as death, sickness, limitations, isolation, responsibility, and meaninglessness are all around. It is not a coincidence that the World Health Organization expects depression to be the most common threat to well-being and health in 2030 (Lépine & Briley, 2011). Not only will existential themes be increasingly present in private practices, a growing group of therapists is already working in specific settings such as refugee camps, oncology hospitals, palliative care, and so forth, where existential themes are paramount. However, patients are largely dissatisfied with the attention given to their existential struggles (Dezutter et al., 2017). At the same time, satisfaction with the attention given by practitioners to the existential domain – compared to attention given to the physical, psychological, and social domain – is the strongest predictor of life satisfaction, less depressive symptoms, and lower pain in chronic pain patients (Dezutter et al., 2017). As therapists are facing problems which can't be *solved*, medical and solution-focused therapy models might lose their efficacy.

For these reasons, there is a high need for a theory and practice that can deal with these challenges. Although returning to the source – and learning from Otto Rank, Carl Rogers, Rollo May, Eugene Gendlin, and many others – is absolutely meaningful and inspiring, we also want to remember the lessons learned in the years since. Therefore, the real challenge is to integrate the micro-process research – which has largely been conducted by focusing-oriented and emotion-focused scholars – into a theory that would support our actual being-with-ourselves-and-our-clients. From my point of view, the *experiential–existential approach* could serve as such a framework. In its core, this approach is strongly based on Gendlin's philosophical tenets, is influenced by other existential writers and models (such as Buber, Tillich, May, Yalom, Frankl, van Deurzen), and is person-centered and experiential in its therapeutic format (Madison, 2010, 2014a, 2014b). Instead of having intellectual talks with clients about their existence, experiential-existential therapy helps to be with the bodily-felt existence of the client (and therapist) in the here-and-now. Being both existential and experiential, this approach might pave the way for a deeper integration of the best of both therapeutic approaches.

In this chapter, I will introduce experiential-existential psychotherapy as an emerging framework, delineate how micro-processes could be understood from an existential point of view, and finally make suggestions for future research and practice.

Experiential–existential psychotherapy

Experiential-existential psychotherapy has emerged from the experience that the integration of an existential understanding of the client's concerns within a focusing-oriented framework (and vice versa) can help facilitating, deepening, and broadening therapeutic change (Madison, 2010, 2014a; Leijssen, 2014, 2016; Vanhooren et al., 2015). In our experience as therapy trainers, the aforementioned authors found that discovering the existential roots of experiential therapies helps us to be more present with our clients. Experiential psychotherapists who took an in-depth course on existential therapy[1] repeatedly shared how this training helped them to be more present. Moreover, the existential approach – infusing a certain amount of darkness into their humanistic optimism – helped them to be more grounded and to feel more confident to engage with the existential challenges of the client. They experienced a heightened awareness for existential themes and felt freer to explore, re-experience, and communicate their empathy. This is remarkable, considering that most of these students had been practicing person-centered, focusing-oriented, Gestalt, or emotion-focused therapy for a number of years. Existential understanding seems to facilitate a different type of therapeutic presence and it even fosters the experiential work itself. When the existential reality comes into the experiential picture, focusing becomes accessing existence again. One might ask how an existential understanding could broaden and deepen the work of experienced experiential and process-experiential psychotherapists. There are different answers to these questions.

Facing one's own existential challenges

A first answer might be found in the fact that facing one's own existential challenges helps the therapist to connect with the client in a deeper way. Existential training courses in Flanders (Belgium)[2] have been based on experiential learning right from the start. Students are not only asked to learn about existential psychology but also to scrutinize their own existential realms. In a way, working through one's own existential issues broadens one's capacity to be with the ultimate concerns of the client (Leijssen, 2013). By not having to avoid themes such as finitude, isolation, freedom, guilt, responsibility, and meaninglessness, therapists experience themselves more open to pick up the existential layers of the client's presence. They have a broader vocabulary that helps them meet the client at this level. They are more able to be with darkness on the one hand and to see the light through the cracks on the other hand.

As Madison (2014b) argues, infusing darkness into the optimistic bias of humanistic and experiential therapies helps the therapist being with whatever comes. This "being with what is really there" and the capacity to resonate with the inescapability of certain existential givens, is the main road to what Otto Rank calls change (Kramer, 1995). Change within the proto experiential-existential framework of Otto Rank is not about altering these existential tensions, but rather about changing how one lives with and within these givens (Kramer, 1995). Tillich (1952/2000) would say that change means finding the courage to be while facing not-being, and by creating new meaning which embraces meaninglessness. Likewise, the majority of these students discovered a new courage to be with their existential challenges. Not only did this courage enlarge their capacity to contain their clients' existential concerns; the therapeutic relationship was also transformed in an important way. Therapists experienced themselves more as fellow companions and were more at ease with the fact that they didn't have all the answers.

This increased capacity to be with the client's existential concerns and to search together for meaning is beneficial in different clinical settings. Not only for therapists who work in private practice, but also for therapists who work on oncology, chronic pain, and palliative services in hospitals who feel inspired by this experiential-existential approach. At the moment, new experiential-existential group programs are being launched and studied in hospital settings.

The existential roots of experiential therapies

A second set of answers might lie in the fact that experiential therapies such as focusing-oriented therapy have strong existential roots. Reconnecting to these roots might help therapists to understand their own practice in a more profound way. At the same time, as we noticed in our postgraduate person-centered therapy training (KU Leuven), it helps new students understand that therapeutic interventions are there to support the life process of the client as well as their own being. For example, Gendlin's focusing-oriented therapy has profound existential-phenomenological grounds (Ikemi, 2014). Gendlin (1966, 1973), being both a philosopher and a psychotherapist, reconnected abstract existential philosophical concepts to the here-and-now experience, or to what Bugental (1999) calls *the living moment*. Inspired by the existential and phenomenological philosophies of Heidegger, Merleau-Ponty, and Sartre, Gendlin (1966, 1973, 1990) understands human existence as *Dasein* (being-in-the-world). For Gendlin, to be human means that we are primarily and constantly in interaction. Moreover, we are our interaction *and* situation. What we sense when we are practicing psychotherapy is our being-ourselves-with-our-client, and the client's existence at that very moment is being-with-her-with-the-therapist. In this way, this being-together already means a first element of change (both for the client and the therapist).

Gendlin (1973, 1978) proposes a direct way to access this being-in-the-world or existence which he calls *focusing*. Existence is primarily bodily felt and our felt sense is the result of our bodily-environment interaction (or being-in-the-world here and now, or existence). Attending to our bodily senses in the here-and-now-moment reveals the implicit meaning of our actual life situation (Gendlin, 1962/1997). Our implicit and often unattended existential needs become explicit by symbolizing (or giving meaning to) our felt sense. At the same time, we are in touch with our situational or larger direction in life. Remarkably, attending to our existence in this direct way carries our existence further: our life process moves in a more *authentic* way (Gendlin, 1973). We are becoming our own *truth* (Madison, 2014b).

It is not a coincidence that Gendlin's focusing has been adopted within the *existential-humanistic approach* (Hoffman, 2009; Schneider & Krug, 2010). For existential therapists without experiential background, using focusing brings the existential concepts to life (Madison, 2014a). Existential concerns are not merely talked about but can be directly experienced. Klagsbrun (2014) gives examples of how focusing helps sick and dying clients meet their existential challenges. Moreover, as Missiaen (2016) suggests, approaching the existential challenges in an experiential way can help clients contain their challenges. By helping clients to connect to their bodily felt senses and to search for a bodily-located safe place, an experiential haven can be created from where clients can explore anxiety-provoking themes. Whatever comes, the client can always return to his or her bodily existence.

The level of access a person has to his or her bodily-felt existence has also been called one's *openness to experience*. Rogers and Gendlin developed an experiencing scale which was later further elaborated by Mathieu-Coughlan and Klein (1988). Research based on these experiencing scales and other instruments has been very clear about the significance of deepening the client's experience in terms of therapy outcome (Cain, 2016; Angus et al., 2014). The therapist's own level of experiencing would be essential for deepening the client's experiential awareness (Sachse and Elliott, 2002).

However, deepening the level of experience of the client is not just about deepening the experience as such. It is about opening to one's bodily felt being-in-the-world. Interestingly, understanding anew the existential corner-stones of Gendlin's theory sheds a totally different light on the research findings concerning the level of experiencing. If it is not merely about the level of experiencing but about one's being-in-the-world, then how can we understand micro-processes?

Micro, meso, and macro searching

Micro-processes can be understood as tiny steps or moments in the larger process of psychotherapy. Where Rogers (1961) was primarily studying the therapeutic process as a whole, Gendlin (1978) and later Greenberg, Rice and Elliott (1993) took a more microscopic look at processes which influenced the larger process in a significant way. This endeavor gave birth to what today is called focusing-oriented therapy (Gendlin, 1996) and emotion-focused therapy (EFT) (Elliott et al., 2004). The theoretical framework of emotion-focused therapy is completely different from Gendlin's existential-phenomenological philosophical approach. EFT combines dialectical constructivism with contemporary cognitive science and emotion theories (Greenberg et al., 1993). The micro-unit is not *Dasein* as in Gendlin's theory but the *cognitive-affective scheme*. It is through this lens that processes are understood and interpreted in EFT.

Thanks to this research, the person-centered approach is recognized as an evidence-based treatment in certain countries for categories such as depression and others (Angus et al., 2014; Greenberg & Watson, 2006). However, from an experiential-existential point of view, using the EFT framework and language to explain these processes results in leaving the existential layer unexplored or *implicit*. A good example of this unattended existential layer is the way *meaning* is discussed in EFT.

Meaning

In EFT, meaning is understood as a dialectical constructivist process (Angus & Greenberg, 2011; Elliott et al., 2004; Greenberg et al., 1993; Greenberg & Pascual-Leone, 2001). Inspired by focusing – but without adopting the underlying existential-phenomenological theory – EFT considers the creation of meaning to be a bottom-up process induced by attending to the felt sense combined with the process of symbolization (Greenberg & Pascual-Leone, 2001) or narrating/contextualizing unclear emotions (Angus & Greenberg, 2011). This creation of meaning would influence higher-order affective-cognitive schemes such as the self-image, identity, worldview, life narrative, etc. Angus & Greenberg (2011) extracted from case study research an interesting list of meaning problem markers and meaning-making markers. Surprisingly, in their study on meaning, existential meaning (Vos, 2015) and spiritual meaning (Leijssen, 2014) are not included. Likewise, the possibilities of meaninglessness (not as a problem but as a possible reality) or *groundlessness* (Yalom, 1980) are not considered.

In a way, one could say that meaning as understood in EFT includes meaning as a result of a *micro* search for meaning (e.g. "What does this felt sense mean?"; meaning of specific feeling, behavior, situation) and a *meso* (identity) search for meaning (e.g. "Who am I?"; self-image, self-narrative, worldview). However, EFT does not attend to *macro* searching in an explicit way (e.g. "why am I?"; existential meaning and mattering, spiritual meaning). Contrary, existential frameworks often do not attend to micro searching. For example, meaning-centered therapies (e.g. Breitbart & Poppito, 2014) put a lot of effort into meso (identity) and macro searching (sources of existential meaning), but don't include micro searching as part of their therapy program.

From an experiential-existential point of view, all three levels of searching contribute to a fuller and deeper experience of meaning. Depending on the needs of the client, more time might have to be spent on a micro, meso, or macro searching level. For example, micro searching will be an important step for clients who are overwhelmed by their emotions or who have a hard time contacting their feelings or felt sense (Leijssen, 2007). Without having the ability to find meaning on this micro-level, a search for meaning on a macro-level (what's the meaning of my life) might be a fruitless endeavor.

However, all levels of searching come together in one moment, for example during a focusing session. Leijssen (2007) explains how focusing on a bodily felt sense can open the door for the transcendent. In the same way, all levels of searching seem to crystallize in moments of what Mearns and Cooper (2005) call *relational depth*. Since meaning is basically about connecting, a search for meaning at each level might evoke a change in one's Dasein or being-in-the-world.

From I-Me and I-it to an I-I and I-Thou relationship

An important part of EFT's micro-work is about evoking an experiential access to specific "cognitive-affective schemes" such as the inner critic (Elliott et al., 2004). Based on Gendlin's philosophy, we know that experiencing is about having deeper access to one's existence. EFT-tasks such as empty chair work and chair dialogues can be understood as ways of helping clients reconfigure their inner relationships, or their being-with-one's-self, or their *Eigenwelt*. Inspired by Buber (1923/2003), Cooper (2015) describes how clients often feel alienated from their inner existence. Instead of truly meeting their inner existence, people often treat their inner life in an object-like way. Cooper calls this distancing relationship to one's self an I-Me relationship, whereas having an authentic and open relationship to one's self is called an I-I relationship. These kinds of inner I-Me relationships have serious implications for the way people connect with others (Gunst and Vanhooren, in press; Vanhooren et al., 2017). At the core lies an existential alienation from their inner experience (I-Me) and from the others (in Buber's terms I-it) at the same time. They have lost touch with their own existence. May (1983) states that clients sometimes give up their existence in order to survive. Or in other terms, they accept "nonbeing in order that some little being may be preserved" (May, 1983, p. 27).

Just like in focusing, EFT micro-tasks such as chair dialogues could be understood as an active way to help clients to move from an I-Me to more of an I-I relationship. When it works, the shift in their being-with-one-self is accompanied by a search for meaning on a micro-level ("How can I understand what just happened during this experience?") often followed by meso searching ("How does this fit into my life story?"), and – in our experience – also followed by macro searching ("What does this mean on a spiritual level?").

Gendlin's (1973) *interaction first* principle helps us understand that a more I-I relationship is often transferred into a more authentic relationship with the therapist and with others (an I-Thou relationship in Buber's terms) and the other way around: our experience of the other and of ourselves is part of the same interactional reality. Gendlin's idea about experiencing as having access to one's existence also helps us understand thatdeeper I-I and I-Thou relationships are accompanied by experiencing deeper levels of meaning in life. For Gendlin (1973), accessing one's existence, becoming more deeply related to one's self through the help of a deeply related other, discovering meaning, and finding direction in life all come together.

One could question whether a change of framework from a scheme-based thinking toward a being-in-the-world thinking would really make any difference. From an experiential-existential point of view, the answer is yes. By using a different theory in order to understand the micro-processes, therapists and researchers might notice different aspects of the same micro-processes. On a therapeutic level, knowing about macro searching might help the therapist be aware of and actively attend to the existential consequences of micro shifts. For researchers, being aware of the existential layer might help identify and name these aspects while studying process-outcome research. For example, an often used qualitative measure called Helpful Aspects of Therapy (HAT) (Llewelyn, 1988) doesn't contain any category that refers to existential searching or meaning: some categories are about gaining insight but don't distinguish between our described levels of meaning. As a result, the existential aspects cannot be scored and remain unnoticed. Being unnoticed, these existential aspects are not included in newer theories. Considering the fact that therapists may face an increasing amount of existential issues, and that these same therapists feel rather unequipped to meet these existential concerns (Hill, 2016), a huge challenge is waiting for the whole psychotherapy and counseling community.

The therapist is fully implied

One way to respond to this challenge is to revisit the therapeutic process with fresh eyes and ears. Reclaiming the existential and experiential sources of humanistic psychotherapies – which can be traced back to Otto Rank (Kramer, 1995) – can help us understand anew what therapy is all about. This is not only helpful for the individual practitioner but also for the researcher. Re-evaluating measures on their compatibility with the existential foundations might help bring the existential layer of the therapeutic process back into the picture.

In order for therapists to be more equipped to face the existential challenges of their clients, micro, meso, and macro levels of searching and existential functioning have to be studied. Research on micro searching and the shift from an I-Me to an I-I relationship could possibly reveal new aspects. Likewise, meso and macro searching need to be implied in both research and practice. From a process-researcher's point of view, a lot is unknown about these latter levels. For example, we might know how focusing works, but we know less about what exactly happens after we have completed a focusing cycle.

However, knowing more about these different levels of existential searching will not be sufficient. As the therapist is a fundamental part of the client's being-in-the-world – at least when she or he is in the therapy office – the therapist's avoidance in meeting his or her own existential challenges might prevent change in the client (Gendlin, 1973; May, 1983). Therefore, therapists should not only be trained in how to deal with micro-processes but should also develop an enduring encounter with their own existential layers. It is not the therapist's *knowledge* but his/her *level of experiencing* – the ability to access one's own existence in the here and now – which helps the client contact the existential layer (Ikemi, 2014).

According to Gendlin's (1973) interaction first principle, it is not only the therapist who is part of the client's being-in-the-world, but the client too is part of the therapist's existence during therapy. This explains why experiences of relational depth touch the therapist in his or her deepest core (Mearns & Cooper, 2005). Likewise, the problems of the client often feel particularly palpable in the therapeutic relationship and can leave a deep trace in the therapist's existence. *Alliance ruptures* (Safran & Muran, 2000) between client and therapist are experientially noticeable in the therapist and dealing with these ruptures is not only for the sake of the client. As the therapist is also the subject of change in a therapeutic encounter (Gendlin, 1973; May, 1983), existential support and spiritual nourishment might not be a luxury. Existential scholars such as Leijssen (2013), Schneider (2013, 2017), Hoffman (Hoffman et al., 2009), and Yang (2017) have picked up on this need and provide inspiring frameworks for therapists.

Concluding thoughts

After developing his theory and noticing the similarities with existential writings, Rogers (1980, p. 39) realized that his approach was a sort of a "home-grown brand of existential philosophy." Although many have discussed whether or not person-centered therapy could be identified as an existential approach (e.g. Stumm, 2005; Cooper, 2012), Rogers deepens his "therapy is of the essence of life" in his last book. While contemporary therapists experience the scattering of the person-centered approach in different tribes and styles (Sanders, 2012) the existential background of person-centered theories could serve as a compass to navigate different person-centered and existential methods. In the spirit of Rogers, May, and Gendlin, therapy is about *being with existence*. Using this benchmark, the therapist does not have to solve the existential challenges of the client. Instead, therapy becomes – for the client as well as for the therapist – a vehicle to engage with life and its challenges in a fuller and more authentic way. A therapeutic framework that adopts this point of view sheds a different light on how we can understand change in therapy. Even on a micro-level, change is not so much about solving but about fully meeting every fiber of the client and giving every aspect its right to exist and speak. It is through the meeting of the therapist and the client, and the meeting of the client and his or herself, that one's inner and outer relationships will shift (Leijssen, 2007). Every meeting has the capacity to bring forth new meaning. On an intrapersonal level, meeting one's bodily felt existence helps to make implicit felt meanings explicit (Gendlin, 1962/1997). On an inter- and meta-personal level, meeting the other person or life itself at the fullest can change one's own being and meaning in life (Buber, 1923/2003). Therapists can only meet their clients if they are willing to meet themselves and are willing to be touched by what happens during therapy. *Being* with the client is essentially also being with one's self. As a result, therapy is not only an adventure for the client but for the therapist as well.

Notes

1 These students took the course "Specialisatiejaar Existentiële Psychotherapy" at Focus on Emotion (Belgium).
2 There are three existential training courses in Flanders (Belgium): "Specialisatie Existentiële psychotherapie" (Focus on Emotion and KU Leuven), Existentieel Welzijn (KU Leuven), and the Edx Massive Open Online Course Existential Well-Being: A person-centred and experiential approach (KU Leuven).

References

Angus, L. E., & Greenberg, L. S. (2011). *Working with narrative in emotion-focused therapy: Changing stories, healing lives*. Washington, DC: American Psychological Association.

Angus, L. E., Watson, J. C., Elliott, R., Schneider, K., & Timulak, L. (2014). Humanistic psychotherapy research 1990–2015: From methodological innovation to evidence-supported treatment outcomes and beyond. *Psychotherapy Research*, Advance online publication. doi:10.1080/10503307.2014.989290.

Breitbart, W. S., & Poppito, S. R. (2014). *Meaning-centered group psychotherapy for patients with advanced cancer*. New York, NY: Oxford University Press.

Buber, M. (1923/2003). *Ik en Jij*. Utrecht, the Netherlands: Bijleveld.

Bugental, J. F. T. (1999). *Psychotherapy isn't what you think*. Phoenix, AZ: Zeig, Tucker.

Cain, D. J. (2016). Toward a research-based integration of optimal practices of humanistic psychotherapies. In D. J. Cain, K. Keenan, and S. Rubin (Eds.), *Humanistic psychotherapies: Handbook of research and practice, second edition* (pp. 485–535). Washington, DC: American Psychological Association.

Cooper, M. (2012). Existentially informed person-centred therapy. In P. Sanders (Ed.), *The tribes of the person-centred nation*, Second edition (pp. 131–160). Ross-on-Wye, GB: PCCS Books.

Cooper, M. (2015). *Existential psychotherapy and counseling: Contributions to a pluralistic practice*. London, UK: Sage publications.

Dezutter, J., Offenbaecher, M., Vallejo, M. A., Vanhooren, S., Thauvoye, E., & Toussaint, L. (2017). Chronic pain care: The importance of a biopsychosocial-existential approach. *The International Journal of Psychiatry in Medicine*, Advance online publication, 1–13. doi:10.1177/0091217417696738.

Elliott, R., Watson, J. C., Goldman, R. N., & Greenberg, L. S. (2004). *Learning emotion-focused therapy: The process-experiential approach to change*. Washington, DC: American Psychological Association.

Gendlin, E. T. (1962/1997). *Experiencing and the creation of meaning: A philosophical and psychological approach of the subjective*. Evanston, IL: Northwestern University Press.

Gendlin, E. T. (1966). Existentialism and experiential psychology. In C. Moustakas (Ed.) *Existential child therapy* (pp. 70–94). New York, NY: Basic Books.

Gendlin, E. T. (1973). Experiential psychotherapy. In R. Corsini (Ed.), *Current psychotherapies* (pp. 317–352). Itasca, IL: Peacock.

Gendlin, E. T. (1978). *Focusing*. New York, NY: Everest House Publishers.

Gendlin, E. T. (1990). The small steps of the therapy process: How they come and how they help them come. In G. Lietaer, J. Rombouts, & R. Van Balen (Eds.), *Client-centered and experiential psychotherapy in the nineties*. Leuven: Leuven University Press.

Gendlin, E. T. (1996). *Focusing-oriented psychotherapy*. New York, NY: The Guilford press.

Greenberg, L. S., & Pascual-Leone, J. (2001). A dialectical constructivist view of the creation of personal meaning. *Journal of Constructivist Psychology*, 14, 165–186. doi:10.1080/10720530125970.

Greenberg, L. S., Rice, L. N., & Elliott, R. (1993). *Facilitating emotional change: The moment-by-moment process*. New York, NY: The Guilford Press.

Greenberg, L. S., & Watson, J. C. (2006). *Emotion-focused therapy for depression*. Washington, DC: American Psychological Association.

Gunst, E., & Vanhooren, S. (In press). The destructive pattern: An experiential and existential theory-building case study. *Person-centered & Experiential Psychotherapies*.

Hill, C. E. (2016). Therapists' perspectives about working with meaning in life in psychotherapy: A survey. *Counselling Psychology Quarterly*. Advance online publication, 1–19. doi:10.1080/09515070.2016.1173014.

Hoffman, L. (2009). Introduction to existential psychology in a cross-cultural context: An East-West dialogue. In L. Hoffman, M. Yang, F. J. Kaklauskas, & A. Chan (Eds.), *Existential psychology East-West* (pp. 1–67). Colorado Springs: University of the Rockies Press.

Hoffman, L., Yang, M., Kaklauskas, F., & Chan, A. (2009). *Existential psychology East-West*. Colorado Springs, CO: University of the Rockies Press.

Ikemi, A. (2014). A theory of focusing-oriented psychotherapy. In G. Madison (Ed.), *Theory and practice of focusing-oriented psychotherapy: Beyond the talking cure* (pp. 22–35). London, UK: Jessica Kingsley Publishers.

Ikemi, A. (2017). The radical impact of experiencing on psychotherapy theory: An examination of two kinds of crossing. *Person-centered & Experiential Psychotherapies*, Advance online publication. doi:10.1080/14779757.2017.12323668.

Klagsbrun, J. (2014). The body knows the way: Working with clients facing illness and death. In G. Madison (Ed.), *Emerging practice in focusing-oriented psychotherapy: Innovative theory and applications* (pp. 154–165). London, GB: Jessica Kingsley Publishers.

Kramer, R. (1995). The birth of client-centered therapy: Carl Rogers, Otto Rank, and "the beyond". *Journal of Humanistic Psychology*, 35, 54–110.

Leijssen, M. (2007). Making space for the inner guide. *American Journal of Psychotherapy*, 61, 255–270.

Leijssen, M. (2013). *Leven vanuit liefde: Een pad naar existentieel welzijn*. Tielt: Lannoo.

Leijssen, M. (2014). Existential well-being counselling. In G. Madison (Ed.), *Emerging practice in focusing-oriented psychotherapy: Innovative theory and applications* (pp. 138–153). London: Jessica Kingsley Publishers.

Leijssen, M. (2016). Massive Open Online Course Existential well-being counseling: A person-centered experiential approach. https://www.edx.org/course/existential-well-being-counseling-person-kuleuvenx-ewbcx

Lépine, J.-P., & Briley, M. (2011). The increasing burden of depression. *Neuropsychiatric Disease and Treatment*, 7, 3–7. doi:10.2147/NDT.S19617.

Llewelyn, S. P. (1988). Psychological therapy as viewed by clients and therapists. *British Journal of Clinical Psychology*, 27, 223–237.

Madison, G. (2010). Focusing on existence: Five facets of an experiential-existential model. *Person-Centered & Experiential Psychotherapies*, 9, 189–204.

Madison, G. (2014a). The palpable in existential counselling psychology. *Counselling Psychology Review*, 29, 25–33.

Madison, G. (2014b). Exhilarating pessimism: Focusing-oriented existential therapy. In G. Madison (Ed.), *Theory and practice of focusing-oriented psychotherapy: Beyond the talking cure* (pp. 113–127). London, UK: Jessica Kingsley Publishers.

Mathieu-Coughlan, P., & Klein, M. H. (1988). Experiëntiële psychotherapie: Beslissende gebeurtenissen in de interactie tussen cliënt en therapeut. *Psychotherapeutisch paspoort*, 2, 505–549.

May, R. (1983). *The discovery of being*. New York, NY: Norton & Company.

Mearns, D., & Cooper, M. (2005). *Working at relational depth in counselling and psychotherapy*. London: Sage Publications.

Missiaen, C. (2016). Existentiële demonen in de ogen kijken [Facing your existential demons]. *Tijdschrift Persoonsgerichte Experiëntiële Psychotherapie*, 54, 37–44.

Rogers, C. R. (1942). *Counseling and psychotherapy*. Boston: Houghton Mifflin Company.

Rogers, C. R. (1951). *Client-centered therapy*. London: Constable.

Rogers, C. R. (1961). *On becoming a person*. Boston: Houghton Mifflin Company.

Rogers, C. R. (1980). *A way of being*. Boston: Houghton Mifflin Company.

Safran, J. D., & Muran, J. C. (2000). *Negotiating the therapeutic alliance: A relational treatment guide*. New York, NY: The Guilford Press.

Sanders, P. (Ed.) (2012). *The tribes of the person-centred nation: An introduction to the schools of therapy related to the person-centred approach*, second edition. Ross-on-Wye, UK: PCCS Books.

Sachse, R., & Elliott, R. (2002). Process-outcome research on humanistic therapy variables. In D. J. Cain & J. Seeman (Ed.), *Humanistic psychotherapies: Handbook of research and practice* (pp. 83–116). Washington, DC: American Psychological Association.

Schneider, K. J. (2013). *The polarized mind: Why it's killing us and what we can do about it*. Colorado Springs, CO: University Professors Press.

Schneider, K. J. (2017). *The spirituality of awe: Challenges to the Robotic revolution*. Cardiff, CA: Waterfront Press.

Schneider, K. J., & Krug, O. T. (2010). *Existential-humanistic therapy*. Washington, DC: American Psychological Association.

Stumm, G. (2005). The person-centered approach from an existential perspective. *Person-centered & Experiential Psychotherapies*, 4, 106–123. doi:10.1080/14779757.2005.9688375.

Tillich, P. (1952/2000). *The courage to be*. New Haven: Yale University Press.

Vanhooren, S. (2014). De moed om niet te weten, het lef om niet te kunnen. *Tijdschrift Cliëntgerichte Psychotherapie*, 52, 100–115.

Vanhooren, S., Leijssen, M., & Dezutter, J. (2015). Posttraumatic growth during incarceration: A case study from an experiential-existential perspective. *Journal of Humanistic Psychology*, Advance online publication, 1–24. doi:10.1177/0022167815621647.

Vanhooren, S., Leijssen, M., & Dezutter, J. (2017). Ten prisoners on a search for meaning: A qualitative study of loss and growth during incarceration. *The Humanistic Psychologist*, 45, 162–178. doi:10.1037/hum0000055.

Vos, J. (2015). Meaning an existential givens in the lives of cancer patients : A philosophical perspective on psycho-oncology. *Palliative and Supportive Care*, 13, 885–900. doi:10.1017/S1478951514000790.

Yalom, I. (1980). *Existential psychotherapy*. New York: Basic Books.

Yang, M. C. (2017). *Existential psychology and the way of the Tao: Meditations on the writings of Zhuangzi*. New York, NY: Routledge.

PART III
Person-centred therapy and spirituality

12

FROM THE SCIENTIFIC TO THE MYSTICAL IN THE WORK OF CARL ROGERS

Michael Sivori

Introduction

> I have felt an increasing discomfort between the rigorous objectivity of myself as a scientist and the almost mystical subjectivity of myself as therapist.
> *(Rogers, 1961, p. 200)*

Carl Rogers was an 'accidental mystic'. Over a lifetime he produced a huge body of work on the science of the psychotherapeutic relationship. He was the first person in its history to receive both the APA's Scientific Contribution Award and latterly the Professional Contribution Award. The citation for this first award recognised his work in:

> developing an original method to objectify ... the analysis of the therapeutic process, for formulating a testable theory of psychotherapy and its effects on personality ... and for extensive systematic research to exhibit the value of the method and explore and test the implications of the theory ...'
> *(American Psychological Association, 1957, p. 125)*

Shortly before his death, in 1987 aged 85, he had also been nominated for the Nobel Prize for Peace, recognising his work with communities in conflict in Latin America and Northern Ireland amongst others. His scientific contribution to psychology, and to the inception and growth of Person-Centred Therapy (PCT), particularised the essential components of successful therapeutic personality re-structuring and for the first time demonstrated empirically that successful therapy is the outcome of the quality of relationship between therapist and client. In so doing, it challenged the notion that the psychotherapist was the agent of change and that their ability to diagnose and interpret was the key driver for this. Instead, Rogers demonstrated that all people have the capacity for self-interpretation and self-ordering and the function of the therapist was to facilitate this in a relational climate of genuineness, acceptance and empathic understanding.

Beginning in December 1940, and up until his major theoretical publications in the late 1950s, he had been among the first psychologists to harness the new technology of the day – magnetic recording discs, the precursor to tape – to actually record the encounters between therapist and client. Rogers' pre-eminent contribution to the science of psychotherapy was to quantify the essential elements of this climate, based on years of analysing '*in very minute detail*' the phrasings and sentences, even specific words, used by therapists where the client had benefited or had been impaired by the counsellor's intervention: 'I cannot exaggerate the excitement of our learnings as we clustered about the machine that enabled us to listen to ourselves, playing [the recordings] over and over ... We gained a great deal from that microscopic study' (Rogers, 1980, p. 138).

But what happens when a scientist, in the process of their work, seemingly stumbles upon mystical experience? What happens when phenomena are noticed for which there is no scientific vocabulary? Steeped in the experimental method, through Teachers' College, Columbia University, and Dewey's philosophical school of Pragmatism, Rogers began as a Freudian analyst in Rochester, NY in the 1930s but by 1940 had evolved. He would go on to pioneer the application of the experimental method to therapy, formulating rigorous, testable hypotheses and objective measures of personality change in psychotherapy (Rogers, 1961). He undertook major experimental studies that sought to confirm, or not, his theory. By the early 1960s his seminal volume *On Becoming a Person* (Rogers, 1961), written whilst Professor at the University of Wisconsin, consolidated his experimental work and summarised his major theoretical statements. But it also set out a vision of what he saw as a more human science – he wrote in the first person and at length about his own development, to underline his concurrent philosophical stance that sought to humanise psychology.

In a chapter titled 'Persons or science?' (Rogers, 1961) he wrote:

> I have become increasingly conscious of the gap between these two roles ... the better therapist I have become, the more I am aware of my complete subjectivity when I am at my best in this function. And as I have become a better investigator, more 'hard-headed' ... I have felt an increasing discomfort between the rigorous objectivity of myself as a scientist and the almost mystical subjectivity of myself as therapist.
>
> *(p. 200)*

In this chapter there is also a first, strong hint of mysticism; although Rogers did not profess any religious convictions.

He describes moments of intensely subjective encounters with clients where at:

> the deepest parts of therapy [there] seems to be a unity of experiencing ... When there is this complete unity, singleness, fullness of experiencing in the

relationship, ... a timeless living in the experience which is *between* the client and me.

(ibid., p. 202)

This was published in 1961, it would be some twenty years later before Rogers referred publicly to this type of experience again.

Why? Most likely because his work was so committed to testing and confirmation, or not, of his theories that he did not want to lessen the scientific standing of his work by discussing phenomena that sounded unscientific. In an interview posthumously published in 1987, Rogers once again referred to that experience of 'timelessness' and 'unity' in the therapeutic encounter from 1961. Now, this time it is less couched in philosophical terms and is explicitly mystical in its language:

[When] I am in a slightly altered state of consciousness in the relationship, then whatever I do seems full of healing. Then simply my presence is releasing and helpful. At those moments it seems that my inner spirit has reached out and touched the inner spirit of the other. *Our relationship transcends itself, and has become part of something larger.*

(Rogers, 1987, p. 148, my emphasis)

I want to focus in this chapter, on the parts of both statements that refer to the relationship, where the being of both therapist and client is sensed as a whole; the experience where separateness has given way to unity. I refer to the relationship itself, yet calling it a relationship is misleading since the individuals relating to each other, although physically present, have lost their relatedness; that is – their relating to each other through individual consciousness, has, instead been superseded by a 'communal consciousness'. The existential situation of the physical and psychological encounter *between* therapist and client has transcended itself, and experiences itself as a whole which is also part of a greater whole. The meeting of two people, or two individual minds, has broken through the soil, emerged into daylight and flowered into a more profound sense of communal being.

But how can that be? How can two people sitting there, transcend and become a part of 'something larger'? And what is this larger thing that they have become a part of?

Here lies the reason perhaps why Rogers did not discuss this or subject it to the experimental method: there is nothing quantifiable here; as consciousness cannot as such be measured objectively. By what criterion may we measure 'a unity of experiencing'?

The accidental mystic

Rogers might be reasonably described as an 'accidental mystic' since he had not set out to prove the existence of the phenomena of 'unity'. He had in fact stumbled across it in the course of his work, and as such, ever the pragmatist, he had given it due regard – valuing its therapeutic benefit – but limited his discussion of it.

An analogy here could be that the therapeutic situation is a glass of tea, and the individual consciousness of the therapist and client are each a sugar cube. When the sugar cubes are immersed in the glass of tea and interact, they dissolve, to enhance the sweetness of the tea. If the analogy works, then it highlights the absence of a credible scientific language to discuss these aspects of human experience.

What Rogers' work tells us is that this type of unity is achieved, in part, through simultaneously immersing oneself wholeheartedly into the 'here and now' of relationship, while at the same time, stepping out of one's need to have anything happen in that relationship. An intimate letting-go with the faith that this is therapeutically valuable; it requires courage and sincerity in the therapist.

It begins with the quality of attentiveness and sensitivity to the other and from subjective immersion into the subjective world of the other that points the way to unity:

> When I can really hear someone … it enriches my life (and) there is (a) peculiar satisfaction in really hearing someone: it is like listening to the music of the spheres because beyond the immediate message of the person, no matter what that might be, there is the universal. Hidden in all psychological communications which I really hear there seem to be orderly psychological laws, *aspects of the same order we find in the universe as a whole.*
>
> (Rogers, 1980, p. 8, my emphasis)

A tantalising allusion by Rogers that falls short of explaining what that order might be, or perhaps, it is a knowing that is beyond words and their meanings.

Perhaps in Sufi terms we can consider that Rogers is describing a fleeting movement between the particular intellect and the universal intellect. In comparing Sufism with psychoanalysis, Dr Javad Nurbakhsh describes the particular intellect, which is our personal intellect, as the gatekeeper of the ego. It is able to learn but is incapable of knowing the Truth. Whereas the universal intellect is 'heart-consciousness'; a state of consciousness that a person arrives at through concerted effort on the Path including: devotion to the Master, letting go of attachments, service to creation, maintaining a cheerful countenance in the face of hardship and trial, lightening the hearts of others, and constant remembrance of God. 'When the heart becomes cleansed of the rust of multiplicity, it will reflect the Truth as it is … And the source of … knowledge or insight … is called the universal intellect or "heart-consciousness"' (Nurbakhsh, 1990, p. 6).

The traditional model of psychoanalysis is that in order to get to 'the light' one must delve into the dark recesses of the subconscious first. However, this could be criticised as a western reductionist approach. Writers from spiritual traditions have pointed out that one cannot go into the dark (of the subconscious) unless one has the light of a higher consciousness or 'superconscious'. In his biography of Sri Aurobindo, Satprem writes:

> You must know the whole before you can know the part and the highest before you can truly understand the lowest … Psychoanalysts … look from

down up and explain the higher lights by the lower obscurities; but ... the [superconscious], not the [subconscious], is the true foundation of things. The significance of the lotus is not to be found by analysing the secrets of the mud from which it grows.

(Satprem, 1993, p. 206)

So Rogers is describing in his terms a moment whereby he is operating in the realm of the superconscious or which in Sufism is called 'seeing with the eye of the heart' (Nurbakhsh, 1990, p. 5). That is, perceiving existence as it truly is, in its wholeness – from the top down.

The mystical moment and Rogers

I believe that what Rogers could not and would not articulate, because he had no empirical base, was that the reciprocal intensity of a deeply immersed subjective relationship lifts the energy of the interpersonal field to such a degree that perception with the eye of the heart is possible for a moment.

I choose the word *moment* carefully, not just as a temporal measure but in fact to allude to its quality of timelessness; something reported by most therapists participating in Geller and Greenberg's qualitative study (Geller & Greenberg, 2011).

This sense of 'timelessness' leads again to terms in the spiritual lexicon. For example, in volume 8 of the *Farhang-e Nurbakhsh (Sufi Symbolism)*, Dr Nurbakhsh provides the definitions by past Sufi Masters of the term 'moment', writing that 'moment' or 'waqt' 'describes "time present" when the entry of a Divine infusion ... or the stimulus of Divine attraction in the Sufi's heart so preoccupies one that one loses all sense of past or future' (Nurbakhsh, 1994, p. 105).

Shah Nimatullah Wali in the same volume on this subject is cited thus:

> Be present in your (moment) ... Let past and future go, do not lose your (moment), for consciousness of the past spoils the present moment and thinking of the future causes it to pass. Hence it has been said that the Sufi is the 'child of the moment'.
>
> *(ibid.)*

The experience of timelessness occurs in many situations – at an exciting sports event, or at a music gig. A band walk onstage – they are feeling good tonight, they begin their performance, it reaches their audience and lifts their spirits; in turn the people in the audience respond enthusiastically and this enhances the band, which in turn lifts the audience higher, and so on. The dynamic field of potentiality exists and is present in all interpersonal interactions. Surely I am amongst many of you who have witnessed that phenomenon in music: from the grand orchestral concert halls to Traditional Irish folk sessions in tiny pubs: the symbiotic enhancement of the communal experience where, with music as a vehicle, the veil between performer and audience is dissolved. Where, the day after, you feel somehow enhanced by the experience of having been a part of that event.

This dynamic energetic field exists between therapist and client, lover and beloved, master and disciple and the focused immersion into it heightens the subjectivity to such a degree that separateness is felt to be passing away, and a new wondrous plain of consciousness is experienced. Imagine the therapeutic possibilities if this could be predicted. And this is the challenge for those who want to seriously extend Rogers' work. How do you make a scientific case for this?

What best to give to the interpersonal field to raise the energy dynamic to such a degree that the field unifies the consciousness of individuals within it?

I'm sure many therapists would immediately tell me that 'mindfulness' does that. But I'm not so sure. Yes, it might, or it might be other qualities that contribute. Or maybe it is how much of yourself – your being – you give, and not just to the other person but to the situation. How much of your 'sugar-ness' will you give to that tea? How much of your professional façade, or self, will you put aside or sacrifice so that you can enter into that realm?

Rogers was clear about how much to give of himself to the therapy relationship:

> I launch myself into the relationship ... not as a scientist, not as a physician who can accurately diagnose and cure, but as a person, entering into a personal relationship. I risk myself ... I let myself go into the immediacy of the relationship where it is my total organism which takes over and is sensitive ... I live the relationship on this basis.
>
> *(Rogers, 1961, p. 202)*

He had found himself, when doing this, unwittingly experiencing mystical moments on countless occasions in his work with individuals and groups. But he did not turn towards consciously engaging with mysticism until much later in life.

As scientist and pragmatist, he did not want his theory to be the last statements on the therapeutic relationship, but instead urged further experimentation. He continued his life's work of reconciling the scientific with the subjective world of personal and spiritual experience, and the 'new science' of Chaos theory and his own philosophy were closely aligned.

Rogers had described the psychologically healthy person – the fully-functioning person (1961) – as a person continually in the process of becoming (their potentialities), adapting positively to the feedback and interaction they have with their environment. The fully-functioning person moves creatively 'towards ever greater complexity of experiencing'. This is the marker of a person in the process of becoming their potential.

In the years before he died, he was excited to see that his findings in the science of psychotherapy were reflected in other fields such as chemistry and mathematics and with the emergence of 'Chaos theory'. In other words, the fully-functioning person is 'an open system' – a principle in Chaos theory – interacting with their environment and integrating these new experiences to adapt, as they proceed.

There are clear implications in his later work that, although as yet scientifically untestable, Rogers' personal experience had led him to apprehend a spiritual reality; that he saw this as part of our evolution as a species, or our potential as individuals, but that he did not believe he could responsibly convey this without sufficient empirical evidence.

It could well have been that Rogers would have gone on to use 'open systems' theory to begin to synthesise the scientific with the spiritual. According to Ruth Sanford, his close companion in his later years, he believed that living as an open system, being a fully-functioning person and moving towards ever greater complexity '*does not rule out transformation to another form of existence*' (Sanford, 1993, p. 259).

The potential for this to be embodied in the relationship between therapist and client is a marvellous aspiration.

Note

This is an edited version of an article originally published in *Sufi – Journal of Mystical Philosophy and Practice*, 93 (Summer 2017), Khaniqah Nimatullahi Publications, London. With many thanks to the journal for granting permission.

References

American Psychological Association. (1957, March). Distinguished Scientific Contribution Awards for 1956 – Carl R. Rogers. *The American Psychologist*, 12, 125–133. Geller, S. M. & Greenberg, L. S. (2011) 'Therapeutic Presence: Therapists' experience of presence in the psychotherapy encounter', *Person-Centred and Experiential Therapies*, 1(1&2). http://www.tandfonline.com/doi/abs/10.1080/14779757.2002.9688279

Nurbakhsh, Dr Javad. (1990) 'Sufism and Psychoanalysis; Part Two: A Comparison between Sufism and Psychoanalysis', *Sufi: A Journal of Sufism*, 6, 5–6.

Nurbakhsh, Dr Javad. (1994) *Sufi Symbolism VIII*. London: Khaniqah Nimatullahi Press.

Rogers, C. R. (1961). *On Becoming a Person: a therapist's view of psychotherapy*. London: Constable.

Rogers, C. R. (1987). *The Carl Rogers Reader*. Edited by H. Kirschenbaum & V. L. Henderson. Boston, MA: Houghton Mifflin.

Rogers, C. R. (1980) *A Way of Being*. New York: Houghton Mifflin.

Sanford, R. (1993) 'From Rogers to Gleick and Back Again' in D. Brazier (Ed.), *Beyond Carl Rogers*. London: Constable.

Satprem (1993) *Sri Aurobindo, or the Adventure of Consciousness*. Mount Vernon, WA: Institute of Evolutionary Research.

13

LIVING FROM THE 'FORMATIVE TENDENCY'

'Cosmic congruence'

Judy Moore

Introduction

> I hypothesize that there is a formative directional tendency in the universe ... This is an evolutionary tendency toward greater order, greater complexity, greater interrelatedness.
>
> (Rogers, 1980, p. 133)

Over the past thirty years my understanding of how the theory and practice of the person-centred approach could potentially bring about radical social transformation has grown as I have deepened my understanding of the embodied nature of spirituality. This understanding has grown alongside my experience as a therapist, as a trainer on a person-centred counselling course (renowned for its inclusion of the spiritual dimension of the person) throughout much of the 1990s, and, up until four years ago, as director of a person-centred counselling service at the University of East Anglia (UEA).

The journey of understanding what I outline here reflects a particular strand in the evolution of the person-centred approach since the 1950s. Many writers within the approach have written about the core condition of congruence; many have contributed to our deeper understanding of the spiritual dimension, not least my early colleague, Brian Thorne. But, for the purposes of this chapter, I confine myself to tracing a very distinct thread in terms of the meaning and implications of 'congruence' and how it can manifest as deeper spiritual awareness. I first consider Rogers' (1961) *On Becoming a Person*, the inspirational text that first drew me to the person-centred approach. I then consider Gendlin's (1959) early conceptualisation of congruence and how his 'process' view deepens understanding of this core condition and underpins the work of Peter Campbell and Edwin McMahon, the originators of Bio-Spiritual Focusing. Their view is that embracing an embodied spirituality enables us to live from a state of *agápe*, selfless, unconditional love that contains the potential for revolutionary social transformation. This means, as I will try to demonstrate, living from 'the formative tendency' in a state of what Campbell and McMahon define as 'cosmic congruence'.

Underpinning this journey is a recognition that the world in which the theory of the person-centred approach was first formulated – and even the more recent world in which the person-centred approach could flourish in higher education – is very different from the one we inhabit today.

On becoming a person

First published in 1961, Carl Rogers' *On Becoming a Person* includes many statements about what our lives might mean both individually and collectively, with a clear vision for our potential as human beings. It consists of papers written over the previous ten years, a rich and creative decade in which much of the theory of the approach was formulated.

What strikes me today on re-reading *On Becoming a Person* are the simple human truths that resonated so deeply when I first discovered this seminal work over thirty years ago. At its heart is the recognition that each of us is asking the same basic questions: 'Who am I?' and 'How may I become myself?' Given the right conditions, Rogers argues, any human being will become:

> … a person who is more open to all of the elements of his organic experience; a person who is developing a trust in his own organism as an instrument of sensitive living; a person who accepts the locus of evaluation as residing within himself; a person who is learning to live in his life as a participant in a fluid, ongoing process, in which he is continually discovering new aspects of himself in the flow of his experience.
>
> *(Rogers, 1961, p. 124)*

The aim of therapy (clearly expressed in 'A process conception of psychotherapy') is that the client should eventually be enabled to live 'as a participant in a fluid, ongoing process', a state that Rogers regards as optimal: 'Life, at its best, is a flowing, changing process in which nothing is fixed' (Rogers, 1961, p. 27).

There is optimism inherent in Rogers' view of the person: 'It has been my experience that persons have a basically positive direction' (ibid., p. 16). This positive vision of the person and the trustworthiness of inner experiencing ('Experience is, for me, the highest authority' (ibid., p. 23)) is nevertheless set against a deep concern for the broader social context in which he was writing:

> Man's awesome scientific advances into the infinitude of space as well as the infinitude of sub-atomic particles seem most likely to lead to the total destruction of our world unless we can make great advances in understanding and dealing with interpersonal and inter-group tensions.
>
> *(Rogers, 1961, p. x)*

Rogers goes on to describe his aim in putting together the collection of papers that constitutes *On Becoming a Person*:

> I hope for the day when we will invest at least the price of one or two large rockets in the search for more adequate understanding of human relationships. But I also feel keenly concerned that the knowledge we *have* gained is very little recognized and utilized. I hope it may be clear from this volume that we *already* possess learnings which, put to use, would help to decrease the inter-racial, industrial and international tensions which exist. I hope it will be evident that these learnings, used preventively, could help in the development of mature, nondefensive, understanding persons who would deal constructively with future tensions as they arrive.
>
> (Rogers, 1961, p. x)

On reading more deeply through the essays in *On Becoming a Person*, I find myself admiring Rogers' optimism and agreeing wholeheartedly with most of what he writes. I realise that I take much of what he says for granted and can see how deeply imbued my own worldview is with such assumptions as the fact that the 'good life is a *process*, not a state of being' and that life is 'a direction, not a destination' (ibid., p. 186). I agree that if the learning from the approach could be somehow be translated to a broader social context the world would indeed be a better place.

The question is *how*? My experience is that some behaviours that Rogers advocates in *A Way of Being* simply don't work – and can even be harmful – in a more formal or an institutional context. For example, is it *always right* to do what 'feels right' in a given situation? We don't exist in a solipsistic vacuum. Even though '[t]he person who is fully open to his experience would have access to all of the available data in the situation' (ibid., p. 190), he (or she) would only have access to his/her *personal* data; they do *not* have equally trustworthy access to data about someone they might choose to angrily confront or have full knowledge about a situation that they perceive as particularly unjust.

I am reminded of an incident several years ago with an angry trainee counsellor, who had been working with her training group on her need to be more open in expressing her anger. One day, fired up by her colleagues, she stormed into the Counselling Service, slammed her bag on the reception desk and angrily demanded to be told why she hadn't been allocated more clients. Whatever relief the trainee experienced in giving vent to her feelings did not justify the distress this outburst caused to the innocent receptionist who was on its receiving end.

The trainee did not know the 'bigger picture' – perhaps that there was a genuine shortage of clients, perhaps that there were concerns about the quality of her work and it had been decided to hold back on allocating her new clients for the time being – and did not wait to find out before expressing what she 'needed' to express at an immediate, surface level. My working life has been punctuated by such incidents of equally unhelpful 'self-expression', where counsellors – both trainee and qualified counsellors – would justify hurtful and even damaging outbursts in the workplace in terms of what they saw as their need to give expression to strong surface feelings, often justified as a 'need to be congruent'. *Always*, apart from in the protected environment of the therapy room, the training group or possibly an encounter group, the need for self-expression has to be balanced with awareness of the 'bigger picture'. A way of being that is powerfully effective in a person-centred training group or an encounter group simply does not work in an institutional context and – when it 'leaks out' of an environment where person-centred ideals hold sway into the wider institution – can cause irreparable damage to the reputation of the approach. In such a case, the impact of the person-centred approach ends up being the opposite of Rogers' hopes and dreams for how it might benefit society in the future.

This points to the need for a more refined and more contextualised view of 'congruence'.

'Congruence cannot be defined as explicit symbolization'

Rogers' team at the University of Chicago was enriched from the mid-1950s by the presence of Eugene Gendlin, who was at that time a young philosophy graduate student. I have described the early collaboration between Rogers and Gendlin – and, in particular, the influence of Gendlin's concept of 'experiencing' on Rogers and his team – in more detail elsewhere (Moore, 2016). It is clear that Rogers' and Gendlin's was a rich and inspiring association in the early years of their work together. They shared an understanding of how life as process and the process nature of experiencing found their fullest expression in 'the fully functioning person' who understands that 'Life, at its best, is a flowing, changing process in which nothing is fixed' (Rogers, 1961, p. 27). Gendlin's influence is clearly visible – and openly acknowledged – in Rogers' work.

Rogers adopted a 'process' view of empathy, describing it as 'a process rather than a state' in 'Empathic: an Unappreciated Way of Being' (Rogers, 1980) but never accepted a process view of congruence, still describing congruence in terms of emotional content: 'Congruence, or genuineness, involves letting the other person know "where you are" emotionally. It may involve confrontation and the straightforward expression of personally owned feelings – both negative and positive' (Rogers, 1980, p. 160).

The limitation of this view is clear. I have known congruence to be narrowly interpreted as 'confrontation' on several person-centred training courses and it is certainly this perception of congruence that drove the behaviour of the 'angry trainee'.

In an early unpublished paper, entitled 'The concept of congruence reformulated in terms of experiencing', Gendlin (1959), who was at that time very much engaged with Rogers and his team in the development of the theory, endeavours to re-frame congruence as a more refined concept that can admit greater complexity than simply 'letting the other person know where you are'. Gendlin defines the aim of his paper in the following terms:

> This paper will attempt to show that the major conclusions of Rogerian theory can be supported and clarified, if an addition to the theory is made. This addition, implied in the theory itself, is the *function* (rather than the content) of experiencing.
>
> *(Gendlin, 1959, p. 1)*

'Experiencing', he explains, is 'pre-conceptual' and 'felt, rather than conceptually known by the individual' (ibid., p. 9). The danger of symbolising congruence in an over-simplified way derives from the fact that it is 'often felt as one "this way I feel"' (p. 7). Nevertheless, 'it can usually be differentiated and explicated as many different feelings and meanings [and one] physical feeling may later be said to have implicitly included many ideas, experiences, assumptions or attitudes' (p. 7). Too simple an interpretation or the identification of one dominant feeling that seeks expression is explained through the example of 'hatred': 'One might experience hatred and symbolize it as hatred, yet it might not become integrated with other experiences. Thus awareness of hatred could simply lead to a distorted perception and a destructive behavior' (ibid., p. 16).

If experiencing can be accepted as part of the organismic process, with the emphasis being on a 'subjectively felt referent' (or, as it later became known, as 'the felt sense') rather than on the emotional 'content' that strongly and immediately presents itself (in the above example, 'hatred'), then a more complex awareness can be allowed to form:

> A genuine therapist's expression will not be some single feeling such as pure impatience or disturbance ... Thus a therapist can be advised to be genuine all the time and this does not imply that he would discriminate and express each single personal experience, *nor does it imply the symbolic expression of single unintegrated feelings. It implies the use of the therapist's present experiencing as a basis for response.*
>
> *(ibid., p. 28; my emphasis)*

From the perspective of this 'process' view of congruence, the complexity of what is present both in the person (past and present) and in their environment, needs to be given attention:

> Complete congruence thus means that all experiences *function* to determine perception and behavior. Therefore congruence cannot be defined as explicit symbolization (as the theory now holds). All experiences can not be *explicitly* symbolized in awareness simultaneously. Rather than an awareness of explicitly symbolized *contents*, congruence implies an *implicit* awareness in which very many experiences *function* in any one moment.
>
> *(ibid., p. 29)*

Had this early view of congruence been integrated by Rogers, the theory of the person-centred approach over the past fifty years or so would probably have evolved in a very different way. It makes complete sense to me that 'all experiences can not be *explicitly* symbolized in awareness simultaneously' and this accounts for my own longstanding discomfort with what increasingly seemed too simplistic a version of this particular core condition. It is unfortunate that Gendlin's perceptive analysis and his pointing to congruence as a complex, *implicit* awareness that can never be fully articulated has remained so little known. I was unaware of it myself until I began to read Gendlin's early writings some years after my direct involvement in UEA's person-centred professional training had ceased.

I hypothesise that Rogers never integrated Gendlin's view of congruence at least in part because of the rift that eventually split the group that left the University of Chicago to engage in the ill-fated Wisconsin Project between 1957 and 1963 (Kirschenbaum, 2007, pp. 281–295). Rogers was even threatened with legal action by Gendlin as part of the fallout and it was many years before they were reconciled. As a result of Rogers' adherence to a more 'static' view of congruence it has been left to later generations to interpret and research congruence, to discover the relevance of Gendlin's contribution through his published works and to inspire more sophisticated thinking around the concept (e.g. Wyatt, 2001; Cornelius-White, 2007, 2013; Grafanaki, 2013).

'Presence' as congruence

Gendlin's emphasis on listening to the felt sense rather than simply to our feelings *grounds* the person-centred approach in something deeper and richer than emotionalism. We can sense and bring attention to our pre-verbal knowing, to the full complexity of our experiencing if we are willing to stay with the physical sensations that underpin the feelings that we might otherwise be too quick to express.

In an earlier article (Moore, 2004) I explored how Carl Rogers' later work, particularly *A Way of Being* (Rogers, 1980), invites us to develop ourselves as fully and deeply as we can, developing our quality of 'presence' and opening ourselves to experience 'a transcendent awareness of the harmony and unity of the cosmic system, including humankind' (Rogers, 1980, p. 133). I link this process to the Buddhist notion of 'forgetting' the 'self', finding a trustworthy place of 'not knowing' from which we can not only live more deeply, but also work more effectively, especially with deeply-troubled clients. Adomaitis (1992), quoted by Haugh (2001, p. 6) connects Rogers' well-known statement on the quality of 'presence' with a mystical level of 'congruence':

> When I am at my best, as a group facilitator or as a therapist, I discover another characteristic. I find that when I am closest to my inner, intuitive self, when I am somehow in touch with the unknown in me, when perhaps I am in a slightly altered state of consciousness, then whatever I do seems to be full of healing. Then simply my *presence* is releasing and helpful to the other. There is nothing I can do to force this experience, but when I can relax and be close to the

transcendental core of me, then I may behave in strange and impulsive ways in the relationship, ways which I cannot justify rationally, which have nothing to do with my thought processes. But these strange behaviours turn out to be right, in some odd way: it seems that my inner spirit has reached out and touched the inner spirit of the other. Our relationship transcends itself and becomes a part of something larger. Profound growth and healing and energy are present.

(Rogers, 1980, p. 129)

Haugh is dismissive of Adomaitis' view that Rogers' explanation of presence 'suggests there can be a deep, spontaneous self, a self whose presence is innately healing', explaining that since 'Rogers never made any formal theoretical statement of this fourth facet of congruence, Adomaitis' suggestion can only be speculation' (Haugh, 2001, p. 6).

If we return, however, to Gendlin's definition of congruence as 'an *implicit* awareness in which very many experiences *function* in any one moment' (Gendlin, 1959, p. 29) there is no reason why the 'inner, intuitive self', 'the unknown in me', the 'slightly altered state of consciousness' should *not* be part of congruence. My view is that if the rift between Rogers and Gendlin had not taken place, had they continued to work together on the theory beyond 1960, this 'fourth facet' would have become a widely accepted aspect of congruence and our view of 'the person' within the person-centred approach expanded in a very straightforward way to encompass the spiritual dimension.

This development was, however, carried forward in the work of Peter Campbell and Edwin McMahon.

'Congruence as story'

Edwin McMahon (1930–2013) and Peter Campbell (b. 1935) have devoted their lives to understanding and teaching how we can listen more deeply to ourselves to create better lives for all, including for the next generation. Trained as Jesuit priests and in the psychology of religion, both were taught and influenced by Gendlin, whose work they discovered in the late 1960s; Edwin McMahon was also taught by Carl Rogers. Their lifelong quest to help relieve suffering was inspired by the work of Teilhard de Chardin, whose dream was to found an institute to investigate the question: 'Is there some organic, spiritual motivational energy for life inside human beings that can be awakened to guide us into a transformed way of living?' (http://www.biospiritual.org/the-campbellmcmahon-library). In 1975 Campbell and McMahon founded the Institute for Bio-Spiritual Research, carrying this dream forward with knowledge they had acquired from their background in Christian theology. Intrinsic to their work is also their learning from what was then the 'new psychology' of the person-centred approach. McMahon (1993) makes an interesting distinction between the contributions of Rogers and Gendlin to the development of this theory:

... much like electricity, while Rogers knew *that* congruence worked, he did not fully [understand] *how*, or what actually happened within the person that made it all possible.

[...] Carl Rogers had uncovered the barest tip of it all, 'When I can be my feelings, then they change.' But what did this actually mean and how was it such a crucial ingredient in the very process of transformation itself? With the kind of creative leap that so characterizes many great discoveries in science, Gendlin isolated a further piece in the experience of congruence.

(pp. 235–236)

McMahon goes on to explain Gendlin's discovery that finding the 'right' word leads to a 'felt shift', a sense of 'rightness' in the body – a process with which we are all familiar from everyday conversation as well as in the context of therapy. He then quotes from Gendlin's 'Theory of personality change' to explain the 'interactive' and 'process' nature of what happens when a knowing that is *implicitly* held within the body is accurately symbolized, pointing to the significance of its *implicitness*:

Implicit meaning units are *incomplete*. They are not hidden conceptual units. They are not the same in nature as explicitly-known meanings. There is no *equation* possible between implicit meaning and 'their' implicit symbolization. Rather than an equation, there is an *interaction* between felt experiencing and symbols (or events).

(Gendlin, 1970, p. 135; quoted in McMahon, 1993, p. 238)

McMahon continues:

That was the key! *There is not 'equation' but 'interaction' between symbol and felt meaning.* With this careful observation, the true nature of congruence could unfold. Felt-meaning is not some vague shadow form of more clearly-defined, rational concepts already conceived in the mind ... The emphasis in this experiencing is not upon *information* but on *forward movement* in the body's knowing. Felt-meaning (or felt-sensing) represents an organismic step not simply toward some new 'content' of knowledge but into an actual experiencing of *the 'process' of wholeness itself.*

(McMahon, 1993, p. 238)

McMahon explains that we come to an increasing awareness of the *'forward movement'* of our lives as our own individual 'story' unfolds:

Part of what draws us all to a story is the felt ongoing-ness of it, the flow, the being carried along. The actual details become secondary. They provide a convenient structure within which some more primal process can unfold. There is a fundamental urge for such 'going-forwardness' which lies inside

> each person. The interaction between symbol and felt-meaning brings this into awareness through an evolving of congruence. But the actual goal of such body-experience appears to be an unfolding of some greater wholeness within the human organism itself.
>
> *(ibid.)*

It is this explicit acknowledgement of the importance of giving attention to the 'unfolding of some greater wholeness' within us that is distinctive to Bio-Spiritual Focusing. It fascinates me that this profound discovery should have been so explicitly rooted in the core condition of congruence: 'Congruence as "story" is our most primal experience of forward movement into a deeper current called "Spirit", as this evolves within human consciousness' (McMahon, 1993, p. 239).

> Bio-spirituality ... has grown out of an experience of congruence (wholeness, holiness) as this unfolds within the human body. What makes the bio-spiritual movement different is not the appearance of new or unusual ideas. Instead, the very ground rules of discussion and exploration have been shifted away from ideas and explanations toward what might best be described as some kind of 'resonance' with *a bodily-felt process of congruence* that expresses what we have heretofore called 'Spirit'.
>
> *(ibid., p. 241)*

For Campbell and McMahon this *'process of congruence'* is seen very specifically within the context of a Christian theology and the movement towards greater wholeness to which we are drawn they regard as a movement of 'grace'.

'Cosmic congruence'

The learning from Bio-Spiritual Focusing can encompass all spiritual disciplines, but its early formulation in the language of the person-centred approach makes it especially appealing to me as an explication of the process whereby Rogers' 'quality of presence' and alignment with the 'formative tendency' might be achieved.

In 2004 my colleagues and I ran a conference at the University of East Anglia entitled 'The Spiritual Dimension in Therapy and Experiential Exploration'. The conference papers were collected into a book, *Spirituality and Counselling: Experiential and Theoretical Perspectives* (Moore & Purton, 2006). The most frequently quoted words in the book were Rogers' statement on 'presence'. The view held by many of our contributors was that 'presence' constitutes not only a 'facet' of congruence (as held by Adomaitis), but that it is a 'fourth condition' in itself. The paradox of this view is that 'presence' is something to be sought as a 'goal', which may be achieved by certain gifted or more advanced practitioners and can be cultivated to some extent, but *not* that it can develop as the outcome of a teachable process, such as that outlined in Bio-Spiritual Focusing.

The work of Campbell and McMahon was unknown to me at the time of the 2004 conference (and there is no reference to them in any of the presentations in the conference book), but I am aware of what a fresh and inspiring perspective would have been brought, especially to the person-centred element of the audience (the vast majority of the conference attendees) by their view:

> 'Spirit' has always been intended to identify that capacity which somehow transcends limitations of the flesh. What Rogers and Gendlin offer is a fresh perspective on where this transcendence actually lies within the human organism and how it expresses itself. It does not function as some nonmaterial *content*, labelled 'the faculty of intellect' or 'soul'. Rather, it is an experience of *'self-process'*. [...]
>
> 'Spirit comes into being by the development of the body'. Now, we can begin to make the necessary precision about such development. *Spirit becomes visible 'as' the graced unfolding of congruence in the body!* There is no such thing as 'a' self. What exists is either the gift of ongoing *self-process*, the congruent movement into greater wholeness, or there is blocked self-process, frittering existence away in the myriad addictions that litter our human landscape.
>
> *(McMahon, 1993, p. 240)*

The centrality of bodily awareness to spiritual development has been explored by others who have built on Gendlin's theories of process and experiencing, but it is through the work of Campbell and McMahon that I have found a the 'necessary precision' of articulation that completes my own understanding within the language and concepts of the person-centred approach.

In the original Introduction to *Bio-Spirituality: Focusing as a Way to Grow* (1985, re-published in an expanded second edition in 1997), the implications of the focusing steps and method that Campbell and McMahon have evolved are presented:

> We believe that the regular use of Focusing can support significant movement toward a humane valuing process. This is valuing that is not drawn from the mind's distinction between right and wrong but from a deeper sense for direction, purpose, and content within the cosmos. There is support within our bodies for unitary consciousness. Focusing, we believe, can contribute to a spirituality that nourishes *cosmic congruence* irrespective of a person's religious affiliation.
>
> *(Campbell & McMahon, 1997, p. xxix; my emphasis)*

The path to 'cosmic congruence' is not an easy one. There is not space to describe the steps of Bio-Spiritual Focusing in any detail here; indeed they require teaching and careful practice over time. Critical to the process, however, is the establishment of a caring, feeling presence inside ourselves that can metaphorically hold whatever comes to us in our inner experiencing, however stuck or frightened or painful that may be. The aim is that we should be with our experiencing with the tenderness and care that we would bring to a sick child or an injured pet. We welcome whatever is there – however uncomfortable – as part of our unfolding 'story'. Accepting what is there, allowing ourselves to experience it just as it is, enables it to shift and, in shifting, opens us to what McMahon (Campbell & McMahon, 1997) describes as 'the congruent movement into greater wholeness' within ourselves.

This conscious choice to stay with what is painful and difficult at the level of the felt sense is the opposite of the 'blocked self-process' that comes when we choose to distract ourselves, 'frittering our existence away in the myriad addictions that litter our human landscape'. Campbell and McMahon point to the danger in what Gendlin terms 'process-skipping', where instead of giving full attention to an uncomfortable or painful situation or feeling we substitute it with another behaviour 'rather than becoming congruent with, owning and processing what is real, thereby allowing it to unfold and tell its story so the body-feel of it can be carried in a different way' (Campbell & McMahon, 1997, p. 179). Campbell writes:

> Process-skipping structures are not just obvious things like drugs, alcohol, sex, work, or pleasing other people. Prayer, meditation, volunteer work, anything that can be substituted for a congruent owning of what is real inside me contains the negative potential for contribution to a process skipping pattern of addiction.
>
> *(ibid., p. 181)*

The potential for distraction today is even greater than when these words were written two decades ago. In particular, the internet offers constant potential for easy distraction and it feels in many ways harder than ever to carve out the time and the space needed to bring a caring, feeling presence to the uncomfortable thoughts and feelings that arise as part of our daily existence.

But if we *can* succeed in being with the painful and difficult thoughts and feelings that beset us, then something eventually begins to shift – bringing not only immediate relief and insight, but also opening us to awareness of the bodily feel of the self-process, or, as McMahon (1993) describes it, '*a bodily-felt process of congruence*' (p. 241).

Allowing this 'bodily-felt process of congruence' enables movement into a more expansive awareness of 'cosmic congruence' that recalls Rogers' description of the 'formative tendency':

> I hypothesize that there is a formative directional tendency in the universe, which can be traced and observed in stellar space, in crystals, in micro-organisms, in more complex organic life, and in human beings. This is an evolutionary tendency toward greater order, greater complexity, greater interrelatedness. In humankind, this tendency exhibits itself as the individual moves from a single-cell origin to complex organic functioning, to knowing and sensing below the level of consciousness, to a conscious awareness of the organism and the

external world, to a transcendent awareness of the harmony and unity of the cosmic system, including humankind.

(Rogers, 1980, p. 133)

Carl Rogers' 'presence' as *agápe*

As we have seen, Edwin McMahon makes a very interesting distinction between Rogers and Gendlin when describing their respective positions in relation to the concept of congruence, asserting that Gendlin sought to understand exactly *why* congruence 'worked' while Rogers simply knew that it *did*: '… much like electricity, while Rogers knew *that* congruence worked, he did not fully [understand] *how*, or what actually happened within the person that made it all possible' (McMahon, 1993, p. 235–236).

The same holds true of Rogers' oft-quoted description of the quality of 'presence', where *how* this state comes about is left vague ('somehow…' 'perhaps…'). There is almost a sense of surprise that 'healing' comes, but Rogers nevertheless clearly asserts that what happens is 'releasing' and 'helpful' to 'the other':

> I find that when I am closest to my inner, intuitive self, when I am somehow in touch with the unknown in me, when perhaps I am in a slightly altered state of consciousness, then whatever I do seems to be full of healing. Then simply my *presence* is releasing and helpful to the other.
>
> *(Rogers, 1980, p. 129; Rogers' emphasis)*

The fact that Rogers never explained *how* he might have *arrived at* this quality of presence (or how others might consciously work to achieve this state) is reflected in the extent to which 'presence' became a dominant theme for speculative exploration at our 2004 'Spirituality' conference.

Edwin McMahon had significant personal experience of Rogers' 'quality of presence' and describes this experience in a chapter in his and Peter Campbell's most recent book, one which is directed quite specifically at the Christian community, entitled *Rediscovering the Lost Body-Connection within Christian Spirituality* (2010):

> Many years ago, when I was studying with Carl Rogers, what fascinated and touched me most deeply was his quality of presence in the relationship both to himself as well as with the person whom he was companioning. The experience was a powerful teacher. At the time, I had already read just about everything he had written, but never did I expect to learn so much from the physical presence of the writer himself.
>
> *(Campbell & McMahon, 2010, p. 133)*

McMahon links Rogers' quality of presence with *agápe* love as it is understood in the Christian tradition:

> As my training program with Dr Rogers progressed, I came to realize that what he was teaching us as potential healers stood out for me as the missing link with pastoral Christianity for empowering each person to tap into the gift of *agápe* love within their own body.
> ... I found it so freeing and hope-filled that a fellow psychotherapist could not only practice but grow personally through his research, knowing in my Christian bones that this might be closest I would ever come to experiencing in my own body the human qualities of a presence in *agápe* love that so many with open hearts must have felt in the presence of Jesus.
>
> *(ibid., p. 135)*

This is a powerful tribute to the state that Rogers achieved through a lifetime of working with clients, developing self-awareness and investigating the human conditions for growth and change. Again, McMahon makes explicit what is not explicit in Rogers' own writings – the link between 'congruence' and 'presence':

> The issue of human wellness and healing, or wholeness, revolves around an experience of inner *congruence* directly experienced and felt within the human organism. For us, congruence means, *being able to feel your feelings physiologically and allowing them to symbolize themselves accurately*. Developing a body-sense of congruence *within yourself* and learning to take care of your inner environment balances your inside ecology so you can then bring this same caring quality of presence toward your outer environment. The process of your inner congruence then becomes your teacher for how you present yourself and interact in the world around you. But this process first begins *inside your own body*. Your developing sense for inner congruence, or wholeness, can then guide your quest for growing in *the body-experience* of being an integral part of something greater than yourself.
>
> We introduce the topic of congruence here because a growing inner sense for this experience directly relates to maturing in the capacity for *agápe* presence.
>
> *(ibid., pp. 137–138)*

He goes on to identify how this 'maturing in the capacity for *agápe* presence' manifests in a person, expressing it terms borrowed from Rogers' theory: 'The Experience of Being Fully Received', 'Empathic Presence' and 'Unconditional Acceptance' (or 'Unconditional Positive Regard') (ibid., pp. 138ff). His view represents an in-depth understanding of the person-centred approach, which logically extends to the spiritual dimension.

The social dimension

The 1993 text in which Edwin McMahon explains so clearly how Bio-Spiritual Focusing evolved from Rogers' and Gendlin's thinking is entitled *Beyond the Myth of Dominance: An Alternative to a Violent Society* and it is dedicated 'To all who search for a way to heal themselves, their children and the planet'. Spiritual development is not for oneself alone, but for the benefit of all who inhabit our planet, as he goes on to explain: 'Once we learn how to treat whatever is real inside us, then we will know how to treat others and the planet we live on' (McMahon, 1993, p. 13).

In the section of the Bio-Spiritual Institute website that explains the origins of the Institute's work (http://www.biospiritual.org/welcome/our-origins/) the link between personal growth and the vision of Teilhard de Chardin is explained in terms of how accessing the 'felt sense' can lead to a 'Teilhardian sense for evolution within human awareness'. The human body, 'with its innate knowing potential' is regarded as 'the doorway to future human progress' and presented as 'a vast, untapped evolutionary resource'.

Campbell and McMahon offer a complete vision for how humanity can move forward. With deep understanding, they have built on the many strands of their respective backgrounds and experience, including carrying forward and developing the inspirational work of both Rogers and Gendlin.

In *On Becoming a Person* Rogers (1961) describes how it would be if an individual were to live fully what it means to be a human being: 'It means ... that one lives fully and openly the complex process of being one of the most widely sensitive, responsive, and creative creatures on this planet' (p. 178).

It has become clear to me, through my own experience, that this vision, created in the optimism of post-war America, can still inspire individuals, but is not so easy to live in an institutional context.

The changing face of an institution

In 2012 Peter Campbell kindly agreed to be a keynote speaker at a conference ('Spirituality and Physicality: Crossing the Thresholds', 1–5 July 2012) at the University of East Anglia. This conference was organised on behalf of the International Association for Children's Spirituality by the then-Director of the Centre for Spirituality and Religion in Education. Unable at that time to travel to the UK, Peter Campbell joined us through Skype link; his colleague, John Keane, from Ireland, was physically present to give a complementary presentation. I introduced them both and facilitated the discussion that followed. The abstract for Peter Campbell's presentation reads as follows:

> Rev. Peter A. Campbell, PhD, together with his colleague in the USA, Rev. Edwin McMahon, PhD, have spent the better part of their professional lives working within an area best described as *the Psychology of Religion*. This includes both the broader implications of what in religion and spirituality moves toward health and human wholeness within the person, and what tends toward pathology in religion and religious practices. It also includes a more careful examination of the body's role in spiritual development.

It was a very successful event and many people commented afterwards on how inspiring the idea of bio-spirituality was to them. It was also the first time that there had been direct collaboration between the Centre for Spirituality and Religion at UEA and the Centre for Counselling Studies (of which I was then Director). It was an inspiring moment, full of potential.

Sadly, and very paradoxically, even at the time that this event took place, both the Director of the Centre for Spirituality and Religion and I had received intimations that our 'centres' were under threat and that our own creative time at the University was drawing to a close. The University now wanted its 'centres' to be highly-rated 'research centres' and we simply no longer fitted the description of what a 'centre' was meant to be. That we did not 'fit' was presented to us as personal failure. Creative, organic growth, such as we had enjoyed in the Centre for Counselling Studies since it was founded by Brian Thorne in 1992, was no longer possible and the university decided to shrink the work of the Centre to a 'teaching-only' function. Within two years the Centre for Spirituality and Religion and the Centre for Counselling Studies ceased to exist, and both I and the Director of the Centre for Spirituality and Religion left our substantive posts at UEA (at the time I was also Director of the University Counselling Service). Ironically, the title 'Centre for Counselling Studies' was eventually 'resurrected' for marketing purposes, but no replacement director was appointed.

In the Spring of 2017 it was decided to close all the person-centred counselling courses at UEA, a devastating, but not unsurprising move. Similar trainings had already closed in other UK higher education institutions and, in an article that assesses the context and impact of the closures, Andy Rogers (2017) identifies how they form part of a national trend across sectors:

> This is exactly what's been happening in other sectors, of course, particularly the NHS, where instrumental, short-term approaches (therapy-lite, if you will) have become dominant. These approaches are ideally adapted to the current, highly medicalised regime around mental health, with its diagnose-treat-cure approach to human distress, which in its atomised conception of people and its quick-fix mentality is in turn ideally suited to our current political and socio-economic conditions – what is often referred to as 'neo-liberalism' – in which therapy's job is perceived by the State and its agencies to be returning 'ill' workers (or students), to their jobs (or studies) after a short course of 'evidence-based treatment'.
>
> At all levels of education, one impact of the neo-liberal order has been to prioritise the needs of business over both critical thinking and holistic personal development. In higher education (HE) especially, organisations are run as businesses themselves, with students considered consumers and staff expected to be compliant employees.
>
> (p. 32)

The course closures were probably, more than any other factor, down to the recent increase in undergraduate student fees (to £9,000+ per year) in the UK, meaning that undergraduate degrees had become more financially profitable than professional post-graduate level person-centred trainings that demanded a high staff to student ratio. Meanwhile, small-scale qualitative research projects such as we had undertaken into the effectiveness of the person-centred approach (e.g. Lane & Moore, 2012) were not the kind of undertaking that was likely to attract multi-million-pound research grants. In all areas, we had ceased to 'fit' the business model of the university.

The university was no longer a place where investigation could have continued into what was described in the abstract for Peter Campbell's presentation as 'the broader implications of what in religion and spirituality moves toward health and human wholeness within the person'.

Coming full circle

Shortly after his lecture, Peter Campbell emailed me with an afterthought for which I am extremely grateful:

> I thought of one more book I would really recommend to anyone attempting to understand Bio-Spiritual Focusing. Carl Rogers' *On Becoming a Person*. You might mention this if you think it's relevant. This work is so fundamental for appreciating the farther extension that Gendlin has made upon his original mentor. It also opens a far richer understanding and appreciation of what *agápe* is all about – and therefore has implications for spirituality.
>
> (Campbell, personal communication, 2012)

These few words have been more helpful to me than I could ever have imagined. They have enabled me to uncover a rich vein of material for a chapter that I never dreamt of having the time or the opportunity to write when I was so embroiled in institutional issues back in 2012.

I am very aware of the paradox that it is only now that I am finally removed from the pressure of trying to keep the person-centred approach alive in an institutional context that I have been able to find the inner space to re-connect with a view of the person, a way of looking at life that has never ceased to inspire me. I have also needed time to contact the very real sadness I feel at the ending of the person-centred vision at UEA, a process that for me was going on at a private level for some time before the more recent course closures were announced.

If I were still to be involved in person-centred training, I would undoubtedly want to integrate and promote the deeper understanding of congruence that I've presented in this chapter. But I question whether I – or any of us – could have actually *lived* this way of being within the university as it is now. Institutions are very disorientating places with their own rules and conventions. It is easy to get caught up in the daily whirlwind of conflicting demands, political games, the battle with other departments for resources, even the compulsion of fighting to save what one believes in. These compelling – potentially addictive – activities all invite 'process-skipping', the very thing that takes us away from allowing into awareness the sadness, the hurt, the anger that we first need to accept in order to become the process to which the person-centred approach aspires, whether that be defined as 'cosmic congruence', a state of '*agápe*' or 'living from the formative tendency'.

Conclusion

Promoting and maintaining the person-centred approach became, in my experience, increasingly difficult and eventually impossible in the context of a higher education institution.

However, connecting more deeply than I have ever done before with the development of congruence from Rogers and Gendlin to Campbell and McMahon – all of whom have continued to work to the end of their lives for the good of humanity – gives me renewed cause for optimism. Carl Rogers (1961) writes, 'life, at its best, is a flowing, changing process in which nothing is fixed' (p. 27). Discovering the wisdom inherent in living such a process requires stopping and listening to the truth of our inner experiencing as it expresses itself at the bodily level of the felt sense. This is a step-by-step process that needs time and patience and it now needs to find nurturance in contexts other than business-led institutions. It feels important at this time for those of us committed to the person-centred vision to find people and places – and organisations – where the *whole* of the person can be received, where it is possible to live the fullness of one's humanity. Asking the questions 'Who am I?' and 'How can I become myself?' are in themselves part of the process by which we can move to a fuller and more grounded understanding of who we are and what we may eventually become. Living in 'cosmic congruence' and from the 'formative tendency' can serve as an inspiring aspiration, but it is one that requires perpetual grounding in 'what is real inside us', supported by social contexts – and maybe new kinds of institutions – where this is regarded as a valid and worthwhile way of being.

References

Adomaitis, R. (1992) On Being Genuine: A Phenomenologically Grounded Study of the Experience of Genuineness and its Place in Client-Centered Psychotherapy. Unpublished PhD Dissertation, Northwestern University, USA.

Campbell, P. and McMahon, E. (1997) *Bio-Spirituality: Focusing as a Way to Grow*, 2nd edition. Chicago: Loyola Press.

Campbell, P. and McMahon, E. (2010) *Rediscovering the Lost Body-Connection within Christian Spirituality*. Minneapolis, MN: Tasora Books.

Cornelius-White, J. (2007) Congruence: an integrative five-dimensional model, *Person-Centered and Experiential Psychotherapies*, 6, 229–239.

Cornelius-White, J. (2013) Congruence, in O'Hara, M., Schmid, P. and Bohart, A. (eds.) *The Handbook of Person-Centered Psychotherapy and Counseling* (2nd edition). Basingstoke: Palgrave Macmillan.

Gendlin, E. (1959). The concept of congruence reformulated in terms of experiencing. *Counseling Center Discussion Papers*, 5(12). Chicago: University of Chicago Library. From http://www.focusing.org/gendlin/docs/gol_2077.html.

Gendlin, E. (1970) A theory of personality change, in Hart. J. and Tomlinson, J. (eds) *New Directions in Client-Centered Therapy*. Boston: Houghton Mifflin.

Grafanaki, S. (2013) Editorial: Experiencing congruence and incongruence. *Person-Centered and Experiential Psychotherapies*, 12(3), 183–185.

Haugh, S. (2001) A historical review of the development of the concept of congruence, in Wyatt, G. (2001) (ed.) *Rogers' Therapeutic Conditions: Evolution, Theory and Practice, Vol. 1: Congruence*. Ross-on-Wye: PCCS Books.

Kirschenbaum, H. (2007) *The Life and Work of Carl Rogers*. Ross-on-Wye: PCCS Books.

Lane, K., and Moore, J. (2012) Giving 'a face' to the university: the value of an embedded counselling service. *AUCC Journal*, November, 19–12.

McMahon, E. (1993) *Beyond the Myth of Dominance*. Kansas City: Sheed and War.

Moore, J. (2004) Letting go of who I think I am: Listening to the unconditioned self. *Person-Centered and Experiential Psychotherapy*, 3(2), 117–112.

Moore, J. (2016) 'Focusing' and 'experiencing': Gendlin's early contribution to client-centred theory and its implications for practice, in Lago, C. and Charura, D. (eds) *Person Centred Counselling and Psychotherapy: Origins, Developments and Contemporary Applications*. Milton Keynes: Open University Press.

Moore, J., and Purton, C. (eds) (2006) *Spirituality and Counselling: Experiential and Theoretical Perspectives*. Ross-on-Wye: PCCS Books.

Rogers, A. (2017) Standing the edge. *Therapy Today*, September, 30–33.

Rogers, C. (1961) *On Becoming a Person*. London: Constable.

Rogers, C. (1980) *A Way of Being*. Boston, MA: Houghton Mifflin.

Wyatt, G. (ed.) (2001) *Rogers' Therapeutic Conditions: Evolution, Theory and Practice*, Vol. 1: *Congruence*. Ross-on-Wye: PCCS Books.

14

"A KIND OF LIKING WHICH HAS STRENGTH" (CARL ROGERS)

Does person-centred therapy facilitate through love?

Peter F. Schmid

Introduction

Many years ago, a prominent Viennese psychoanalyst replied cynically in the course of a theoretical discussion with me. "Does this mean that you believe in therapy through love?" He could also have said: "Are you really so naïve?"

This question has been in my mind since then. Is it love that brings about change? Is it love that helps clients grow and come to grips with their life? If we speak of love, what do we mean by a word that obviously has so many meanings? Do we love our clients? Can it be professional to love? Can giving love be something we can learn? Can one have a training in love? Do clients see a therapist because they look for love? Do they want to be loved by the person they consult? Or do they want to be told: "You are loveable"?

I will concentrate on a few fundamental questions and try to examine to what extent the different facets or ways of love resonate with the therapeutic relationship and with therapy theory.

What does love mean? – A phenomenological investigation

All you need is love, the Beatles famously claimed (Lennon, 1967). But what is meant by love?

Everybody has his or her own ideas about love, his or her individual concept of love, a conception that is often not reflected, and most likely not systematically reflected. Romantic love is usually the first that comes into one's mind. Religious people may think of God's love and brotherly love, charity. There is "to make love" as a euphemism for "have sex". Within it, there is a broad variety from respect to lust, from intimate closeness via joy to intellectual desire. Love is both a very common and a multi-faceted and highly personal phenomenon.

Some basic facts

One can love a person, something one does or experiences (e.g. playing chess, cooking or being caressed), one can love another creature (a dog, a flower), a thing (one's car, another's outfit, money) or an idea (freedom, truth, home, one's country, the world, universal connectedness).

Basically, according to Haeffner (1997, p. 908), thinking of persons, one can distinguish between the following:

- *parental love* (and child's love towards the parents),
- *love in partnership* (of different or same sex),
- *friendship* (a love that needs some form of equality or that creates it),
- *self-love* (not to be mixed up with egoism, a twisted form of self-love).

We think that love can be strong, it comes upon us, it may be there suddenly; we think of it as something we do not ourselves create but that draws us in. Love occupies our thinking and feeling. Love makes fools of us. We do things which we never thought we would do. Love can change our perception drastically. Love also may make us think about the meaning of our life, how we want to live it, where we want to go – or it may let us forget thinking about the future and just take the present moment hoping it will last eternally. Neglected love can immediately switch into hate, which can be as strong as love was before. On the other hand, love can come about silently, starting with a little bit more interest in something or somebody, with sympathy (*amor benevolentiae*, a precursor of love, characterized by benevolence, friendliness) – or, at the opposite pole, with an unclear but noticeable dislike or reluctance, before it shows its true face and we start loving what we did not at all like at first sight.

In any case love implies affection, attachment to something or to somebody. Love is an intensive emotional *relationship* (Meyers Enzyklopädisches Lexikon, 1986). Another characteristic of love is that – at least intentionally – its value is seen beyond the category of purpose and means, e.g. in the sheer existence of the beloved "it is good that you are or exist", to paraphrase Fromm (1956) or in the act of loving itself. This means that love is to be attributed neither solely to the subject nor to his or her opposite, but has its place *between* the lover and the beloved, in their imagination or experience. And this "between", to use Buber's (1953) term, has an impact, helps the persons involved develop, changes their existence – all of the above demonstrating that love can be very strong.

Love in religions and theologies, philosophies and psychologies

Different religions deal differently with love: *Polytheistic religions* (e.g. the religions of the ancient east and those of Greeks, Romans, and Germanic people) with specific gods or goddesses that impersonate love (e.g. Eros, Aphrodite, Venus, Ishtar). *Hinduism* considers love to god as devotion (*Bhakti*) as the way to redemption,

Buddhism the all-encompassing kindness (Metta, universal loving kindness) and the all-encompassing compassion (Karuna) as the way to overcome suffering.

Monotheistic religions regard love as part of their image of God. Jews, Christians, Muslims love God and feel loved by God. The Bible explicitly states that "God is love" (John 4:8,16; 1 John 3–5). For Christians, Jesus was *the* prophet of love, even incarnation of God's love. According to the Jewish-Christian double commandment love to God, love to the fellow human and self-love is one and the same (Matthew 22:37–40). So, love is ranked top in Christian ethics with love of one's enemies as utmost consequence (Matthew 5:43–45a). The theologoumenon (or theological statement in the area of individual opinion) of a Tri-une God, the trinity, is based on the idea that God in himself is community whose characteristic is mutual love; the Holy Spirit is understood as God's love in humans (Schmid, 1998a).

Modern psychological concepts about love are often based on ancient philosophical concepts. This is true for the Eros theory of Freud (1920, see below), Fromm's (1956) work on the art of loving and in a way also for Maslow's (1954) theory of the hierarchy of needs that places self-actualization at the peak. He maintains that those who have reached self-actualization are capable of love. Sternberg (1986) developed the triangular theory of love in the context of interpersonal relationships with the components of intimacy, passion and commitment.

For psychotherapy, it can be rewarding to compare the understanding of love in different cultures and times. Here I will concentrate on having a closer look at the four most prominent types in Western understanding and examine whether or not they have something to do with the psychotherapeutic endeavour and the therapeutic relationship and if we can gain something from their understanding for our own understanding and practice of therapy.

Traditionally the different dimensions of love are named after the four ancient Greek words for what we call love (cf. Lewis, 1960) – see below.

Many forms of love – *or One* Love

Eros (amor complacentiae)

Eros (ἔρως), the Greek god of love (in Latin *Amor* or *Cupidus*), is one of the oldest gods according to Hesiod's (2002) *Theogony*, and according to Parmenides (400 BC), even the first of all the gods to come into existence (Kraus, 2013).

As an allegory of friendship and love between youths and men, Eros was worshipped together with his brother *Anteros*, the god of requited (returned or counter-) love who, as a punisher of those who spurn love, was the avenger of unrequited love.

In the classical world, erotic love as the passionate love was generally referred to as a kind of madness: *theia mania* (divine madness, madness from the gods).

The first philosopher to deal extensively with Eros was Plato in his *Symposium* (Boll & Buchwald, 1989). He developed an idealistic concept of Eros, which proved to be very influential in modern times. Describing the nature of Eros, Plato asserts that it is the result of the great love for another person. The lover, inspired by beauty, is filled with divine love and filling the soul of the loved one with love in return. As a result, the loved one falls in love with the lover, though the love is only spoken of as friendship. They experience pain when apart, and relief when they are together. Later, Plato refined his own definition: although Eros is initially felt for a person, with contemplation it becomes an appreciation of the beauty within that person, or even becomes appreciation of beauty itself.

So, Eros originally meant the passionate desire for the good, true and beautiful. Its main characteristic is permanent aspiration and desire. Even when Eros seems to give, it continues to be a desire to possess. Thus, for Plato, Eros always remains an egocentric love: it leans towards conquering and possessing the object that represents a value for a human. To love the good signifies to desire to possess it forever. Love is therefore always a desire for immortality (Schmid, 2015a).

Later it became the meaning of intimate love, characterized by a search in supplementing one's own limitations. Nowadays, the notion of Eros is always connected to sensual, genital desire and enjoyment, to the passionate, aphrodisiac, the sexual pleasures (it goes without saying that acted out sex definitely has no place in psychotherapy, because there is no sex without interest).

What does Eros have to do with psychotherapy?

The psychotherapy scientist who most radically thought the connection of any relationship with Eros was undoubtedly Sigmund Freud. His metapsychology refers to the Platonic view of Eros, as expressed in the "Symposium", and to Schopenhauer. In his paper "The resistances to psycho-analysis", Freud (1925) confronts his adversaries for ignoring such great precursors and for tainting his whole theory of Eros with a *pansexual* tendency by mixing up Eros with sex as related to primary genital activity. In Freudian psychology, Eros, not to be confused with libido (which is the energy "behind"), is not exclusively the sex drive, but our life force, the will to live. It is the desire to create life. Eros favours productivity and creativity. In early psychoanalytic writings, instincts derived from Eros were opposed by forces stemming from the Ego. But in later theory, Eros is opposed by the destructive death instinct of Thanatos, the death drive. So, for Freud Eros is *the* motor in anything that fosters, builds, develops life. However, it must be noticed that Plato sees Eros as a spiritual energy initially, which then "falls" downward; whereas in Freud Eros is a physical energy which is "sublimated" upward.

Herman Nohl, a German social pedagogue, coined the term "pedagogic eros" referring to Plato and Wilhelm Dilthey, describing the unselfish, altruistic basic attitude to foster self-development in adolescents (Nohl & Pallat, 1988). This concept is based on experience and can later be found in the works of Gendlin and Rogers.

In contrast to Freud's image of the human being, according to which life is the result of different conflicting motives, of a "war" between opposites, Carl Rogers put forward the notion of one motive in life, namely the actualizing tendency, the outcome of the development of one force, which in itself can be split when the self-actualizing tendency differs from the organismic valuing due to introjections of conditions of worth. The result is incongruence between self and organism which in severe cases results in so-called psychopathology. According to this view of the human, *the* way to overcome such forms of incongruence is through unconditional positive regard (UPR), which reduces the defences that hinder the actualization tendency to do its work because of the anxiety that comes along when change is required. In an accepting, acknowledging relationship, anxiety can be reduced and a more realistic view can more easily develop. One way to foster this is psychotherapy. Another one is a loving relationship, be it a friendship or a partnership. This brings UPR into connection with love of the Eros type and raises the question whether it is the same kind of love as in the love of partners.

Storge (affectus)

Storge (στοργή) is used to characterize familial love, natural affection, connectedness, especially of parents towards their offspring and vice versa. It's the common and natural empathy, like that felt by parents for their offspring. Storge is a wide-ranging force: between family members, friends, owners towards their pets, companions or colleagues; it can also blend with and help underpin other types of love such as passionate love or friendship. Thus storge may also be used as a general term to describe the love between exceptional friends (or partners in marriage), and the desire for them to care compassionately for one another. Storge can be love between married couples, who are committed, and plan to have a long relationship together.

Another interpretation for storge describes it as a sexual relationship between two people that gradually grew out of a friendship – storgic lovers sometimes cannot pinpoint the moment that friendship turned to love. Such lovers are friends first, and the friendship and the storge, can endure even beyond the breakup of the sexual relationship. They want their significant others to also be their best friends. Storgic lovers place much importance on commitment, and find that their motivation to avoid committing infidelity is to preserve the trust between the two partners.

Is storge a dimension of a therapeutic relationship?

Relationships such as the ones described come along with and can only exist with a sufficient degree of empathy. It is empathy-bond love (Lewis, 1960). Storge is a natural ability of humans as is empathy. Storge is the kind of loving relationship where empathy plays a major role, can be developed and refined. And empathy begets UPR and vice versa.

Undoubtedly there are commonalities between a parent-child relationship and a therapeutic relationship, e.g. in terms of imbalance in power, a certain one-sidedness (parents care and are responsible for their children, at least for some time; this is not true vice versa in the same way; clients do not need to care and are not responsible for their therapists). And it is not true regarding the limited time. Rogers' (1975) exchange with Gloria about father and daughter comes to mind, as does Freud's theory of transference and the later developed theory of countertransference. Here it becomes very clear how the image of the human being influences the understanding of the question whether there is a place and which place there is for love in therapy.

But the differences are also obvious: a therapeutic relationship is not intended to last longer than necessary and is always thought to be only a temporary substitute for a relationship the client him- or herself can have in his or her private life.

Philia (amor amicitiae)

Philotes is a goddess in Greek mythology whose equivalent in Roman mythology is Amicitia (friendship). She is said to be the personification of philia.

Philia (φιλία) means pure, friendly interest in others, love between friends, "brotherly love". Others describe philia as dispassionate virtuous love. It is the very opposite to phobia. Mostly this kind of affectionate regard is translated as "friendship", usually between equals, characterized by caring and sympathy. Philia is expressed variously as loyalty to friends, family, and community, and requires virtue, equality, and familiarity.

While Plato can be seen as the philosopher of Eros, Aristotle (1999) in his *Nicomachean Ethics* deals with philia (Pechriggl, 2009, p. 49). Aristotle (1380b36–1381a2) defines the activity involved in philia as "wanting for someone what one thinks good, for his sake and not for one's own, and being inclined, so far as one can, to do such things for him." He takes philia to be both necessary as a means to happiness ("no one would choose to live without friends even if he had all the other goods", 1155a5–6), and noble or fine in itself.

The Austrian philosopher Augustinus Wucherer-Huldenfeld (1997) proved that philia characterizes a common realization of community. Philia, as seen from the person-centred image of the human being, is a beautiful example of interconnectedness. Richard of St. Victor, among others, and the 20th century philosopher Emmanuel Levinas speak of "con-dilectio", of shared love, co-love, when two lovers together love a third one, e.g. a child (see Schmid, 1991; 1994).

Is therapy love of the philia type?

Is therapy a kind of friendship? There are obvious similarities in the way of being-with each other and counter to each other (thus developing both the relationship and themselves as individuals) as it is with good friends. The most important commonality from a person-centred point of view is that both relationship and therapy spring from a fundamental common We (see below) – the understanding of which comes close to this interpretation of the Aristotelian view of philia as described.

But there are important differences. Friendships are mutual; friends usually have an interest in mutuality. A one-sided friendship could last for a certain period (e.g. when one of them is in need) but needs to be balanced in the long run. The therapist-client relationship does not need to be mutual; it can slowly grow towards a mutuality of sharing, but as soon as this is reached, therapy comes to an end. Furthermore, friendships have to do with mutual interests, whereas therapy is only for the sake of the client. It may happen *after* therapy that therapist and client become friends. But this must be carefully reflected and therapy should never have this as a goal.

Agapē (caritas, amor benevolentiae, dilectio)

Originally the word did not have a specific religious connotation as it later had under the influence of the translations of the Bible. Agapē (ἀγάπη) embraces a universal, unconditional love that transcends philia and serves regardless of circumstances. In the biblical use of agapē attention and caring (charity) are the dominant characteristics of agapē. It is saying yes to the other and therefore doing all that one can do for an Other. The foundation for it lies in God's love to all humans and in the participation in this, in God's love.

If you express this understanding of love in a more general, contemporary, "spiritual" language, you might speak of *universal love*. Such love is not only based on the conviction of a fundamental We of the human being, but also, in an analogous sense, of everything in the universe. In its exact and profound meaning agapē aims at wholeness, at the connection with the universe. I consider *personal love* (Schmid, 1996, pp. 533–540) to be an adequate English term for agapē, given that "personal" is understood in the sense of the person-centred notion of "person" (see below).

Agapē is a type of love that:

- is beyond the reciprocity of giving and taking, more than the fulfilment of one's own duties, more than ethical social behaviour;
- is entirely non-possessive – the dominant characterization is not desire but confirmation of the other as the Other, i.e. as he or she is;
- uniquely serves (as the only type of love) regardless of changing circumstances;
- – is at one and the same time love of the Other (the others, the world) and love of myself, whereas the important point is that it is completely about the Other and not about myself in the Other; it is about empathy not about cognitive social perspective taking (Binder, 1996);
- is co-love or co-operation (Ledermann, 2011).

Is therapy agapē?

Rogers (Schmid, 1996) used love in the explicit meaning of agapē several times to characterize the dimension of the therapeutic relationship he called unconditional positive regard. If we take the original meaning of agapē into consideration as a turn towards the Other, as loving devotion to the cosmos, we can see that Rogers – he had studied four semesters of theology – uses the term correctly. Other therapeutic theoreticians did likewise (ibid.).

Agapē is devotion to the whole. From this view, each therapeutic agapē is both an affirmation of the client and an affirmation of life as such. Each of us feels, has, *is* two seemingly contradictory desires: to be fully connected with the universe, to be in uni-ty, to be united *and* to be individual, uni-que, fully and freely oneself. Both are included in the meaning of agapē.

There are several coincidences: agapē is the only love that serves regardless of changing circumstances; this love is fully directed towards the other without intention of self-regard; this love is bound to self-love.

But there are also differences, the most important of which is that love in therapy should not be enduring for the whole life, it is not "eternal". And agapē in other circumstances than therapy does not depend on the need or wish of one person as it does in therapy.

Beyond this four, further terms include *sexus* (σέξ, Latin *amor concupiscentiae*), which denotes the sensual, voluptuous desire (lust) and thereafter way of relating, and *philautia* (φιλαυτία), self-love – either narcissistic or enhancing the self-concept thus becoming able to give more love to others. This is unquestioned in psychology today, but it can already be found as a central statement in the Bible (which does not say: do love the other instead of or more than yourself, but makes mature self-love, equalling the love to the Other even a measure for love to God). (For further characteristics of the meaning cf. Bierhoff et al., 1993.)

Varieties of one *love?*

Obviously, there is love in different forms or gestalts. Is it *one* love that expresses itself in diverse forms, colours or flavours – or do these different performances in human life, experiences and acts have a different motivational origin? Could it be that it is not by coincidence that modern languages like English, German or French only have one word for all these variant expressions for love – for our natural need to transcend ourselves?

Can these expressions exist separately? Is each love in some way erotic love? Is each form of love in some way estimation and care? What has a more abstract, spiritual love of the universe got to do with the body, with physical love? Has a quickie, a one-night-stand or seemingly sheer masturbation, called "self-satisfaction" or "self-gratification", something to do with universal agapē or even love to God?

Are not in all these forms physis, psyche and mind (bodily sensations, emotions and spiritual attitudes) mutually interactive albeit in diverse intensity? Isn't love always a holistic, bio-psycho-spiritual-social phenomenon, however in different manifestations, peculiarities, flavours, shaping?

This short overview not only showed that there is much overlapping but also that among all four forms of love some things are similar and some are different.

Types of love in therapy

Thus, it is not accurate to compare love in therapy with agapē only. This is so for several reasons. One of them is that the four forms *apply to different aspects of therapy:*

- *Eros* is the "driving force" that may motivate a person to work in psycho-social areas and induces the attention and care for the concrete work with a certain client. If you understand Eros as the motivation for the altruistic basic attitude to foster self-development, as in "pedagogic eros", psychotherapy definitely needs this kind of Eros – even building on Plato's notion: to discover and appreciate the beauty within a person – could this perhaps be an adequate description of person-centred therapy?
- *Storge* relates to empathy as a given resource in humans. With its natural origin and its fidelity storge may be seen as the *cantus firmus*, the "firm song" or pre-existing melody which underpins a therapeutic relationship and makes it possible to withstand the difficulties Eros might have incurred.
- *Philia* regards the Other as a peer, ranked equally, and emphasizes mutuality in the relationship. It is based on the idea of a fundamental We. Together with agapē, an in-depth understanding of philia shows that love is only love when it is *embedded in the community*, which has many sociological, political and socio-therapeutic consequences (Schmid, 2014; 2015b).
- *Agapē* as the unconditional caring for the client finally "centres" in the Other and is only for his or her sake – the crucial point of a person-*centred* psychotherapy.

This said, we must be careful not to overlook *that self-love and love towards the Other are mutually dependent*. No love that deserves its name is without self-love. No turn towards another in a loving attitude is really possible without standing on one's own ground, being clear about one's being-oneself. There is no relationality without substance. There is no selflessness in love; pure altruism is impossible – meaning that the caring person would not be involved in love. The idealization of the negation of the I was, among others, detected, disclosed and interpreted as missing strength, even more: covered, hidden selfishness.

Love and the image of the human being as person

Furthermore, it is becoming clear that all types of love mentioned are connected to the specific image of the human being which humanistic philosophy calls "person".

Love is always also physical love. Not only is the psychoanalytic view of an erotic drive as a fundamental force to life built on this conviction; also in humanistic therapies body, psyche and mind are seen as permanently involved in what a person does. This is also true for love. There is no love that is purely spiritual and without physical involvement; even in an act of love towards God, the body of the loving person is involved. Love is always bound to corporeity and can only be experienced through the body (the way one looks, the glance in the eyes, words, deeds, symbols). You can encounter the beloved human, animal, plant or thing only through his or her body or its material form. If this is true, then the same happens in therapy. Love in therapy always also has its bodily dimensions; but in no case, not even where love is more or mainly about satisfaction of needs, can this be seen as love, if the partner is only a bodily object of desire.

Love to others always has to do with transcendence of oneself, albeit for different reasons. Although love may be a very private thing, it has always effects in and on community. And in a certain way even the Eros-related (and definitely the other forms of love) are explicitly *community-bound*.

Love, understood as personal quality with its substantial and relational notion (Schmid, 1991; 2013) *is always about personalization*, about the process of being and becoming a person – regarding both the Other and oneself, even though this might sometimes be true only to a minimal degree. Therefore, *love is more than a subject of ethics* – it is a subject of anthropology, of understanding who and how we humans are.

Love in the PCA

With some exceptions for quite a long time the word "love" did rarely appear in person-centred literature except in transcripts of therapies. Thinking about love in therapy was a marginal issue – apart from the important contributions of Brian Thorne (1985; 1998; 2005), who committed himself to a theological, Christian understanding of the person-centred approach (PCA) and examined the attitude of "tenderness". This has changed somewhat with authors like Dieter Tscheulin (1995), Suzanne Keys (2009), Divine Charura and Stephen Paul (2014) among others. But from the very beginning there is one outstanding exception: Carl Rogers.

Carl Rogers: UPR as agapē

Rogers adopted the (quite technical) term *unconditional positive regard*, coined by Standal (1954), and explained it – among many other descriptions – as love.

The term UPR used by Rogers (1957, for example) was obviously created to avoid misunderstandings and to discern what Rogers discovered to be essential for therapy from other forms of love. He always tried to use a language as close to experience as possible, but he was also careful not to be misunderstood. (Sentences like "the therapist loves the client" or "the therapist appreciates being loved by the client" might easily be misinterpreted). The essential aspect of UPR is the lack of conditions for acceptance, in other words: the client is accepted as the person he or she is.

In 1959 Rogers defined UPR as "one of the key constructs of the theory" and refined the definition in later years.

> if the self-experiences of another are perceived by me in such a way that no self-experience can be discriminated as more or less worthy of positive regard

than any other, then I am experiencing unconditional positive regard for this individual. To perceive oneself as receiving UPR is to perceive that of one's self-experiences none can be discriminated by the other individual as more or less worthy of positive regard.

(Rogers, 1959, p. 208)

Rogers (1957) thought that the term might be a little unfortunate as it had an "absolute all-or-nothing" ring to it (Tudor & Merry, 2002, p. 146). Other terms used include non-possessive warmth, emotional warmth, respect, regard, liking and prizing and – love.

As early as 1951, Rogers wrote that unconditional positive regard is love, "easily misunderstood though it may be" (Rogers, 1951, p. 159), and stressed its importance as a therapeutic agent, when he emphasized that:

> the client moves from the experiencing of him- or herself as an unworthy, unacceptable, and unlovable person to the realization that he is accepted, respected, and loved, in this limited relationship with the therapist. *"Loved" has here perhaps its deepest and most general meaning – that of being deeply understood and deeply accepted.*
>
> *(Rogers, 1951, p. 160, my emphasis)*

And in 1962:

> Positive regard means a kind of love for the client as he is, providing *we understand the word love equivalent to the theologian's term agapē, and not in its usual romantic and possessive meanings.* What I am describing is a feeling which is not paternalistic, nor sentimental, nor superficially social and agreeable. It respects the other person as a separate individual, and does not possess him. *It is a kind of liking which has strength, and which is not demanding.* We have termed it positive regard
>
> *(Rogers, 1962, p. 94; my emphasis).*

Although he tried to avoid terms with "misleading connotations" (Rogers, 1959, p. 208), Rogers (1962) deliberately used the biblical term "agapē" to denote the love he was speaking of. On another occasion, he adopted Tillich's term of listening love (Rogers & Tillich, 1966). And towards the end of his life he sensed that "the strongest force in our universe is not overriding power, but love" (Rogers, 1980, p. 204).

Personal love: the art of acknowledgement

After extensive work on the anthropological, epistemological and ethical foundations of the term "person" and related terms (Schmid, 1991; 1998b; 2013), where I have found how essential the concise phenomenological investigations of the authors of encounter philosophy are to understand the underlying image of the human being, I came to conclude that love – in a unique and very precise understanding – is indeed an adequate term to describe the motivation for person-centred work and its impact on personality change. It's in this context that many key stances of person-centred theory can be comprehended in their profound meaning and inner connection. (Here I only can name these briefly and give references for more in-depth reading.)

Based on dialogical terminology, I've referred to UPR as *acknowledgement*, a term among others used by Buber (1953). Acknowledgement without conditions denotes an attitude towards life which confirms *the Other* in his/her being truly an Other, a unique person, different from me. It accepts the Other as he or she is – the Other is neither evaluated nor assessed nor judged. Ac–knowledge–ment is an active and pro-active way of *deliberately saying yes to the Other as a person* (Schmid, 2001). To acknowledge somebody has nothing to do with "excessive friendliness or 'niceness'" (Tudor & Merry, 2002, p. 146). It is an affection for the person based on respect, a way of approaching the Other with emotional warmth, "a warm interest without any emotional over-involvement" (Rogers, 1951, p. 44), a way of caring without taking possession. It means to be with the Other whatever might happen to, or in, him or her – this is what storge love is about. It is an expression of trust in the person and his or her actualizing tendency.

Acknowledgement means that *the person as such is "ap-preciat-ed" in his or her worth and dignity* – esteemed as a "precious" being. This does not imply imagining what the Other might actually want to say (cf. Rogers, 1975, p. 50), but bona fide, in good faith and without hidden suspicion or evaluation, to take ("ac-cept") the Other as he or she describes, exposes, discloses him- or herself, namely, "at face value" (see Schmid, 2001).

The Other is not a variant of myself, *not an alter ego* – which means that he or she can never be understood by drawing conclusions from me to him or her or by generalizing my experiences, but only through empathic communication when the Other opens up and discloses him- or herself. This requires a *Thou-I-relationship*, where the movement of relating and understanding goes from the Other to me – the posture of *encounter*. In dialogic philosophy, such a personal encounter (understood as being touched by the essence of the opposite, Guardini, 1955) is described as an existential interplay, an authentic game of love from person to person (Schmid, 1998c; 2006; 2014; Schmid & Mearns, 2006).

The meaning of *person* – the prominent term in our approach – developed in the western tradition values equally one's own individuality and autonomy (the substantial dimension of being), *and* one's interconnectedness and interdependence, the capability and need for reciprocal solidarity (the relational dimension of becoming) in a dialectical way (Schmid, 1991; 1998b). The intersubjectivity of this notion equals that of the aspects of love to oneself and the Other.

The relationship where a person relates to the Other as a person is termed *personal encounter*, which is thought to be *the* healing element in therapy. As a radical contrast to any solution-oriented idea, the person-centred relationship is characterized by the unique stance that relationship is not used for anything, e.g. therapy; rather *relationship is itself therapy*, not a pre-condition for it. The essence of an encounter relationship is to be surprised, to be open to meet the unexpected, not to observe, check and not at all to diagnose. To my knowledge it is best expressed in the famous sentence of the Lithuanian philosopher Emmanuel Levinas (1983, p. 120): "Encountering a human being means being kept awake by an enigma." Personal encounter is a relationship *face to face*, as agapē is described in the Bible (1 Corinthians 13; Schmid, 1994; 1998b; 2013).

The epistemological stance of encounter – instead of investigation, expertise and goal- or solution-orientation – outlines the distinguishing characteristic of PCT. In contrast to looking for more and more sophisticated techniques to be used as methods to make clients what therapists think they should make of them, euphemistically and misleadingly called therapy – when in fact it's sheer social engineering – the notion and surprising richness of the adventure and art of encounter describes what happens when you are *present* to and with another person. It is the exact opposite of checking, figuring out, apprehending everything and everybody and thus exerting control, domination, and exercising power – the age-old wish to be like God. The person-centred posture is the exact opposite of techniques that aim at bringing nature under control, of techniques aimed at controlling both our own psyche and the psyche of others: psychological techniques, therapeutic techniques, management techniques – all geared towards gaining influence, being the master, making the world like *I* want it to be. The alternative to "make" something happen is the power of love – however, not an easy task, full of risk (Schmid, 1996, p. 540).

In order to be able to acknowledge, the therapist tries to be as *present* as possible as the basic "way of being with". The three Rogerian conditions of empathy, acknowledgement (UPR) and authenticity are three dimensions of *one* attitude, comprehensively called "presence" (Schmid, 2001; 2002). Presence is – beyond therapy and helping relationships – an elementary constituent of human communication and the human condition in general. It means to be fully in the *kairos* (Schmid, 2014), the given moment, living UPR as acknowledgement, empathy and authenticity – triggered and maintained by the therapeutic Eros. This dialogic approach is related to what Thorne (1985) has called "tenderness" and Mearns and Cooper (2005) have come to name "relating at depth". It is based on the conviction of a *fundamental common We* of the human being (Schmid, 2003), and, in an analogous sense, of all in the universe – which is the perspective and dimension of philia and particularly that of agapē.

Acknowledgement is the personal response to another person's call – a response, which we owe each other. But what people do owe each other is *love*. Such love is inseparably an attitude towards oneself as well as love towards the Other. Because of the notion implied in the understanding of a human as a person I've come to term love in PCT as "personal love" (Schmid, 1994, p. 278; 1996, pp. 533–540). Personal love means: somebody is loved as a person by a person.

In a nutshell: I am convinced we truly can say that *love in therapy is the art of acknowledgement*.

Acknowledgement, understood as personal love, can be seen as the "art of responding" (Pagès, 1968; Schmid, 2002, 2013): a way of responding to the other person and the world, out of inner freedom – not by giving simple answers but by *being a response* as a person oneself. It is a matter of courage; it needs courage to trust in the client's and one's own abilities instead of falling back on behaviours, methods, and techniques which seemingly provide security because we think we *know* what will come next. The risk is to *ac-know-ledge* what is opening up and disclosing itself, to be surprised by the mystery of the Other and to dare to receive, to ac-cept, to ap-preciate.

It needs bravery to see oneself as a therapist, as an "artist of responding" and as somebody who is capable of "a kind of liking which has strength", as Rogers (1962, p. 94) says. Simply put, it is the question whether we dare to love our clients.

Summary: the PCA is about the power of love

Is therapy love? Yes, definitely. Is it Eros, storge, philia or agapē? No, none of these in the classical sense and not in the traditional or usual meaning; it has aspects of all of them but all these forms do not describe it fully.

PCT is a relationship of its own character. Whatever else it may be, PCT is a unique form of love. It has elements of other forms of love, is similar to some of them but not equal. It is *personal love* in the special relationship between client and therapist.

Special characteristics of love in therapy are, among others:

- It does not aim at being mutual (although this may happen).
- It is a relationship that is destined to come to an end.
- It is a permanently supervised and thus well-reflected relationship.

How one thinks about love is a question of one's personal image of the human being. Each of us has his or her *personal love concept*. And so each of our clients has a personal love concept. To empathize with it is a primary task in psychotherapy.

According to the understanding illustrated above, it is not only possible to call what we do in therapy love as a metaphor, but it is most adequate to regard the person-centred therapeutic relationship as a loving relationship. Even more: the person-centred approach is about the power of love. This is a non-intrusive rather than imposing power; it is the power to accept, not the power to make. Love plays a central role in person-centred thinking and acting. As shown, the person-centred anthropological, epistemological, and ethical core terms try to grasp the notion of love.

Such love is an existential response based on our human response-ability to the client, whom we see both as a fellow human and as the Other whom we never can comprehend and know but can encounter. The true quality of love is present where a human being confirms, says yes to the being-there and the way of being of the Other or the Others and enjoys their potential to say yes to him- or herself. Our love becomes visible and perceptible by our reliable presence, and our trust in the self-agency and actualization of the clients. It is love as the ultimate expression of what we think is the foundation of the person-centred relationship, the fundamental We. It is love that means being- and becoming-together.

Person-centred therapy is a special form of personal love. It is an art of acknowledgement unparalleled in other forms of therapy or other relationships in life. However, to talk about love in therapy needs careful explanation as to what we do mean by it in order to avoid misunderstandings. A theory of love in therapy is a specialization of a theory of personality and of relationship that can and must be described in detail.

It is true, as St. Augustine said: *"Dilige et quod vis fac"* ("Love and do what you wish", Augustine, 2002, Tract. on ep. John, 7,8). But this is the very opposite of "anything goes". The love we talk about is not at all an arbitrary, nice, or warm attitude or behaviour or reliance on spontaneous creativity alone.

To allow yourself to love a client also has nothing to do with harmlessness nor with romance. It is, in contrast to John Lennon's song, not "easy". It is a risk to allow yourself to open up and be touched by the client's experience. It needs ongoing careful training by personality development, theory development and supervised practice. It needs permanent reflection and learning in order to work *lege artis* (in accordance to the rules of the art or craft), and not use the clients for our own needs – which is definitely an abuse. There is no love without self-love, no self-love without reflected experience in relationships. To learn to love oneself is one of the things that personality development in therapy training is about. The task is to vigilantly and wisely avoid seeing as love the acting out of our own wishes, desires, curiosities, of our needs to be seen as good, as the seemingly altruistic ones. The adequate way of being with clients needs permanent engagement and life-long learning – as does love (Schmid, 2014; 2015b).

One last important aspect can be briefly mentioned here: The possibility to love requires conditions where love is possible, structures where there is the freedom of loving. Thus, therapy cannot only be individual *psycho*therapy or counselling in smaller or larger groups. It must aim at including society as such and therefore also become *socio*therapy which requires political engagement (Schmid, 2015c).

References

Aristotle (1999). *Nicomachean ethics*. Indianapolis: Hackett.
Augustine (2002). *Opera. Werke*. Paderborn: Schöningh.
Bierhoff, H.W., Grau, I. & Ludwig, A. (1993). *Marburger Einstellungsinventar für Liebesstile*. Göttingen: Hogrefe.
Binder, U. (1996). Empathie und kognitive soziale Perspektivenübernahme. In: C. Frielingsdorf-Appelt et al. (Eds.), *Gesprächspsychotherapie* (pp. 131–143). Cologne: GwG.
Boll, F. & Buchwald, W. (Eds.) (1989). *Platon: Symposion*. München: Artemis.
Buber, M. (1953). *Das dialogische Prinzip*. Heidelberg: L. Schneider.

Charura, D. & Paul, S. (Eds.) (2014). *Love and therapy*. London: Karnac.
Freud, S. (1920). Jenseits des Lustprinzips. In *Studienausgabe*, vol. III (pp. 213–272). Frankfurt a.M.: Fischer, 1975.
Freud, S. (1925). The resistances to psycho-analysis. In *The Standard Edition of the Complete Psychological Works of Sigmund Freud*, vol. XIX (pp. 211–224).
Fromm, E. (1956). *The art of loving*. New York: Harper & Brothers.
Guardini, R. (1955). Die Begegnung. *Hochland* 47, 3, 224–234.
Haeffner, G. (1997). Art. Liebe. In Kasper, W. (Ed.), *Lexikon für Theologie und Kirche, vol. VI*. Freiburg i.Br.: Herder.
Hesiod (2002). *Theogonie*. Zurich: Artemis and Winkler.
Keys, S. (2009). Love in therapy: spiritual, sexual, political and ethical aspects. Conference "Person and Dialogue" in honour of Peter F. Schmid, Vienna.
Kraus, M. (2013). Parmenides. In H. Flashar et al. (Eds.), *Frühgriechische Philosophie* (pp. 441–530). Basel: Schwabe.
Ledermann, C. (2011). Altruismus in der Psychotherapie (pp. 95–136). In: H. Petzold & J. Sieper (Eds.), *Menschenliebe heilt*. Vienna: Krammer.
Lennon, John (1967). All you need is love. In The Beatles, Album *Magical Mystery Tour*.
Levinas, E. (1983). *Die Spur des Anderen*. Freiburg: Alber.
Lewis, C.S. (1960). *The four loves*. New York: Harcourt.
Maslow, A. (1954). *Motivation and personality*. New York: Harper & Row.
Mearns, D. & Cooper, M. (2005). *Working at relational depth in counselling and psychotherapy*. London: Sage.
Meyers Enzyklopädisches Lexikon (1986). Liebe. Mannheim: Bibliographisches Institut.
Nohl, H. & Pallat, L. (Eds.) (1988). *Handbuch der Pädagogik*. vol. 1. Frankfurt/Main: Fischer.
Pechriggl, A. (2009). *Eros*. Vienna: Facultas.
Pagès, M. (1968). *La vie affective des groupes*. Paris: Dunod.
Rogers, C.R. (1951). *Client-centered therapy*. Boston: Houghton Mifflin.
Rogers, C.R. (1957). The necessary and sufficient conditions of therapeutic personality change. *Journal of Consulting Psychology* 21, 2, 95–103.
Rogers, C.R. (1959). A theory of therapy, personality, and interpersonal relationships, as developed in the client-centered framework. In S. Koch, (Ed.), *Psychology: A study of a science*, vol. III (pp. 184–256). New York: McGraw Hill.
Rogers, C.R. (1962). The interpersonal relationship: The core of guidance. *Harvard Educational Review* 4, 32, 416–429.
Rogers, C.R. (1975). Client-centered therapy. In E. Shostrom (Ed.), *Three approaches to psychotherapy*, Corona del Mar: Psychological Films.
Rogers, C.R. (1980). *A way of being*. Boston: Houghton Mifflin.
Rogers, C.R. & Tillich, P. (1966). *Paul Tillich and Carl Rogers – a dialogue*. San Diego: San Diego State College.
Schmid, P.F. (1991). Souveränität und Engagement: Zu einem personzentrierten Verständnis von "Person". In: C.R. Rogers & P.F. Schmid, *Person-zentriert: Grundlagen von Theorie und Praxis* (pp. 15–164). Mainz: Grünewald.
Schmid, P.F. (1994). *Personzentrierte Gruppenpsychotherapie*. Vol. 1: *Solidarität und Autonomie*. Cologne: EHP.
Schmid, P.F. (1996). *Personzentrierte Gruppenpsychotherapie in der Praxis*. Vol. 2: *Die Kunst der Begegnung*. Paderborn: Junfermann.
Schmid, P.F. (1998a). *Im Anfang ist Gemeinschaft*. Stuttgart: Kohlhammer.
Schmid, P.F. (1998b). "On becoming a person-centered approach": A person-centred understanding of the person. In B. Thorne & E. Lambers (Eds.), *Person-centred therapy: A European perspective* (pp. 38–52). London: Sage.

Schmid, P.F. (1998c). "Face to face". The art of encounter. In B. Thorne & E. Lambers (Eds.), *Person-centred therapy: A European perspective* (pp. 74–90). London: Sage.

Schmid, P.F. (2001). Acknowledgement: the art of responding. In J. Bozarth & P. Wilkins (Eds.), *Unconditional positive regard* (pp. 49–64). Ross-on-Wye: PCCS Books.

Schmid, P.F. (2002). The necessary and sufficient conditions of being person-centered. In J.C. Watson et al. (Eds.), *Client-centered and experiential psychotherapy in the 21st century* (pp. 36–51). Ross-on-Wye: PCCS Books.

Schmid, P.F. (2003). The characteristics of a person-centered approach to therapy and counseling. *Person-Centered and Experiential Psychotherapies* 2, 2, 104–120.

Schmid, P.F. (2006). The challenge of the Other: Towards dialogical person-centered psychotherapy and counseling. *Person-Centered and Experiential Psychotherapies* 5, 4, 241–254.

Schmid, P.F. (2013). The anthropological, relational and ethical foundations of person-centred therapy. In M. Cooper, M. O'Hara, P.F. Schmid, & A. Bohart (Eds.), *The handbook of person-centred psychotherapy and counselling*, 2nd edition (pp. 66–83). Houndmills: Palgrave Macmillan.

Schmid, P.F. (2014). Psychotherapy is political or it is not psychotherapy. The Person-Centered Approach as an essentially political venture. *Psychotherapy & Politics International* (Special Issue) 12, 1, 4–17.

Schmid, P.F. (2015a). Memento mori and carpe diem: Love and death. In D. Charura & S. Paul (Eds.), *Love and therapy* (pp. 117–128). London: Karnac.

Schmid, P.F. (2015b). Encounter-oriented learning programs for person-centered psychotherapists. *Person-Centered and Experiential Psychotherapies* 14, 1, 100–114.

Schmid, P.F. (2015c). Person and Society: Towards a person-centered sociotherapy. *Person-Centered and Experiential Psychotherapies* 14, 3, 217–235.

Schmid, P.F. & Mearns, D. (2006). Being-with and being-counter: Person-centered psychotherapy as an in-depth co-creative process of personalization. *Person-Centered and Experiential Psychotherapies* 5, 3, 174–190

Standal, S. (1954). The need for positive regard. Unpublished PhD. thesis, University of Chicago.

Sternberg, R.J. (1986). A triangular theory of love. *Psychological Review* 93, 2, 119–135.

Thorne, B. (1985). *The quality of tenderness.* Norwich: Norwich Centre Publications.

Thorne, B. (1998). *Person-centred counselling and Christian spirituality: The secular and the holy.* London: Whurr.

Thorne, B. (2005). *Love's embrace.* Ross-on-Wye: PCCS Books.

Tscheulin, D. (1995). Heilung durch Liebe? In J. Eckert (Ed.), *Forschung zur Klientenzentrierten Psychotherapie* (pp. 51–69). Cologne: GwG.

Tudor, K. & Merry, T. (2002). *Dictionary of person-centred psychology.* New York: Routledge.

Wucherer-Huldenfeld, A. (1997). Zur philosophischen Theologie des Aristoteles. In *Ursprüngliche Erfahrung und personales Sein* (pp. 243–278). Vienna: Böhlau.

PART IV
Person-centred learning and training

15

ENTER CENTRE STAGE, THE CASE STUDY...

Deborah A. Lee

Prologue

Narrator:
'Prepare to welcome the "case study"!
A fictional/academic/ethnotheatre hybrid!
A "narrative approach" – person-centred and existentially-informed!
Magical encounters in relational ethics and shared humanity!
A public psychotherapy for the stage!'

★

Playwright's notes: A name in bold means that person is on-stage; more than one audience member is being signified by **AM**; artistic licence has been taken with the cast!

★

Act 1

(The curtain rises.)

McLeod (2010), standing in a spotlight, muses: 'There has been relatively little methodological innovation within the narrative approach ...' (p. 27).

Zeldin (2015) enters, observing: 'Each meeting between two people that is not merely superficial is an opportunity to enlarge [life] beyond the banal, through discovery and invention' (p. 395).

Bourriaud (1998) (introduced with a flourish by Jones, 2006, p. 72) takes both their hands, and declares: 'Relational art ... [is] a set of artistic practices which take as their theoretical and practical point of departure the whole of human relations and their social context' (p. 133).

('Clinical' bright light blinds the audience; it's freezing cold...)

Voice off: 'It's the CASES!'
The 'cases' enter; signs covering their faces.
'I'm borderline'
'I'm depressed'
'I'm anxious'
... **'I'm a healthy control'**'s sign doesn't obscure his smile.

(The lights soften. The cast list appears on-screen.)

'The "case" – forty-six+ audio-recorded fifty-minute encounters, between Kate Smith (a self-chosen pseudonym) (38, female, heterosexual and in a relationship) (the "client") and Deborah Lee (44, female, heterosexual and in a relationship) ("the psychotherapist-in-training"). In the wings, an experienced/enigmatic female supervisor (her choice of words). All encounters are UK-based.'

'And here, a supporting cast of many (Ayckbourn's [2002] rule that "economy often equals better art" [p. 13] is cast aside!)'

(The screen displays the following.)

'Assessment of the "presenting problem"? People are "a dynamic flow, continually changing over time" (Cooper, 2015, p. 55). Worsley (2006) says of Levinas: "we cannot know others or ourselves for we are creatures of inexhaustible possibility" (p. 213).

Ayckbourn (2002) interjects: "A good DSM is like gold" (p. 157). The only DSM here is the Deputy Stage Manager!

The intervention? "Dialogical exchange" (Cooper, 2015, p. 73).
How was the case study done? It was a collaboration.
The outcome? The relationship is ongoing; Kate's judgement is paramount.'

AM: 'She's ... HUMANISED the case! She doesn't know how to do assessment and formulation! Where's she studying?'

Two cognitive-behavioural therapy (CBT) therapists, **Shorey and Stuart** (2012) read from their assessment/formulation: 'Henry was a 26-year-old, single, non-Hispanic Caucasian male who was self-referred ... for possible treatment for symptoms related with anxiety. Henry lived alone, was employed part-time as a cashier at a local retail company and was also a full-time student ... Henry's presenting diagnosis was SAD [social anxiety disorder]. The therapist was a 2nd year male undergraduate student in clinical psychology supervised by a licensed clinical psychologist' (p. 36).

Shorey and Stuart (2012) add: 'He reported living alone ...' (p. 37).

AM: 'We heard you the first time.'

Shorey and Stuart (2012) continue, after treatment: 'he was currently engaged to be married' (p. 44).

AMs: 'Didn't you do well!'

The therapists smile.

Cooper (2003) shakes his head: 'It-ification' (p. 134).

Friedberg, Tabbarah and Poggesi (2013) object, declaring 'presence' ('a way of being' which 'enables authentic connection' [Tannen & Daniels, 2010, p. 1]) important in CBT: when 'therapists add presence, immediacy and transparency ... increased patient involvement and therapeutic momentum is likely to be realised' (p. 2).

AM: 'Feels like a technique.'

Person-centred therapists, **Stephen, Elliott and MacLeod** (2011) share 'their' social anxiety case. 'Lucy ... was 40 years old. ... A Scottish female, living alone, Lucy was employed in a professional role ... The therapist assigned to work with Lucy was trained as a psychologist and a PCT psychotherapist, with 12 years' post-training experience' (pp. 57–58). After therapy, 'she had developed a lasting relationship'! (Stephen, Elliott & MacLeod, 2011, p. 60).

(Confetti rains down.)

AM: 'Was Lucy white? How old was the psychologist?'

A voice off muses: '"presence" was probably there in the *encounter* with "*Lucy*", but it feels like the "clinical case study's" structure jars with person-centredness?'

'Yes!' says **Madison** (2010): 'The pathology-centred form of encounter gives rise within psychotherapeutic literature to medical attitudes expressed in adjectives such as "clinical". [Then] the therapist takes an objective quasi-physician role in order to deliver the experimentally derived intervention' (p. 194).

Van Deurzen (2010) tweets: 'existential therapy does not consider anxiety to be evidence of pathology, but rather an essential reminder of our vibrant and dangerous aliveness' (p. 238).

AM: 'McLeod (2010) says "it is the most troubling, embarrassing or shameful aspects of [a client's] life that are being most closely scrutinised [in a case study]" (p. 54), so maybe there's better to come ...'

MacLeod and Elliott (2014) muse that the 'skeptic' stance of their hermeneutic single-case efficacy design (HSCED) studies may be problematic '[because] the client may access and read public accounts of their experience' (p. 308).

McLeod (2010) concurs, clients 'may discover what their therapist really thought about them' (p. 55).

(Offstage, women laugh.)

A psychodynamic therapist, **Jacobson** (2000) introduces the 'case' of 'Pierre': '[My supervisor said] "I should let him leave if he needed to, since two years is about as long as these kinds of borderlines remain in treatment"' (p. 4).

Geller and Greenberg (2012) assert that psychodynamic therapy 'emphasise[s] the importance of creating a lively, genuine relationship with the patient' (p. 20) to effect change.

AM: 'The "genuine relationship" sounds good ... But "these" borderlines? Are we seeing how the "clinical case study" can objectify? Is this ethical? Does it prize diversity? Is this what psychotherapists-in-training need to hear?'

Leavy (2015) says that arts-based research (ABR) work (like this) can 'jar people into seeing and thinking differently' (p. 25).

(It starts warming up.)

Narrator: 'We've started to see "case studies" questioned, with regard to diversity (or "intersectionality" – Collins and Bilge (2016) explain that "power relations are to be analysed both via their intersections ... as well as across domains of power, namely structural, disciplinary, cultural and interpersonal" (p. 27) and "relational ethics" ("a co-constructed ethical and moral encounter, with associated relationship experiences and processes, that both influences and in turn is influenced by the complex multidimensional context in which the relationship occurs" [Gabriel & Casemore, 2009, p. 1]), so let's take a closer look at "case studies".

McLeod (2010) identifies five "genres" (p. 17): (i) "single subject studies ... an observable and measurable target behaviour would be identified, and the frequency of this behaviour would be monitored" (McLeod, 2010, p. 19); (ii) "theory building case studies" (McLeod, 2010, p. 21); (iii) "pragmatic case studies [in which] the practitioner is required to collect as much information as he or she can on a case" (McLeod, 2010, p. 24); (iv) "HSCED studies ... [which ask] is this a good outcome case? Can the outcome be attributable to therapy?" (McLeod, 2010, p. 26); and (v) "narrative case studies ... [which look at] what the therapy was like" (McLeod, 2010, p. 27). In addition, there have been "autobiographical and fictional narrative case studies" (McLeod, 2010, p. 203), which haven't been received with great interest (McLeod, 2010, p. 204).

"Single subject studies" raise questions in viewing a case "as if it were an experiment" (McLeod, 2010, p. 20); "theory building case studies" challenge therapists who fear questioning "conceptual edifices" (McLeod, 2010, p. 23); "pragmatic case studies" imply that there are "different types of client" (McLeod, 2010, p. 25) when Worsley (2006) draws on Levinas to talk of people as "infinite" (p. 218); and the "judicial framework" (McLeod, 2010, p. 26) of HSCED studies makes the client "a key witness" (MacLeod & Elliott, 2014, p. 296) rather than the judge. Of the "narrative approach", McLeod (2010) says "much more needs to be done, in terms of method development..." (p. 206) or work may be unpublishable.

As we saw just now, "case studies" can reduce clients to first names, their identities encapsulated selectively – and meaninglessly. That "Lucy" is "40" (Stephen,

Elliott & MacLeod, 2011, p. 60) signifies nothing in the text. People become "presenting problem(s)" which clever therapists (identified by their experience) "fix" – preparing them for (more) social control. For is a "lasting relationship" (Stephen, Elliott & MacLeod, 2011, p. 60) really the pinnacle of therapeutic success? Are we hearing a distasteful suggestion that "Lucy" was gathering dust? Samuels (2015) talks of psychotherapy's "fairly bad record" (p. 9) in relation to "diversity".

McLeod (2010) explains that: "there has been little work on case study ethics" (p. 58). Therapists' decisions must not just be about "ethical procedures" advises McLeod (2010, p. 71) but about "moment-by-moment ethical decision making". Carroll and Shaw's (2013) conceptualisation of "ethical maturity" (p. 137) – to be able to make/implement "good or better" decisions, to take responsibility for them, and to learn/grow from them – involves "relational ethics": "with such importance on human relationships for life, development, growth and happiness, is it any wonder that a relational ethics should find its way into the heart of ethical maturity?" (Carroll & Shaw, 2013, p. 103).

The narrative/ABR approach offers a relationally-ethical approach which respects complexity. Leavy (2015) defines ABR as "an engaged, moral, and at times political activity" (p. 29). Leavy (2015) contends that public ABR can generate "empathy" and "self-reflection" (p. 2). Willis et al. (2014) say that this sort of approach is now "attracting increasing attention in the field of counselling and psychotherapy" (p. 526), citing Meekums' (2011) special issue of the *British Journal of Guidance and Counselling* as one example. Speaking of ethnotheatre, Saldana (1999) explains that only editing which "will not affect the integrity of the voice or quality of the data" (p. 63) is permitted. This is what Deborah has done here. Such work calls for "new and more ambiguous [evaluation] criteria" (Gergen & Gergen, 2011, p. 8). Leavy (2015) declares that "usefulness" (p. 27) is highly important.

Deborah is committed to the British Association of Counselling and Psychotherapy's (BACP's) (2016) ethical principles: being "trustworthy", "[respecting] the client's right to be self-governing", "promoting the client's wellbeing", "avoiding harm to the client", being "fair" and self-caring (p. 2). There was "no inducement or pressure" (McLeod, 2010, p. 64) for Kate to participate (informed consent for the work went through two negotiated iterative informed consent forms). The "ongoing" (Abrahams, 2007, p. 241) nature of Kate's consent was recognised.

Bond (2013) refers to an "ethically mature" research as involving "discussion with clients" (p. 339), but he doesn't suggest collaborating. MacLeod and Elliott (2014) refer to a client undergoing a "battery of quantitative measures" (p. 296), which sounds like an imposition. Here, Deborah and Kate spent time dialoguing about their relationship (prior to, or after therapy sessions). For one dialogue, "helpful/unhelpful" events (Elliott, 1986, p. 307) was used. All dialogues were audio-recorded (McLeod, 2010, p. 69), with consent; material selectively quoted was transcribed, and approved by Kate. Kate approved the final version of the work.

As the focus is upon process, personal material was kept minimal. While "intersectionality" demonstrates "complexity", revealing all of anyone's identity jars with ethics: instead, Kate chose how she wished to be described, and Deborah mirrored her choices. There are some personal identity similarities evident in these descriptions (above) but clearly Deborah and Kate are different (Lago & Christodoulidi, 2013, p. 116), and the social structures in which they are located matter even if they are not explored here in order to be respectful of ethics.

Deborah feels this approach is consistent with her therapy room encounters. Adame and Leitner (2011) point out that Buber's meaning of "dialogue" is "literal spoken conversation but also how our choices and actions in life are a way of dialoguing or being-in-the-world" (p. 44). She follows Yalom (2002), seeing client/therapist as "fellow travellers" (p. 8).

Kate is a current, not ex-client (in comparison with Etherington, 2000). This means that issues arising may be processed in the relationship.'

Voice off: 'We know that clients can defer to therapists, how do we know that Kate didn't defer to Deborah in this study?'

(The screen displays messages from the enigmatic supervisor.)

(Before the research): 'Kate is a unique client. I believe she will benefit a lot from a deep reflective process and she will equally be able to decline things she does not want to do.'

(During the research): 'I listened to the research dialogue and noticed that while Deborah was in the role of researcher as well as being Kate's therapist, Kate remains Kate as she is in a therapy session; and Deborah had no difficulty in resuming only the therapist role afterwards'.

(After the research): 'While doing research will take a client in a direction that they aren't going in spontaneously, you'll see something therapeutically interesting come out of this collaboration!'

Deborah: 'There's, of course, a power dynamic here, in that I need to quote my supervisor's support of my decisions ... But I also trusted my internal supervisor!'

★

Act 2

Noises off: POLICE SIRENS, CAR DOORS SLAMMING, PEOPLE SHOUTING (but no-one blinks an eyelid). A clock appears on the screen, and time passes very quickly.

(Two women appear in a soothing cream light.)

Deborah: (a professional statement, addressed to **Kate**).

'Until recently, I saw myself as a "classical-client centred" (CCT) psychotherapist-in-training.

I like CCT's political nature: Rogers (1978) talks of challenging inequalities (p. 273). I've also always liked "the model's elegant economy" (Barrett-Lennard,

1998, p. 104). It emphasises, as I do, the relationship (Merry, 2012, p. 21). I concur with Geller and Greenberg (2002) that "presence" (being "fully there" [Schmid & Mearns, 2006, p. 176]) is "the foundation of ... empathy, congruence and unconditional positive regard" (p. 83).

I believe that being "genuine", "the more helpful [the relationship] will be" (Rogers, 1961, p. 33), and "the more acceptance and liking I feel towards [an] individual, the more I will be creating a relationship which [she] can use" (Rogers, 1961, p. 34); and I feel "a sensitive empathy with each of the client's feelings and communications" (Rogers, 1961, p. 34). Like Rogers (1961, p. 35), I believe in people's tendency to actualise. Like Franke, Rachlin and Yip-Bannicq (2012), I notice that "nondirective therapy" "directs" (p. 205).

I agree with the CCT "rejection of diagnostic assessment and labelling" (Merry, 2012, p. 21); and I am increasingly confused by a perceived mismatch between this and Rogers' (1961) ideas of "psychological maladjustment" (p. 37).

This has led me towards existentially-informed person-centred therapy. Above, Van Deurzen (2010) (a prolific tweeter) said: "existential therapy does not consider anxiety to be evidence of pathology, but rather an essential reminder of our vibrant and dangerous aliveness" (p. 238). I agree.

I'm increasingly questioning "certainties", so with any approach to therapy I'm aware how: "the theory's 'gaze' ... both opens up and reflects realities and closes down and deflects realities" (Goodman, 2016, p. 81). The most exciting work I read recently is Madison (2010), explaining an experiential-existential model. Madison (2010) says: "the body, rather than an inert object, is an experiential process interacting with and responding to its environment" (p. 192). As such, "therapists offer invitations to the client to stay with what is felt but not being paid attention to" (Madison, 2010, p. 196). This speaks to me'.

Kate (who is the only one qualified to assess the impact of Deborah's therapeutic responses): 'I've felt quite open to the way that you work, and kind of trust the way that you have worked with me, for it to work ...'

(Then ... we go back in time ...)

'Phase A: the beginning phase' (Barrett-Lennard, 1998, p. 106)

Deborah (wrote notes after listening again to session 2, and Kate read them): 'I heard a lot of the processes [or interventions] that are still present. (They came naturally "embedded within a fluid, dialogical exchange" [Cooper, 2015, p. 73] rather than being "intents"): "active listening" (Cooper, 2015, p. 76), "if a therapist comes in too quickly ... it may interrupt clients from connecting at [a deep] level"; "minimal encouragers" (Cooper, 2015, p. 76), "brief interjections that let clients know that they are being listening to, received and understood"; "reflecting, paraphrasing and summarising" (Cooper, 2015, p. 76) which show clients that "their experiences are intelligible" (Cooper, 2015, p. 77); and "asking open-ended questions" (Cooper, 2015, p. 78).

Deborah: '...you were sharing a lot with me (some types of therapists might have "asked for" what you said, to do an "assessment" ... my intention was not to "ask for" anything, only to receive whatever you wanted to say – your "assessment", in fact, of whether you wished to share with me) ...'

Kate: 'I've always felt very comfortable with you'.

Sexton et al. (2005) comment: 'the early client-therapist connection was largely established in the first session. The level of the client-therapist connection was quite stable from the first to the second session' (p. 112).

Deborah: 'At 8.16 minutes into the session, you say (rather profoundly) that: "now is all we have" and observe that might sound "a bit poncey". You then tell me, laughingly, that "you're shaking your head", I say: "it's not poncey!", and you agree. It felt like there was already a connection developing between us'.

Barrett-Lennard (1998) observes that at the end of the 'beginning phase', there's a move from 'monologue to duologue ... communicating with a person now felt and coming into view as a distinctive other person' (p. 107).

The middle

Deborah: 'Something that stood out for you [in our relationship] later? I know what mine is [laughing]'.

Kate: 'You tell me what yours was [laughs]'. (**Deborah**: 'ok')

Deborah: 'There's a bit of self-disclosure in it, I hope that's going to be ok, and we can talk about it afterwards. I nearly didn't train for psychotherapy in case people brought a certain thing and there was a day when you did bring that thing and the relational depth [explored below] took over and I facilitated you saying more about the thing I probably didn't want to hear about and I think you cured me'.

Kate: [pause] 'Oh gosh. (**Deborah:** 'yes') I don't know what to say. (**Deborah:** 'mmm') Oh, I might cry. I feel quite emotional hearing that'.

Barrett-Lennard (1998) says: 'personal realness and transparency works to disarm and evoke trust in the other' (p. 113).

Deborah: 'Rapport/alliance building, assessment, interventions – they're ongoing processes. New patterns emerge from relating'.

'Phase D ... clients now experience new levels of personal change' (Barrett-Lennard, 1998, p. 117)

Kate: 'There's been a lot of reflection on how some of the processes in me are changing, particularly this [deleted] element. And I remember when I first started coming to see you, that I couldn't put my finger on what I was missing (**Deborah:**

'mm'), it was almost like grasping at candy floss, or ether, and it's become clearer, it's become clearer what it was that was missing, and then what's happened is that I feel the [deleted] now, I'm more connected with it'.

Barrett-Lennard (1998) observes, 'a helping relationship does not literally produce change but works by releasing or nourishing inbuilt recuperative and actualising tendencies' (p. 89).

Edgar (2009) observes that 'clocks' are a regular theatrical '*device*', (p. 156) but here, time seems to be passing at the speed of light!

Act 3

Noises off: POLICE SIRENS, CAR DOORS SLAMMING, PEOPLE SHOUTING (but no-one blinks an eyelid). A clock appears on the screen, and time passes very quickly.

Narrator: 'Let's now fully unpack the meaning of the clocks and the noises off.

Geller and Greenberg (2002) define "presence", as: "the ultimate state of moment-by-moment receptivity and deep relational contact" (p. 85).

In Geller and Greenberg's (2002) work, "therapists [from a variety of modalities] described actively clearing a space [for presence]" (p. 77). In "presence", therapists felt "flow, energy and calm" (Geller & Greenberg, 2002, p. 80); "time and spatial boundaries seem[ed] to drop away" (Geller & Greenberg, 2002, p. 81).

"[Presence] involves being with the client rather than doing to the client" (Geller & Greenberg, 2002, p. 85); this raises questions about whether "presence" is really present in some of the modalities now explored.

Geller and Greenberg (2012) say that: Freud referred to "receptivity, and described it as emerging from an impartial, non-judgemental, evenly applied attention" (p. 18); it was not communicated to the analysand. As we saw earlier, current psychodynamic work uses the relationship instrumentally. Gauna et al. (2015) talk of "moments of high receptiveness" in clients, when therapists can "produce change" (p. 65).

CBT now also values how relationship affects outcomes (Geller & Greenberg, 2012, p. 34) (see Friedberg, Tabbarah & Poggesi [2013, p. 2] above). But Geller, Greenberg & Watson (2010) compared "presence" in CBT, process-experiential and process-experiential/client-centred therapists; CBT therapists scored lowest (p. 607).

"Presence", in existential theory, "helps people confront, accept and tolerate ... the inevitability of the conditions of living" (Tannen & Daniels, 2010, p. 2). For Yalom and Bugental, "the cultivation of presence" (Krug, 2009, p. 330) "goes beyond, experiences or moments of deep connection with self and other" encompassing also "that each person's past is present in the here-and-now" (Krug, 2009, p. 331). Therapy then involves "connection" and recognition of "how specific behaviours and attitudes block [a client] from these deeper connections" (Krug, 2009, p. 331).

In person-centred therapy, Schmid & Mearns (2006) say that: "we are looking for a deeper sense of meeting than simply a working alliance" (p. 178). For Focusing-oriented therapists, "presence of the therapist is central to clients who are learning to listen to their own emotional experience" (Geller & Greenberg, 2012, pp. 29–30). Geller and Greenberg (2012) note that: "even though humanistic therapists espouse the value of presence, they have not clarified how to be fully present" (p. 34).

Geller (2013) feels that therapist "presence"/inviting client "presence" "can allow for moments of relational depth" (p. 175). Variations of "relational depth" occur across modalities (Wiggins, Elliott & Cooper, 2012, p. 140). Mearns & Cooper (2005), person-centred therapists, define "relational depth" as "a feeling of profound contact and engagement with a client" (p. 1); it is "fundamentally dyadic" (Mearns & Cooper, 2005, p. 113); it can be "moments" or "enduring experiences" (Mearns & Cooper, 2005, p. 1)'.

Kate: (to whom Deborah had previously said she didn't notice time passing in their meetings, and who had just read some notes about 'relational depth' written by Deborah) 'So, it's a "thing"!' [**Deborah:** 'mmm!'] [both laugh].

Narrator: 'Wiggins, Elliott & Cooper (2012) contend that there being a "timeless atmosphere" seemed to be about "moments" only (p. 150)'.

Deborah: 'The reason I put bold around 'enduring' (in the notes), is because that's the one they don't write about as much, but that is what I feel here, it's not every now and again, to me, if feels enduring. I don't know how it is for you?'

Kate: 'I'm not aware of what's happening outside, not aware of anything else'.

Narrator: 'Knox and Cooper (2011) say that their interviewees compared experiencing relational depth with not experiencing it with previous therapists (p. 68)'.

Kate: 'Whereas all the other times [of having person-centred therapy], yes I've connected with people on a level, and, you know, I've got a lot from it, it's not been the same connection, I don't think, as it has been with us'.

Narrator: 'When relational depth didn't happen for clients: "a recurring theme was the unwillingness of the client to 'let go'" (McMillan & McLeod, 2006, p. 288)'.

Deborah: 'I wrote that (on the materials Kate read) because there were a few sessions where you said you were censoring ... I was thinking [pauses] perhaps this [what has been written before] isn't quite right, that you *can* still be censoring and still have relational depth, there can still be some things that you're thinking how you can say it for your own ...'

Kate: '... safety, yes.'

Deborah: 'Yes, and it doesn't mean you can't have connection. They might have missed something.'

Kate: '… when I've been holding things back, it's not been because I don't trust you, it's maybe because I don't trust myself with it, what those feelings mean and then get carried away with it, and open Pandora's box. … But, that doesn't mean to say that I'm not engaged.'

Bazzano (2014) observes of ideas of clients not 'letting go' that: 'the therapist's frustration can be a great teacher' (p. 210).

Narrator: (She throws her script aside): 'Deborah and Kate, I find your interpretation more interesting!'

Kate: '…that's a whole other paper!'

Deborah: 'It is!' [both laughing].

Narrator: 'Bazzano (2014) introduces the term "togetherness", referring to "aloneness, autonomy and conflict alongside relatedness and interdependence"' (p. 205).

(Off-script again; she's building up her part.) 'That doesn't jettison relational depth, and it offers the existentially-informed approach that you're developing, Deborah'.

AM: 'Doesn't time fly?'

Epilogue

Narrator: 'When Deborah and Kate reflected upon their research dialogues, something interesting happened …'

Deborah: 'We've been doing what we do, but before [this process], we hadn't sort of done a review of how we are doing it, to me it feels a very helpful thing to know more about how you feel about it'.

Kate: 'Yes, definitely. I've had quite a lot of counselling and stuff and I've not had that kind of dialogue'.

Deborah: 'Would you like for us to reflect on being together more often?'

Kate: 'Yes, maybe, yes, I think that would be good'.

Deborah: 'How would you like that to be initiated?'

Kate: 'Shall we do it every month. Does that sound ok?'

Narrator: 'Bond (2013) distinguishes between therapy/research, contending that research "is primarily for the benefit of people other than the patient" (p. 338). As has just been shown, that need not necessarily be so.

This outcome suggests a pluralistic framework. Cooper and McLeod (2007) explain that it: "maintains that the client's view on what is helpful and not helpful in therapy is as valid as the therapist's" (p. 139).

This development is available to Deborah and Kate because of Deborah's personal work on "certainties" – previously she would have been too "classical client-centred" for "reviews"!'

Deborah: 'I've written this case study in a way that might not have been expected, as a piece of ABR in which "client" and "psychotherapist-in-training" collaborated.

Leavy (2015) explains that evaluation of ABR provokes "much debate" (p. 266), with people considering if the "standards" present for qualitative work should be applied to it, or if "new" means of evaluation are needed.

Leavy (2015, p. 267) is opposed to a "gold standard" of evaluation for ABR, for she judges assessment of ABR to be "a messy terrain" (Leavy, 2015, p. 268).

Nevertheless, Leavy (2015, p. 266) says that "there is no question that we need ways to evaluate this work". Evaluation methods may reflect researchers' locations in the sciences/arts (Leavy, 2015, pp. 267–268) and are outlined in Leavy (2015, pp. 266–289).

Earlier, McLeod's (2010, p. 203) misgivings about "autobiographical and fictional narrative case studies" were cited. Those preferring more "standard" "case studies" may be challenged by the collaborative approach and the ABR here. But, as Leavy (2015, p. 285) observes: "no research product can be all things to all people".

Taking Leavy's (2015, p. 267) advice that any "individual criteria" for evaluation need to be applied "as appropriate to a specific project", I follow Leavy (2015, p. 273) in being particularly drawn to the concept of "usefulness" as a means of evaluating this present work.

I perceive (as explained above) that psychotherapy "case studies" usually tend to define "clients" by their "problems" and "psychotherapists" by their "training/experience", and that this creates flat/objectified characters, an "us" and "them" situation of deep inequality – in which some people are deficient and others "fix" them – rather than revealing complex human beings who have more in common than might be supposed. Such writings create a sterility to psychotherapy which does not resonate with me, and a situation in which I feel "ethical practice" (Leavy, 2015, p. 280) is compromised.

In contrast, in collaborating with my "client" to explore our sessions together and drawing on that material here, I hope the warmth of the encounter between us two "multi-dimensional" (Leavy, 2015, p. 281) human beings has been shown. In editing this work for publication, I have repeatedly agreed with Meekums (2011) that ABR provokes "emotional/embodied reactions" (p. 382): I have felt/feel deep honour and pleasure that I meet with Kate. And if I have been able to convey at least some of the warmth of the relationship and its relating then this is primarily, for me, how this work should be evaluated – a "usefulness" (Leavy, 2015, p. 272) which I would also hope might influence ethical principles in psychotherapy "case study" research (see Leavy's [2015, p. 274] comments on influencing policy) – for I feel that psychotherapists need to take all opportunities available to stop seeing "clients" as "other", including how "we" write about "them"; I believe that ABR has enabled me to start to develop this "research goal" (Leavy, 2015, p. 273).

Bourriaud (1998) says art has a "co-existence criterion ... does this work permit me to enter into dialogue?" (p. 1089). Bringing many voices on-stage, I sought/ seek to encourage the voices of you, the audience, maybe particularly those of you who are in psychotherapy training or delivering it. Might you conceive of "case studies" differently through this arts-based research?'

(The curtain falls.)

Note

This chapter was originally published as: Lee, D.A. (2017) 'Enter centre stage the case study'. *British Journal of Guidance and Counselling.* http://dx.doi.org/10.1080/03069885.2017.1310368 © 2017 Informa UK Limited, trading as Taylor & Francis Group.

References

Abrahams, H. (2007). Ethics in counselling research fieldwork. *Counselling and Psychotherapy Research*, 7(4), 240–244. doi:10.1080/14733140701707068.

Adame, A. & Leitner, M. (2011). Dialogical constructivism: Martin Buber's enduring relevance to psychotherapy. *Journal of Humanistic Psychology*, 51(1), 41–60. doi:10.1177/0022167810379959.

Ayckbourn, A. (2002). *The crafty art of playmaking.* London: Faber & Faber.

Barrett-Lennard, G. (1998). *Carl Rogers' helping system. Journey and substance.* London: Sage.

Bazzano, M. (2014). Togetherness: intersubjectivity revisited. *Person-Centred & Experiential Psychotherapies*, 13(3), 203–216. doi:10.1080/14779757.2013.852613.

Bond, T. (2013). The ethics of research. In Carroll, M. & Shaw, E. (2013) *Ethical maturity in the helping professions.* London: Jessica Kingsley.

Bourriaud, N. (1998). *Relational aesthetics.* Dijon: Les presses du reel.

British Association for Counselling and Psychotherapy (BACP) (2016). *Ethical framework for the counselling professions.* [Online] Available from: http://www.bacp.co.uk/ethics/EFfCP.php.

Carroll, M. & Shaw, E. (2013). *Ethical maturity in the helping professions.* London: Jessica Kingsley.

Collins, P.H. & Bilge, S. (2016). *Intersectionality.* Cambridge: Polity.

Cooper, M. (2003). "I-I" and "I-Me": transposing Buber's interpersonal attitudes to the intrapersonal plane. *Journal of Constructivist Psychology*, 16, 132–153. doi:10.1080/10720530390117911.

Cooper, M. & McLeod, J. (2007). A pluralistic framework for counselling and psychotherapy. *Counselling and Psychotherapy Research*, 7(3), 135–143. doi:10.1080/14733140701566282.

Cooper, M. (2015). *Existential psychotherapy and counselling: Contributions to a pluralistic practice.* London: Sage.

Edgar, D. (2009). *How plays work.* London: Nick Hern Books.

Elliott, R. (1986). Helpful and non-helpful events in brief counselling interviews: an empirical taxonomy. *Journal of Counselling Psychology*, 32(3), 307–322.

Etherington, K. (2000). *Narrative approaches to working with adult male survivors of child sexual abuse.* London: Jessica Kingsley.

Franke, M., Rachlin, H. & Yip-Bannicq, M. (2012). How nondirective therapy directs: The power of empathy in the context of unconditional positive regard. *Person-Centred & Experiential Psychotherapies*, 11(3), 205–214. doi:10.1080/14779757.2012.695292.

Friedberg, R., Tabbarah, S. & Poggesi, R. (2013). Therapeutic presence, immediacy and transparency in CBT and youth: carpe the moment! *The Cognitive Behaviour Therapist*, 6(12), 1–10. doi:10.1017/S1754470X13000159.

Gabriel, L. & Casemore, R. (2009). Introduction. In Gabriel, L. & Casemore, R. (Eds.) *Relational ethics in practice*. London: Routledge.

Gauna, M., Roibal, M., Ruiz, J., Fernandez, J. & Bleichmar, H. (2015). Active change in psychodynamic therapy: moments of high receptiveness. *American Journal of Psychotherapy*, 69(1), 65–86.

Geller, S. (2013). Therapeutic presence as a foundation for relational depth. In Knox, R., Murphy, D., Wiggins, S. & Cooper, M. (Eds.) *Relational depth*. Basingstoke: Macmillan.

Geller, S. & Greenberg, L. (2002). Therapeutic presence: therapists' experience of presence in the psychotherapy encounter. *Person-Centred & Experiential Psychotherapies*, 1(1–2), 71–86. doi:10.1080/14779757.2002.9688279.

Geller, S. & Greenberg, L. (2012). *Therapeutic presence*. Boston, MA: American Psychological Association.

Geller, S., Greenberg, L. & Watson, J. (2010). Therapist and client perceptions of therapeutic presence: the development of a measure. *Psychotherapy Research*, 20(5), 599–610. doi:10.1080/10503307.2010.495957.

Gergen, M. & Gergen, K. (2011). Performative social science and psychology. *Forum: Qualitative Social Research*, 12(1), 1–11.

Goodman, D. (2016). The McDonaldization of psychotherapy: processed foods, processed therapies and economic class. *Theory and Psychology*, 26(1), 77–95. doi:10.1177/0959354315619708.

Jacobson, G. (2000). Case presentation – a perfect transference. *Psychoanalytic Social Work*, 7(3), 3–18. doi:10.1300/J032v07n03_02.

Jones, K. (2006). A biographic researcher in pursuit of an aesthetic: the use of arts-based representations in "performative" dissemination of life stories. *Qualitative Sociology Review*, 11(1), 66–85.

Knox, R. & Cooper, M. (2011). A state of readiness: an exploration of the client's role in meeting at relational depth. *Journal of Humanistic Psychology*, 51(1), 61–81. doi:10.1177/0022167810361687.

Krug, O. (2009). James Bugental and Irvin Yalom: Two masters of existential therapy cultivate presence in the therapeutic encounter. *Journal of Humanistic Psychology*, 49(3), 329–354. doi:10.1177/0022167809334001.

Lago, C. & Christodoulidi, F. (2013). Client-therapist diversity: Aspiring towards relational depth. In Knox, R., Murphy, D., Wiggins, S. & Cooper, M. (Eds.) *Relational Depth*. Basingstoke: Macmillan.

Leavy, P. (2015). *Method meets art: Arts-Based research practice*. New York: Guildford Press.

Macleod, R. & Elliott, R. (2014). Non-directive person-centred therapy for social anxiety: a hermeneutic single-case efficacy design study of a good outcome case. *Person-Centred & Experiential Psychotherapies*, 13(4), 294–311. doi:10.1080/14733145.2011.546203.

Madison, G. (2010). Focusing on existence: five facets of an experiential-existential model. *Person-Centred & Experiential Psychotherapies*, 9(3), 189–204.

McLeod, J. (2010) *Case study research*. London: Sage.

McMillan, M. & McLeod, J. (2006). Letting go: The client's experience of relational depth. *Person-Centred & Experiential Psychotherapies*, 5(4), 277–292. doi:10.1080/14779757.2006.9688419.

Mearns, D. & Cooper, M. (2005). *Working at relational depth in counselling and psychotherapy*. London: Sage.

Meekums, B. (2011). Editorial. *British Journal of Guidance and Counselling*, 39(5), 379–384. doi:10.1080/03069885.2011.617146.

Merry, T. (2012). Classical client-centred therapy. In Sanders, P. (Ed.) *The tribes of the person-centred nation*. Ross-on-Wye: PCCS Books.

Rogers, C. (1961). *On becoming a person*. London: Constable.

Rogers, C. (1978). *Personal power*. London: Constable.

Saldana, J. (1999). Playwriting with data: ethnographic performance texts. *Youth Theatre Journal*, 13(1), 60–71. doi:10.1080/08929092.1999.10012508.

Samuels, A. (2015). *A new therapy for politics?* London: Karnac.

Sexton, H., Littauer, H., Sexton, A. & Tommeras, E. (2005). Building an alliance: early therapy processes and the client-therapist connection. *Psychotherapy Research*, 15(1–2), 103–116.

Schmid, P. & Mearns, D. (2006). Being-with and being-counter: person-centred psychotherapy as an in-depth co-creative process of personalisation. *Person-Centred & Experiential Psychotherapies*, 5(3), 174–190.

Shorey, R. & Stuart, G. (2012). Manualised cognitive-behavioural treatment of social anxiety disorder: a case study. *Clinical Case Studies*, 11(1), 35–47. doi:10.1177/1534650112438462.

Stephen, S., Elliott, R. & Macleod, R. (2011). Person-centred therapy with a client experiencing social anxiety difficulties: a hermeneutic single case efficacy design. *Counselling and Psychotherapy Research*, 11(1), 55–66. doi:10.1080/14733145.2011.546203.

Van Deurzen, E. (2010). *Everyday mysteries*. London: Routledge.

Tannen, T. & Daniels, M.H. (2010). Counsellor presence: bridging the gap between wisdom and new knowledge. *British Journal of Guidance and Counselling*, 38(1), 1–15. doi:10.1080/03069880903408661.

Wiggins, S., Elliott, R. & Cooper, M. (2012). The prevalence and characteristics of relational depth events in psychotherapy. *Psychotherapy Research*, 22(2), 139–158. doi:10.1080/10503307.2011.629635.

Willis, A., Bondi, L., Burgess, M.C., Miller, G. & Fergusson, D. (2014). Engaging with a history of counselling, spirituality and faith in Scotland: a readers' theatre script. *British Journal of Guidance and Counselling*, 42(5), 525–543. doi:10.1080/03069885.2014.928667.

Worsley, R. (2006). Emmanuel Levinas: resource and challenge for therapy. *Person-Centred & Experiential Psychotherapies*, 5(3), 208–220. doi:10.1080/14779757.2006.9688410.

Yalom, I. (2002). *The gift of therapy*. London: Piatkus.

Zeldin, T. (2015). *The hidden pleasures of life*. London: Quercus.

16

SHEEP OF TOMORROW

Manu Bazzano

Introduction

> [The persons of tomorrow] have an antipathy for any highly structured, inflexible, bureaucratic institution. They believe that institutions should exist for people, not the reverse. [...] These persons have a trust in their own experience and a profound distrust of external authority. They make their own moral judgments, even openly disobeying laws that they consider unjust.
> *(Rogers, 1980, p. 351)*

> Still, when illusions burn out, they leave embers.
> *(Di Benedetto, 2017, p. 175)*

The author of this person-centred learning journal, left in the kitchen bin on the ground floor of the *Macondo Institute*, a therapy training centre sited in affluent suburbia, would be surprised at seeing its publication, even in the heavily edited version you are about to read. None of the four notebooks – pale brown cover of the sort they sell at Muji bound together with an elastic band, wrapped in an orange Sainsbury's carrier bag – bear a name, a contact number or a postal/email address. My first, sagacious thought was to leave the bundle where I had found it. A moment later I thought to hand it in at reception. In the end, a fiercer, less noble impulse prevailed: curiosity. Or perhaps something that was even less splendid: the irresistible itch to unearth gossip, secrets or scandalous revelations. After all, although the diarist had thrown it away, he or she had not cared to destroy it and this, I thought wistfully, could only mean one thing: they had wanted someone to find it and read it.

At any rate, my decision to hold on to the notebooks for a while came after scanning, next to the kitchen bin, the first few words on the first page. I found them compelling – although, to be 'entirely congruent' (as they say around here) with *you*, my dear reader – I cannot say exactly *why* they were compelling. Enough. I knew only one thing: I wanted to read more, right away. I left Macondo's premises with a spring in my step, pulling my hat lower to hide a conspiratorial smile, and obscured my face further by tucking it into the raised collar of my coat. I magically summoned, in short, all feasible detective stories platitudes, including the melancholy gathering of shadows on a drizzly and dreary November dusk.

I went to my favourite place a block away – a local Romanian cafe where the coffee is strong, where they don't over-foam the milk nor draw daft heart-shapes to the chagrin of the newly heartbroken who come by after their weekly counselling session at the low-cost Macondo Counselling and Psychotherapy Services. In this cafe all waitresses are pretty, and waiters handsome; here you can spot lonely punters staring into the distance wistfully while gay and hetero young couples post YouTube compilations as a way to share their love while unfriending expired lovers on Facebook.

I found a quiet table at the corner where the depressingly cheerful muzak could not reach my ears; I ordered a double macchiato and started reading the first notebook, blissfully undisturbed. I found the reading captivating, to say the least, and managed to read a good chunk of the entire journal there and then.

The following passages from the journal are arranged in chronological order. Words and sentences are unedited: intact and unpolished, given that the author was not writing for an audience but solely for him/herself. The division into sections is arbitrary hence the narrative drive is entirely of my own making.

After eventually reading all four notebooks, I couldn't help feeling that I knew a little about the author. Presumptuous of me, but isn't it what we do, even when we read fiction? We assume that most fiction is autobiographical and are compelled to look for the shameful revelation, the embarrassing detail, the fall from grace and the ordinary but potentially tragic illness that turns the hero into an ordinary human being who is allowed to become a hero again only if she or he has survived the addiction, crushed his/her demons, and declared readiness to sing along a narrow-minded tune. We seem to want a *pathography* rather than a fiction or a biography. I am digressing, so I just take the opportunity to state the following: 1) No person-centred therapist or trainee was harmed during the writing of this chapter. 2) My sincerest apologies to all sheep the world over for using the term of this gentle creature in the colloquial sense. No insult is meant; it's just that language sometime does not allow for subtleties and ambivalences.

This is the dawning of the age of the fish bowl

8 September 2005

On the train back from the Introductory Course in Person-centred Counselling. a group of twenty-four people. Tired; how come, given I've just sat all day talking and listening?

Question: What is my *potential*? Are the commuters in this crowded carriage on the Central Line (tourists, first-daters, bored couples with kids, old folks with newspapers, folks with their face illumined by the light on their mobile phone like medieval saints) *actualized*? Are tourists *more* actualized than commuters because they have more space to see and feel and imagine? And: am *I* actualized? I don't think so, though I could do with a holiday. Boy, I'm getting paler by the minute. Here I am, anyway, learning: how to be a *peeeerson*, as this Glaswegian shrink said of Carl Rogers who is btw the head and founder of PCT when introducing him to his mates: 'This is Carl, he's not a man, he is a *peeeerson*'. This guy, whose name was Ronnie Laing, wrote great books they tell me and also loved his drink as well as Kierkegaard and also said that Carl, who's the Supreme Chief of this therapy thing, he said Carl wouldn't survive in a Glasgow pub. Which makes you think. Brings to mind that time in Harlesden when we played a Sunday gig in this noisy pub and they would talk loud all over our set, they showed no respect this bunch of middle class Sunday trippers and their boring girlfriends. So I kissed the mic with my lips up real close and shouted *Shut the fuck up!* They were startled and the bass player who is a gentleman looked at me like I was nuts which I was really with all the ganja in my Southern lungs etc. But really, now that I think of it: if I learn this PC therapy will I then become a super softy half-man/half-frangipane who's scared shitless of his own shadow? Will I turn into one of those weedy men who have to ask their girlfriends first before they decide to do anything? Will I survive in a Glasgow pub or a Harlesden pub? I noticed the other men in the group today, there were four of us in all including me, all the others were women, twenty women and four men! I looked at the men and they had this apologetic look of moral resignation and they looked at the women with fear and awe and I was thinking what the f...? This guy then during 'group process' as they call it was 'sharing', which means talking openly and saying what you feel including private stuff. This guy said, I'm knackered, we had an argument last night and she shut me out of the house and won't let me in, but I *deserved* it, so I slept rough and it was cold though not really cold, we are only in September thank God, he said with a smile. Everybody was nodding meaningfully and he carried on and said the argument was nothing really but no, he said it wasn't nothing, it was important, she wants me to dedicate more time to her, doesn't like it when I read by myself or listen to music or just chill out. Thing is, he went on, it's my flat and since she's moved in she took over, you know, all her things spread out in the living room and I don't get to watch documentaries or Herzog or Wenders anymore, she wants us to be together and watch *Strictly* and I hate it to be honest I fucking hate it as I'm strictly bored to death to watch that shit but then I think she's right maybe I'm too poncey for my shirt and I should like normal things. At this point the facilitator, Emma, said, looking empathically in the eyes of the sharing bloke whose name is John, she said 'Does anyone feel like taking a leap and be a counsellor to John for the next twenty minutes?' and so John and a volunteer, Gemma, brave of her I thought, sat in the middle which is called 'fish bowl' which btw made me laugh a little private laugh as I thought: Should I tell them now that I'm no tame little red fish in an aquarium and if they piss me off I can bite their head·off? I was thinking my own thoughts rather than, you know, being in the zone, *presence* they call it which is big in these circles I think. So I drifted, which is not OK. I drifted and thought of the Age of Aquarius, aquariums as fish bowls, the world a better place if everyone was person-centred and doing regular fish-bowl all transparent like a Crystal Palace with no secrets and lies and stuff. Aquarium: ideal and peaceful and universal, shiny happy women and men holding hands around a campfire, humming OM or Halleluiah or La-di-dah and whatever turns you on and turns you into the Big Love. Bring it on! A future where everyone, having done lots of fish bowls and sharing and PC counselling, I mean *really* done those things, you know, not just going through the motions, having *really* done this stuff empathically and congruently and with generous helping of love and fraternal benevolence for our fellow beings in this Friendly Smiley Planet, which is also btw benevolently actualizing, a big well-meaning Organism floating among the stars and the moon and the sun and moving everyday towards greater clarity, consciousness and good behaviour, a Pally Planet actualizing as we speak, like everything else in existence if you see what I mean. This is not your average pub banter, btw it's cosmic stuff Emma calls it *Formative Tendency*. Everything has a Purpose, you know. You smoke your little smoke, drink your little drink, chew your silly spearmint but you have no idea do you little man? You have *no* fucking idea. You are *actually* actualizing, I'm telling you. And you could actualize a lot faster if you weren't a lazy sod. And did you know? Your actualizing helps our Big Friendly Planet in a benevolent empathic and congruent universe that showers unconditional love to all living things every single moment, for instance even when I'm watching *Strictly* on the telly consciousness rises and become shinier every minute.

11 September 2005

All this actualizing of potential could turn out to be pretty boring with no one going to the pub because being so soft and empathic and actualized they couldn't survive in there like Ronnie Laing said of Chief Carl who to be honest at first looks kind of weedy to me in those videos but he means what he says I give you that and this Gloria girl liked him in the end the way one likes a caring Dad, which is not at all like a Sugar Daddy, oh no, that's another ballgame altogether, right? No sugar here, only generous helping of saccharine and what's wrong with that I ask, especially if you are confused and battered by life, what's wrong if someone listens to you and nods and makes friendly humming sounds and repeats the words you just said so that you really know that she or he is listening to you; and how rare is that in the world we live in? Even your two-bit friends, let's face it, they give you advice and what do they know? The GP gives you prescriptions, and your band mates give you drugs, so it is rare and precious to have a nice geezer or woman nodding and listening and rephrasing and paraphrasing and humming away so that you begin to know and understand, get it?

13 September 2005

It's good to see once a week someone who prizes you and accepts you as you are, even though you haven't got a clue what or who you are in the world or even if he also doesn't have a clue in the world but is so kind and nice and perceptive that somehow you begin to like yourself a bit more and then start making good decisions instead of crap ones like *I* did so many times.

Here I am, at 42, re-training as they say, *me* a *therapist*? 'A shrink?' my ex band mate asked me in disbelief. That's when it dawned on me. When I signed up I thought, well, it's another step towards self-discovery or whatever.

[...]

Re actualization: I just remember that during the lunch break at our introductory course someone pointed at a group of people coming out of the room opposite ours. 'They are third year – she said – they must be self-actualized, or at least *more* actualized than us. Look how they walk, how they talk and smile at each other; they look so ... present.' I nodded, unconvinced. What am I getting into? Well, it started quite naturally anyway. Started therapy two years ago, as I wanted to get myself sorted. Don't we all?

14 June 2006

This afternoon during fish bowl exercise, rather than writing down feedback to Carole who was being therapist to John who was being client, I just wrote down whatever came up, feeling the room out, the general feel of it, drifting in and out of what John was saying and Carole was saying and this is what came up. It was fun to do and did I learn something? I did in fact but couldn't really put it in an essay or speaking it at a Viva or anything like that and by the way it's not poetry either I don't think nor could I give it as a feedback but I think it's related to what Carole was saying and to what John was saying, so here it goes:

> Work-like, brittle. Connection, as when something fits in a painting. Enclosure, the ground under my feet, something wanting to go down. Low voices. Silence. Testing the walls: how solid? How safe? Hemmed in. Warmth. Distant sounds drifting. Can everything be allowed? World waiting to be called in. Filled suspension. Do come in, into a false oasis of cries and whispers and drafts settling down, lapping the floor. The secret can't be known. Nope – it doesn't want to be known. Traffic on a busy street. We can't stop. Not allowed to. Come closer, closer and cry as much as you like and talk and play, kindergarten play, yes play over the top. Here by the river, still water, muffled sound. These words rising, suspended and fading, passing away absorbed by the carpet. Craving so badly, held tenderly on the red carpet, change and face the strange. The room says 'change will happen anyway', the room says it.

The name of the father

25 June 2006

My first residential weekend: on arrival, I saw the three tutors having dinner in the corner of the cafeteria and ask Caroline, my tutor, 'What's the plan?' She gives me a broad smile and in response to my question opens her arms wide. I was perplexed and a bit embarrassed. Maybe it was her way of saying 'Let me have my dinner in peace'. Don't know. Was I wrong in asking? I'm paying to attend this weekend after all and I'd rather not be here but away with my new girlfriend as it's been awhile since we had 'quality' time together. But anyway, I talked about this with Joanna, who has done another course before and knows this sort of thing. Her take is that Caroline probably meant that it is all open, it is an *encounter*, a giant two and a half day group process where we can be ourselves and there is no leader and there is no plan. Hence the wide open arms, meaning acceptance and love and unconditional regard big time and with a large group. But does this mean that *anything* goes? With a group of *forty* people? Never mind. I'm all cosy in bed with a short story by James Salter, and soon I'll switch off the light and tomorrow is another day.

27 June 2006

On the train back to London, I'm reminded of what the only male tutor said this morning in the large group. He mentioned Kafka's letter to his father where he accused him of being too permissive, too accepting: 'Go out my son, do whatever you like!' And what is more disabling, more castrating than that? The tutor seemed to imply that assuming that we can sit around in an 'open encounter' is a misleading notion, that maybe the injunctions are internalized, what other psychologists call, I think, the Name of the Father: necessary, to exercise our claws, our sense of limitations and boundaries, and a lot more useful than this naive humanistic stuff of the 'we're all free'. That's what I understood anyway. And in any case is not like we were free at all. It seemed clear to me that Caroline was running the show. I mean, she was condescending towards the male tutor whose name is Rudy, for each time Rudy spoke she would either correct him or thank him for his contribution which is not the sort of thing you say to a co-facilitator I don't think but more to a student, no?

Infernal locus of evaluation

6 July 2007, 12.20pm

En route to the person-centred Conference with the ghost of a faint summer bleeding on this green and pleasant land, I breathe with relief. Fields and trees, mute in their green and pleasant disregard of all things human, save for our comical despair that makes us go in search of a shrink, i.e. someone like me.

Then the Virgin train-of-never-ending-broadcasts leaves me stranded in some backwater with not a soul in sight but a Scandinavian lady, Agnek. Both of us amble religiously around our suitcases in front of a semi deserted pub. It turns out Agnek loves London and so do I. But what are we doing here in the sticks? Over apple juice (me) and beer (her) we convince a punter to take us to the Conference – 'we are psychologists, you know' using concerted beaming of UPR and the promise of a large tip. I end up giving too much money out of clumsiness, out of this fucked-up idea of being the Buddhist champion of the downtrodden.

So this is the famous Conference: sunset on green fields; boys shouting, playing football while I talk on the phone to my sweetheart left behind in North London where civilization still reigns on the other side of the Watford Junction.

7 July 2007, 11.40 a.m.

Today I learned that Carl Rogers was human and not a 24/7 super hero of empathy. What a relief! He wrestled with demons in the small hours! He drank (not just apple juice)! He had *affairs*! He also wanted to make sure that no Rogerian Church would see the light of day in the US, something he could not manage on these shores obviously. Fat chance buddy, for here in Europe there is great, inferiority-induced clamour and incitement for the PCA to become professional, with some person-centred celebrities berating the sceptics and inciting the faithful to grow and multiply, to metamorphose from a small commando of well-meaning and awfully-nice people to sharp suit-wearing non-expert doctors who will enter the walls of the city where, however, from Plato onwards no gypsy, refugee and spiritual anarchist has ever entered.

7 July 2006, 11pm

Community meetings are the thing here. They remind me of my student movement days – the worthy aspirations, the populism: despotism of the majority, chatterbox consensus … All together now, but is this another middle-class confraternity? I bet most therapists here own their home or at least have a mortgage. As I tucked in the third meal of the day, I gazed in wonder at the dignified interiors of the dining hall: the revolution will have to wait 'til after dinner.

[…]

This morning I was challenged by someone called Marianne. Mind you, she didn't address me directly but asked Agnek whether she had minded being 'taken over' by me. Backtrack: last night at the community meeting Agnek started speaking while *I* was speaking. I carried on talking rather than being a gentleman and let the lady speak first. So this morning this Marianne asks *her* whether she felt 'shut down by that other person, that *man*'. I felt stunned. For a good five minutes I sat there with mixed feelings, mainly anger. I hesitated. Someone else talked. Then I asked for the mic and said how really pissed off I felt. Who was she? A public prosecutor? And why was she not addressing me directly? She responded while pacing up and down the room, in a way that reminded me of my brief stint with physical theatre. Someone interrupted me, 'can't you see she is upset?' I have an urge to stand with my feet on the chair and strike a dramatic pose to show that I too was upset, big time. The debate raged on, others got involved. I glanced at Marianne – she was sitting on the far left across the line of chairs – I could see her tears. I felt an unexpected a surge of tenderness and a desire to speak and cry with her but didn't do any of that, I just couldn't. As the meeting ended, I was surprised that some people – mostly women – expressed their support to me. It also felt strange that no men, for what I recall, spoke at the time. Marianne had framed her intervention around the issue of gender, but where were the men? I am fairly new to PC World. What do men do in here? Try to be good and soft and considerate? Beats me. Maybe they are shitting themselves and distract others' attention from the fact by quoting Rogers and Clouds of Unknowing.

PS I just read the line above and feel embarrassed. Am I a cynic? Must erase it from the final version.

UPR for all

15 December 2007

I'm confused. A guy from the third year made a joke at the general meeting of tutors and trainees, saying how dismayed he was that London had a toff as a mayor and this posh tutor objected to his 'racism'. I thought racism means calling a black person a nigger, or referring to Jews as mean and more generally to say nasty things about any historically oppressed group. But most of the group agreed. They said person-centred is about acceptance and you can't call a toff a toff. It's discriminatory. I'd thought all along that PCT came out of, you know, the anti-Vietnam war, May '68, humanistic psychology, being on the side of the underdog, fostering progressive change, being freedom-loving and radical and rebellious and (kindly) sticking two fingers up to all the privileged, domineering, patronizing classes whose behaviour exacerbated mental distress etc. But no. Turns out PCT is a sort of liberal, centrist, tolerant view where we all get along with one another. Reminds me of New Labour. Not in the least incompatible with smiley, recycling, tolerant, *nice* conservatism and even why not, right-wingers and monarchists – provided you are, you know, really nice and meaning it.

24 January 2008

What can I say? I read Jean Genet to keep sane. I read Genet in the way Genet read Proust – to understand how to write, which is a lot more than a skill, methinks. My own writing has been contaminated by too much psychology and academic garbage. OK, it has helped me to convey thoughts in a certain way; it has helped me publish some academic papers here and there and even the odd article in *Therapist Monthly*. So? I just can't betray my love of poetry and philosophy and all for what? To have my articles dissected by anonymous grumpy reviewers. To have them desiccated and anesthetized? Get me out of here!

2 February 2008

I get it: Macondo is a family. Is this why I can't *breathe*?

24 February 2008

Clients come and go and forget to close the door.

15 April 2008

Yesterday I met Giorgio. We had lunch together. He had soup and tea – left the tea bag brewing forever in the milky paper cup. I had a sandwich and a coffee. I was glad he found time to meet, him so well-known and all that. His workshop organized by Macondo in a town hall a month ago or so came at the right time. I was about to give up the training but something in the way he presented the seminar made me think it's OK to have doubts, you don't have to be a card-carrying member of a cult in order to be a therapist. Anyway, he said how tired he is of working in an institution where courses are organized for what exactly other than making money? We both laughed, but I know that he practically *is* the institution, while I'm just a little schmuck, really. Is that the freedom of those who are past expertise, who mastered their metier and can afford a carefree ride?

The florist near where he lives got it into his head that he is an old hobo and greets him with a touch of condescension, 'How's things today?' 'Have just come back from a conference in Sweden.' 'Oh, really? (incredulous) I'm sure you have, I'm sure you have!' Giorgio's work has that touch of creativity that restores therapy to the arts. Psychotherapy needs strong poets to inject life into the stale recycling of knowledge in academia where to succeed means to conform. Are therapists aspiring to be artists? I know many who don't but maybe a few are. Anyway, he wanted to get to know what I want to do with all this therapy thing.

17 April 2008

I have done well so far. I stayed at the blooming course and it's now Diploma final act. My therapist Tony is waffling and shuffling in his brown leather chair. A Byronic portrait of himself at 28 years of age on the wall. His little dog came in today and barked at the portrait. Did I bring ghosts back into this apartment? He waffles at times but he is so affable and considerate; he mentions TV programmes as examples. We had a good discussion on the DSM and why some person-centred writers are so damn obsequious to this shite and what I can do to balance, i.e.

absorb, learn, feel the mounting rage against the stuff I'm being fed and then take a healthy distance.

Sheep of tomorrow

5 May 2008

An international figure came to give a one-day seminar at Macondo day before yesterday. It was a big deal and they put posters up months before and book signing and webinars and what not and it was all about how the PCA according to Chief Carl wasn't just about clinical work, no, it's all about Thinking Big, Changing the World, Building the Future, Creating the Persons of Tomorrow. The name of the big shot is Eileen and she studied with the Chief in Person and she said it was a super dynamic whirl of transformative energy and really deep stuff that was going on and some of my course mates had said if you are receptive it will rub off you this good positive stuff, and you may come out of the day actualized just like that or at least with some insight that in due course will grow massive. Eileen also talked Big Love and reminded me of Marianne who had said the same thing which btw comes from the Christian Bible I think. Were we not supposed to be free of all this religious stuff and walk around with less baggage? My real fear is that the PCA is basically smuggling back blooming Christianity after we worked so very hard all those years to push it back and leave us alone and let us live our sweet and sorrowful lives, our short life on this poor crust of a planet but no. Eileen went on, it was about *agape*, big love with no strings attached whatsoever, because love is great and love will win. We shouldn't be afraid to love our clients, to be of great service, we, the big-love therapists, Eileen was saying; we shall usher in a new world of collaboration and open dialogue. This is because we are all interconnected, we are one, you and me and he and she; and human suffering can be defeated at the dawn of this new era that will see the birth of the persons of tomorrow. They will be fully therapized; they will dream in colour, the persons of tomorrow never ever will they dream in black and white. Mental distress can be defeated right now if all of us hold hands congruently and empathically. But there is work ahead of us, a tremendous amount of work to do, she added. I looked around at the packed room in Macondo full of counsellors to be, all taking notes and breathing deeply. Anxiety is not necessarily part of existence, she added. It is created by social circumstances. But there is no need to bring about a revolution. This is *not* an anti-institutional battle. We still can work in the same old institutions and bring change from within, Eileen said, and as she said that I noticed the group of tutors in the right corner giving big sighs of relief. This is an *inner* revolution, you know. Like, we can still churn out the same old course notes and show the same old *PowerPoint* presentations and quote from the very same old books. Just add some new jargon from neuroscience, a bit from attachment theory and find a good healthy link between PCT and CBT. And make sure trainees repeat all the stuff in their essays and most importantly at their VIVA examination. They shall usher in the future. They shall see the Birth of the Sheep of Tomorrow.

One hundred plus years of solitude

3 April 2009

Can't believe I'm still dreaming of Macondo a year after I graduated. It hangs around like a dysfunctional family home, like a small town you dug your way out of with your nails.

In the dream Mark and I were walking around; we had both dropped acid and some big event had just finished and it was night and we were looking and looking the whole night for the exit, like, how do we get out of this effing place? I mean, it's nice and all, but can we please get out now, please? Only around 7am or so we finally found the front door and out there it was a magical winter morning with fluffy snowflakes and there was a guy straight out of a Mantegna painting selling red apples, it was a fruit market in Milan and I bought one and my god it was delicious. We were out of the blooming Garden of Eden at last, and the forbidden apple was the best thing, for who wants to live in a bloody empathic prison and be showered with Love, and giving birth to the Persons of Tomorrow? And when I woke up I thought, yeah makes total sense, in Garcia Marquez's novel too (Garcia Marquez, 2014) Macondo is an insular place cut off from the world. Was it not a Biblical injunction to marry within the tribe and worship the One and Only Righteous God? My God, they have a name for people like that, it's hey *endogamous*! And in Macondo too, you see, we were not allowed to find a therapist or supervisor outside the Macondo-approved list of therapists and supervisors so that the whole incestuous, controlling and auditing to-and-fro could continue 'til the sheep come home and we could then churn them out the Sheep of Tomorrow, the Empathic Agents of Conformity and Banality that will make sure that the same blooming nonsense is repeated for a few more generations.

I bit the apple, mmh yes it was delicious and thank god I'm free at last.

References

Di Benedetto, A. (2017) 'Ace.' *The Paris Review*, Issue 222, pp. 155–176.
Garcia Marquez, G. (2014) *One Hundred Years of Solitude*. London: Penguin.
Rogers, C. R. (1980). *A Way of Being*. Boston, MA: Houghton Mifflin.

17

WHAT DO I KNOW AND HOW DO I KNOW IT?

Theories of knowledge and the person-centred approach

Dot Clark

Introduction

When you first read the title of this chapter, did you wonder if the questions posed might be answered here? I start by asking this because I want to defuse any assumptions which may be in play arising from the context in which this piece is presented: a chapter in a book, probably looking solidly academic and thereby carrying authority. I know my own intake of breath on sitting down to read someone else's ideas, and my own willingness to give them 'the benefit of the doubt' and take on what they may be saying. However, my desire as I embark on this exploration is to engage you, the reader, with your internal locus of evaluation fully in play, in a discussion about what we know and how we know it in the community of the Person-Centred Approach (PCA).

The historical background to asking the questions which open this chapter is the undermining of overarching truth claims regarding knowledge which has been an ongoing process in a variety of conversations since the 'subjective turn' in philosophy last century. People thinking in the fields of postcolonialism, feminism, theology and philosophy have been asking 'whose truth prevails here?' – is it that of the Colonisers, the Patriarchy, God, Rationality? And of course such challenges to truth claims open up the other extreme where it might be claimed that the only truth of importance is mine. Claiming truths to be universal can stifle fruitful conversation, but prioritising subjectivity can undermine the basis for having any conversation at all.

The challenges of these extremes are familiar within the PCA; the development of congruence can go through a stage where the primacy of the individual's experiencing is claimed, and at the other end of the spectrum Carl Rogers can be quoted as if his word outranks that of others. Practitioners wrestle with the demands of attempting to receive another with unconditional acceptance while being conditioned beings. We negotiate constantly between inner experiencing and the shared world, especially because the art of listening is located right at the heart of that negotiation.

As counsellors and psychotherapists we know the tensions at play in our profession. The person-centred commitment to encounter another person in all their uniqueness with acute attention and open acceptance can feel at odds with a profession which increasingly values academic qualifications for practitioners, research to validate our interventions and regulation according to a fixed set of criteria. The person-centred community necessarily lives in the tension between developing trust in individual experiencing and the need to justify our practice in professional terms, thus the relevance of wider conversations about the relationships between subjective and objective, social construction and deconstruction, empirical truth and phenomenology, the absolute and the relative.

My aim in this chapter is to draw on conversations associated with this theme in the hope of refreshing person-centred thinking and practice. Rather than sketch a brief outline of the philosophical history of various subjective challenges to Enlightenment objectivity, I wish to take as my starting point that human beings have the capacity to attend to and know the world and ourselves in different ways. In the implicit dualism of the endlessly looping subjective/objective debates, I recognise my own experience of feeling the absolute truth of my own values and beliefs, while also knowing what it is to experience a more open and uncertain approach to the world and its differences. This is where I live, and it is where the challenge of personal development is played out. My responsibility is to examine and loosen the conditions of my situatedness which inform *what* I know while trusting that the continued effort to explore *how* I know develops my capacity to create space to encounter the other. In noticing that my knowing moves between a fixed picture of *what* I know and a more fluid process of *how* I know it, I recognise that two different epistemological strategies are available to me.

My reference point here is Iain McGilchrist's book *The Master and His Emissary: The Divided Brain and the Making of the Western World* (McGilchrist, 2009). In discussing the two hemispheres of the divided brain, McGilchrist is not addressing the absurd "popular travesty" of thinking simplistically that the left hemisphere is "hard-nosed and logical ... somehow male" and the right is "dreamy and sensitive ... somehow female" (McGilchrist, 2009, p. 2). Rather he argues that both hemispheres are involved in reasoning and language and creativity. His thesis is that the bihemispheric structure of the brain underpins our capacity to contain different versions of reality and modes of experiencing.

Building on McGilchrist, my contention here is that the brain has two epistemological strategies available to it at all times which pay different modes of attention to the world. However the 'both/and' fullness of our capacity for knowing has been lost in an 'either/or' struggle between these different modes, with the knowledge structures of the left hemisphere having come to dominate in the Western world: the Emissary has become the Master which, according to the tale told by Nietzsche and quoted by McGilchrist (2009, p. 14) in explaining the title of his book, leads to the domain collapsing in ruins. My intention here is to explore the ways in which the person-centred community can stay open to our different capacities for knowing without becoming subsumed by our culture's dominant mode.

The divided brain

To begin it seems necessary to clarify the two epistemologies, or theories of knowledge, represented by the left and right brain hemispheres. McGilchrist (2009) argues that a right hemisphere mode of awareness is comfortable with not knowing, tolerant of uncertainty, open to the movement of process, appreciates paradox and the implicit, and relates to the world with care: the left hemisphere values fixity, clarity, certainty, the explicit and the capacity to represent and manipulate the world. As always, McGilchrist strongly resists the temptation to binary thinking here: the brain is split into two halves but '[w]orking out what it means is not in itself to dichotomise: it only becomes so in the hands of those who interpret the results with Cartesian rigidity' (2009, p. 11). And so at the outset and throughout his extensive discussion, McGilchrist insists on the importance of both aspects and the ways in which they depend on each other.

> Experience is forever in motion, ramifying and unpredictable. In order for us to *know* anything at all, that thing must have enduring properties. If all things flow ... one will always be taken unawares by experience, since nothing being ever repeated, nothing can ever be known. We have to find a way of fixing it as it flies, stepping back from the immediacy of experience, stepping outside the flow. Hence the brain has to attend to the world in two completely different ways, and in so doing to bring two different worlds into being.
>
> *(McGilchrist, 2009, pp. 30–31)*

The pre-reflective world of the right hemisphere embraces complexity in a gestalt which experiences the relational 'betweenness' of connection; the reflective world of the left hemisphere delineates, separates and can identify differences such as objective and subjective. The right hemisphere experiences the world as changing, evolving, interconnected, implicit, incarnate, never fully graspable and imperfectly known. It experiences things as 'present', has a consciousness of the Other, and it relates to the world thus known with care. The left hemisphere uses denotative language and abstraction for clarity, and it manipulates things that are fixed, static, isolated, decontextualised, explicit, disembodied, general and lifeless. Knowledge thus known is a closed self-referential system, where things are 're-presented' as the idea of the thing (McGilchrist, 2009, pp. 174–175). Ultimately we need both capacities in play to be most fully ourselves. However, the default position of what we have come to valorise as knowledge and truth in the West is denotative language, linear sequential analysis, clarity and precision.

According to McGilchrist, experience of the world when dominated by left hemisphere knowing has the following characteristics: loss of the broader picture;

narrow focus; information replaces knowledge; skill and judgement are not valued except as far as they can be reduced to procedures; abstract, conceptual, virtual re-presentations abound; technology and bureaucracy expand; uniqueness is lost (McGilchrist, 2009, pp. 428–429).

> Family relationships, or skilled roles within society, such as those of priests, teachers and doctors [and I would add therapists], which transcend what can be quantified or regulated, and in fact depend on a degree of altruism, would become the object of suspicion.
>
> *(ibid., p. 432)*

They would be mistrusted and subjected to bureaucratic control. 'As a culture, we would come to discard tacit forms of knowledge altogether. There would be a remarkable difficulty in understanding non-explicit meaning, and a downgrading of non-verbal, non-explicit communication' (ibid., p. 433). Reading this paragraph, a peal of bells is ringing for person-centred practitioners as we regard the counselling and psychotherapy profession today.

Recognition of the description above gives us a sense of the prevailing imbalance between the epistemological strategies available to us in our current climate. Awareness of our different capacities for knowing can also encourage us to attend to the tension between them and the potential for imbalance. Zooming in from the cultural perspective, I contend that we can notice this process at play in our daily lives, moment to moment. It is familiar and explicit in counselling and psychotherapeutic practice through the monthly rhythm of taking our professional experience to supervision in order to reflect on and represent what we have been up to in the light of our theoretical knowledge; we then return to our work with new knowing from the integration of right and left perspectives. It can be identified in our personal development as the challenges of disagreement, difference or the unfamiliar invite us to revisit our fixed conditioning and beliefs, and return to encounter with an expanded capacity to hear. It is also recognisable in descriptions of learning processes such as David Kolb's Experiential Learning Cycle which goes through the four stages of concrete experience, reflective observation, abstract conceptualisation, active experimentation and back then to experience (Kolb, 1984). These are all indications that knowledge is an active process; that *what* we know can only be fixed briefly before the next challenge arrives from *how* we know, demanding that we revisit what we thought was known.

In the next section, I want to look at some examples of the rehabilitation of right hemisphere awareness in twentieth century thought. I have written about some aspects of this elsewhere (Clark, 2016); my emphasis here is on the reintroduction of movement in the process of knowing. The challenge of our age, played out in the PCA as well as elsewhere, is to reclaim the fluidity of right hemisphere knowing and destabilise the fixity of left hemisphere knowledge which occupies the dominant ground. I want to look at examples of moves in this direction from which we may learn: firstly, I discuss deconstruction as a general move against fixed structures of meaning, language and power as exemplified by aspects of the thinking of Jacques Derrida; I then turn to Michael Sells' exploration of apophatic language as an exemplar of destabilising the tendency of meaning to solidify; and finally I bring in John Caputo's theology of the event which draws attention to whatever is dynamic rather than fixed in our encounter with the world.

Deconstruction

Derrida has been described as 'questioning our preconceived ideas about meaning and evoking a radical and paradoxical structuring and de-structuring of truth that can never be directly stated, grasped or defined' (Shakespeare, 2009, p. 6). However, this does not imply giving up on meaning or truth because it cannot be fixed.

> Derrida understands meaning differently, not as an underlying truth, but as the interweaving of forces. Meaning, on this account, cannot be gathered into a simple presence. It differs from itself and always arrives too late for that. But this is not the end of meaning: *it is how it works*.
> (Shakespeare, 2009, p. 20, italics added)

The relevance of Derrida to us here concerns his interest in unsettling the border between

> universal truth and individual life. Individuality or singularity cannot simply be incorporated into a grand narrative. Rather, it is a piece of grit in the eye of the all-seeing system. It is the secret without which there could be no truth, no responsibility, no decision.
> (Shakespeare, 2009, p. 8)

Carl Rogers wrote in *On Becoming a Person* that 'What is most personal is most general' (Rogers, 1961, p. 26). I quote this not to appeal to Rogers as a higher authority (of course not!) but to remind us that the gritty meeting of the personal and the universal is at the heart of the person-centred endeavour and Derrida shows us the depth of the challenge contained in this responsibility.

For Derrida, understanding the other requires:

> a repeated breaking-up of all the versions of the Other that the Same constructs for itself. Constant interruption is the necessary instability that provides the conditions for glimpsing the otherness of the Other through the broken ruins of one's own constructions.
> (Almond, 2004, p. 43)

Deconstruction requires constant movement; it draws on play and paradox to disrupt whatever settles again and again. It can be understood as the subversion of left hemisphere knowledge in favour of right hemisphere modes of knowing and attending and, as such, it offers a model of such practice to nourish the PCA.

At times Derrida has been criticised for relying on certainty, truth and presence in order to challenge the very existence of these attributes by deconstructing them. This challenge can be seen as a left hemisphere misunderstanding of a right hemisphere dynamic which expects the latter to be 'pure' and stand alone while failing to see the inseparability and interdependence of the two epistemological strategies. The totality of our knowing emerges from the movement between fixity and fluidity with meaning being located in the tension between the two.

Apophasis

Another mode of discourse we can identify in deconstruction is *apophasis*, unsaying whatever has been said. It addresses the general problem of expressing reality in language, a problem present in the experience of therapeutic encounter. This particular form of dialogue is familiar in the field of negative theology. I do not wish to engage here in the debate regarding whether aspects of deconstruction can be understood as being akin to theological thinking. Rather I am interested that there are moves which are recognisable in the realm of theology which can support us when we are reflecting on our processes of knowing and challenging the fixity of structures. In the following discussion I draw on the book *Mystical Languages of Unsaying* by Michael Sells (1994).

Originating in the theological paradox of speaking of the transcendent which is ineffable (beyond words), a mode of discourse emerged which is described as *apophasis* in Greek, unsaying or speaking away (Sells, 1994, p. 2). 'Any saying (even a negative saying) demands a correcting proposition, an unsaying. But that correcting proposition which unsays the previous proposition is in itself a "saying" that must be "unsaid" in turn' (ibid., p. 3). Meaning is in the tension and the tension must be continually performed. Sells recognises such language in writers such as Levinas, Bion and Lacan: he argues that apophatic language in psychoanalysis is not 'the same thing' as mysticism, but in both instances:

> the effort to engage 'the real' in language leads to a continual turning back of language upon itself. The real is unknowable, yet that unknowability, rather than resulting in silence, becomes the dynamic of a new discourse ... The real is ultimately not locatable in the self or the other (soul and deity, self and neighbour, analysand and analyst), but is 'radically dialogic'.
>
> *(Sells, 1994, p. 220)*

This speaks of a dialogue between the wider-than-words experience of the right hemisphere being expressed in words by the left with the inadequacy of the result sending the effort round the cycle again to unsay and re-say, the knowing being held in the whole movement rather than in any one part.

> At the heart of that unsaying is a radical dialectic of transcendence and immanence. That which is utterly 'beyond' is revealed or reveals itself as most intimately 'within' ... When the transcendent realises itself as the immanent, the subject of the act is neither divine nor human, neither self nor other.
>
> (Sells, 1994, p. 7)

In these texts, logic and semantic structures are broken down in an effort to touch the extraordinary, 'but the extraordinary, the transcendent, the unimaginable, reveals itself as the common' (ibid.). While apophatic language addresses the openness and not-knowing of the therapeutic stance, it also demonstrates how difficult it is to talk about leaving room for no-thing. Apophasis uses language in ways which try to elucidate non-linguistic modes of being and knowing: holding open space, not diagnosing, letting experience unfold. Thinking of the PCA, what is being articulated is the practice of someone who has integrated their theory so fully that the therapist, while being a professional practitioner, claims no expertise other than skill in holding a space in which another can simply be.

What I aim to illustrate here is that the mystical and contemplative strands of religious traditions have expertise in right hemisphere knowing and attending from which we can learn as we seek to revivify our processes of knowing and attending in the PCA. The performance of saying then unsaying entails continual movement from knowing to not knowing and back, which captures a sense of perplexity at the edge of what can be known in whatever conditioned context we find ourselves. Rather than getting lost down the road of wondering if the apophatic language of negative theology brings us in some way to mysticism, Sells understands unsaying as a practice which evokes a sense of mystery rather than being mystical.

> This mystery might be viewed through the prism of three 'names': the mystery of being, the mystery of being alive, and the mystery of being aware (the mystery of consciousness). Such an experience of mystery does not insulate the worldviews in which it is found from criticism or scrutiny; on the contrary, it is an invitation for continual reevaluation of them as the limited constructions they are.
>
> (Sells, 1994, pp. 216–217)

Such continual re-evaluation takes effort and remembering. It requires a readiness to let go of certainty and to loosen our grasp of knowledge as a fixed thing. And to tolerate uncertainty and not knowing is risky; it opens our vulnerability and touches our humanity.

Before leaving this consideration of saying and unsaying, I want to highlight the role of *both* of our epistemological strategies in supporting practice here. Any anxieties that may arise about a therapeutic stance of not knowing becoming a licence for all sorts of wacky or even abusive treatment of clients do not value the role the left hemisphere plays in rooting us in a particular theory, culture and tradition. To draw on the Sells quotes above, we cannot escape having some kind of worldview which is the product of conditioned construction and habitual thought; it is the humility to keep revisiting this that roots our practice in experience and reality, and keeps us constantly learning and growing.

A theology of the event

Thus far, my contention is that the acknowledgement of how we move between saying and unsaying, knowing and not knowing, certainty and bewilderment can deepen the knowledge processes of PCA practitioners. I now want to consider the writing of John Caputo, a postmodern philosopher and theologian, who offers us a dynamic which has more to do with our attention than our words. In exploring a theology of the event, for Caputo an event is not what happens but 'something going on *in* what happens ... it is not something present, but something seeking to make itself felt in what is present' (Caputo in Robbins, 2007, p. 47). By event, Caputo is trying to catch something different from what is conditioned and therefore deconstructible like names or things. Events are 'never present, never finished or formed, realized or constructed' (Robbins, 2007, p. 48). Rather Caputo is talking of something dynamic, a movement, a pulse. Not being present, events are provocations and promises, having 'the structure of what Derrida calls the unforeseeable "to come"' (Robbins, 2007, p. 48).

The relevance of the 'event' to the PCA is that Caputo offers an understanding of a dynamic which we might recognise as present in the actualising tendency (Rogers, 1961, p. 351). 'The event is the *unconditional* that is astir in these local conditions, what is undeconstructible in any historical construction or discursive practice' (Caputo in Robbins, 2007, p. 53). Throughout deconstructive thinking, we meet a challenge to any easy person-centred assertion of being unconditional. Being elsewhere than our situated selves is impossible to claim as a simple move. However, the event or the actualising tendency might be understood as what is left when we get out of the way as fully as possible.

As well as a philosopher, Caputo is a theologian. He is interested in talk of God while recognising the death of the God of power when deconstruction did the work of 'burning off the old metaphysics of omnipotence' (ibid., p. 67). He is left talking of the weakness of God using the term not as 'an abstract logical possibility but of a *dynamis* that pulses through things (*rei*), urging them, soliciting them, to be what they can be' (ibid., p. 65). Here we recognise Rogers' anecdotal formula 'what I am is good enough if I can just be it' which invites us to trust what is astir in ourselves and others. Something is trying to happen and even though we cannot know what that is, we can contribute to the process by clearing space for it, in itself no small act but one of great responsibility.

Caputo argues that events have 'the power of powerlessness' to which we are called on 'to respond, to realize or actualize them, to make them happen, which here means to make *God* happen, to give God body and embodiment, force and actuality' (in Robbins, 2007, p. 64, original italics). Caputo asserts:

it is precisely because the face of God is transcendent that the only form in which you will ever find the face of God is in the face of the neighbour, which is where you should direct all your attention.

(in Robbins, 2007, p. 79)

Talk of God will not be to everyone's taste here; my own understanding of the word in this context is that it carries a weight of meaning, is profoundly situated at the heart of daily life and informs how we choose to pay attention. The call implied by this God-language will be familiar to many drawn to counselling and psychotherapy by the impulse to engage with the world in the interests of love, compassion and justice.

The wisdom of centuries of theological effort to explore whatever is beyond the structures of our understanding is carried in this postmodern theology which is humble, rooted in the everyday and acknowledges the intensity required to pay attention to what can never be fully known but which may be astir. Such attention requires our trust, our willingness to get out of the way, our commitment to listen to what moves in our own organismic valuing process as well as beyond ourselves. In touching on the sometimes heated and often tedious question regarding the relationship between the PCA and spirituality, my contention is that traditional religions carry expertise accumulated over centuries in right hemisphere modes of knowing and attending from which, if we are not too hubristic about the specialness of our own tradition, the PCA can learn.

Conclusion

What I have been attempting to explore so far is the contribution other conversations can make to enrich our person-centred understanding of 'what' and 'how' we know. Thinking about the divided brain can help us recognise that all of us move through different processes of knowing and that these constantly interact and work together. However, our current culture can prioritise the fixed 'what' of knowledge over the dynamic 'how' of knowing, challenging person-centred practice which relies on a willingness to open our attention beyond what we already know in order to fully encounter the other.

The contributions I have drawn on here from Derrida, Sells and Caputo excite me, as I recognise their effort to engage and elaborate the 'how' of knowing while writing about the experience in words in books, just as I am doing now. However, when I am reading the works of these men, I also recognise the endless looping of left hemisphere attention around trying to express in language something about the relationship between language and a wider form of non-verbal attention which does not lend itself to linear strings of words on a page. Getting stuck in its own mode of expression is such a left hemisphere dilemma! But when the academic debates go on and on, there comes a moment when I step out of the conversation saying 'Thank you folks, I've got something useful, carry on by all means, but I'm leaving you now'. Any reading of texts which includes the right hemisphere, which takes place in the heart, which is embodied and relates to the particular, that reading seeks life and practice to fully know the meaning being carried in the words.

The moment to step out is arriving for me now. What I write here is intended to support our practice, our relating, our attention and our being in the world, not our tendency to endlessly write to each other. I see the irony! The fundamental model which underpins this chapter is that of the divided brain. The immediate energy of the right hemisphere in meeting the present can be understood as a horse which pulls the wooden cart of the left hemisphere's effort to represent that experience and reality. They are two different but inseparable entities. In the person-centred community we need the capacity of the cart to carry our theory, our tradition and our ability to reflect on what we are up to; we can only move and grow when the horse of the right hemisphere is in harness. This is where we live. The best we can do to keep our person-centred community alive and growing is to remember not to put the cart before the horse.

References

Almond, I. (2004). *Sufism and Deconstruction: A Comparative Study of Derrida and Ibn 'Arabi*. London: Routledge.

Clark, D. (2016). Thinking about the other: conversations and context, in Lago, C. and Charura, D. (Eds.), *The Person-Centred Counselling and Psychotherapy Handbook*. Maidenhead: Oxford University Press.

Kolb, D. A. (1984). *Experiential Learning: Experience as the Source of Learning and Development* (Vol. 1). Englewood Cliffs, NJ: Prentice-Hall.

McGilchrist, I. (2009). *The Master and his Emissary: The Divided Brain and the Making of the Western World*. New Haven and London: Yale University Press.

Robbins, J.W. Ed. (2007). *After the Death of God: John D. Caputo and Gianni Vattimo*. New York: Columbia University Press.

Rogers, C.R. (1961). *On Becoming a Person*. London: Constable.

Sells, M.A. (1994). *Mystical Languages of Unsaying*. Chicago & London: University of Chicago Press.

Shakespeare, S. (2009). *Derrida and Theology*. London: T&T Clark International.

18

THE EMPATHOR'S NEW CLOTHES

When person-centered practices and evidence-based claims collide

Blake Griffin Edwards

Introduction

Carl was a boy. He was a boy who loved to work hard. He was a boy who loved to play. He was a boy who loved to laugh. He was a boy who cared for people. By the time Carl became a young man, neighborhoods had changed. Fewer children ran between houses and into fields giggling with one arm straight out to their side with hula hoop spinning over a mud puddle here, bumping over a curb there. New homes were built with smaller yards and taller fences, neighborhoods with narrower streets but faster cars. These were dangerous places for play, and more and more kids stayed indoors. New toys were made with wires connected to screens. Kids spent hours, then days, then years clicking buttons on controllers connected to the wires and watching the people on screen having such fun and adventure.

Carl became busy. And sad. He had grown up. He missed friends he had so many years ago spent endless time with, jumping and rolling and throwing and exploring. He remembered his grandfather had told him many years ago, "Laughter is the best medicine." Carl fondly remembered being tickled by his grandfather. Carl moved far away in hopes of finding a land of play and laughter. He found a school where he could learn more about the sadness he saw in people all around him – and that he himself felt at times – and he became a doctor of tickle medicine. Dr. Carl, the tickle doctor, found people all over who had forgotten how to play and laugh, and the Tickle Doctor helped many of them. As the Tickle Doctor grew older, he taught many how to become tickle doctors. He demonstrated his gifts in tickle medicine on stages, like a magician, and he wrote books telling tales and sharing ideas.

The students loved their teacher. They studied what he said and did, and the Tickle Doctor grew even older. New systems of care determined that the effectiveness of tickle medicine could not be proven. Sad people sought tickle doctors, yet they could no longer be paid for their work. Dr. Carl tried to continue his good work, yet tickle medicine became outlawed. Signs were posted across the land calling for the arrest of "the Tickle Monster." Many tickle doctors continued to practice tickle medicine in small caverns below streets and in offices hidden above flower shops, some in schools and hospitals and the like, discreetly incorporating tickle medicine into their work. Tickle medicine is still alive and well, but few know the secrets of the great tickle doctor. His students continue to provide help covertly, working to shape a world where people will know how to play and laugh and experience joy together.

Psychotherapy from a manual

Over the past several decades, there has risen an increasing call for evidence-based practice (EBP) in the field of psychotherapy, which has inevitably led to a kind of sorting – those models which have not been quantitatively validated, to the historical dust bin of shame; and those which can, into managed care. What we are seeing nationwide and possibly on a global scale are turf wars that vie for a share of the market. In 2016, I participated in a training process for one such aspiring new model called Common Elements Treatment Approach (CETA), whose proponents, in my view, offer an excellent sampling of the kind of models fighting for credibility, visibility, and eventually, viability in the marketplace. Here was my experience –

8:45am–12:15pm on day one

The first morning of a two-day training conference, we spent an hour discussing symptoms of anxiety, depression, and post-traumatic stress disorder. After this, the facilitators emphasized the importance of utilizing formal clinical measures, including the PHQ-9 and PCL-C. A fair amount of time was devoted to role-playing how to conduct clinical assessment. We broke out into small groups to role-play how to present semi-scripted feedback to a client regarding their clinical measures. The training, thus far, struck me as not offering a unique model of intervention, especially after having heard bold claims by CETA proponents in the weeks prior and having been intrigued by the scant CETA literature.

1:15pm–5:00pm on day one

After lunch, we were taught how to develop basic crisis and safety plans, talked about providing psychoeducation, including how to draw out more feedback from clients, as well as how to "normalize" clients' symptoms. We role-played how to present the structure of therapy sessions to a client so as to encourage engagement rather than overwhelm or put off the client. The facilitators instructed us on cognitive coping using the thinking-feeling-behavior triangle, a useful CBT tool for helping clients understand how thoughts, feelings, and behaviors are connected.

A participant raised his hand and asked the presenters whether these components constituted "evidence-based practices." The presenter answered that as CBT itself is "evidence-based" and these components are "essentially CBT," then "yes." Can you make claims of a new "evidence-based" model on the basis that it is built from component parts of another? – I thought. The last portion of day one was centered on unpacking trauma memories. A basic lesson on exposure, regarded as a key ingredient in the treatment of anxiety, was the focus, yet with limited focus on how to use it.

8:30am–12:00pm on day two

The beginning of day two began with learning how to help clients identify irrational thoughts. The T-F-B triangle was brought in again as a tool in this endeavor. Time was spent role-playing progressive logical questioning, or how to help a client identify discrepancies between current beliefs and what is more accurate in reality. After a break, we lightly discussed relaxation techniques, such as deep breathing and muscle relaxation. Before lunch, we discussed gradual exposure using ladders to help illustrate a fear hierarchy with clients. We role-played the use of gradual exposure at-length.

1:00pm–2:30pm on day two

After lunch, the topic was behavioral activation. This included tools to motivate clients toward change, widely accepted as necessary for therapy to be at all successful with depressed clients. We were told to role-play in small groups how to assign homework activities.

2:45pm–4:00pm on day two

As the training wrapped up, the facilitators began outlining CETA in more detail; that is, the trainers explained the designed order of interventions, contingent on diagnosis. Ultimately, CETA was branded as an approach based on common treatment components widely accepted as either necessary or effective: administering basic clinical measures; engaging clients; helping clients identify their thoughts, feelings, and behaviors, and the linkages between; helping clients replace distorted thinking; helping clients learn to self-soothe and relax; helping clients heal from trauma through gradual therapeutic exposure; prioritizing safety throughout therapy; and motivating clients toward change.

4:00pm–5:00pm on day two

At this time, we were chided to sign-up to participate in a nine-month biweekly phone consult group. This would involve inputting clients' clinical measures into an online toolkit database for the training institute and consulting on our use of

CETA. The therapists who came with me and I opted out of continuing with CETA. Neither the training nor the model offered them new knowledge, skills, or abilities but rather, in my view, an overly prescriptive, overly uniform approach to treating clients.

EBPs are important, but EBPs are only useful if they are appropriately matched to practitioners who gain in scope or depth of practice, particularly when their professional developmental level as a psychotherapist indicates the need for a limiting focus, clear parameters for practice, and a semi-scripted methodology. I have concerns, however, about a culture change in the field marked by increasing blind assumption of research validity and expanding regulation related to EBP.

The largest concern that I have about CETA is not the methods that are present in the model – which are in large part, as the trainer explicitly stated, a re-packaging of the basics of CBT – but the value and cost to agencies in having therapists already trained in, for instance, CBT skills spend additional time becoming certified in CETA which offers only a less advanced, highly scripted version of these skills. There are more efficient and economical ways to go about brushing up basic skills and more robust EBPs that offer master's level clinicians a more advanced set of clinical skills. Why, then, do we see the increasing spread of such patchwork, manualized practice models in the psychotherapy marketplace?

Do you remember when all Starbucks stores used manual La Marzocco machines? Nowadays, by using automatic machines, Starbucks is able to make more drinks in a shorter time. And, it's a lot easier to teach a barista how to press a button than how to properly grind, tamp, and pull a shot. Ultimately, it saves in labor costs and in training time, resulting in faster on-boarding and greater consistency overall. Starbucks is as great a corporation as it's ever been, but you could argue that it's lost the magic of the art it once wielded. It was a major compromise on quality. In fact, it has nearly eliminated the craft of coffee within Starbucks, yet to be fair, it is also more difficult now to make a bad coffee. The net result is much fewer exceptional cups of espresso beverage but also much fewer terrible cups of espresso beverage. Was it worth it? People are not coffee, yet the analogy has some merit. For the field of psychotherapy, "manualization" refers to the need, in order to research a model's effectiveness and ensure a model considered effective is being closely followed, to have psychotherapists maintain fidelity to the requirements of a particular model's protocol manual. The potential for an excellent cup of joe significantly decreases in the automatization of the craft. I contend that the manualization of psychotherapy similarly shoulders significant risks.

Low fidelity isn't fidelity

I criticize blind and sweeping EBP claims and regulation on the basis of the sort of concerns I have presented about my experience and perspective of CETA and other aspiring practice models, some of which hope to ride on the coattails of more established and more robust EBPs. Additionally, many models claiming to be evidence-based do so on the basis of small, potentially faulty, and untested research trials. CETA itself admits in one of the only journal articles chronicling its primary trials in southern Iraq and in Thailand near the border of Burma that "all pilot clients were survivors of systemic violence and/or torture and were predominantly a convenience sample," citing client samples of only twelve pilot research participants in Iraq and twenty-two in Thailand (Murray et al., 2014, p. 118). At the time of writing, there have been far from sufficient trials of CETA, yet the model's thin base of spliced evidence is being marketed within the statewide evidence-based practice machinery where I live, which I'll translate as meaning it is in the pipeline for eventual consideration as a SAMHSA registered EBP. CETA is, in my view, appropriately cast as a trauma-focused brief intervention model for use by lay counselors in post-disaster and post-political imprisonment, yet I witnessed CETA trainers make bold claims that its evidence-based methodology and findings, so called, may be generalized to use by highly-trained counselors with *most* American community-mental health center clients experiencing more or less severe forms of anxiety or depression.

Proponents of EBP such as Scott Lilienfeld offer trenchant critiques of EBP criticism, exposing straw man arguments against use of EBPs. Lilienfeld (2014) wrote,

> Nothing in evidence-based practice implies that treatment decisions should be based exclusively on the results of single studies; quite the contrary. Instead, the rationale is that all else being equal, treatments [that] have been shown to work in multiple, independently replicated, well-designed studies (especially when confirmed by meta-analyses, that is, quantitative summaries of the literature) should be accorded higher priority in treatment selection than treatments that haven't.

Fair enough. Yet a number of evidence-based practice claims in the marketplace do remain insufficiently tested, and too many of these remain insufficiently challenged. Additionally, a large number of therapists implementing EBPs may well be failing to replicate the methodologies of particular EBPs studies. I do not intend this as a wholesale critique of EBP research design nor of EBP-utilizing therapists but a critique of the widely held assumption that therapists trained and certified in particular EBPs are implementing in practice the methodologies of those EBPs to a level of fidelity comparable to that carried out by the therapists participating in the original research studies. The reality is that if therapists implement the methodologies of an EBP but do not implement it to a satisfactory level of fidelity, their practice is not evidence-based, yet very broad allowances are being made in the coding of EBPs within managed care to satisfy the increasingly strict regulatory requirements for the levels of EBP implementation, resulting, I fear, in a net reduction in depth and quality of psychotherapy practice rather than an increase in fidelity to effective psychotherapy intervention.

Many EBPs rigidly structure for therapists and, thereby, for clients, systems of levers to pull should the client's esteem tip this way or should the client's fears tip that way. In my experience, evidence-based practice cadres often *do not have an interest in the personal agency of the client* – in their capacity to choose for themselves and innate strengths and resilience that can emerge given the right kind of supportive conditions. While the spirit and principled mindset of a field of evidence-based practice is appropriately postured to mitigate potentially negligent and dangerous practices, far more widely than is widely acknowledged, EBP implementation takes the form of naive acceptances of poorly tested interventions and, in effect, may or may not ultimately ensure better therapy.

Donald Berwick, a Harvard-based quality-improvement expert, himself noted for employing evidence-based methods in the field of medicine, wrote in 2005 that we had "overshot the mark" and turned evidence-based practice into an "intellectual hegemony that can cost us dearly if we do not take stock and modify it" (Berwick, 2005, p. 315). In 2009, advocating for "patient-centered care," he declared, "evidence-based medicine sometimes must take a back seat" (Berwick, 2009, p. 561). His sentiment applies to the field of psychotherapy as well, in my view.

A common critique by EBP skeptics in light of researchers' claims of tightly controlled studies goes, "If your effect is so fragile that it can only be reproduced under strictly controlled conditions, then why do you think it can be reproduced consistently by practitioners operating without such active monitoring or controls?" If fidelity to a manualized modality cannot be ensured beyond the randomized controlled trials that stamped it "evidence-based," how do we know, in the marketplace, that it *is* so? These, in my view, are valid concerns. Reminiscent of Hans Christian Andersen's brief, illuminating tale about the two weavers who promise an emperor a new suit of clothes that they say is invisible, many EBPs may be wearing no clothes, if you catch the analogy.

Research findings based on the application of treatment manuals have led to endorsement of treatment brands which assume that these are practiced in a manner consistent with the research treatment manuals. Very often, they are not. In effect, the endorsement of a brand name treatment is a shortcut to and a means of defining de facto clinical practice guidelines and gaining a market monopoly. The American Psychological Association unveiled a policy in 2005 recognizing that to practice from an evidence base, *findings based on research are insufficient*. The policy characterizes evidence-based psychological practice (EBPP) as incorporating evidence about treatment alongside expert opinion and an appreciation of client characteristics. Three components – evidence for treatment, expert opinion, and patient characteristics – are essential to writing clinical practice guidelines and thereby enhancing the delivery of evidence-based treatments (APA Task Force on Evidence-Based Practice, 2006).

The APA policy stated, "A central goal of EBPP is to maximize patient choice among effective alternative interventions" (p. 284). Many practices claiming to work from an "evidence base" in practical fact *minimize client choice*. CETA, for instance, guides therapists implementing its model to fidelity to follow a prescribed CETA intervention flow that provides a specific order for interventions on the basis of diagnosis, risking the preclusion of space needed for a client to meaningfully choose. Never once in the course of CETA training or consultation were participants trained on the necessity of maximizing client choice among effective alternative interventions. Additionally, systems-wide Medicaid regulation continues to evolve toward an increasing incorporation of EBP requirements, specifically an increase by percentage of service encounters coded with an EBP against total service encounters. I have witnessed throngs of agencies rushing to choose the EBPs they wish to invest their resources in and often this has as much to do with which consortium or initiative a particular agency may benefit from increasing its ties to as it does with anything. And here is the rub: once agencies hitch their wagons to particular EBPs, the therapists they employ have little choice but to embrace those particular EBPs and anchor the lion's share of their professional development and practice within that agency to them; neither the therapists nor the clients, in these scenarios, have much choice, and let me be clear – this is not an anomaly within isolated quarters but the shape of the vast expanses our current professional landscape.

There is no wholesale dismissal of evidence here, only of the errors of blind acceptance of a widely criticized and underperforming field of EBP research that has oversold to the unscientific public the merits of many findings.

The babies and the bath water

I mentioned that the therapists I took with me to the CETA training and I opted out of continuing with CETA. Well, that is not the end of the story. One of the trainers contacted the corporate office of my organization and complained that in registering for the training, there was an expectation that we would continue on with the nine-month consultation process, and, fearful of any potential negative harm to our agency's reputation, in terms of its participation in statewide evidence-based practice initiatives, I was told by a corporate administrator I was given no choice but to enroll myself and my therapists in the full nine-month CETA consultation process. During that process, we utilized CETA with several clients each and inputted required clinical measures and other data into an online database to be used for aggregation and evaluation by the research center administering the consultations.

Therapist participants shared during multiple case consults their own concern that they had strayed outside of the bounds of fidelity to CETA, yet again and again, consultants encouraged these therapists against their protests that they had demonstrated fidelity. These participants seemed uncomfortable with these conclusions. I certainly was. I assumed that the motive of the facilitators must have been to enhance the data being reported and increase both the number of successfully certified CETA clinicians as well as decrease any potential misgivings about the usefulness of the model. From my own understanding based on others' anecdotal experiences, subjective aspects within and incentives related to such research leave the field vulnerable to corruption in study data that may be construed as "evidence." We, as practitioners and consumers should be asking, "But evidence of *what*?"

Robert McNamara was the U.S. Secretary of Defense from 1961–1968. McNamara saw the world in numbers. He spearheaded a paradigm shift in strategy at the Defense Department to implement large-scale metric tracking and reporting that he contended would help minimize individual bias among department experts. A core metric he used to inform strategy and evaluate progress was body count data. "Things you can count, you ought to count," argued McNamara. His focus, however, created a problem because many important variables could *not* be counted, so he largely ignored them. This thinking led to wrongheaded decisions by the U.S. and resulted in an eventual need for withdrawal from the Vietnam conflict. Daddis (2009) instructed, "While McNamara contended that factual data had not supplanted judgment based on military experience or intuition, senior uniformed officials perceived their expertise being minimized as systems analysis took hold within DoD" (p. 56). Social scientist Daniel Yankelovich (1972) coined the term, the "McNamara fallacy," pointing out a human tendency to undervalue what cannot be measured and warning of the dangers of taking the measurably quantitative out of the complexity of its qualitative context:

> The first step is to measure whatever can be easily measured. This is OK as far as it goes. The second step is to disregard that which can't be easily measured or to give it an arbitrary quantitative value. This is artificial and misleading. The third step is to presume that what can't be measured easily really isn't important. This is blindness. The fourth step is to say that what can't be easily measured really doesn't exist. This is suicide.
>
> *(Yankelovich, 1972, p. 72)*

Sociological researcher William Bruce Cameron (1963, p. 13) put it another way, "Not everything that counts can be counted, and not everything that can be counted counts."

Clinicians, agencies, and entire systems of mental health care are beginning to identify themselves with particular EBP brands and hold increasingly rigid methodological expectations that drive skillful, humanistic practitioners to the fringes. In fact, in some cases, agency EBP czars are acting to weed out noncompliance at early stages of understanding and implementation, ignoring therapists' feedback, remaining willfully blind to nuanced considerations, and disallowing any divergence. Yet critics of psychotherapy research such as James Coyne, a psychologist who teaches critical thinking in health research in the Netherlands, warn of methodological design flaws in and false claims regarding the outcomes of vast swaths of psychotherapy research around the globe. Coyne (2014) argued:

> As it now stands, the psychotherapy literature does not provide a dependable guide to policy makers, clinicians, and consumers attempting to assess the relative costs and benefits of choosing a particular therapy over others. If such stakeholders uncritically depend upon the psychotherapy literature to evaluate the evidence-supported status of treatments, they will be confused or

misled ... [Psychotherapy] randomized controlled trials are underpowered, yet consistently obtain positive results by redefining the primary outcomes after results are known. The typical RCT is a small, methodologically flawed study conducted by investigators with strong allegiances to one of the treatments being evaluated. Which treatment is preferred by investigators is a better predictor of the outcome of the trial than the specific treatment being evaluated. Many positive findings are created by spinning a combination of confirmatory bias, flexible rules of design, data analysis and reporting and significance chasing. Many studies considered positive, including those that become highly cited, are basically null trials for which results for the primary outcome are ignored, and post-hoc analysis of secondary outcomes and subgroup analyses are emphasized. Spin starts in abstracts and results that are reported there are almost always positive

I wish the reader will simply take for granted that I do not intend to throw the baby out with the bath water – that there are, of course and indeed, many good reasons our field should be expanding research in and implementation of evidence-based practices. I assume, however, that on the basis of what I have written thus far, many readers are at risk of concluding that I am simply ignoring the case for evidence-based practice and EBP research. That being said, let me erase that assumption: the continued development of niche cadres of evidence-based practices, within proper bounds and with proper accountability, has great promise. In short, I see three primary benefits of EBP:

1. Research-backed therapy interventions operationalized in manuals and delivered by trained therapists offer significantly increased efficacy in treating certain disorders (Wampold, 2001; Roth & Fonagy, 1997; Nathan & Gorman, 1998).
2. Consistency in treatment intervention can reduce therapist variability which will likely increase efficacy in treating certain disorders (Luborsky & Barber, 1993).
3. When we emphasize the need for evidence-based skill sets, we elevate in value and priority the significance of ensuring effective therapeutic treatment with clients, including our knowledge about what works and with whom (Norcross, 2002).

To be clear, and lest I gain a reputation for what I am against: I support online toolkits that integrate and track data collection as part of EBP research and case consultation; I support any time systems of care promote and validate the complementary paradigm of "practice-based evidence," providing a means for therapists to generate support of what works for clients based on professional experience; I support grant funding for promising practices; I support serious implementation of confidential and peer-reviewed feedback systems; I support specialized practice cadres which promote niche clinical skills and clinical integrity intending to promote positive therapeutic outcomes; and I support epistemological pluralism, a contrast to placing value through reductionism on only certain aspects of therapeutic outcome – one of my primary criticisms of CETA.

Common factors

In 1936, researcher Saul Rosenzweig argued that factors common to different therapy models have a greater importance to client outcome than the model itself (Rosenzweig, 1936). His use of the term, "Dodo bird" was a sideways reference to Alice in Wonderland in which a number of characters had become wet, and a Dodo bird proposed a race in which they would all run around until they were dry. No one had prepared any good way to measure a winner. It remained unclear how far each had run or for how long, who had become driest and when. The Dodo bird proclaimed, "Everybody has won and all must have prizes." Saul Rosenzweig proclaimed back in the 1930s that the only data available indicated that psychotherapies were effective to certain extents but that there was not a significant discrepancy between how effective one therapeutic approach is versus another. Psychotherapy researchers ever since have battled to either overturn or support Rosenzweig's hypothesis, which remains highly controversial.

Since then, researchers have conducted studies that paint a better picture of what common factors psychotherapies share. Grencavage and Norcross (1990) identified 35 specific "common factors." Researcher Michael Lambert (1992) estimated on the basis of meta-analytic data that "extratherapeutic" factors having nothing at all to do with formal therapeutic work account for roughly 40% of therapeutic progress, that therapeutic relationship factors account for roughly 30%, client expectation or mindset and what is known as "the placebo effect" account for roughly 15%, and techniques unique to specific therapy models account for roughly 15%. These studies sparked a new wave of interest and engagement in research on common factors.

Common factors remain hotly contested. It is widely accepted that there are factors common to different therapeutic approaches that contribute to therapy progress; what is contested is the degree to which the common factors influence therapy outcomes. Common factor theorists contend that common factors are causal agents in therapeutic work. These theorists do not disregard particular schools or modalities; to the contrary, what is acknowledged at this point by nearly all is that, in fact, psychotherapists tend to better employ these common factors in their work when they operate from a coherent model which provides a framework for understanding and intervening with client problems. The Dodo research battle over the years has resulted in at least this certainty: *nothing works for everyone.* Therapists and clients alike need choice, as although ultimately there may exist common factors contributing to therapeutic effectiveness across different models of therapeutic work, at the same time, empirical evidence indicates that not all therapeutic approaches work equally well for all therapists or for all clients. Again, unique models and approaches are very important, and it would be impossible to devise a therapeutic modality based on "common factors."

Mark Hubble, Barry Duncan, and Scott Miller (1999), themselves assertive spokesmen for the role of common factors, asserted:

> There is no reason for those who are devoted to the development and testing of specific techniques to discount the obvious benefits of common factors and particularly the importance of therapist attitudes of respect, caring, understanding, and concern. By the same token, those of us who are convinced of the primary importance of the therapist, as a person, would be well served by remaining open to the likelihood that specific techniques, when offered within the safety of the therapeutic relationship, will appreciably add to the therapeutic encounter.
>
> (Hubble, Duncan & Miller, 1999, p. 49)

Yet ultimately faith, hope, relationship, and an unfathomable number of other factors impossible to quantify or procedurize, many external to the therapeutic enterprise, may catalyze therapeutic transformation. We must, therefore, be cautious of increasing demands for "evidence" and remain wary of evidence-based claims. Many evidence-based practice models are designed with oftentimes unrealistic controls in mind. For instance, some EBPs such as CETA rely on diagnostic controls in which EBP therapists are to follow certain intervention protocols on the basis of a client's particular diagnostic formulation. Yet what controls exist to ensure *diagnostic* precision? Over my years of practice, I have witnessed countless cases in which clients have been assigned disparate diagnoses across systems of care, in which psychotherapists, clinical psychologists, neuropsychologists, psychiatric providers, and primary care providers have committed to incompatible diagnostic conclusions, in which time and again proactive and conscientious cross-silo, interdisciplinary case collaboration has proven ineffectual to remedy. Ultimately, we must grapple with the more substantive and unassailable reality that there is a vast gulf between the diagnosable problems as seen through the lens of clinical expertise and the essence and worth, strengths and hopes of the person before me.

The curious paradox

A young man – let's call him Wesley – wanted desperately to break free from his own arrogance, isolation, and bouts with meaninglessness. Wesley exemplified an unremitting curiosity of his own depths. During one session, I became distant and agitated, recognizing that I hardly knew him, the warm-blooded creature who sat before me, albeit with an intriguing mythology – that the liveliness with which he philologized – the significance of histories, occurrences, and distresses within the text of his own personal epic was eclipsed by my growing repulsion for him. I wondered if others had felt this way, if anyone loved or even liked him enough to tell him. I recognized that if I withheld my own reflection from this existential encounter, I would be of little use and a mere Rorschach inkblot from which to affirm pre-existing and self-defeating assumptions.

And so I told him. I shared my early affinity for his apparent drive toward self-betterment, and I described my growing gut-level frustration at his incessant self-questioning. I recounted that day after day, and now week after week, he had woven poetical meaning retrospectively of his long-dissolved childhood family, the trials of his teen years, and his now grand despair in failing yet to decipher a sense of his own destiny which would provide, he felt, the key to present choices being meanwhile avoided. To what end? I felt convinced that he would find no such key. He remained unsuspicious of his own motives in justifying virtual inaction toward his stated aspirations – peace with himself, connection with others, and purpose in life – but here he slumped, having for weeks not shown any sign of life outside his own archeological dig into dynamics of disconnection he had long since calibrated to a science. I found Wesley self-absorbed and unaware of his egotism.

Wesley had to attend frequent meetings at work, a vast number of human beings for whom he had little regard. I suspected he spent as much time in meetings as anywhere. And so, painstakingly, I coaxed Wesley to talk me through his meetings, to share with me the aura of the hallways with their sounds of wood soled shoes – ca-clap-ca-clap-ca-clap – reverberating off the walls, the niceties at entry. *What did he feel* when his counterparts looked at him? No, no – not what he *thought of them*! I had to continually redirect – "Wesley, surely they look at you? They say things? Glance your shoulder or hand? Question you during the meeting? In your breathing, your muscles, your posture ... how or what do you feel?" "Kind of voyeuristic, don't you think?" Wesley guarded his discomfort and loss of control with jest. *Touché*. Wesley squirmed in his seat. Half-rolling his eyes, he countered with a proposal – "I'll tell you what I felt if you really want to hear." I did. "What I feel – down in my bones, in the fibers of my being – is that they don't give a flying you-know-what about me. They're all just dicks in the mud." I chuckled. "Sticks?" In the next twenty or so minutes, I met Wesley.

In *On Becoming a Person*, Carl Rogers (1961) observed, "Each individual appears to be asking a double question: 'Who am I?' and 'How may I become myself?'" (p. 123). Wesley had begun to "drop one after another of the defensive masks with which he has faced life." Rogers asserted, "The curious paradox is that when I accept myself as I am, then I change" (p. 17).

"I'm my own person. I've always had to be." A psychologically fragile kid from an emotionally volatile home, Wesley had learned how to be a real "a-hole" (*his word, not mine*), yet in the remaining minutes of that session, he leaned forward in his seat with his nose toward the ground, occasionally peering up at me, gauging my reactions to disclosures that seemed raw, honest, and cathartic.

Wesley's life had become quite tidy. He had invested mountains of time in its curation – who can blame him? – yet that work nearly kept him from it. He had lost touch with instincts for spontaneity, creativity, and love. Wesley distanced himself from that which he had once found meaningful, sacrificed in the economy of time and the geography of ambition. Wesley had experienced troubles during critical seasons of his childhood that were well beyond his control. In the course of his oppressions, he had learned to think his way out of corners he had been backed into, to fend for his own interests. Yet Wesley's troubles had long since faded into the decades on the one hand, into a haunting anxiety on the other. Wesley longed to grow beyond a racing self-reflection and compulsive isolation.

In his *Sonnets to Orpheus*, Rainer Maria Rilke (1922, trans. 2001) wrote of a creature who lived in a state of being "unpeopled," who was nourished with, rather than food, only "the *possibility* of being" [italics mine]. As Wesley grew in age, he had become increasingly surrounded by people and yet increasingly unpeopled, who rather than finding nourishment through vulnerable and proximal relationship, had opted to snack only on the possibility of being. As I sat with Wesley, related to, became irritated at, listened with an overwhelming sense of pain and care, laughed, facilitated reflection, offered reframe, engaged in limited disclosure, challenged, gave space, sat back, leaned in, and wrestled, I began to see more fluidity and risk-taking in our give-and-take, yet found myself questioning whether he could meaningfully shift this way or that, could truly change.

To become increasingly flexible and resilient, clients must experience freedom within felt pushes and pulls of powerful self-perpetuating forces in which problems maintain themselves. One of my graduate professors, Bill Collins, taught me that "pathology" is a dangerous and untenable categorization of a person's experience. He contrasted "providing treatment to people" with "puzzling through a process with someone." As an illustration, he told of one friend whose father, growing up, would never let him finish anything without taking over. His friend would, as his father asked, begin to screw in a nail with a screwdriver, and before he could finish, his father would grab it from him and say, "Oh, just give me that." Those kinds of experiences, he noted, leave long-lasting impressions on a person in regard to self-worth and one's competencies. Bill advised that we are to "help others to unpack their conclusions about who they are." Then, if a client is to change, transformative experiencing must occur.

Looking along and looking at

I thought about what Bill had taught me as I saw Wesley return again and again, heavy-laden and perseverating about difficulties outside of his control, oblivious to that which was within it, and persistently breathing life into a burdensome caricature of himself. What could I offer him? The therapist has power to offer empathy, and empathy has power to re-shape experience. Once a client experiences himself feeling, thinking, or behaving differently in-session, he will experience himself feeling, thinking, and behaving differently in life.

In his *Critique of Pure Reason*, Immanuel Kant (1781) illuminated the conflict between "reason" and "understanding." He warned that reason devoid of experience risks false understandings. He claimed there can be neither true knowledge nor true understanding apart from experience. The varying faculties of the rational mind analyze and not only extrapolate meaning from information but give it a shape as well, and the mind is shaped in so doing. Kant understood this, and so has, traditionally, humanistic psychology. Kant stressed the consequence of an irrevocable cleft between the rational and the empirical yet posed the possibility of seeing human action through different lenses, and by so doing, resolving contradictions apparent by one lens alone. C.S. Lewis's (1970) essay, "Meditation in a toolshed," provides an instructive anecdote here.

> I was standing today in the dark toolshed. The sun was shining outside and through the crack at the top of the door there came a sunbeam. From where I stood that beam of light, with the specks of dust floating in it, was the most striking thing in the place. Everything else was almost pitch-black. I was seeing the beam, not seeing things by it. Then I moved, so that the beam fell on my eyes. Instantly the whole previous picture vanished. I saw no toolshed, and (above all) no beam. Instead I saw, framed in the irregular cranny at the top of the door, green leaves moving on the branches of a tree outside and beyond that, 90 odd million miles away, the sun. Looking along the beam, and looking at the beam are very different experiences ...
> *(Lewis, 1970, pp. 212, 215)*

Lewis (1970) observed, "It has even come to be taken for granted that the external account of a thing somehow refutes or 'debunks' the account given from inside" (p. 213), concluding that rational investigation of human experience is often "all the apparatus of thought busily working in a vacuum" (p. 214). Freud, for instance, engaged intellectually in psychological mythopoeia and brilliantly so. Yet in the course of mapping the longitudinal, he failed to look *along*. He took long, but he looked at. As for our current situation, I fear that an increasing reliance on research validation of psychotherapy intervention will continue to steer us afield of a focus on the core empathy-driven and necessarily individualized person-centered psychotherapist development that has been long and widely accepted as both foundational and fundamental to good and effective psychotherapy. It must continue to be the work of therapy to acknowledge and provide for this freedom even where it requires a departure from a particular psychotherapy model's prescribed flow of intervention.

I came to one session prepared with a short essay I had written about our time in therapy together, of a new strength I had seen in him over a period of months, of the courage he had embodied in his work with me and, increasingly, in bold decisions he made and actions he took between our appointments. As I read, Wesley's eyes welled up with tears, and he shared with me significant changes he had experienced in his work and relationships that included a significant decrease in irritability and anxiety and a significant increase in compassion and a sense of peace. Wesley and I decided together, somewhat spontaneously, that this would be his final session. His parting handshake gripped tightly, and I glimpsed a glint of newfound confidence and gratitude as we laughed and said our goodbyes.

Conclusion

If a psychotherapist's technique is too technical, his efforts to help may be worthless. Therapy in this case may be little more than a poor excuse for scientific experimentation. There is a great deal of need for and promise in much of the evidence-based psychotherapy research being conducted, yet – and let me be clear that this critique applies as well to many modalities that are clearly not evidence-based – the mechanisms of some psychotherapies undermine their therapeutic value. If a therapist is not fully present as a warm, accepting, genuine, caring person, then the power center of therapy remains turned off and, for all practical purposes, ineffective. This is because, ultimately, the person-centered process – *not* a series of manualized techniques – is the soul of psychotherapeutic change.

Note

In accord with ethical standards of practice, client identity has been protected through alteration of name and unique identifying details.

References

APA Task Force on Evidence-Based Practice. (2006). Evidence-based practice in psychology. *American Psychologist* 61, 271–285. doi:10.1037/0003–066X.61.4.271.

Berwick, D. M. (2005). Broadening the view of evidence-based medicine. *Quality and Safety in Health Care* 14, 315–316.

Berwick, D. M. (2009). What 'patient-centered' should mean: Confessions of an extremist. *Health Affairs* 28(4), 555–565.

Cameron, W. B. (1963). *Informal sociology: A casual introduction to sociological thinking*. New York: Random House.

Coyne, J. (2014, June 10). Salvaging psychotherapy research: A manifesto. Retrieved from http://blogs.plos.org/mindthebrain/2014/06/10/salvaging-psychotherapy-research-manifesto/.

Daddis, G. A. (2009). No sure victory: Measuring U.S. Army effectiveness and progress in the Vietnam War (Unpublished doctoral dissertation). University of North Carolina-Chapel Hill, Chapel Hill, North Carolina.

Grencavage, L. M., & Norcross, J. C. (1990). Where are the commonalities among the therapeutic common factors? *Professional psychology: Research and practice* 21(5), 372–378.

Hubble, M., Duncan, B., & Miller, S. (1999). *The heart and soul of change: What works in therapy*. Washington, D.C.: American Psychological Association.

Kant, I. (1781/1899). *Critique of pure reason* (Translated by J.M.D. Meiklejohn). New York: The Colonial Press.

Lambert, M. J. (1992). Psychotherapy outcome research: Implications for integrative and eclectic therapists. In J. C. Norcross & M. R. Goldfried (Eds.), *Handbook of Psychotherapy Integration* (pp. 94–129). New York: Basic Books.

Lewis, C. S. (1970). Meditation in a toolshed. In W. Hooper (Ed.), *God in the dock: Essays on theology and ethics* (pp. 212–215). Grand Rapids: Eerdmans Publishing Company.

Lilienfeld, S. (2014, January 27). Evidence-based practice: The misunderstandings continue [Blog post]. Retrieved from https://www.psychologytoday.com/blog/the-skeptical-psychologist/201401/evidence-based-practice-the-misunderstandings-continue/.

Luborsky, L., & Barber, J. E. (1993). Benefits of adherence to treatment manuals, and where to get them. In N. Miller, L. Luborsky, J. P. Barber, & J. P. Docherty (Eds.), *Psychodynamic treatment research: A handbook for clinical practice* (pp. 211–226). New York: Basic Books.

Murray, L., Dorsey, S., Haroz, E., Lee, C., Alsiary, M. M., Haydary, A., Weiss, W. M., & Bolton, P. (2014). A common elements treatment approach for adult mental health problems in low- and middle-income countries. *Cognitive and Behavioral Practice* 21(2), 111–123.

Nathan, P. E., & Gorman, J. M. (Eds.). (1998). *A guide to treatments that work*. London: Oxford University Press.

Norcross, J. C. (2002). *Psychotherapy relationships that work: Therapist contributions and responsiveness to patients*. New York, NY: Oxford University Press.

Rilke, M. R. (1922). *Die Sonette an Orpheus* [*Sonnets to Orpheus*], translated by A. S. Kline, 2001. Available online: https://www.poetryintranslation.com/PITBR/German/MoreRilke.php, retrieved 28 June 2017. Rogers, C. R. (1961). *On becoming a person: A therapist's view of psychotherapy*. Boston: Houghton Mifflin Company.

Rosenzweig, S. (1936). Some implicit common factors in diverse methods of psychotherapy. *American Journal of Orthopsychiatry*, 6, 412–415.

Roth, A., & Fonagy, P. (1997). *What works for whom? A critical review of psychotherapy research*. New York: Guilford Press.

Wampold, B. E. (2001). *The great psychotherapy debate: Models, methods, and findings*. Mahwah, NJ: Erlbaum.

Yankelovich, D. (1972). *Corporate priorities: A continuing study of the new demands on business*. Stamford, CT: D. Yankelovich Inc.

PART V
Challenging some aspects of person-centred practice

PART I

19

CHALLENGING SNOOPERVISION[1]

How can person-centered practitioners offer new alternatives to the fracturing of the person in the supervision relationship?

Zoë Krupka

Introduction

Quietly, supervision has become like management, a profession in its own right. The lyrics of this particular version of the siren song of professionalism have focused in large part on the division between "expert knowledge" and "personal knowing". This has framed the difficult experiences of therapists as deficits and attempted to contain emotional and personal expression in supervision in order to surgically define a "clean" separation between supervision and therapy.

While person-centered approaches to supervision have tried to step aside from this fragmented treatment of supervisor, therapist and client, they remain widely criticized and under threat from current legal and ethical guidelines of practice.

In this chapter, I explore the links between current conceptualizations of supervision and neoliberal frameworks of belief.[2] These beliefs prioritize the compartmentalization, neutralization and eradication of personal issues from the workplace, and create a mythical disembodiment of the supervisory space, magically cleansed of the contaminants of the therapist whilst confining the client to a narrow, static realm of never-ending otherness.

This chapter is a call for a politically creative and imaginative approach to congruent person-centered supervision practice in order to more fully articulate and advocate for its alternative voice.

The extinction of the species

In *The Art of Cruelty*, Maggie Nelson writes:

> For not only do our work and words speak beyond our intentions and controls, but compassion is not necessarily found where we presume it to be, nor

is it always what we presume it to be, nor is it experienced or accessed by everyone in the same way, nor is it found in the same place in the same way over time.

(Nelson, 2011, p. 9)

A very long time ago, I took some trouble to learn to be a dog trainer. The man who taught me was small and compact, earnest and kind. Warm and solidly effusive, not unlike a bull terrier. He began our rudimentary training by asking us to question everything we thought we knew about dogs. He told us: "Say to yourself: but what if I'm wrong about everything? It is from this place of suspension of belief that you may begin to listen to her; to the Pug, the Wolfhound, the Rottweiler, and you will have some chance of hearing what she says".

You may know, if you have a dog yourself, how literally counter-cultural this approach was. Dogs and behaviorism are now virtually synonymous in the Western conceptual view of canine-human relationships. Reward and punishment, crating and the imposition of middle class manners are the order of the day if you're a pet dog. To ask us to meet each dog as a being separate from us but infinitely open to our connected understandings, was to ask us to leave the everyday world behind and to create a new one. In one sense he was simply requesting that we suspend our prejudices and try to let go of the sedimentations of belief that could act as isolating carapaces, objectifying each dog we would encounter. But he was also asking us to do something rarely demanded of those who come to learn. He wanted us to listen to our own experience. Yes, to profoundly question it, but also to rely upon it, to use it as a springboard to other more relational inter-species imaginings. In the process of my training, my love of dogs was empathically explored, turned over like a smooth stone in the hand and sometimes painfully exposed as something from a galaxy far, far away from love. Ultimately I learned to assist in the relationship between people and dogs through a process that was intentional, introspective and relational. It was a profoundly unprofessional training experience. I learned to profess nothing and to be curious about everything. I like to think of this teacher as my first anti-clinical supervisor. I think of him often, particularly when I am caught by the shiny allure of professionalism or by the many safety hooks of accreditation.

My first psychotherapy training had much of the quality of this early teaching relationship. Sitting next to my now dear friend Brendon, we were asked on our first day what we thought therapy was about. He said many things, but what I remember most clearly was his pronouncement that *people aren't crabs; you don't have to crack them open to get the good stuff out*. My initial impression was that he was a kind of Labrador, quick to love and with a deep desire for intimacy. Unfortunately, I'm a bit more of a nervous Whippet, and I took some time to appreciate him, but amongst the many eager student responses offering parallels to mentoring, midwifery and even mountain climbing, his crab analogy won me over.

Carl Rogers suggested early on in his career that we pay more attention to the selection of curious and intelligent prospective therapists than to the content of their training (Rogers, et al., 1989) and my teachers had taken this to heart. Our interviews were rigorous, demanding and emotionally open experiences, and for the most part our classes were shared as much as taught. However, when after a number of years post-qualification I began to supervise other therapists, the tinted one-way glass of professionalism already had a firm grip on this area of practice, and process had long ago given way to manualized content and the misleading comforts of rigid format.

A double bind

Twelve years have passed since I began to work as a supervisor. In that time, both the separation and conflation of our personal and professional lives has become so marked that we almost need superpowers to hold and make meaning of the now divergent areas of our lives and selves. Many people across all professions are working significantly longer hours (Bannai & Tamakoshi, 2014), while at the same time expected to pursue some kind of ideal of work/life balance. We are meant to be professionals at work, keeping our private, emotional lives contained elsewhere, while many of us are also expected to maintain the imposed standards of our disciplines in our public and socially-mediated expressions of self. This is a double bind whose intensely pressured knot conceals the fallacy of the separation of the personal from the professional. It holds us to the myth of separate selves, while simultaneously requiring the personal to be professional. Perhaps when we had more time, the pressure of this dilemma was easier to ignore. Now that most of us do not have adequate time outside of our work, the illusion that we can both hive off our so-called personal lives while at the same time collapsing them with our professional identities, has become untenable.

This personal/professional double bind is arguably also one of the impacts of the increasing regulation of both psychotherapy and supervision. While most of the evidence for the effectiveness of psychotherapy points to the personal qualities of the therapist (Norcross & Lambert, 2011), accreditation and registration have nonetheless supported a clinical practice model, which professionalizes the personal, narrowing the options of expression and stiffening interpersonal flexibility. In Australia for example, and more recently in Aotearoa New Zealand, counselling, psychotherapy and supervision have become, despite the absence of any sound supporting evidence, increasingly regulated, placing both overlapping professions within the realm of "health", with all of the medically-modeled clinical oversight that accreditation of this kind entails (Tudor, 2013).

Over the past ten years, a western proliferation of specialized and predominantly evaluative supervision training has invaded our practices with the determination of Crown of Thorns starfish. Colleges of supervision with strict entry requirements have sprung up within our peak bodies, and a search of

Amazon.com reveals over seven hundred guides on how to perform supervision published during this period (Amazon, 2017). In short, supervision, like management, has become a separate profession, and you could be forgiven for thinking that it appears to be one struggling, not unlike management, with a sense of its identity and purpose.

The institution of psychotherapeutic supervision is now a structure solidly built on the idea of the compartmentalization of the person. Therapists and supervisors exist within this overly-landscaped construct as either person or professional – as if self and world were not inextricably co- and inter-dependent. A cornerstone of this compartmentalization is the current prohibition within most models and codes of supervisory practice, on addressing the life struggles of the therapist within the supervision relationship, in any profound or extensive way. While some guidelines have designed small corners for addressing the "personal issues" of the therapist as a way of encouraging improvement in their work with clients, each ultimately demands that therapists direct any personal issues to therapy which threaten to invade the supervision space, in order to "protect" the vulnerable client by draining our potentially infectious interpersonal wounds elsewhere (American Psychological Association, 2010; Australian Psychological Society 2004; Barnett & Molzon, 2014; Corey, Corey & Callanan, 2011).

Person-centered approaches to supervision have benefited from a well-articulated position of responding to the whole of the organism, where any proposal or mandate to fragment the therapist along personal/professional lines and the focus of supervision into supervisory/therapeutic issues is understood to be not only undermining of greater honesty in supervision, but also of a fundamentally embracing, existential and holistic relationship (Tudor & Worrall, 2007). Person-centered therapy has also profoundly rejected the managerialism of a virtuous hierarchy model of supervision, in favor of an approach that makes room for a practice of loving witness, in which "… the supervisor is a partner rather than an educator; a witness rather than a monitor; a fellow explorer rather than a fount of wisdom" (Lambers, 2006, p. 274).

There have been several other articulately constructed responses to this violent parsing of the person of the therapist in the context of supervision, perhaps most powerfully within narrative therapy where the social constructivist and activist roots of practice have profoundly challenged a-contextual and fragmented models of the person. These critiques also confront approaches to the regulation of supervision that come from a model of therapist deficit, a premise antithetical to person-centered theorists and practitioners (White, 1997).

But is it possible to work as a loving witness within this increasingly narrow structure of supervision, or are person-centered supervisors who hope to protect the individual supervision space from a premise of hierarchical deficit simply working in *bonsai* form? It is the fraught enculturated relationship between thought and feeling and the uneasiness around not only personal wholeness but also our inescapable interconnectivity and inter-responsibility far outside of the supervision dyad, that I believe sits behind this question.

Trigger warnings

> It is an impossible debate. There is too much history lurking beneath the skin of too many people. Few are willing to consider the possibility that trigger warnings may be ineffective, impractical, and necessary for creating safe spaces all at once. The illusion of safety is as frustrating as it is powerful.
>
> (Gay, 2014, p. 151)

The distinction between what is now allowable within the context of supervision and what is not, is part of a social and political framework that justifies both overtly and covertly, the parsing not only of the organism of the therapist, but of course by necessity, their clients and supervisors. The organization of the work of supervision into personal and professional selves, working and non-working selves, is a rapidly growing structure that by its very existence has begun to lock even the most dedicated of person-centered practitioners out of a more inter-connected and inter-responsible realm of experiencing. Even the British Association of Counselling and Psychotherapy, historically a place of great inclusiveness in its approach to the definition of counselling and supervision practice, has begun to focus greater attention on the problematically defined and utilitarian ideals of client outcomes and evidence-based practice (British Association of Counselling and Psychotherapy, 2016).

The separation of "personal issues" from supervision, and even the idea that exploring these issues can be useful *in the service of the client*, speaks to a practice across all therapeutic traditions that both fragments and objectifies each point of the therapeutic triangle of client, therapist and supervisor. To argue against the inclusion of personal issues in supervision or to argue for the *utility* of addressing them, is in a sense the same thing. Both positions tacitly endorse the idea of a separation of the organism – both are fragmentations of the person, even though one places the unwanted pieces into the garbage can and one into the compost bin. In this compartmentalization, all three roles become othered: the client as the most vulnerable and to-be-protected other; the therapist, as the idealized supported healer, seeking to improve their capacity to create a safe working space, and the supervisor, as the facilitator, making room for each of the "parts" of the therapist in this sanitized process. Even arguing for there to be space for "everything" the therapist brings to supervision *in order that the client may benefit*, is deeply connected to this objectified divisibility of the person.

One example of this double-binding separation is the concept of vicarious trauma, a central concern within the field of supervision. Ostensibly the recognition that the witnessing of pain and injustice can affect not only the person directly harmed, but also those who have witnessed that harm in some way, was a significant improvement in developing a more relational understanding of both human relationships and the rippling effects of violence. It challenged the notion that what harmed you did not harm me and that I could be of service to you without our permeable relationship having a permanent impact on my experience of myself and of the world.

However the concept of "vicariousness" when applied to trauma has some long whiskers on it. There are two problems here: both the idea of "vicariousness" and of whom this category is allowed to include. Underlying the idea of something being vicarious is the belief that there is a rightful owner, or recipient of a particular experiential happening. This "owner" is meant to be a kind of ground zero of a traumatic event, and others around them, the witnesses, those who hear their story, read or transcribe the event, are meant to be spaced out in concentric and ever widening circles which are ideally less and less impacted by what has happened and have less and less legitimacy attached to their feelings of emotional and psychological distress. To the person directly affected in this construct, it is a violence to be both borne and repaired. To the witness, it is a potentially toxic substance, illegitimately invading their person. The more distant the experience, the more illegitimate the impact.

The concept of vicarious trauma then, cements the idea that some trauma or painful reckoning is surrogate or derivate experiencing and needs to be challenged through various means, including compassion, reducing empathic connection and sometimes more physiologically distancing and buffering strategies (Rothschild, 2006).

But why shouldn't we be traumatized by the brutalization of others, either known or unknown to us? Why should our witnessing pain be pathologized in this way? Should we be protected from the impacts of forces that are much greater than the individual? Even *the concept of post-traumatic growth* (Tedeschi & Calhoun, 1996) *assumes an individualized phoenix-like transformative use of the pain of others*. In this new supervision world, pain is seen as either threatening or useful, but not as informative and never as structurally inevitable.

This separation of what happens to you and what happens to me not only legitimates a false demarcation of experience, but simultaneously obscures those happenings that do *only happen to you and not to me*, cementing the places where our different positions in the world mean that we are more or less vulnerable to pain and trouble.

These different positions are also cemented in the relational imbalance of the research focus in the field of supervision, where very little attention is paid to how psychotherapeutic work affects the life of the therapist, and even less to what therapists learn from their clients (Jensen, 2016). This lack of attention then serves to obscure further the co- and interdependent relationship between self and world.

Seeing the deleterious effects of witnessing the hurts of others as something to manage individually (*Look After Yourself!*) is also part of a supporting structure that personalizes cruelty and distress themselves as well as the strategies to address them. There have been person-centered challenges to the idea of managing the trauma of others by practices that reduce empathy, pathologize the sufferer (Lee, 2017) and that point instead to empathy's role in promoting personal growth (Brockhouse, et al., 2011; Joseph, 2004). But if we are to truly embrace the ethos of person-centered supervision, we will see our links, connections and interpersonal responsibilities as extending far beyond the supervision room. This means both resisting a self-serving approach to Rogers' nuanced concept of actualization (Bazzano, 2012; Warner, 2009) and instead opening ourselves to an understanding that what we hear in both the supervision and therapy spaces reveals not simply individual experience but also the social process of how trauma is transmitted from generation to generation, and how these socially-mediated processes can swallow us, the helpers, up into their cycles of transmission.

Central to the therapeutic perpetuation of this cycle of traumatic transmission I believe is the framing and allocation of what emotions are, and who is legitimately allowed to have them. Rather than seeing emotions simply as something we "have" or that belong to us, or even as sensations that "make sense" in the light of what is happening, they can be seen as *expressions that make meanings in the world* and so have a creative impact rather than simply a function (Ahmed, 2004). Some emotional experiences are also privileged while others are not, and we need to be aware that feelings, affect and emotion are all culturally embedded ideas and processes with their own rules of retention and expression, and are not the realm of psychology alone (Cvetkovich, 2012).

In so many of the professionalized stories of supervision, the organizing metaphors appear to be deficit and emotional contagion. In these narratives, the therapist is living in an experience of socially-sanctioned deficit, where emotion is meant to be contained and transmission of distress prevented, and the supervisor is caught in the framed position of a provider of a kind of decontamination or decompression chamber, either safe from or growing as a result of the therapist's affect-charged narratives. These metaphors of deficit and emotional contagion then serve to separate therapist, client and supervisor from their environments, making each solely and personally responsible for their troubles, and direct the creativity of their responses towards a narrowly defined notion of self-care.

A story

Stephen and I are talking about one of his supervisees. A young man, overwhelmed with too many clients, limited line management supervision, poor pay, not enough holidays, burnt out, disillusioned and coming undone. Together we talk about what to do to support him at the end of what to us as supervisors is now an unfortunately familiar tether. I find myself offering advocacy strategies, telling Stephen how to get a GP to call him back, how to advocate for something resembling a reasonable amount of leave, how to help his supervisee avoid the pitfalls of punitive performance management. These are skills related to activism, advocacy. They are sisters to the tasks called for in social work supervision. If we are to have any hope of supporting person-centered practice in the increasingly risk management focused helping professions, then activism and advocacy must become central pillars of our supervisory practice (Beddoe, 2010). But even knowing this, even fired up with an activist spirit, at the end of this discussion we are both left feeling helpless and angry.

This is not just a story of supervision. It is also a story of our common and uncommon humanity. Of the gulf between what this overworked man needs and what Stephen can give him; between his emotions and a safe place for them to fall; between his needs and those of his clients; between the reality of his personal power and the fantasy of his personal control – and of course, between his power and position and his employer's, his power and position and ours. This story cannot hope to be a transformative one if it does not cause us pain or teach us a lesson about the links between our work and the normalization of distress.

Post-truth

And above all, I will argue the necessity for preserving, against all shame, a demanding question of revolution itself, a question about utopia that keeps pushing its way through a field of failed aspirations, like a student at the back of the room who gets suddenly, violently, tired of being invisible (Berlant, 1994, p. 133).

Many years ago, when my daughter was quite small, she told her father and me a story about an animal with glowing eyes who came into her bedroom at night. *She eats the fruit you leave for me*, she said.

I puzzled over her dreams, re-imagined the stories we read together before bed.

The tiny bites taken out of the fruit in the bowl underneath the kitchen window, left open for the comings and goings of the cats, remained outside of my awareness.

Sometimes dreams can seem very real, I said to her. I spoke to friends about her story, received a kind of supervision from them. All of us supporting each other in our beliefs; that children dream lucidly, that children make up stories, that in our urban world there are very few secret animals that come in the night.

Then one evening I was passing by her bedroom, and I saw the glowing eyes myself. A large possum, by her bed, eating the pear slices meant to delay her early morning progress to us. I got a towel, threw it gently over the animal, took her outside. How long she'd been stuck in the house, living on my daughter's fruit, I'll never know.

I feel an arguably healthy mortification recalling this story. The hubris of my grown up position, thinking that time on earth could be substituted for experience. The memory of that parental dismissal reminds me of much of my expected role as a supervisor, and leaves me with a penitent heart.

Supervision now has very little room for the restless doubt that keeps us alert to the possibility that we are in the presence of an important question. Instead, we are more and more likely to miss the possums in the night because of the increased pressure to function as gatekeepers and evaluators whose worth rests upon seniority. Within the widely endorsed definitions of supervision, this function is the most chilling to me, because of its current ubiquity in programs of supervisor training and accreditation. Here is a just one of many such examples:

> An intervention provided by a more senior member of a profession to a more junior member or members of that same profession. This relationship is evaluative and hierarchical, extends over time, and has the simultaneous purposes of enhancing the professional functioning of the more junior person(s); monitoring the quality of professional services offered to clients that she, he, or

they see; and serving as a gatekeeper for those who are to enter the particular profession.

(Bernard & Goodyear, 2009, p. 7)

It is not lost on me that I was once a dog trainer, and that dogs are most often pets, unpaid workers or feral outcasts, and that training does little to address their domesticated subjugation. And I am known now officially as a *Clinical* Supervisor, with all of the violent medicalization of the person, including my person, inherent in that title. There has been no escaping this de-personalization, despite repeated calls for person-centered political activism (Elder, 2015; Lee, 2017; Sanders 2006; Sanders & Tudor, 2001; Schmid, 2014; Zucconi 2011) and the hard social activist work of many. Our offices and workplaces are not truly sites of safe haven, even if they may offer a brief respite from the relentless demands to be all we can be in the service of the few. I think we must agree that our heartfelt calls to arms have been largely unsuccessful in slowing the domination of an increasingly narrow and engineered view of our profession. I hope we can also agree that this does not mean we must stop calling.

I am not a great one for the building of systems, and I will not propose an inevitably surplus one here. We now have so many supervision manuals, so many rules, an abundance of strategic calls to action and so much available training. This affluence can only mean that we feel vulnerable, always alert to a potential display of our theoretical nakedness. But while I don't think we need more systematized guidelines, I do have an understanding of how a neatly drawn map with a clearly labeled *You are Here*, boldly in red, can calm a person enough to allow them to move forward into the area that borders that map, to the so far unexplored territory, into *Terra Incognita*. However, were I to draw such a map, based on what is currently understood as the territory of supervision and its relationship to the holistic ideals of person-centered practice, I suspect it would be as useful as those maps in shopping centers; temporarily clear and comforting, but difficult to conjure up once a few forks in the fake marble road are passed.

After many decades of research, even though we know it's effective, we don't really know what psychotherapy is; there are ingredients within our healing relationships that are closer to a kind of magic that will never be illuminated by positivist scientific research (Miller & Hubble, 2017). If we don't really know what psychotherapy is, how can we be so grandiose as to profess to know the boundaries of supervision? While psychotherapy has proven to be effective, the links between supervision and better work with clients are tenuous at best (Watkins, 2011). Person-centered supervisors have been sent on a fool's errand, to police the indefinable, and we have strongly resisted this violent and disenfranchising errand and claimed an inherently political space for person-centered practice.

But we need to remember that we are not just inevitably political because of our choice to work within a person-centered ethos. We were *already* political creatures, already formed in our socio-cultural Petri dishes. We are the "ones prepared earlier". I believe we need to reflect more deeply, to actively re-imagine our work, to question our practice, its form, its pace and especially its home, in order to find more space to breathe within the narrow structures we've been permitted to inhabit. To ask ourselves *What is a supervisor and how am I playing one? How can I re-imagine myself outside of the roles I've been given to play?*

I don't in any way want to ask for an end to action. We must continue to actively engage in the discussions about supervision requirements; to challenge the evidence and the lack thereof and especially the dearth of attention paid to the evidence already in existence. To allow supervision to be and to continue to be a place of intentional activism. To fight for a widening of the field of supervision, openly challenging the professionalization of the person, and the pathologizing and allocated ownership of emotion. To resist the impulse to be part of creating new research evidence based on paradigms of isolation and exclusion. To continue to resist clinical monikers, status, manualization and the medicalization of our training. To continue to voice our objections to institutionalization and regulation and to expose the violence inherent in these structures and their relationship to our violent nation states. And to refuse to embrace the unbearable, appropriated construct of resilience, with its built-in assumption of history erasing, individual responsibility and traumatic hierarchies, and instead to embody a more connected idea of stout-heartedness.

This is not a time to be reassured but a time to experiment. So rather than a map, may I suggest an active re-imagining and re-visioning of a more "unowned" space for supervision, a space off the grid not so much of expectation, but of planning and design. Space to be both discovered and created. To imagine places outside of the punitive frame of current supervision standards, and not simply to advocate for them. And to make room in our creations, for everyday acts of resistance.

★

Not long ago, I was sitting through a symposium, trying to stay awake, in a state alternating between fury and depression. We were listening to a spokeswoman from a major psychology regulatory body regale us with the idea that we needed to crack down on "rogue" approaches to psychotherapy and supervision. She took animal assisted therapies as an example of the worst kind of quackery. I felt like a sulky teenager. I'm sure I was pouting, all my energy closed down against this assault of false scientism. But the woman next to me was invigorated somehow, free, still accessible by imagination. I could sense her, alive and awake in her chair. *It sounds like it's been a long time since you've really felt loved by a dog*, she said, out loud, without raising even one of her hands. And the room, once deadly with silence, erupted with laughter.

Notes

1 Like many an unknowing plagiarist, I thought I came up with this term myself. However the moniker "snoopervision" has been used quite a number of times, particularly within the management and education literature. The term can be traced originally to the pages of the *Lutheran Quarterly* of 1927. "We are satisfied that supervision (not '*snoopervision*') is an essential in every well regulated school" (Anonymous, 1927, p. 242).

2 For the purpose of this chapter, I am working from one of George Monbiot's (2016) excellent and comprehensive definitions of neoliberalism. "Neoliberalism sees competition as the defining characteristic of human relations. It redefines citizens as consumers, whose democratic choices are best exercised by buying and selling, a process that rewards merit and punishes inefficiency. It maintains that 'the market' delivers benefits that could never be achieved by planning. Attempts to limit competition are treated as inimical to liberty. Tax and regulation should be minimised, public services should be privatised. The organisation of labour and collective bargaining by trade unions are portrayed as market distortions that impede the formation of a natural hierarchy of winners and losers. Inequality is recast as virtuous: a reward for utility and a generator of wealth, which trickles down to enrich everyone. Efforts to create a more equal society are both counterproductive and morally corrosive. The market ensures that everyone gets what they deserve."

References

Ahmed, S. (2004). *The cultural politics of emotion*. Edinburgh, UK: Edinburgh University Press.
Amazon. (2017). Amazon books. August 1. Retrieved from https://www.amazon.com/books-used-books-textbooks/b?ie=UTF8&node=283155.
American Psychological Association. (2010). *Ethical principles of psychologists and code of conduct*. Retrieved 12/8/17 from http://www.apa.org.ez.library.latrobe.edu.au/ethics.
Anonymous. (1927). Snoopervision. *The Lutheran Quarterly*, 57, 242.
Australian Psychological Society. (2004). *APS ethical guidelines: Guidelines on supervision*. Melbourne, Australia: Author.
Bannai, A., & Tamakoshi, A. (2014). The association between long working hours and health: A systematic review of epidemiological evidence. *Scandinavian Journal of Work, Environment & Health*, 40(1), 5–18. doi:10.5271/sjweh.3388.
Barnett, J., & Molzon, C. (2014). Clinical supervision of psychotherapy: Essential ethics issues for supervisors and supervisees. *Journal of Clinical Psychology*, 70(11), 1051–1061.
Bazzano, M. (2012). Immanent vitality: Reflections on the actualizing tendency. *Person-Centered & Experiential Psychotherapies*, 11(2), 137–151.
Beddoe, L. (2010). Surveillance or reflection: Professional supervision in 'the risk society'. *British Journal of Social Work*, 40(4), 1279–1296.
Berlant, L. (1994). '68 or something. *Critical Inquiry*, 21(1), 124–155.
Bernard, J. M., & Goodyear, R. K. (2009). *Fundamentals of clinical supervision*. (4th ed.) Upper Saddle River, NJ: Merrill.
British Association for Counselling and Psychotherapy. (2016). *Good practice in action: Research and literature overview of supervision within the counselling professions*. Lutterworth, UK: Author.
Brockhouse, R., Msetfi, R. M., Cohen, K., & Joseph, S. (2011). Vicarious exposure to trauma and growth in therapists: The moderating effects of sense of coherence, organizational support, and empathy. *Journal of Traumatic Stress*, 24(6), 735–742.
Corey, G., Corey, M.S., & Callanan, P. (2011). *Issues and ethics in the helping professions*. (8th ed.). Belmont, CA: Thompson Brooks/Cole.
Cvetkovich, A. (2012). *Depression: A public feeling*. London, NC: Duke University Press.
Elder, S. (2015). Off the couch and into the streets: Psychotherapy and political activism. *Smith College Studies in Social Work*, 85(4), 373–386.
Gay, R. (2014). *Bad feminist*. New York, NY: HarperCollins.
Jensen, P. (2016). Mind the map: Circular processes between the therapist, the client and the therapist's personal life. In A. Vetere, & P. Stratton (Eds.), *Interacting selves: Systemic solutions for personal and professional development in counselling and psychotherapy*. (Chapter 3). Milton Park: Routledge.

Joseph, S. (2004). Client-centred therapy, post-traumatic stress disorder and post-traumatic growth: Theoretical perspectives and practical implications. *Psychology and Psychotherapy: Theory, Research and Practice*, 77(1), 101–119.

Lambers, E. (2006). Supervising the humanity of the therapist. *Person-Centred and Experiential Psychotherapies*, 5(4), 266–276.

Lee, D. A. (2017). A person-centred political critique of current discourses in post-traumatic stress disorder and post-traumatic growth. *Psychotherapy Politics International*, 15(2). https://doi.org/10.1002/ppi.1411.

Miller, S. & Hubble, M. (2017). How psychotherapy lost its magick. *Psychotherapy Networker*, 42(2). Retrieved from: https://www.psychotherapynetworker.org/blog/details/1173/how-psychotherapy-lost-its-magick.

Monbiot, G. (2016). Neoliberalism – the ideology at the root of all of our problems. *The Guardian*, 15 April. Retrieved from: https://www.theguardian.com/books/2016/apr/15/neoliberalism-ideology-problem-george-monbiot.

Nelson, M. (2011). *The art of cruelty: A reckoning*. New York, NY: W.W. Norton & Company.

Norcross, J.C., & Lambert, M.J. (2011). Psychotherapy relationships that work II. *Psychotherapy*, 48(1), 4–8.

Rogers, C. R., Kirschenbaum, H., & Henderson, V. L. (1989). *The Carl Rogers reader*. Boston, MA: Houghton Mifflin.

Rothschild, B. (2006). *Help for the helper: The psychophysiology of compassion fatigue and vicarious trauma*. New York, NY: W.W. Norton & Co.

Sanders, P. (2006). Why person-centred therapists must reject the medicalisation of distress. *Self & Society*, 34(3), 32–39.

Sanders, P., & Tudor, K. (2001). This is therapy: A person-centred critique of the contemporary psychiatric system, in C. Newnes, G. Holmes & C. Dunn (Eds.), *This is madness too: Critical perspectives on mental health services* (pp. 147–160). Llangarron, UK: PCCS Books.

SchmidP. (2014). Psychotherapy is political or it is not psychotherapy: The person-centred approach as an essentially political venture. *Psychotherapy and Politics International*, 12, 4–17, doi:10.1002/ppi.1316.

Tedeschi, R. G., & Calhoun, L. G. (1996). The posttraumatic growth inventory: Measuring the positive legacy of trauma. *Journal of Traumatic Stress*, 9(3), 455–471.

Tudor, K. (2013). Be careful what you wish for. *New Zealand Journal of Counselling*, 33(2), 46–69.

Tudor, K. & Worrall, M. (2007). Supervision as continuing professional development, in K. Tudor, & M. Worrall (Eds.), *Freedom to practise, Volume II: Developing person-centred approaches to supervision* (pp. 169–175). Ross-on-Wye, UK: PCCS Books.

Warner, M. S. (2009). Defense or actualization? Reconsidering the role of processing, self and agency within Rogers' theory of personality. *Person-Centered & Experiential Psychotherapies*, 8(2), 109–126.

Watkins, C.E. Jr., (2011). Does psychotherapy supervision contribute to patient outcomes? Considering thirty years of research. *The Clinical Supervisor*. 30(2), 235–256. http://dx.doi.org/10.1080/07325223.2011.619417.

White, M. (1997). *Narratives of therapists lives*. Adelaide, Australia: Dulwich Centre Publications.

Zucconi, A. (2011). The politics of the helping relationship: Carl Rogers' contributions. *Person-Centered & Experiential Psychotherapies*, 10(1), 2–10.

20

RE-VISIONING PERSON-CENTRED RESEARCH

Jo Hilton and Seamus Prior

Introduction

In this chapter, we return to Carl Rogers' early development as a researcher in order to provide the basis for a potential re-visioning of person-centred research for our own times. We argue that both his practice and his conceptualisation of research were profoundly reflexive, grounded in an appreciation of the subjectivity of both researcher and the researched, informed by life contexts and experiences of power, and produced in and through the professional wisdom of clinical practice.

We demonstrate how important strands of influence on Rogers' early writing and theorising seem to have been under-acknowledged within mainstream person-centred training and research in the UK. In particular, we highlight the strong influence on Rogers' thinking of the pioneering work of psychiatric social workers Jessie Taft, Virginia Robinson, and Frederick Allen in Philadelphia in the 1930s, themselves followers of the psychoanalyst, Otto Rank, with whom Rogers also had a meaningful exchange early in his career.

In developing this perspective of Rogers as a reflexive researcher, we bring back to the research table the value of forms of research that include the reflexive process of the researcher, rather than viewing this as bias that needs to be set aside or bracketed.

Against the backdrop of the rise of the evidence-supported validated therapy research paradigm (House & Loewenthal, 2008), with its importation of research instruments from academic psychology and medicine, we recall Rogers' characterisation of his psychotherapeutic research as a *social science*. As you read our chapter, we invite you to consider research approaches that are congruent with person-centred theories of what it means to be human and person-centred practices which prize subjectivity and inter-subjectivity.

This chapter is written in the form of a personal narrative. It tells the story of how the first author (Jo) came to discover Carl Rogers – the person, practitioner, theorist and researcher in an iterative way over more than a decade of immersion in person-centred scholarship and practice. The second author (Seamus) has served as a partner in dialogue with Jo, helping to shape her ideas and ultimately her writing. While the bulk of this chapter is Jo's work, Seamus too has had an important hand in its creation and is named as a co-author.

Jo's narrative of encountering Rogers

I present my account of re-visioning Carl Rogers as a reflexive researcher in a reflexive way, referring to my own experience of reading the work of Carl Rogers and the body of scholarship that has grown up around him. This is not because I believe my perspective to be uniquely accurate in some objective way – quite the reverse, my position is highly subjective. Rather, I am interested in how subjective experience can contribute to a debate within the person-centred approach, especially a debate about the influence of subjective experience.

Encounter 1: Early readings of Rogers

My first reading of Carl Rogers' life story was Brian Thorne's biography (Thorne, 2003). My memory of this account was of encountering Rogers' life as a collection of key facts in a slim volume. It felt important, to me, for some reason, to know Rogers the man as well as the theorist. I read the story of a boy who grew up in a somewhat traditional, religious family in Oak Park, Chicago. After a spell at agricultural college and a trip to China and Japan, he changed direction once or twice, moving through the fields of history and theology before transferring to the study of psychology, finding work in a child guidance setting in Rochester, New York. One day a mother of a child who was attending the centre asked if he would see adults. He spent some sessions with her and, so the story goes, the field of person-centred counselling was invented.

According to Thorne (2003), Rogers and colleagues discovered the value of recording client work using the glass discs that were available at the time and brought a step towards a more "objective" science to the study of therapy, hitherto only accessible to those who had completed a psychoanalytic apprenticeship at great expense. They discovered six "necessary and sufficient conditions for therapeutic change" (Rogers, 1957, p. 95). Rogers went on to develop his work by focusing on large groups and the potential of group work to help address conflict in communities.

I liked this view of Rogers; it felt safe and reliable. I felt as if I could trust him. His life, as told by Brian Thorne, resonated with some of my own story, coming from a family where religion was important, not in a pious way, but in a genuinely prayerful way, at least before bedtime and at church on Sundays. At other times my family was all about science, the teaching of science and mathematics, knowing the "right" way to apply a formula and getting the "right" answer.

Later at university I had learned another side of mathematics as a student of the subject, mathematics as an art and as a form of philosophy. I was introduced to the concept of "uncertainty" in quantum physics. This theory overturned a world view based on a belief in determinism, where causes could be linked to associated "determining" effects in a highly predictive way. It also challenged the very idea of neutral, unbiased observation and of objectivity itself. This chimed with Donna Haraway's (1988, p. 590) suggestion that feminism seeks "better accounts of the world" that do not pretend "to be from everywhere and so nowhere".

In recent years, Wolter-Gustafson (2013, p. 107) has discussed Rogers' position as a non-linear, non-dualistic approach to the organism, respecting "the complexity of the organism's tenacious tendency to maintain and enhance health, wellness, and optimal functioning, as well as the way it becomes disorganized and dysfunctional". This fits well with my earliest reading of the PCA, with experience being understood as having an *influence* on complex developmental processes rather than setting off some kind of knowable, causal chain of events.

Another strand of my interest in how life evolves was rooted in my experience of conflict. I had grown up in the 1970s and 1980s when the fallout from the "Troubles" in Northern Ireland had led to bombs and bloodshed in Manchester, my first home, and central London, my second. I found comfort in hearing that Rogers did not restrict himself to the counselling room, but was active in helping people meet to work with difference and division. It seemed like a very powerful approach that foregrounded the potential for human encounter to support the healing of rifts within and between communities.

As I went on to read more of his writing (Rogers, 1951, 1957, 1961, 1980; Rogers & Stevens, 1967), I felt drawn to a man who seemed to have a very open relationship with his readers, able to act as a communicator of ideas that came out of collaborations with others. I had come across the idea of *reflexivity* in practice in the work of Donald Schön (1983) and I saw Rogers' way of writing about and learning from his work to connect to the idea of *reflective practice*, even though I did not find this perspective echoed in the secondary sources.

Encounter 2: The philosophy years

As I progressed through my training, practice and my own scholarship, I became fascinated by the worlds of ideas in which Rogers and his colleagues engaged. I saw the approach as very much rooted in philosophy and I devoured philosophical theories, although often I struggled to read far enough beyond what was being said to make my own sense of what was being said. I read Rogers' dialogues with Buber and May (Anderson & Cissna, 1997, Rogers, Henderson & Kirschenbaum, 1989), Buber's (1959) *I and Thou* and the philosophical explorations of Gendlin (1997). I tried to learn enough about philosophy to find a key to the person-centred approach. I felt drawn to Heidegger (1976) and the ethical perspective of Levinas (Levinas, Cohen and Poller, 2006), alongside the work of Schmid (2017) in trying to articulate the underlying philosophy of the approach. While some of the concepts fitted well at times, in terms of a core way of addressing the problem of living, I felt my ideas were becoming less grounded in something that felt personally meaningful.

As I was also studying the development of object relations theory in Scotland, I wondered about how the Scottish enlightenment philosopher Adam Smith's (2011) view of "sympathy" in relationship and John MacMurray's (1991, 1998) thoughts on personhood and relationship might be linked to person-centred theory. The core underlying principles of the person-centred approach seemed to me to be less about individuals and their wants and needs, and more about the "self as agent" (MacMurray, 1991) and "persons in relation" (MacMurray 1998, Kirkwood 2002, 2003, 2005).

As I moved into my own research, the work of David Rennie (1998, 2007) offered further insight into how a radically reflexive position, where reflexivity is defined as self-awareness "and radical reflexivity as awareness of self-awareness" (Rennie, 2007, page p. 53) can help identify ways in which a client's sense of agency develops as a significant aspect of the counselling process. Rennie links his work to Gendlin's (1997) focus on *explicating the implicit* which privileged "experiencing". I wondered how the researcher's experience and sense of agency might be included in therapy research, as my reading of many counselling research papers seemed to exclude this aspect of the story or identify it as "bias". Although these ideas felt important, it seemed to take me further away from where I started. I could not find one perspective that fully spoke to me in the way that that first encounter with Rogers did.

Encounter 3: Turbulence

I began to experience uncertainty and doubt and for a while I was unsure if the turbulence I experienced was internal or external. Perhaps, I thought, this is an essential part of finding a way in a world that asks complex questions that cannot be answered easily. Maureen O'Hara and Graham Leicester (2012, p. x) describe their experience of working with colleagues to discover ways to "become more effective and responsible in action in a world we don't understand and can't control". I think that my own "conceptual emergency", to borrow their phrase, led me to wonder what was valuable in the person-centred approach if we were to move towards Rogers' (1980, p. 339) suggestion of the attributes of "persons of tomorrow"?

Certainly my early confidence in following Rogers' espoused path as a pure, empirical scientist had long faded. It had promised a lot but had not seemed to fit the complexity of what I was trying to understand in my research which was looking at moments in a therapy relationship. The act of observation, I was taught in quantum theory classes during my first degree, cannot help but change what is being observed. The empirically-supported evidence-based approach, with its epistemological foundation in rationalism and positivism, seemed to me to suffer from as much epistemological inconsistency and blindness to what it means to be truly human as early biological determinism.

My second area of concern lay in the idea that there are "tribes" of the person-centred approach. I have found that Margaret Warner (2000) characterizes the fragility that I experience in clients, friends, colleagues and myself in the least pathologizing way that I know. Garry Prouty (Prouty et al., 2002) extends the ways in which therapists can reach others when the first condition, psychological contact, feels only attainable in snatches. The arguments around the primacy of some aspects of theory over others became foregrounded for me when I heard Jerrold Bozarth characterize approaches that direct clients towards "emotion" (Greenberg, Rice & Elliot, 1993; Greenberg, 2004) or the "felt sense" (Gendlin, 1997) as "mutations" (Bozarth, 2015). That metaphor felt harsh to me at first, but when he explained it to me in terms of tomatoes, rather than viruses, it felt more accepting of change and growth; an organic movement reaching beyond the original perspective of what the person-centred approach might mean.

As my interest in process-experiential, emotion-focused therapy (Greenberg, Rice & Elliot, 1993; Greenberg, 2004) and the approach overall grew, I was introduced to a person-centred research active community that seemed to function happily with research methods favoured in clinical and academic psychology. Although I was impressed with the inroads they were helping to make into the evidence-based research model (Saxon et al., 2017), I started to feel less at home there. They seemed to me to be moving further away from therapy research as a social science, as the study of people in relation, than where I wanted to locate myself.

Encounter 4: A return to the early days of Rogers

In my confusion and uncertainty at this time, I was reminded that it had not only been Rogers the scientist that had appealed to me, but Rogers the person, and I returned to Rogers' personal story to revisit my experience of him.

Reading the twenty-year-old Rogers' account of his journey to China in 1922 (Cornelius-White, 2012) helped me reconnect with the young Rogers who was an acute observer of the world. I was fascinated that he had hauled a 25lb typewriter with him, so he could capture his observations, whether of world religions, political systems, the industrial splendour of the Golden Gate Bridge or the raw beauty of Mount Fuji. This reminded me of the idea that narrative can *not only be a way of describing something you already know, but of learning something new, possibly even becoming someone new* (White & Epston, 1990).

Fellow researchers, including some of my more psychodynamically oriented colleagues, had been working more explicitly with narrative as inquiry for a long time (Etherington, 2000, 2001, 2004; Denzin & Lincoln 2000; Lee & Prior, 2016; Wyatt 2016). I recognized it was a strand in my own life and process of inquiry that I had lost connection with, as I had immersed myself in the work of others and the more ascendant evidenced-based research tradition.

I looked again at Rogers' early writings and remembered a passage in Brian Thorne's (2003) book about Rogers' making reference to Jessie Taft. While I knew her to be a key link back to psychoanalysis as the biographer of Otto Rank, I had no idea of her as a writer in her own right and I had not come across any direct evidence of her work in my original person-centred training.

I turned to a number of original texts, including those included in Howard Kirschenbaum's *Carl Rogers Reader* (Kirschenbaum & Henderson, 1990) and found that Taft went unmentioned in the index. Yet she was there, quietly, buried in a reference to his time in Rochester, where Rogers said that he felt much more at home with the psychiatric social workers and did not feel that he was a psychologist at all:

> During this period I began to doubt if I was a psychologist. The University of Rochester made it clear that the work that I was doing was not psychology … The psychiatric social workers however seemed to be talking my language.
> *(Rogers, 1957, p. 12).*

Having earlier reflected that he saw the psychoanalysis of his early Freudian learning and the statistical, objective approach of the Teachers College at Columbia University as "never the twain shall meet" (ibid.,, p. 11), it was interesting to note the shift when Rogers came across Otto Rank, described here:

> during the second half of this period there were several individuals who brought into our group the controversial therapeutic views of Otto Rank and the Philadelphia group of social workers and psychiatrists whom he had influenced. Personal contact with Rank was limited to a three-day institute we arranged; nevertheless his thinking had a very decided impact on our staff and helped me to crystallize some of the therapeutic methods we were groping toward.
> *(Rogers, 1959, p. 187)*

The unnamed Philadelphia social workers, who had developed relationship therapy, linking their work to Otto Rank's "will therapy", were Jessie Taft, Virginia Robinson, and Frederick Allen, according to Roy de Carvalho (1999). Keith Tudor (2017, p. 199) notes that this early *relationship therapy* pre-dates the "relational turn", that is usually attributed to Greenberg and Mitchell (1983), by half a century.

Nathaniel Raskin (1948) attempts to unravel this period to detect some of the ways in which their work was to influence Rogers. He suggests that their attraction for Rogers, based on his experiences of working in a social work context rather than with psychologists, was their interest in a less directive, more relational approach to clients. They recognized the significance of working in the "here and now" with their young clients, in an attuned way, working with acceptance of the client in their world, rather than with theories that privilege the therapist's role in guiding the client towards insight. This influential group of social worker-therapists used the words, "reflective, passive, and non-invasive" to describe their technique (de Carvalho, 1999, p. 139).

For the first time, I could reconnect to my early reading of Rogers. I saw that in bringing in his own experience, he was borrowing from what we might now think of as a reflexive form of discourse and that was, at some point in his experience, very valuable to him.

Raskin (1948) suggests that Rogers did not have a great deal of time for reading the work of European analysts and that most of his learning came partly from meeting Rank, but also from reading Taft's work and working alongside her. This does not surprise me as Taft, like Rogers, writes evocatively. See this example:

> One might fairly define relationship therapy as a process in which the individual finally learns to utilize the allotted hour from beginning to end without undue fear, resistance, resentment or greediness. When he can take it and also leave it without denying its value, without trying to escape it completely or keep it forever because of this very value, in so far he has learned to live, to accept this fragment of time in and for itself, and strange as it may seem, if he can live this hour, he has in his grasp the secret of all hours, he has conquered life and time for the moment.
>
> *(Taft, 1933, p. 17)*

This writing of Taft's resonates with the Rogers I had first connected with, a highly reflexive writer, who attends to narrative unfolding and intersubjective relating as a way of learning.

Rogers expressed his dissatisfaction with the psychology of the day, arguably because he had so often inhabited the role of "other". He was not just working alongside social work colleagues in a child guidance clinic, he was exposed to a field of practice, learning and research that had been systematically excluded from what then constituted the academic field of psychology. Like Freud before him, Rogers found himself, his practice and his thinking excluded from the mainstream of orthodox academia.

As I have argued, Jessie Taft is very much part of this story. Taft was not just the biographer of Rank, a link to a field of study that was important in American understanding of the human condition; she was also a leading player in the field of sociology, described by Mertens (2012), as one of the few fields open to her after the completion of her PhD in 1913. Mertens (2012) writes:

> No university job awaited her. Reason and intellect, it was thought, belonged properly to men; women should concern themselves with maternal care and domestic virtue. And so, like many other talented young women of her day, Taft turned to social work – seen as an extension of maternal care and thus open to women.

Further exploration of this theme by de Carvalho suggests that:

> female social workers were important disseminators of both Rank's and Rogers' views. Most American followers of Rank were women working in the fields of child guidance and social work. Rogers himself had a long-standing

connection to both fields. The Rankian and Rogerian emphasis on nurture and empathy in therapeutic relationships appealed to female professionals who felt constrained by a strict subordination to psychiatric (i.e., male) supervision and desired to gain a toehold in the independent practice of psychotherapy. Professional conflicts before and after the second world war between male-dominated psychiatry and female clinical professions over the autonomous practice of psychotherapy contributed mightily to the early popularity of person-centered psychotherapy.

(de Carvalho, 1999, p. 133)

In terms of our theme of research, Taft is acknowledged by Raskin (1948, p. 100) as believing, like Rank and other psychoanalysts, that therapy is "purely individual, non-moral, non-scientific, non-intellectual" and that it is "non-scientific ... and not open to research at the moment". Taft and her colleagues could not see their work as belonging in the mainstream of psychiatric and psychological research as defined in 1930s and 1940s America, yet we can reclaim them today as the pioneers of the reflexive research tradition in psychotherapeutic research which Rogers did so much to popularize. De Carvalho (1999, p. 139) argues that by 1951 Rogers had adopted, adapted and replaced "Rankian terms such as passive, non-invasive, and reflective with the terms non-directive and client-centered".

Based on de Carvalho's (1999) description of the politics of the day, Rogers actively chose to dissociate himself from the more sociologically-framed form of inquiry developed by Taft and colleagues to espouse a more empirical perspective. Maureen O'Hara (1995) identifies some tension between Rogers' writing as an objective scientist and his later work, arguing that his writing could also be understood as the act of a radical subjectivist.

Although Rogers describes his involvement with his social work colleagues' thinking and practice as highly influential in the development of his early thinking about relational therapy, by 1942 he was able to write with excitement about his experience of recording client sessions on film and the opportunities this opened up for him. His narrative here seems very clearly imbued with a sense of therapeutic research as a science and something that is objective. This makes sense to me as a reaction to the potential for a therapist, whether relying on psychoanalytical interpretation or psychological interviewing techniques, to offer the only story of a session. Rogers was excited by the potential to see inside the room as an outside observer, without the intrusion of having to be physically present. He writes:

> These brief illustrations may serve to point out the way in which vague therapeutic concepts can be given life and meaning and definition through presenting them, not in abstract form, not from the point of view of a biased observer, the counsellor, but in a completely factual manner as mechanically recorded.

(Rogers, 1942, p. 431)

Based on what has been said before, I have difficulty accepting his reliance on the outside observer as being an objective viewer of the therapy.

I would echo Jessie Taft in suggesting that the science here might be somewhat overstated. Rogers was not, in any way, a neutral, dispassionate observer. He was a highly skilled therapist by then, who had absorbed a great deal, not just from the theories of the day, including his interest in a Rankian perspective on psychotherapy, but also from his travels, his engagement with others interested in therapy and social work. His observations were those of a highly trained man working with colleagues who also had experience and who, it could be argued, were looking at the film with the perspective of experts, drawing on their professional wisdom (Carr et al., 2012) and the wisdom of practice (Bondi & Fewell, 2016).

It is always a problem looking into the past with the eyes of the present, but I wondered if Rogers was ever able to return to this idea of being an objective observer. I found myself considering if he ever acknowledged his own experience of what I would describe as being a reflexive researcher in his writings. I was looking for more than an acknowledgement of the author's bias, as if that could be set aside, or bracketed; I wanted to see Rogers talking about how his reflexivity contributed to his research as if it was a valuable factor, not an inhibiting process.

It took surprisingly little time to have my desire met, and in some ways it is a disappointment to me not to have searched for this sooner. I register an old, somewhat critical voice within myself noticing this error.

I think that if I had been starting to write this narrative all over again, this may have been a worthwhile starting point, but as instead I have followed my interest in subjective experience, I have allowed myself to use writing as a way of unravelling my understanding. I felt the rather knotted ball of wool that has occupied my body as I have been writing this narrative ease a little and I feel myself back on what Dunne (2009) describes, after Wittgenstein, as the "rough ground".

> We have got on to slippery ice where there is no friction and so in a certain sense the conditions are ideal, but also, just because of that, we are unable to walk. We want to walk: so we need friction. Back to the rough ground!
>
> *(Wittgenstein, 2009, p. 51)*

As I read the following extract from Rogers (1949), it confirms my first reading of Rogers as someone able to acknowledge the complexity of the counselling and the research process, able to write personally about professional experience. In short, it confirms my understanding of Rogers as a self-avowedly reflexive researcher.

> Psychotherapy, as it is individually experienced in the office, is a thing of subtlety, of nuances, of delicate shadings in attitude and relationship which produce clinically obvious results. Research seems to be such a plodder. It laboriously uncovers the obvious. It discovers a general principle, but in the process of doing so tramples into the dust so many of the subtleties which may

contain the vital ingredient of therapy. It seems so pedestrian, where clinical intuition is a galloping steed. Yet as our research piles up – not only this series of studies, but the many that preceded it, and the many that are presently being carried on concurrently – we have become more satisfied with it. To be sure, it lags in some ways far behind our clinical sensitivity. Yet as it turns the blazed trail into a solid roadway, it discovers new vistas and new truths of its own. Furthermore, as the body of evidence accumulates it begins to suggest pathways which have been undiscovered even by clinical hunch. We feel, with increasing certainty, that the delicate and fragile web of interrelationship which is therapy will steadily yield its secrets to research, to the benefit of the client, the therapist, and most of all, to the whole field of social science.

(Rogers, 1949, p. 152)

And he goes on to argue that he wants his words in this paper to be acknowledged as more than "old fashioned personal testimony" (Rogers, 1949, p. 153). In doing so, he is claiming a legitimate role for reflexivity in research practice.

Conclusion

We argue here that the time has come for us to acknowledge the roots of the person-centred movement in the reflexively grounded and practice-oriented sociology of Taft and colleagues. In re-visioning the future of person-centred research we care about, we need to think about the kind of future research that values the reflexive voice of the researcher, made explicit in our research. We need to conceptualize person-centred research as embedded in a broad view of the whole spectrum of the social sciences. We need to return to the origins of our research tradition, find our voice again and liberate ourselves from the need to speak the research language of the biological and behavioural sciences.

References

Anderson, R., & Cissna, K. N. (1997) *The Martin Buber-Carl Rogers Dialogue: A New Transcript with Commentary*. Albany: State University of New York Press.

Bondi, L., & Fewell, J. (2016) Reclaiming the wisdom of practice in counselling and psychotherapy research. In Bondi, L., & Fewell, J. (eds), *Practitioner Research in Counselling and Psychotherapy. The Power of Examples*. London: Palgrave.

Bozarth, J. (2015) Personal communication.

Buber, M. (1959) *I and thou*. (2nd ed.) Edinburgh: T. & T. Clark.

Canavan, S., & Prior, P. (2016) Rethinking supervision and ethics in experience-near research. In Bondi, L., & Fewell, J. (eds), *Practitioner Research in Counselling and Psychotherapy. The Power of Examples*. London: Palgrave.

Carr, David, Bondi, L., Clark, C. & Clegg, C. (2012) *Towards Professional Wisdom*. Abingdon: Routledge.

Cornelius-White, Jeffrey H.D. (Ed.) (2012) *Carl Rogers: The China Diary*. With a foreword by Natalie Rogers. Ross on Wye: PCCS Books.

de Carvalho, R. (1999). Otto Rank, the Rankian circle in Philadelphia, and the origins of Carl Rogers' person-centred psychotherapy. *History of Psychology*, 2, 2, 132–148.

Denzin, N. K. & Lincoln, Y. S. (2000) Autoethnography, personal narrative, reflexivity. In *Handbook of Qualitative Research* (2nd ed., pp. 733–768). Thousand Oaks, CA: Sage.

Dunne, J. (2009) *Back to the Rough Ground: Practical Judgement and the Lure of Technique*. London: University of Notre Dame Press.

Etherington, K. (2000) *Narrative Approaches to Working with Adult Male Survivors of Childhood Sexual Abuse: The Clients', the Counsellor's, and the Researcher's stories*. London: Jessica Kingsley.

Etherington, K. (2001) Writing qualitative research – a gathering of selves. *Counselling and Psychotherapy Research*, 1, 119–125.

Etherington, K. (2004) *Becoming a Reflexive Researcher: Using our Selves in Research*. London; Philadelphia, PA: Jessica Kingsley Publishers.

Gendlin, E. T. (1997) *Experiencing and the Creation of Meaning: A Philosophical and Psychological Approach to the Subjective* (first published 1962). Evanston, IL: Northwestern University Press.

Greenberg, J. & Mitchell, Stephen A. (1983) *Object Relations in Psychoanalytic Theory*. Cambridge, MA; London: Harvard University Press.

Greenberg, L. S. (2004) Emotion-focused therapy. *Clinical Psychology and Psychotherapy*, 11, 3–16.

Greenberg, L.S., Rice, L.N., & Elliot, R. (1993) *Facilitating Emotional Change: The Moment by Moment Process*. New York: Guilford Press.

Haraway, D. (1988) Situated knowledges: The science question in feminism and the privilege of partial perspective. *Feminist Studies*, 14, 3, 575–599.

Heidegger, M. (1976) *What Is Called Thinking?* New York: Harper Perennial.

House, R. & Loewenthal, D. (2008) *Against and ffor CBT*. London: Karnac.

Kirkwood, C. (2002) Some notes on dialogue. *Counselling in Scotland*, 9 doi:10.1007/978-94-6091-909-1_4. Kirkwood, C. (2003) The persons-in-relation perspective in counselling. *Counselling and Psychotherapy Research*, 3, 186–195.

Kirkwood, C. (2005) Counselling as personal and social action. *Counselling in Scotland*, Spring, 4–6. http://www.cosca.org.uk/docs/COSCA%20Journal%20Spr%202005%20spp04-28-16.pdf.

Kirschenbaum, H. and Henderson, V. (1990) *The Carl Rogers Reader*. London: Constable.

Lee, B. & Prior, S. (2016) "I have to hear them before I hear myself": Developing therapeutic conversations in British counselling students. *European Journal of Psychotherapy & Counselling*, 18, 3, 271–289.

Levinas, E., Cohen, R. and Poller, N. (2006) *Humanism of the Other*. Urbana: University of Illinois Press.

MacMurray, J. (1991) *The Self as Agent*. New York: Humanity Books.

MacMurray, J. (1998) *Persons in Relation*. New York: Humanity Books.

Mertens, R. (2012) Ahead of her time. Jessie Taft, PhB 1905, PhD 1913, was a matriarch of modern social work. *The University of Chicago Magazine*, 109, 4. https://mag.uchicago.edu/education-social-service/ahead-her-time. Accessed: 30 November 2017.

O'Hara, M. & Leicester, G. (2012) *Dancing at the Edge: Competence, Culture and Organization in the 21st Century*. Axminster: Triarchy Press.

O'Hara, M. (1995) Carl Rogers: Scientist and mystic. *Journal of Humanistic Psychology*, 35, 4, 40–53.

Prouty, G., Werde, D. V., & Pörtner, M. (2002) *Pre-therapy: Reaching Contact-impaired Clients*. Ross-on-Wye: PCCS Books.

Raskin, Nathaniel J. (1948) The development of nondirective therapy. *Journal of Consulting Psychology*, 12, 2, 92–110.

Rennie, D. L. (1998) *Person-centred Counselling: An Experiential Approach*. London: Sage.
Rennie, D. L. (2007) Reflexivity and its radical form: Implications for the practice of humanistic psychotherapies. *Journal of Contemporary Psychotherapy*, 37, 53–58.
Rogers, C. R. (1942) The use of electrically recorded interviews in improving psychotherapeutic techniques. *American Journal of Orthopsychiatry*, 12, 429–434.
Rogers, C. R. (1949) A coordinated research in psychotherapy: A non-objective introduction. *Journal of Consulting Psychology* 13, 149–153.
Rogers, C. R. (1951) *Client Centred Therapy*. London: Constable.
Rogers, C. R. (1957) The necessary and sufficient conditions of therapeutic personality change. *Journal of Consulting Psychology* 21, 2, 95–103. In H. Kirschenbaum & V. Henderson (Eds.) (1990) *The Carl Rogers Reader* (pp. 219–235). London: Constable.
Rogers, C. R. (1959) A theory of therapy, personality, and interpersonal relationships: As developed in the client-centered framework. In S. Koch (Ed.), *Psychology: A Study of a Science. Formulations of the Person and the Social Context* (Vol. 3, pp. 184–256). New York: McGraw Hill.
Rogers, C. R. (1961) *On Becoming a Person. A Therapist's View of Psychotherapy*. Boston: Houghton Mifflin. Rogers, C. R. (1980) *A Way of Being*. Boston, MA: Houghton Mifflin.
Rogers, C. R. and Stevens, B. (1967) *Person to Person: The Problem of Being Human*. Lafayette, CA: Real People Press.
Rogers, C. R., Henderson, V. L., & Kirschenbaum, H. (1989) *Carl Rogers: Dialogues: Conversations with Martin Buber, Paul Tillich, B.F. Skinner, Gregory Bateson, Michael Polanyi, Rollo May, and Others*. Boston: Houghton Mifflin.
Saxon, D., Ashley, K., Bishop-Edwards, L. et al. (2017) A pragmatic randomised controlled trial assessing the non-inferiority of counselling for depression versus cognitive-behaviour therapy for patients in primary care meeting a diagnosis of moderate or severe depression (PRaCTICED): Study protocol for a randomised controlled trial. *Trials*, 18, 1, 93.
Schmid, Peter F. (2017) Person-Centred Psychotherapy. Accessed online http://pfs-online.at/1/papers/paper-pct.htm Accessed: 1 August 2017.
Schön, D. (1983) *The Reflective Practitioner: How Professionals Think in Action*. London: Temple Smith.
Smith, Adam (2011) *The Theory of Moral Sentiments*. Los Angeles: Enhanced Media Publishing.
Taft, Jessie (1933) *The Dynamics of Therapy in a Controlled Relationship*. New York: Macmillan.
Thorne, Brian (2003) *Carl Rogers. Key Figures in Counselling and Psychotherapy*. London: Sage.
Tudor, Keith (2017) *Conscience and Critic: The Selected Works of Keith Tudor*. Oxford: Routledge.
Warner, M. (2000) Person-Centred Therapy at the difficult edge; A developmentally based model of fragile and dissociated process. In D. Mearns & B. Thorne (Eds.), *Person-centred Therapy Today: New Frontiers in Theory and Practice* (pp. 144–171). London: SAGE Publications.
White, M. & Epston, D. (1990) *Narrative Means to Therapeutic Ends*. (New York; London: Norton.
Wittgenstein, Ludwig. (2009) *Philosophical Investigations* (Translated By G. E. M. Anscombe, P. M. S. Hacker and Joachim Schulte). Oxford: Wiley-Blackwell.
Wolter-GustafsonC. (2013) Rogers' generative framework of organismic integrity: Scientific evidence challenging academic, medical, and pharmaceutical forces. In: Cornelius-White, J., Motschnig-Pitrik, R., & Lux, M. (Eds), *Interdisciplinary Handbook of the Person-Centered Approach*. New York, NY: Springer.
Wyatt, J. (2016) Working at the wonder: Collaborative writing as method of inquiry. *Qualitative Inquiry*, 23, 5, 355–364.

21

PSYCHOPATHOLOGY AND THE FUTURE OF PERSON-CENTRED THERAPY

Andrew Schiller

> I will remember that there is art to medicine as well as science, and that warmth, sympathy and understanding may outweigh the surgeon's knife or the chemist's drug.
>
> (Orr et al., 1997)

Introduction

The above extract from Louis Lasagna's revision of the Hippocratic Oath serves as an apt reminder of the limitations of science and neopositivism. Indeed, the father of psychopathology, Karl Jaspers, recognised a fundamental problem when considering psychological phenomena that prevents an exclusively empirical approach to understanding them; "there is no actual research object in the traditional sense" (Bumke, 1948 cited in Musalek et al., 2010, p. 845), in other words the soul or psyche is not something that can be examined or reduced to constituent parts. He continues: "The soul is consciousness ... The soul is not a thing, but the Being in its world ... The soul is not a final state, but becoming, growth, development" (Jaspers, 1913, cited in Musalek et al., 2010, p. 845). From a person-centred perspective, one cannot help but notice the resonance of these words with those of Rogers (1959) in expounding his theory of therapy and personality development. Indeed, this resonance is largely a result of a shared existential heritage. In essence, with regard to psychic distress, person-centred and psychopathological theory represent very different approaches to similar existential challenges: how do we cope with what Simone de Beauvoir called the "ambiguity" of human existence (de Beauvoir, 1948)? In our attempts to alleviate our fellow human beings' anguish, how do we understand, as they do, the nature of their pain and reach out across what Jaspers (1968) termed the "abyss"? Is the path to genuine empathic understanding an epistemic or an ontological one, or a combination of the two?

However we choose to answer these questions, it is clear that the future of person-centred therapy is inextricably linked to its theoretical position on diagnosis, psychopathology and the medical model. Current bodies of opinion on this within the person-centred approach (PCA) seem to be divided into three main groups. One comprises the guardians of the classic ideals of the PCA, who claim that any theoretical collusion with the medical model will lead to a dilution of its foundational theory. A second posits that theoretical alignment between the medical model and the PCA is necessary to improve its representation within the mental health system. The third group contends that, despite fundamental differences, co-existence between person-centred and psychopathological theory is possible within the current system without diminishing the theoretical integrity of person-centred therapy.

Through critical analysis of a classical person-centred understanding of psychopathology and consideration of the contemporary attitudes above, I will attempt to show how it is possible for the person-centred approach to maintain a valuable and fruitful dialogue with the mental health system, particularly in the UK, without degrading its core principles or compromising its ethical integrity. To that end, I will draw on examples from my own practice and also identify developments within the UK mental health system which might facilitate such a dialogue.

Carl Rogers and psychopathology

Of central importance to a person-centred understanding of psychopathology is the relevance of diagnosis to psychotherapy. Rogers recognised "the proved effectiveness of diagnostic procedures in the field of organic illness" (Rogers, 1951, p. 220) but concluded from his own experience of practice that they were inapplicable to psychotherapy. His position was clear: "Psychological diagnosis as usually understood is unnecessary for psychotherapy, and may actually be a detriment to the therapeutic process" (ibid., p. 220). Rogers used a series of assumptive statements concerning the "rationale of physical diagnosis" (ibid.) to make his case, and they are useful in this context to highlight how and why person-centred theory is opposed to the principles of traditional medical diagnosis being applied to the process of psychotherapy.

He states, "1. Every organic condition has a preceding cause. 2. The control of the condition is much more feasible if the cause is known" (ibid., p. 220). If applied to psychotherapy, it would therefore follow that if the cause of the client's psychological distress is known by the therapist, then the therapeutic process would have a better chance of a positive outcome for the client. However, Rogers found this not to be the case in his own experience.

He determined, as Lisbeth Sommerbeck (2003) notes, that "the conditions necessary and sufficient for facilitation of the client's most constructive potentials are trusted to be the same for everybody, irrespective of diagnosis" (p. 33). Put another way, as long as Rogers' "six conditions" are present within the therapeutic process, then all clients have the same chance of realising their potential to some degree and any psychiatric diagnosis is irrelevant.

When describing the cause of a medical condition Rogers asserts, "3. The discovery and accurate description of the cause is a rational problem of scientific search" (Rogers, 1951, p. 220). Implicit within this statement are the underlying philosophical theories of logical positivism and logical empiricism, which can be termed collectively as neopositivism. This paradigm dominates the field of psychiatric diagnosis, and I suggest that it is fundamental in explaining the divergence of person-centred theory from the medical model.

This is both a materialist and reductionist point of view which assumes "that all mental life can be explained and understood solely in terms of biological processes and further that these processes can be understood by taking them apart to examine them" (Freeth, 2007, p. 62). Rachel Freeth believes the dominance of this way of thinking in the UK Mental health system has led to what she terms "scientific imperialism", where scientific claims are received by society as dogma and are unquestioned (ibid., p. 61).

What it excludes, however, is a central ingredient of person-centred theory, that of the existentialist notion of the subjectivity of a client's experience which is so crucial to Rogers' "core conditions", empathy. It is through empathy that the therapist is able to attune to the client's frame of reference and thereby facilitate a process whereby, as Rogers asserts, the client:

> moves from generalizations which have been unsatisfactory for guiding his life, to an examination of the rich primary experiences upon which they are based, a movement which exposes the falsity of many of his generalizations, and provides a basis for new and more adequate abstractions.
>
> *(Rogers, 1951, p. 143)*

Interestingly, empathic attunement was described as "not knowing" by Jaspers (Jaspers, 1963 cited in Spinelli, 2005, p. 151), a term which has since been referred to as "unknowing" by Spinelli (ibid.), and which seems to encapsulate well the attempts of the therapist to remove any of their own pre-conceptions when entering the client's world-view. Jaspers' existentialist credentials are significant here because they point to an often forgotten feature of early psychopathology that is especially relevant today within the current environment of scientific dogma; that *there are limits to scientific understanding when trying to explain psychic phenomena*. It is in this way that Jaspers "places empathic understanding at the heart of psychopathology and thus, psychiatry" (Thornton, 2007, p. 99). He recognised that "some of the key phenomena that characterise psychopathology", particularly delusions, "are not understandable". However, as Tim Thornton suggests, "if Jaspers is correct then psychiatry has a fundamental limitation" (ibid.).

A further limitation is perhaps epitomised by the inherent theoretical contradiction pointed out by R. D. Laing; that in order to remain scientifically "objective", psychopathology depersonalises the person as the "object" of study. This leads to the absurd situation where depersonalisation forms a key component of "a theory intended to be a theory of persons" (Laing, 2010, p. 24).

Rogers' next statement concerning the scientific search for a cause in medical diagnosis is that "4. This search is best conducted by an individual with a knowledge of scientific method, and a knowledge of various organic conditions" (Rogers, 1951, p. 220), or in other words, an expert. The application of this proposition within a psychiatric context causes the psychiatrist to be viewed as an expert by the patient and thus creates a power imbalance. Person-centred theory is anathema to this. Rogers contended that it is the client and not the therapist who is best placed to make meaning from his own experiences because it is only he who possesses "the potentiality of knowing the full dynamics of his perceptions and behaviour" (Rogers, 1951, p. 221). He also believed that the "constructive forces", including the "actualising tendency", which bring about positive change "reside primarily in the client, and probably cannot come from outside" (ibid., p. 222).

Rogers therefore deduced that "the very process of psychological diagnosis places the locus of evaluation so definitely in the expert" and that it could accentuate client dependency to the point where he believes that the "responsibility for understanding and improving his situation lies" not in his own hands but in those of the therapist (ibid., p. 223). When referring to client assessments as a basis for therapy, Jerold Bozarth concurs: "external frames of reference are, at best, interferences that effect clients' inclinations to find their own directions and ways at their own pace" (Bozarth, 1998: 127). In short, adopting an expert-led diagnostic approach to person-centred therapy could dramatically limit its efficacy.

Client perceptions of distress

Given that the medical model dominates the mental health system in the UK and that most clients access therapy through referral from a GP, my own experience of person-centred client practice cannot be said to be uninfluenced by diagnostic assessment. In an early session, a recent client expressed a wish to understand whether or not he "sat somewhere on the autistic spectrum" because of his difficulties in accessing emotions in relation to his experiences. I believe that this wish emanated in part from the primacy of diagnosis within the UK mental health system. My empathic response was that this seemed to be an important question for him.

It is interesting, however, that as the number of our sessions increased, his wish for diagnosis did not surface again. This could well have been because he realised that I was not going to provide one. It could also be that as he began to make meaning of his own experiences via a therapeutic relationship, his perceived relevance of an external diagnosis became less important. This experience appears to be a manifestation of Rogers' assertion that "therapy *is* diagnosis, and this diagnosis is a process which goes on in the experience of the client, rather than in the intellect of the clinician" (Rogers, 1951, p. 223).

A key element of "psychopathological" understanding, as represented in DSM V (American Psychiatric Association, 2013), is that severe mental distress is seen in terms of "illness", "disease" or "disorder". Within this framework, a "mental disorder" is classifiable by a wide range of non-specific symptoms which, in behavioural terms, represent a deviation from an arbitrary norm. Person-centred theory does not adhere to this way of thinking. Rogers' theory does not focus explicitly on illness, disease or disorder; he deals with mental disturbance as part of his overall theory of personality. In the person-centred paradigm the subjective notion of "incongruence" is seen as the main driver of mental distress rather than an array of generically applicable symptoms (Rogers, 1959).

From a person-centred perspective, the process of diagnosis can have a damaging effect on a client by labelling them. Diagnosis can thus affect a person's sense of identity through being objectified as an "illness" with the associated stigma that often accompanies it. It therefore fails to take account of an individual's suffering as "a *unique* expression of this particular person in this particular situation" (Schmid, 2005, p. 78) and as Proctor comments, positions "the individual as someone who is disordered, ill or distressed; the problem is located in the individual rather than society" (Proctor, 2006, p. 69).

This is supported by the definition of a "personality disorder" in DSM V as "an enduring pattern of inner experience and behaviour that deviates markedly from the expectations of the individual's culture ... and leads to clinically significant distress or impairment" (American Psychiatric Association, 2013, p. 647). In addition, what constitutes "clinically significant distress" remains undefined and open to interpretation.

Psychopathology also rejects one of the key tenets of person-centred theory: the fluidity of the self-concept. It is much more pessimistic about how much a personality can change. Rogers believed that people had the potential for profound personality change and understood the danger of perceiving clients in terms of their "illness" rather than their potential:

> if I accept the person as someone fixed, already diagnosed and classified ... then I am doing my part to confirm this limited hypothesis. If I accept him as a process of becoming, then I am doing what I can to confirm or make real his potentialities.
>
> *(Rogers, 1967, p. 55)*

Interestingly, a recent study challenges the notion of consistent, life long, personality traits (Harris et al., 2016). Its findings are at variance with previous studies which suggest there is "a relationship between childhood personality and health and wellbeing in later life" (ibid., p. 450). The researchers concluded that "childhood dependability played relatively small roles in influencing older-age health and subjective wellbeing" (ibid., p. 452) and in doing so indicate that we are much more labile than psychologists have previously thought.

This view of a client's limited potential in "diagnostic" terms can also affect the client's perception of their own potential for positive change. A long-term client of mine disclosed a "diagnosis" of "obsessive-compulsive personality disorder" and subsequently often referred to it as an explanation for her behaviour, her felt sense of emotion and the level of anxiety that she should expect to experience. Whilst this seemed to contribute to acceptance of her distress on the one hand, on the other it seemed to promote a sense of resignation to what could be described as a false ceiling to her true potential.

In this way, it seemed at times that the purpose of therapy for her was to maintain a sort of status quo concerning her accepted view of herself based on an arbitrary diagnosis. Whenever the "diagnosis" was mentioned, it appeared to form a barrier to accessing her true potential for change; it was as though as soon as the impact of the "actualising tendency" was felt in her as a result of its interaction with her conditions of worth, she reminded herself, via her "diagnosis", not to trust it. Thus, her "diagnosis" seemed to contribute in a very real sense to her incongruence.

This experience alludes to what could be argued is a fundamental pathologisation of all aspects of human experience within society. Indeed, this perception, as perpetuated by DSM V, even has critics within the UK psychiatric profession itself. As Simon Wessely (2017) asserts,

> We cannot cope with the disorders we have, and we do think there are such things as shy children; we do think there are some quirky, bookish kids ... this is just a normal part of development and personality. It should not be treated, it should not be pathologised.

It is likely that most person-centred therapists would agree with this statement and would also share the ostensibly existential view that "the experience of anxiety is a fundamental 'given' of being-in-the-world" (Spinelli, 2005, p. 154).

Wessely's comments above are interesting in that they suggest common ground between a person-centred outlook and that of the psychiatric profession which is the dominant force within the UK mental health system. I am doubtful as to whether this represents a fundamental sea-change in thinking within the psychiatric profession but it offers hope when considering how best to maintain a dialogue.

A natural consequence of over-pathologising society is an increasing reliance on pharmacotherapy. In 2016, 64.7m antidepressant prescriptions were dispensed in England alone, representing an increase of 108.5% on the number dispensed in 2006 (Prescriptions Dispensed in the Community, Statistics for England – 2006–2016 [PAS], NHS Digital, 2017). Research has indicated that a combination of psychotherapy and antidepressants is more effective in alleviating depression than medication alone (Cuijpers et al., 2014). Despite this, NHS guidelines often suggest antidepressants are used as a first-line treatment for moderate depression before any talking therapies are considered.

Contemporary person-centred attitudes to the medical model

The prospect of a fruitful dialogue is surely dependent upon its participants. So it is therefore apt to ask the question: which point of view should the person-centred approach represent in this dialogue? In order to answer this question, it is necessary to examine the various groupings of opinion within the person-centred approach toward the medical model as it is this model which dominates mental health system in the UK and in the wider world.

There seem to be three main bodies of opinion represented by different authors within the approach. The first group I will call *Principled Idealists* and they are the guardians of the classical ideals of the PCA. One of the writers who epitomises this approach is Pete Sanders who appears to be vehemently opposed to any collusion with the medical model. Central to his point of view is the "invalidity, unevidenced and damaging nature of psychodiagnosis" and that it derives from "the toxic idea that human distress is an 'illness'" (Sanders, 2005, p. 35). He believes that any compromise is unethical as it risks introducing concepts of "illness", "expertise" and "disorder" into person-centred client practice and that could affect efficacy. He contends such compromise would also be futile and merely play into the hands of the "dominant clique". He cites John Schlien: "The lion and the lamb may lie down together, but if it is the lion's den, the lion is probably quite relaxed, looking forward to breakfast in bed" (Sanders, 2005, p. 35).

In addition, he supports vocal opposition to the medical model in the belief that if sufficient noise is made then a valid challenge to medicalisation can be undertaken by therapists' professional bodies. Sanders believes this principled opposition is also important because "the evolution of ideas requires diversity in the pool of ideas" (ibid., p. 38).

I have great respect for the opinions of the *Principled Idealists* and believe they play an essential role within the PCA for ensuring its principles remain undiluted. However, for the very reason that they are unwilling to work within the system governed by the medical model, I would question their suitability to take part in a dialogue with the mental health system.

The next group I have described as *Diplomatic Compromisers* because, broadly speaking, they seek to interpret person-centred theory using the language of the dominant medical model. This group believe that person-centred therapists can be more effective in their challenge to the medical model if they work from within the system and offer alternative theories. Of course, this involves an acceptance of the primacy of the diagnostic framework.

Margaret Warner is a strong proponent of this point of view and her alternative theory of difficult process (Warner, 2005, 2009) is an apposite example. She argues that conditions of worth are not a sufficient cause of the mental distress which results from abuse, neglect or biological factors and in response proposes a theory of processing to enhance Rogers' theory of conditions of worth. She uses the terms *difficult, fragile* or *dissociated process* (Warner, 2005, pp. 93–95) and aligns them with their psychopathological counterparts such as borderline or narcissistic personality disorders. As an aside, it is interesting to note that Hook and Murphy's recent and compelling response to Warner's theory claims that abuse, neglect or biological factors are not in themselves conditions of worth, though conditions of worth are relevant in a causal sense because they affect the way in which these events are responded to (Hook and Murphy, 2016).

Other writers in this group such as Stephen Joseph (2015) regard the PCA as a positive psychology in that both theories consider client distress in terms of unrealised potential rather than deficit, illness or disease. This notion is of course the essence of the PCA's radicalism and I therefore understand the desire for synergy with positive psychology on that basis. However, there are differences that suggest caution when considering an alliance. For example, positive psychology espouses a "rhetoric of resilience" which undermines the core of the PCA's therapeutic tradition, that "fostering acceptance of one's own and others' vulnerability and imperfection" is the "key for healing and change" (Bazzano, 2016, p. 353).

I admire the practical urgency of the *Diplomatic Compromisers* as I believe they operate, as Sanders suggests, from a position based on the necessity to do something "*today* to help bring the PCT tribe back into the mix of funded treatment options wherever it has been excluded" (Sanders, 2005, p. 38). This also explains Sanders' own collaboration with the emotion-focused therapeutic approach in the form of "counselling for depression" (CfD) as a NICE-recommended treatment (Sanders & Hill, 2014). However, as Hook and Murphy's paper illustrates, I fear that should this group dominate a dialogue with the mental health system in the UK, the integrity of person-centred theory may well be the worse for it.

The final group, the *Optimistic Bridge Builders*, represented by practitioners such as Rachel Freeth and Lisbeth Sommerbeck contend that the person-centred approach and the medical model can be complementary without collusion. In their view, it is possible to simultaneously protect the person-centred therapy process and respect other professionals' treatment of the client from the medical model perspective.

Their argument focuses on the philosophical complementary relationship between "explaining" and "understanding" to support the co-existence of the medical model and person-centred practice. As Freeth asserts,

> in effect they represent two different paradigms. Explaining refers to the scientist's interpretation of causal laws ... Understanding, however, relates to an interest in how human beings perceive their reality and in the meaning for the individual of their experience.
>
> (Freeth, 2007, p. 82)

Jaspers understood the importance of this duality when he posited, "It is therefore in principle not at all absurd to try to understand as well as to explain one and the same real psychic event" (cited in Thornton, 2007, p. 97). However, by attempting to combine empathic *understanding*, which is a practice of existential phenomenology, and *explaining*, an empirically scientific endeavour, within the same "objective" paradigm, he created what Laing (2010, p. 24) refers to as a "spiral of falsity".

By recognising the complementary value of two distinct paradigms in their efforts to achieve the same objective, alleviation of mental distress, it is surely possible to operate from a *collaborative* rather than *defensive* position. It is for this reason that I propose that the *Optimistic Bridge Builders* represent the best chance for a continued and productive dialogue with the UK mental health system without eroding the core principles of person-centred theory. In addition, their case is also enhanced by compelling research evidence concerning the successful use of Pre-therapy (Prouty, 1994) and the use of person-centred therapy with "borderline personality" clients (Teusch et al., 2001).

Pockets of hope within the medical model

Of course, identifying the best approach within the PCA for maintaining a valuable dialogue with the mental health system is only half the battle. Much depends on how receptive the medical model is to the PCA's point of view, but there have been some encouraging developments in this area. As Gillian Proctor (2017) notes, within the field of clinical psychology there is a growing acknowledgement that "the subjectivity of researchers" is of relevance to their findings, just as "objective" or "experimental methods" are (p. 349). Whilst this represents a potential shift from the scientist-practitioner model and emphasises the value of reflection and reflexivity, it is also limited in scope because it "is not used to challenge the scientific idea of evidence by considering how the values of individual practitioners influence their choice of interventions" (ibid., p. 350). Nonetheless, this can still be seen as a significant in-road within a discipline formerly unreceptive to the notion of subjectivity yet one that often acts as an intermediary between the fields of psychiatry and psychotherapy.

Furthermore, it also appears that there is a nascent desire within the field of psychiatry for greater openness and partnership with other disciplines. As Stanghellini and Fuchs (2013) assert, these could include "different combinations of clinician/researcher-philosopher pairings, team-working of various kinds, incorporating patients and carers as experts by experience …" (p. xxxv). This is further supported within the field of psychopathology itself by a growing shift away from the sole consideration of "categories of disorder" and is seen in some quarters as essential "in order to shape a future psychiatry in which the whole person once again becomes the measure of all things" (Musalek et al., 2010, p. 850).

Conclusion

I have argued that the *Optimistic Bridge Builders* offer the best chance of a productive discourse with the dominant forces within the mental health system because the former operate from a position that seeks both to safeguard the theoretical integrity of the PCA and utilise its radicalism through collaboration. There are also signs that the medical model may well be receptive to such dialogue, although I follow Deborah Lee (2017) in urging PCA practitioners to be more politically aware and engaged to make best use of this opportunity. When referring to a person-centred understanding of psychopathology, it is possible to claim that Rogers did in fact value the importance of diagnosis within psychotherapy but not from the perspective of a psychopathological paradigm. He recognised two crucial differences: firstly, diagnosis must reside within the locus of evaluation of the client, and secondly, that such a diagnosis is not based on scientific empiricism but on a *felt sense of meaning derived from experience*. Rogers, unlike Jaspers, attempted to straddle the barrier between human and natural sciences without compromise and I believe this challenge is as relevant today if the person-centred approach is not only to survive but thrive in the future.

References

American Psychiatric Association (2013) *Diagnostic and Statistical Manual of Mental Disorders* (5th ed.). Washington, DC: APA.

Bazzano, M. (2016). "The conservative turn in person-centered therapy", *Person-Centered & Experiential Psychotherapies*, 15(4), 339–355.

De Beauvoir, S. (1948). *The Ethics of Ambiguity*. New York, NY: Philosophical Library.

Bozarth, J. (1998). *Person-Centered therapy: a Revolutionary Paradigm*. Ross-on-Wye: PCCS Books.

Cuijpers, P., Sijbrandij, M., Koole, S.L., Andersson, G., Beekman, A.T., & Reynolds, C.F. (2014). "Adding psychotherapy to antidepressant medication in depression and anxiety disorders: a meta-analysis", *World Psychiatry*, 13(1), 56–67.

Freeth, R. (2007). *Humanising Psychiatry and Mental Health Care*. Oxford: Radcliffe.

Harris, M., Brett, C., Starr, J., Deary, I., & Johnson, W. (2016) "Personality and other lifelong influences on older-age health and wellbeing: Preliminary findings in two Scottish samples", *European Journal of Personality*, 30(5), 438–455.

Hook, L., & Murphy, D. (2016). "Related but not replaceable: a response to Warner's reworking of person-centered personality theory", *Person-Centered & Experiential Psychotherapies*, 15(4), 285–299.

Jaspers, K. (1968). "The Phenomenological Approach in Psychopathology", *The British Journal of Psychiatry*, 114: 1313–1323.

Joseph, S. (2015) *Positive Therapy: Building Bridges between Positive Psychology and Person-Centred Psychotherapy*. Abingdon: Routledge.

Laing, R. (2010). *The Divided Self*. London: Penguin.

Lee, D. (2017). "A person-centred political critique of current discourses in post-traumatic stress disorder and post-traumatic growth", *Psychotherapy and Politics International*, 15(2), e1411.

Musalek, M., Larach-Walters, V., Lépine, J., Millet, B. & Gaebel, W. (2010). "Psychopathology in the 21st century", *The World Journal of Biol Psychiatry*, 11(7): 844–851.

NHS Digital (2017). Prescriptions Dispensed in the Community, Statistics for England – 2006–2016 [PAS]. Available at: http://digital.nhs.uk/catalogue/PUB30014 (Accessed 18 August 2017).

Orr, R.D., Pang, N., Pellegrino, E.D. & Siegler, M. (1997). "Use of the Hippocratic Oath: A review of twentieth century practice and a content analysis of oaths administered in medical schools in the U.S. and Canada in 1993", *Journal of Clinical Ethics*, 8: 377–388.

Proctor, G. (2006). Therapy: Opium of the masses or help for those who least need it? In G. Proctor, M. Cooper, P. Sanders and B. Malcolm (eds.) *Politicizing the person-centred approach*. Ross-on-Wye: PCCS Books.

Proctor, G. (2017). "Clinical psychology and the person-centred approach: an uncomfortable fit?" In Joseph, S. (Ed.), *The Handbook of Person-Centred Therapy and Mental Health: Theory, Research and Practice*. Monmouth: PCCS Books.

Prouty, G. (1994). *Theoretical Evolutions in Person-Centred/Experiential Therapy: Applications to Schizophrenic and Retarded Psychoses*. Westport, CT: Praeger.
Rogers, C. (1951). *Client-Centered Therapy: Its Current Practice, Implications and Theory*. Boston: Houghton Mifflin.
Rogers, C. (1959). "A theory of therapy, personality, and interpersonal relationships, as developed in the client-centered framework." In Koch, S. (Ed.), *Psychology: A Study of a Science*, Vol. 3. *Formulations of the Person and the Social Context*. New York: McGraw-Hill (pp. 184–256).
Rogers, C. (1967). *On Becoming a Person. A Therapist's View of Psychotherapy*. Constable: London.
Sanders, P. (2005). "Principled and strategic opposition to the medicalisation of distress and all its apparatus." In S. Joseph & R. Worsley (Eds.), *Person-centred Psychopathology*. Ross-on-Wye: PCCS Books.
Sanders, P., & Hill, A. (2014). *Counselling for Depression*. Los Angeles: SAGE.
Schmid, P.F. (2005). "Authenticity and Alienation: Towards an understanding of the person beyond the categories of order and disorder." In S. Joseph & R. Worsley (Eds.), *Person-centred Psychopathology*. Ross-on-Wye: PCCS Books.
Sommerbeck, L. (2003). *The Client-centred Therapist in Psychiatric Contexts*. Ross-on-Wye: PCCS.
Spinelli, E. (2005). *The Interpreted World*. Los Angeles: SAGE.
Stanghellini, G. & Fuchs, T. (2013). *One Century of Karl Jaspers' General Psychopathology*. Oxford: Oxford University Press.
Teusch, L., Böhme, H., Finke, J. & Gastpar, M. (2001). "Effects of client-centered psychotherapy for personality disorders alone and in combination with psychopharmacological treatment", *Psychotherapy and Psychosomatics*, 70(6): 328–336.
Thornton, T. (2007). *Essential Philosophy of Psychiatry*. Oxford: Oxford University Press.
Warner, M.S. (2005). "A person-centered view of human nature, wellness and psychopathology." In S. Joseph & R. Worsley (Eds.), *Person-centred Psychopathology*. Ross-on-Wye: PCCS Books.
Warner, M.S. (2009). "Defense or actualisation? Reconsidering the role of processing, self and agency within Rogers' theory of personality", *Person-Centered & Experiential Psychotherapies*, 8(2): 109–126.
Wessely, S. (2017). The Life Scientific, BBC Radio 4, 14 February. https://www.bbc.co.uk/programmes/b08dnr3g.

22

PRESENCE

The fourth condition

Sarton Weinraub

Current state of the person-centered approach

While the three core conditions (empathy, congruence, and unconditional positive regard) are widely recognized as the primary theoretical focus of the person-centered approach (PCA), there are a number of branches or "tribes" that in fact make up the whole of what is now referred to as "Person-centred and Experiential Psychotherapy and Counseling" worldwide. Indeed, "[t]he history of psychotherapy is the history of developments, disagreements and splits" (Sanders, 2004, p. ix). Psychoanalysis, for example, has many branches and their variance and popularity often depend upon geography and the personal preferences of the leaders in those communities (Kirsner, 2009). However, the person-centered approach is unique in that throughout its history there has been only one widely recognized progenitor, i.e. Carl Rogers.

Since Rogers' death in 1987 there has been little widely recognized evolution of person-centered theory. In fact, it might be more accurate to state that the person-centered approach has been declining, especially in the United States. In his 2004 edited volume *Tribes of the Person Centred Nation*, Pete Sanders set out to document the predominant tribes of the person-centered approach. For Sanders "a tribe is not simply a new idea" (Sanders, 2004, p. x), but a marker of what is actually occurring within a community. In his edited volume Sanders highlights five main tribes found within the person-centered approach worldwide: Classical Client-Centered Therapy, Focusing, Experiential Therapy, Existential Therapy, and Integrative Person-Centered Therapy. Sanders acknowledges that these may not constitute a complete picture of our approach and "whether or not it is correct to include these approaches, at least now you, the reader, will be better able to judge" (Sanders, 2004, p. ix).

Sanders draws attention to the fact that "since the advent of the World Association for Person-centred and Experiential Psychotherapy and Counseling (WAPCEPC) in 2000, the tribes have had an organizational meeting point where information exchange, challenging debate, support, project developments and international representation can take place" (Sanders, 2004, p. 17). For Sanders, "issues of definition still loom large as the tribes debate the criteria which should determine whether a therapeutic approach falls within the broad definition of the term client-centred (or still, person-centred)" (Sanders, 2004, p. 17). Yet no matter the tribe, Sanders acknowledges that for person-centered practitioners, "the debate continues to return to two core issues, namely directivity/non-directivity and the necessity and sufficiency of the therapeutic conditions" (Sanders, 2004, p. 17).

Person-centered core conditions

Within the person-centered approach we often refer to what are again called the three "core conditions" (empathy, congruence, unconditional positive regard). While Rogers did not support the term core conditions, he did promote the three-condition model, referring to them as being facilitative: "There are three conditions" – he wrote – "that must be present in order for a climate to be growth-promoting" (Rogers, 1980, p. 115). In the world of what was Rogerian or client-centered therapy and is now known as the person-centered approach, we often refer to what are called the six necessary and sufficient conditions for therapeutic change (Rogers, 1957). These six conditions are the backbone of person-centered theory as they outline Rogers' conception of the conditions necessary for his view of therapeutic change.

However, amongst person-centered practitioners it is more common for us to focus on what we call the three core conditions that come from Rogers' six. These core conditions are often "presented on their own over the years in order to simplify the theory and practice of person-centred counseling" (Sanders, 2006, p. 8). Acceptance of the core conditions model and associating the PCA with the three core conditions has become the norm within our communities and beyond. However, our use of the three-core-conditions conception can create the possibility for misunderstanding our theory: "The problem is that it gives the impression that therapy is something the counselor does to the client" (Sanders, 2006, p. 8). Nevertheless, this shorthand, while possibly too simplistic, has taken root and its renown is now acknowledged throughout all psychological schools. There is speculation that towards the end of his life Rogers was theorizing about the concept of "presence" so much so that it would have become a recognized fourth condition. The idea that presence is a fourth condition has become legend within the PCA. Most of us are aware of presence as the fourth condition, are excited by this topic, yet, do not speak about presence often, particularly in groups. Currently, it feels as if the concept of presence is an unwanted stepchild within our theory and practice. In this way, presence is a theory that is often alluded to, yet few have focused on it with enough depth to challenge this revolutionary suggestion.

Presence: the fourth condition

While Rogers did not specifically define presence, nor state it as a fourth condition, in his later years his writings on presence are significant and fundamental in that he connects presence with a "slightly altered state of consciousness" (Rogers, 1980, p. 129). Some person-centered authors have confused this altered state of consciousness with something supernatural. "He injected supernatural elements into the concept that had not been included in his earlier use of the term" (Brodley, 2000, p. 140). However, the term supernatural can be misleading because its popular definition leaves no room for understanding progressive altered states of awareness. Such progressive states can include a heightened sense of self-awareness. Within this self-aware state, our subjective perceptions can be so attuned that our presence alone motivates movement towards congruence in ourselves and in others. "Then, simply my presence is releasing and helpful to the other" (Rogers, 1980, p. 129).

A remarkable investigation of presence comes from Shari Geller and her collaborator Leslie Greenberg of York University in Toronto (Geller, 2009; Geller, 2013; Geller & Greenberg, 2002; Geller & Greenberg, 2012). For Geller, presence is "a foundation and necessary precondition to the relationship conditions of empathy, congruence and unconditional positive regard" (Geller, 2002, p. 85). Within their seminal volume, *Therapeutic Presence: A Mindful Approach to Effective Therapy* (2012), Geller and Greenberg explore the experience of presence within an eclectic array of psychotherapeutic schools. Throughout, they offer a fundamental respect for Rogers and the PCA. For Geller and Greenberg, "presence could be seen as the larger condition by which empathy, congruence, and unconditional regard came to be expressed" (Geller and Greenberg, 2012, p. 68). At the same time, Geller and Greenberg promote the concept of "therapeutic presence" as a useful technique available to every psychotherapist, "as a way therapists monitor their own experience in therapy" (Geller and Greenberg, 2012, p. 7). And while the technique of therapeutic presence is valuable, it differs from the conception and experience of presence being offered here. The difference is that presence is a way of being and not a technique to be applied. Therefore, the core conditions alone are perfect in their holistic ability to meet needs.

The range of the core conditions has expanded and presence is the fourth core condition. Acceptance of presence as a core condition is, in my view, the most significant theoretical expansion of the PCA since Rogers' death. When we look closer at presence, it in fact becomes the first condition through which the others can arise. In other words, by engaging our own presence we open the door to empathy, unconditional positive regard, and congruence. Without presence, those core conditions run the risk of being disingenuous and can become techniques as opposed to a way of being.

What is presence? Presence is not pretense. To be present is to be in the moment. To be present is to be here and now, moving towards being in touch with ourselves, and available to what we are thinking and feeling. When we are fully present, we are flowing, our awareness is growing, and we are becoming more available to others and ourselves. Presence is not mindfulness, although mindfulness practice, as well as many other progressive practices, can increase our ability to access presence. What is important is that presence requires feeling safe. The more we feel safe enough to experience our presence, the easier it becomes to feel safe in new environments. Certainly there are varying degrees of accessing presence that are determined by a variety of internal and external factors. In this way presence is not a sedentary state but a moving force that expands and contracts. To be alive is to have access to presence. Yet, the degree to which we can acknowledge and share our experience of presence can vary widely. In this way only the subjective perception of the individual can accurately measure his or her ability to access presence.

Accessing presence can be a struggle. Because presence is not a sedentary state, it involves a wide range of moving experiences, some positive and some negative. Sometimes we feel we have access to our full awareness. Other times we struggle to stay in awareness. But if you allow for the actuality of presence, partaking in its positive and negative experiences, you are there. And when you are there it is you, positive or negative, it is the best of you at that moment. And from this acceptance, that we are present and therefore doing our best, a state of congruence can emerge. From congruence we naturally have the energy to offer empathy to ourselves and to others. And with empathy, unconditional positive regard is its natural companion.

Presence is relational

Humans are fundamentally social animals and new research is questioning the conception of survival of the fittest. In his book *Born to Be Good* (Keltner, 2009), Berkeley psychology professor, Dacher Keltner suggests that in fact human evolution is based upon survival of the kindest as opposed to survival of the fittest: "Power and status are inevitable facets of hominid social life but are founded on social intelligence more than Social Darwinism" (Keltner, 2009, p. 64). Because presence is not a state but a process, and because we humans are fundamentally social animals, it may be that we cannot fully access presence alone. Certainly we can initiate the subjective process that can with other ingredients become presence. But it may be that presence requires connection to others to be realized and furthered. This begs the question, if a person is present alone in a forest, is their presence full?

Experience is subjective, yet presence is relational. Furthermore, accessing presence with another is healing. To understand the relational importance of presence, let's do what many person-centered authors have done before, and turn to the philosopher Martin Buber with his epic book *I and Thou*. Person-centered practitioners often cite Buber, whose work influenced Rogers. In 1957 Rogers and Buber gave a public discussion at the University of Michigan (Anderson & Cissna, 1997). Within *I and Thou*, Buber states, "the actual fulfilled present exists only insofar as presentness, encounter, and relation exist" (Buber, 1958, p. 63). For Buber, the need for relating to others is inherent in humans and inextricably linked to our need to become present. In Buber's words: "the innateness of the longing for relation is apparent even in the earliest and dimmest stage" (Buber, 1958, p. 77). And for Buber, humans can only reach their developmental potential when our relational needs are engaged, "man becomes an I through you" (Buber, 1958, p. 80).

According to Geller and Greenberg (2012), another philosopher, Emmanuel Levinas, a generation after Buber "went beyond Buber" (Geller & Greenberg, 2012, p. 23). For Geller and Greenberg, Levinas is "concerned with justice and morality ... that we care for the Other and creates a sense of ethical responsibility for the Other's well-being" (Geller & Greenberg, 2012, p. 24). Levinas elevates the relational potential of presence to a social and potentially political level. The political significance of presence is a huge topic that certainly needs further study. Other authors, such as (Senge et al., 2004), attempt to expand presence from the social/political to the business/organizational worlds. However, unless presence is understood as a way of being, its full capacity is neglected.

Presence requires self-care

Self-care is the road to presence. Self-care is a simple concept but it has profound consequences, and few are able to maintain self-care on a constant and progressive scale. For anyone interested in accessing presence regularly, creating a holistic, disciplined, and progressive self-care plan is the only road forward. Geller and Greenberg (2012) devote a section of their book to self-care, which is the missing link in accessing presence for most healthcare professionals. The concept of self-care is widely accepted in popular culture today and understood to mean acts we engage in to sustain our health. But the difficulty in maintaining self-care is engaging in acts that meet our needs holistically, by addressing our mind, body, and spirit. The other difficulty in maintaining self-care is sustaining the practice, or engaging in the practice as a self-generated discipline.

The discipline that promotes self-care is not the same as imposing external demands on oneself. The latter are not, properly speaking, discipline. True discipline is being engaged on an inner, personal or spiritual, level. When we strive towards presence we are forced to look at our needs, rather than our wants, in the present. And when we accept our needs in their authentic state, a protective energetic force of discipline emerges within us to help maintain the boundaries necessary to meet our needs consistently. This self-generated discipline is a force stronger than any externally promoted doctrine. True discipline is the force that awakens us early in the morning to go to the gym before work. True discipline is the force that motivates us to look closely at the foods we put into our body. True discipline is the force that motivates us to engage others with truth and compassion so that we can experience ourselves more fully within the world. And true discipline is the force that helps us to sleep at night having fully exhausted the energy within us, ready and needing renewal. Once accessed, we crave this discipline because we experience it as the force that can connect us to ourselves and others with ever expanding possibility. Self-generated discipline is the strongest drug because at its core is love of life and humanity.

There are many specific self-care practices that are advertised as helpful in accessing presence. However, the key to accessing disciplined self-care is that the practices are self-determined, studied and experimented with, to see if they fit our unique needs. For example, I have chosen the practice of yoga as my main self-care physical disciple. Specifically, I practice what is called Ashtanga yoga. While I love Ashtanga yoga and I have tried my best to suggest it to friends and colleagues over the years, Ashtanga yoga is not for everyone. I spent a number of years experimenting with a variety of exercise practices and discovered Ashtanga yoga by chance. Ashtanga yoga fits my needs because, as a psychotherapist, I spend most of my day sitting and so I need a significant physical practice to help offset my large amount of daily inactivity. Historically, in Ashtanga yoga you practice up to six days a week. Also, Ashtanga is a self-directed practice. In short, this practice matches my person-centered philosophy by helping me to find my unique course of movement daily. In fact, I formulated many of the concepts within this paper during my Ashtanga yoga practice. Also, on a practical note, I live in New York City where the weather is seasonal and because this daily practice is indoors I can maintain my discipline throughout the year. All of these small but important details have helped me to maintain yoga as a self-care practice for the last decade.

Yoga is very important to me, but it is also only one aspect of my self-care disciplined practices. Another self-care practice I engage in daily is my attempt to engage my primary relationship with open honest communication. The specific outcome is not as important as the journey of developing intimacy. And, as every adult learns, open honest communication is the best way to allow for relational intimacy to develop. That said, working towards open honest communication with a partner/partners in whom we have so much invested is yet another struggle and a consequent source of meaning in life. There is much more to be said on this topic.

Another self-care practice I engage in and struggle with is food. In this day and age poor quality and unhealthy food is too readily available. Not to acknowledge this fact can be a true impediment to accessing presence. Why? Well, food is our source of life. Eating involves bringing a substance from the world into our body and combining it with our life force daily. Is there anything more powerful and spiritual than our connection to food? Another area of self-care I want to outline relates to a topic I will discuss in more detail later in this paper, i.e. Rogers' encounter group process patterns. Specifically, I want to look at what he called the "expression of negative feelings" (Rogers, 1970, p. 19). Looking at the expression of negative feelings from a self-care perspective, it seems there are times in life when we need to access a variety of feelings, negative and positive, within ourselves and in relation to others. Therefore, the ability to engage in free expression is in many ways a self-care practice. Does this mean that we need to verbally assault or verbally abuse others? Certainly not. What it means is that for a healthy society to exist, it must recognize that humans are animals and we need to access our full range of emotions with one another. In this way anger is as valid an emotion as is joy. We cannot restrict one emotion and only advance others without the consequence of imbalance and it requires self-care to maintain this awareness.

While self-care may not seem to be relational, and while many elements of it begin from within, every self-care practice has relational aspects because self-care must occur in connection to the world around us. We will not always be able to maintain self-care and for this reason a good degree of self-acceptance is also necessary

Presence engages self-acceptance

It is only through self-acceptance that we can open ourselves and learn to acknowledge that presence is right here within us. As with self-care, it is the struggle with the mundane day-to-day acts that truly promotes self-acceptance. In this way, many of us overthink self-acceptance, equating it with unrealistic expectations that we will enter a perfect state that is unflinching and never changing. But like all true human processes, self-acceptance is a lifelong journey of discovery. That said, there are moments of breakthrough where our connection to self-acceptance becomes more evident and realized. Hopefully, these moments occur throughout our lifetime and each new moment of awareness brings us closer to a feeling of self-actualization and congruence. I want to share an experience that was particularly important to me because it marked the moment that I chose to become a person-centered practitioner.

I moved to New York City to become a psychoanalyst and in the course of my training discovered the PCA. At one point I found myself trapped with my feet in both worlds. I felt I could not find a way to be in either the psychoanalytic or the person-centered worlds, and I was scared I might not survive this professional crisis and consequently be forced to choose a new profession. I felt that perhaps the psychoanalysts were right and I was simply experiencing deep unconscious conflicts which were beginning to overtake me. However, I did not trust my psychoanalytic supervisor and I knew if I showed any hint of theoretical interest outside of psychoanalytic theory he would judge me as "acting out," and furthermore he could instigate my removal from the psychoanalytic training program. At the same time, I was afraid to address this fear with my person-centered supervisor who I was just getting to know; I was unsure if he was honest about his convictions as the person-centered theories he showed me seemed too simplistic. Also, friends in my psychoanalytic training program began to question my mental stability.

It took some courage, but over a number of sessions I explained my situation to both my supervisors. My person-centered supervisor immediately seemed able to relate to my struggle and in fact he explained that he had also been involved in the psychoanalytic community at the beginning of his career, and therefore had first-hand knowledge of the struggle I was experiencing. However, his person-centered community was very limited and I was afraid of being isolated. As for my psychoanalyst supervisor, it seemed to me he could not completely understand my struggle. Instead of understanding me, he attempted to interpret my concerns and suggested I did not fully comprehend psychopathology. Unfortunately, as I explained my struggle to both supervisors, and while they both did their best to offer me support using the tools they thought appropriate, it seemed I was left with the same struggle. I felt no one could solve this for me. I continued to feel this great conflict inside and it was eating me up.

Early one morning I had a breakthrough. I was feeling horrible, sitting on the subway having just left my psychoanalytic supervisor's office, heading to a clinic where later that day I would meet with my person-centered supervisor. I felt as if I could not reconcile these two opposing theoretical stances. I recall thinking that I could not overcome this conflict and I might have to stop working as a psychologist and I began to think of ways I could begin to refer out my clients. But then, just at the breaking point, the image of my father came into my mind. I recall seeing my father standing between my psychoanalytic supervisor and my person-centered supervisor. I visualized him as a tennis ball that kept bouncing between my two supervisors. I began to think about my relationship with my father in greater detail. I realized that he was basically absent during my youth and I felt overwhelmed. A deep longing followed. I continued to long for my father to be there for me and with me. I wanted his unconditional support and acceptance.

I thought of both my supervisors and I compared them with my dad, and then, suddenly, this sharp, fast, and really meaningful thought hit me. My psychoanalytic supervisor was continuing my history of my being ignored and feeling rejected by my father, while my person-centered supervisor was not ignoring or rejecting me. He was not becoming father-like, but an equal partner in my life. It occurred to me that within the psychoanalytic world, rejection of the son and his capacity to be a father is standard because in fact no one can ever be as good as Freud was; therefore, no one can ever take the place of the father. In other words, I realized that inherent in the psychoanalytic ideology is the requirement to be subservient to Freud as the ultimate father. It became clear to me that at that point in my life, I no longer wanted or could handle having a rejecting father. At that moment I understood that I wanted a loving and accepting father. I made my choice. I chose to begin to let go of my attachment to psychoanalytic theory and I began to embrace the PCA.

This entire thought process took place in a matter of seconds, but once I made the choice I felt I had forever changed. I was no longer the same person when I got off that subway. For that day and for the next few weeks I was high from the energy that grew in me. This does not mean that it was an easy choice or that later I did not second-guess myself. But I *had changed* and there was no going back. In hindsight this change was a whole new level of self-acceptance.

Questioning celebrity in order to access presence

It is important that we clarify the issue of celebrity when outlining what is needed to access presence. In this context, celebrity refers to any preconception or ideal one individual holds in regard to another known individual's ability to access presence consistently. This model of celebrity can refer to a known celebrity in one's popular culture or to individuals who are less famous, such as one's teacher, supervisor, or colleague. In each case, the element that needs to be understood is our preconception and possible idealization of the celebrity's ability to access presence over and above our own. Often these celebrity idealizations create feelings of not being good enough and in comparison unable to access presence. While looking to celebrity is an age-old function of the human condition, we need to clarify and question our engagement with it.

For many of us in the PCA Carl Rogers himself was/is an ideal. Many of us watch him on film during client interviews and we feel we should behave like him. Within the PC community many people seem to expect that Rogers' way of being with others is an unspoken expectation as to how we should engage with each other. At the same time, it is known that Rogers did not want people to become Rogerians. In India there is a long history of gurus where a leader becomes the focal point of the spiritual practice. The guru tradition has been around for so long and it seems to help some people access presence. Therefore we must distinguish between celebrity and guru. The main difference between celebrity and guru is the individual's ability and the level with which they can connect with and engage the person, celebrity, guru, teacher or whatever.

In my professional life I have been lucky enough to be very close to a number of well-regarded and senior mental health practitioners and, aside from their fame, it was their ability to connect to me as an equal human being that has left me with a lasting meaningful connection. In other words, regardless of celebrity, a human connection must exist and is the road to presence.

Unfortunately, most of us are unable to have intimate time with celebrities. At the same time, there is much new evidence that celebrities struggle as everyone else, often worse. The 2007 book of Mother Teresa's personal letters called *Mother Teresa: Come Be Light* clearly showed that she suffered extreme personal doubt and anguish. "Darkness would become the greatest trial of her life" (Kolodiejchuk, 2007, p. 3). Many of us refer to the Dalai Lama as an example of a powerful presence who has little need of external relational support. However, a close study of the Dalai Lama's living conditions clearly reveal that he has a strong and close network of social supports whom he lives with, travels with, and who care for him daily. Here the topic of celebrity is another area that could warrant greater investigation in relation to accessing presence.

Presence and directivity versus non-directivity

As I have previously stated, the issue of the therapist directing the sessions as opposed to attempting to engage the client with a nondirective approach has become a hallmark of the Rogerian PCA. The so-called classical PCA is said to hold non-directivity as a sacred standard when the therapist works with disciplined diligence to "not" direct the client in any conceivable way. While for many the idea of non-directivity might seem cold and unengaged, for the classical PCA practitioner, non-directivity is a sacred ideal that must be held to at all cost. Let's consider statements made by the well-regarded Existential-Humanistic Psychologist James Bugental. Bugental is of the generation who first studied psychotherapy through the early teachings of Rogers. And while Bugental clearly shows a deep respect for Rogers, he openly discusses the pitfalls and contradictions he experienced with Rogers and his followers.

Regarding non-directivity, Bugental states "Rogers' first espousal of the non-directive approach in therapy was quite polemic, suggesting that other therapists were directive, i.e., dictatorial" (Bugental, 1987, p. 90). Here Bugental is pointing out the subtle fact that to label an approach nondirective you are automatically vilifying other approaches and thereby creating an "us versus them" environment. At the same time, Bugental "noted also that even the most loyal patient-centered therapists were adding other dimensions to their work" (Bugental, 1987, p. 90). Here Bugental is stating that he experienced most person-centered practitioners to add other, possibly directive aspects to their stated nondirective approach. At the same time, Bugental states that "to his credit, Rogers himself continually outgrows his earlier formulations" (Bugental, 1987, p. 90). Here Bugental is stating that Rogers himself was open to learning and incorporating new knowledge into his approach; he was adaptive and not dogmatic.

Bugental makes it clear that he moved away from the goal of non-directivity and he did so because he began to believe in a more unified understanding of psychotherapeutic theory.

> Those who over many years practice intensive or depth therapy often come to be more similar to each other in their ways of conducting therapy (if not in their theories about therapy) than to those who share clan names and academic histories.
> *(Bugental, 1987, p. x)*

Whether you agree with Bugental or not, his points need to be debated. The PCA is not binary. It is time that we move away from any dogmatism regarding the directive versus nondirective debate within the PCA. Instead, we need to see this debate as an ongoing egalitarian debate, one that will never end because it is this questioning that balances us and helps bring us to the present.

For too long this debate has stifled the evolution of person-centered theory, especially here in the United States. Instead of debating the merits of theory and practice, a judgmental litmus test has emerged around the issue of directivity versus non-directivity, to test whether an individual is person-centered or not. This dogmatic labeling is destructive in that its judgments prevent honoring the subtleties of research and experimentation within our practice. These dogmatic labels have created a war of derision. In this war practitioners must choose sides and work to ensure they are not seen as outside of the range of their chosen group. Many schools of psychological thought have struggled with this debate in their own ways and using their own language. None are better for it.

Rogers' unrecognized path to presence

Many person-centered authors have commented on the topic of presence (Brodley, 2000; Cooper, 2005; Geller, 2009; Geller, 2013; Geller & Greenberg, 2002; Geller

& Greenberg, 2012; Mearns, 1994; Mearns & Cooper, 2005; Sanders, 2004; Sanders, 2006; Schmid, 2002; Thorne, 1992; Wyatt, 2000). Additionally, many of Rogers' statements on presence have been identified (Rogers, 1957; 1980; 1986) and yet Rogers' statements do not offer a clear definition nor does he directly clarify how one accesses presence. In other words, we do not have Rogers' direct quotes to guide our understanding of presence. However, Rogers' wonderful (unfortunately out of print) book, *Carl Rogers on Encounter Groups*, first published in 1970, offers us an interesting examination of the process of the encounter group and of a model that can be understood as outlining the steps necessary to access presence outside of the encounter group. In other words, Rogers' encounter group process patterns present a model that can inform anyone who is studying their subjective perception and moving towards presence.

In his book Rogers' identifies fifteen encounter group process patterns that he states "give a naturalistic, observational picture of some of the common elements of the process which occur in the climate of freedom of an encounter group" (Rogers, 1970, p. 42). These patterns include: 1. milling around, 2. resistance to personal expression or exploration, 3. description of past feelings, 4. expression of negative feelings, 5. expression and exploration of personally meaningful material, 6. the expression of immediate interpersonal feelings in the group, 7. the development of a healing capacity in the group, 8. self-acceptance and the beginning of change, 9. the cracking of facades, 10. the individual receives feedback, 11. confrontation, 12. the healing relationship outside the group sessions, 13. the basic encounter, 14. the expression of positive feelings and closeness, 15. behavior changes in the group.

Looking closely at these process patterns: number four, the expression of negative feelings, stands out as an important step in accessing presence that is often forgotten in the PCA. Rogers states: "curiously enough, the first expression of genuinely significant 'here and now' feeling is apt to come out in negative attitudes toward other group members" (Rogers, 1970, p. 18).

Rogers believed the expression of negative feelings is important to individuals because "this is one of the best ways to test freedom and trustworthiness in a group" (Rogers, 1970, p. 19). Rogers understood the motivation of the individual to access negativity because "deeply positive feelings are much more difficult and dangerous to express than negative ones" (Rogers, 1970, p. 19). Furthermore, Rogers recognized the importance of the expression of negative feelings in helping individuals become present. "Negatively toned feelings tend to be the first here and now material to appear" (Rogers, 1970, p. 19). Because Rogers' book is currently out of print, the process patterns identified in *Carl Rogers on Encounter Groups* have not been widely regarded. Geller and Greenberg (2012) make little reference to the usefulness of working with negative feelings. At one point they allude to the need for therapists to recognize painful experiences in their lives: "To be able to deeply connect yet discern separation from another's painful experience, one must first develop this discernment within by attending to one's inner state and one's own painful experiences with compassion and inner peacefulness" (p. 113). Yet there is no mention of what this "attending to" actually involves.

Considered in light of the current state of the PCA, particularly in the United States, these process patterns need to be reconsidered. When considering them outside of the encounter group, as a whole, these process patterns align with most psychotherapeutic processes where each phase can last for months and sometimes years. Additionally, these process patterns align with every individual's subjective process of acceptance and engagement of conflict and possible growth. Over the years, the encounter group experience has become a valuable, if not crucial practice, within the PCA. It is through my experience of encounter groups that my understanding of this approach has been fostered and deepened. You cannot fully understand the PCA unless you have taken part in a leaderless and prolonged encounter group. Certainly, at their best, presence is "abounding" in encounter groups. Therefore, it makes logical sense that within these process patterns, discovered within encounter groups, Rogers has laid out his experience of how people engage, change, grow, and become present within themselves and towards others. Recognizing the value of the expression of negative feelings, as well as other processes, can motivate us to become more accepting of what is necessary to become present. And when we access presence there are no true labels or unacceptable boundaries.

Presence can save our approach

The PCA has evolved to include a more active acceptance of the role of presence in theory and practice. This new acceptance can help us move away from the directive versus nondirective debate, and can help revive the approach in the United States through a better understanding of experiential approaches and the concurrent connection to active presence. One of the greatest US-based person-centered practitioners was a Harvard professor, John Shlien. His paper on a "Counter-theory of transference" (Shlien, 1984) is my favorite person-centered paper ever written. In a collection of his writings titled *To Lead an Honorable Life: Invitations to think about Client-centered Therapy and the Person-centred Approach: A collection of the work of John Shlien* (Sanders, 2003), Shlien attempts to describe how change occurs from a person-centered perspective. For Shlien, "when love is present, it is an environment for or the consequence of understanding. Though the two are strongly associated, love does not heal. Understanding heals" (ibid., p. 117). Furthermore: "to realize that it is understanding that promotes the healing will direct us to the remaining problem for psychotherapy and psychology: we do not know the mechanism by which understanding promotes healing or even the mechanism of understanding itself" (ibid., p. 118).

I highly respect Shlien's work, but it is time to acknowledge that we do understand the mechanism by which understanding promotes healing, and it is active presence. The quality of responsiveness originating from presence is at the heart of what makes presence healing (Geller & Greenberg, 2012).

My hero John Shlien, like many of us, has been caught up in the fear that what we love within the PCA will be taken away or corrupted.

> Some who use techniques abhorrent to client-centered therapist justify intrusive or domineering ways as being for the ultimate good of the client. Interestingly, some who hold client-centered philosophy in contempt borrow its techniques (such as reflection, tentative understandings) to open up the client in early sessions for deeper probes later.
>
> *(Shlien in Sanders, 2003, p. 210)*

Yet, do we really have the right to judge another's technique or approach? From a place of presence does technique or approach even matter? Many of us feel we cannot access presence; we are intimidated by it. Many of us do not know what to do with unwanted feelings. Do we pretend that feelings or relationships do not exist? Hasn't psychotherapy blindly followed a male, white, heteronormative ideology for too long? Isn't the fear of money or capital really at the core of all judgment of others?

The work of the English psychologist David Smail needs to be more widely known. "To de-centre the self, to suggest that it is an idealist invention that has no autonomous power not only demands that we revise vast areas of received philosophical and psychological opinion, but undermines the very basis of consumer capitalism" (Smail, 2005, p. 106).

And in the end, isn't presence all we have? Bugental (1987) wrote: "Looking back now, it is surprising how long I overlooked the fundamental importance of presence to therapeutic work. It is even more surprising to me how many therapists and therapeutic systems also overlook it" (p. 46).

As has been stated, the PCA has been declining in the United States since the death of Carl Rogers. Related approaches such as Gendlin's (1978) Focusing, Miller and Rollnick's (1991) Motivational Interviewing, Rosenberg's (1998) Non-Violent Communication, and Greenberg and Johnson's (1988) Emotionally Focused Therapy, are growing within the US. There has never been a clear road to connecting these approaches with the person-centered communities in the US. Instead, US based person-centered communities widely consider these approaches as practicing far from the intent of Rogers. Outside of the US, the PCA has grown significantly since Rogers' death where these related approaches are referred to as "Experiential" tribes of the person-centered world.

The World Association for Person-centered and Experiential Psychotherapy and Counseling (WAPCEPC) recognizes these approaches as fundamental partners in any full recognition of the PCA. Following the 2016 WAPCEPC world conference in New York, significant representatives of these experiential approaches were visible side by side and their larger connection was evident. However, as there has been disconnection for some time, is there now an opportunity to unify these connected approaches? And is an evolved understanding of Rogers' fourth core condition for therapeutic change, presence, the missing link in accepting diversity and moving the PCA into the 21st century? We have not compared and contrasted the PCA with all the experiential approaches. That is for another time. But ask yourself this question, when you are present, does the label you follow matter? Does it matter what you call yourself, as long as you are present? I do not care if you are person-centered as long as you are present. When we are present we are always nondirective. Not because being nondirective is right, but because it matches flowing in the next moment. This is presence.

References

Anderson, R. & Cissna, K. (1997). *The Martin Buber Carl Rogers dialogue: A new transcript with commentary*. Albany, New York: State University of New York Press.

Brodley, B. (2000). Personal presence in client-centered therapy. *The Person-centred Journal*, 7(2), 139–149.

Buber, M. (1958). *I and thou*. New York: Touchstone.

Bugental, J. F. T. (1987). *The art of the psychotherapist*. New York, NY: Norton.

Cooper, M. (2005) Therapists' experiences of relational depth: A qualitative interview study. *Counseling & Psychotherapy Research*, 5(2), 87–95.

Geller, S. M. (2009). Cultivation of therapeutic presence: Therapeutic drumming and mindfulness practices. *Dutch Tijdschrift Clientgerichte Psychotherapie (Journal for Client-Centered Psychotherapy)*, 47, 273–287.

Geller, S. M. (2013). Therapeutic presence as a foundation for relational depth. In Knox, R., Murphy, D., Wiggins, S., & Cooper, M. (Eds.), *Relational depth: New perspectives and developments* (pp. 175–184). Basingstoke: Palgrave.

Geller, S. M. & Greenberg, L. S. (2002). Therapeutic presence: Therapists' experience of presence in the psychotherapeutic encounter. *Person-centred and Experiential Psychotherapies*, 1, 71–86.

Geller, S. M. & Greenberg, L. S. (2012). *Therapeutic presence: A mindful approach to effective therapy*. Washington, DC: American Psychological Association.

Gendlin, E. T. (1978). *Focusing*. New York, NY: Everest House.

Greenberg, L. S., & Johnson, S. M. (1988). *Emotionally focused therapy for couples*. New York, NY: The Guilford Press.

Keltner, D. (2009). *Born to be good*. New York, NY: Norton.

Kirsner, D. (2009). *Unfree associations: Inside psychoanalytic institutes*. Updated Edition. Lanham, MD: Rowman and Littlefield.

Kolodiejchuk, B. (2007). *Mother Teresa: Come be my light*. New York, NY: Doubleday.

Mearns, D. (1994). *Developing person-centred counseling*. London: Sage.

Mears, D. & Cooper, M. (2005). *Working at relational depth in counseling and psychotherapy*. London: Sage.

Miller, W. R. & Rollnick, S. (1991). *Motivational interviewing: Helping people change*. New York, NY: The Guilford Press.

Rogers, C. R. (1957). The necessary and sufficient conditions of therapeutic personality change. *Journal of Consulting Psychology*, 21, 97–103.

Rogers, C. R. (1970). *Carl Rogers on encounter groups*. New York, NY: Harper and Row.

Rogers, C. R. (1980). *A way of being*. Boston: Houghton Mifflin.

Rogers, C. R. (1986). Client-centered therapy. In Kutash, I. L. & Wolf, A. (Eds.), *Psychotherapist's casebook: Theory and technique in the practice of modern therapies* (pp. 197–208). San Francisco, CA: Jossey-Bass.

Rosenberg, M. B. (1998). *Nonviolent communication: A language of life*. Encinitas, CA: PuddleDancer Press.

Sanders, P. (Ed.) (2003). *To lead an honorable life: Invitations to think about client-centred therapy and the person-centred approach: A collection of the work of John M. Shlien.* Ross-on-Wye: PCCS Books.

Sanders, P. (2004). *The tribes of the person-centred nation: An introduction to the schools of therapy related to the person-centred approach.* Ross-on-Wye: PCCS Books.

Sanders, P. (2006). *The person-centred counseling primer.* Ross-on-Wye: PCCS Books.

Schmid, P. F. (2002) Presence-Im-media-te co-experiencing and co-responding. Phenomenological, dialogical and ethical perspectives on contact and perception in person-centred therapy and beyond. In Wyatt, G. & Sanders, P. (Eds.), *Contact perception* (pp. 182–203). Ross-on-Wye: PCCS Books.

Senge, P., Scharmer, C. O., Jawoeski, J., & Flowers, B. S. (2004). *Presence: human purpose and the field of the future.* New York: Crown Business.

Shlien, J. (1984). *A counter-theory of transference.* http://www.adpca.org/publicfiles/library/A%20Counter Theory%20of%20Transference_John%20M.%20Shlien_1.pdf, retrieved 2 March 2018.

Smail, D. (2005). *Power interest and psychology: Elements of social materialist understanding of distress.* Ross-on-Wye: PCCS Books.

Thorne, B. (1992). *Carl Rogers.* London: Sage.

Wyatt, G. (2000). Presence: Bringing together the core conditions. Paper presented at ICCCEP Conference, Chicago.

23

A PLACE IN WHICH EVERYTHING CAN GO

Darran Biles

Introduction

> His whole life has been torn between his desire to reveal himself and his desire to conceal himself. We all share this problem with him and we have all arrived at a more or less satisfactory solution. We have our secrets and our needs to confess.
>
> *(Laing, 1990, p. 37)*

> I have always wanted to write about everything. That does not mean to write a book that covers everything – which would be impossible, but a book in which everything can go.
>
> *(Merton, 2006, p. 7)*

In this chapter I shall speak about my hopes for person-centred therapy as a radically hospitable "place in which everything can go". When I first came to the person-centred world, I was desperate for more honest, more fearless, more vital – yet also somehow kinder, more compassionate – ways of communicating that opened up instead of closing down. For years I had felt anguished and oppressed by all that got left out of "normal" conversation regarding both the inner and the outer world (discussion of the problematic nature of such binaries as inner-outer being one example). The first time I remember hearing of Carl Rogers was while learning about Marshall B. Rosenberg's (2003) process of "Nonviolent Communication", which seemed to hold real promise for empowering awareness, understanding and self-expression. In a sense, this chapter will be all about communication – about my quest for free and open speech. But I would like to make explicit that my concern with communication has always been bound up with other concerns.

When I started training, I desired vastly different possibilities for living and relating, and saw person-centred spaces as potential incubators, radically allowing places where such different possibilities might be cultured. I was interested not in therapy per se but in supporting life – not in patching people up but in helping them to flourish, not in individuals alone but in groups, community, the wider web of beings. I hoped that therapists would be active critics, questioning existing structures and conventions. Personally, I felt impelled to challenge marriage and monogamy, money and property, our use of animals for food, and ecological destruction. In person-centred working, which extended well beyond the bounds of individual psychotherapy and implicated a practitioner's total way of being in the world, I thought that I had found a vehicle for engaging with such issues. Free communication was integral to these concerns; so while in this chapter I shall ostensibly be speaking of communication, my investment in these other matters won't be far away.

Congruence and saying everything

> We young people have ... very little appreciation of you. You are too solemn for us, Excellency, too vain and pompous, and not outright enough. That is, no doubt, at the bottom of it – not outright enough.
>
> *(Hesse, 2001, p. 112)*

The most compelling thing about the person-centred approach when I discovered it was the essential element of congruence. I was most excited by the communicative aspect of this quality: congruence entailed, approximately, being "honest, genuine, authentic, real, natural, spontaneous, open, whole, transparent" (Mearns & Thorne, 2007, pp. 119–123). The idea of congruent communication evoked for me the artist's dream of total self-expression and Dostoevskian scenario of purgative confessions in the marketplace, the terrific possibility of "saying everything" – being fully seen, fully known.

I soon learned that while different person-centred writers had different ideas about what congruence meant, they seemed unanimous that it did not mean saying everything. "[Rogers'] interpersonal theory is designed to foster better understanding, improved adjustment and mutual satisfaction among people", advises Barbara Temaner Brodley (2001, p. 65).

> How is it possible that in this context Rogers could be advocating the behaviour of saying what one thinks and feels in a given moment? Such behaviour often includes judgments, criticisms, insults, accusations, interpretations of other people etc. All of these behaviours are generally recognised as destructive. They are usually destructive to communication, to personal well-being and to satisfaction between people. Could Rogers be naïve? No, he most likely means something else by congruent communication.
>
> *(ibid.)*

Talking specifically of congruent communication in therapy, Mearns and Thorne (2007, p. 139) are similarly dismissive: "plainly not all the counsellor's sensations are appropriate to the counselling contract. The counsellor cannot simply express whatever she is feeling in the moment".

The majority of my colleagues too appeared to take this as a given. For my part, I was ready to allow that saying everything we think and feel (in the therapist role or otherwise, and in therapy or elsewhere) might not be desirable or even possible – yet I felt disappointed. When I had first heard of congruence, I thought it could have great potential for transforming how we talk, calling into question what is "generally recognised" or "appropriate" and broaching domains of experience which might usually go unacknowledged. Yet in the literature and among practitioners, I found little active questioning of communicative norms, and little curiosity in opening the discourse to other possibilities.

What do I mean by "domains of experience which might usually go unacknowledged" and "opening the discourse to other possibilities" (a phrase I take from Updike 1990, p. 144)? Well, consider this perception from Nicholas Spice (2004, p. 11):

> One of the many scandalous realities we choose to ignore because we cannot assimilate it is the fact of unexpressed thought. Consider it. Next time you are sitting at dinner with friends or people you don't yet know, stop for a moment and listen out for the inaudible murmur of concealed thoughts: the things going through your head that you are not speaking, the things going through the heads of the others. On the bus, in a Tube carriage filled with silent strangers, at the breakfast table with your loved ones, in the office or the pub: remember how the secret thoughts are swarming, seething; chattering like millions of bats in an underground cave, rustling beneath the surface of the day like cockroaches.

Despite their claims to congruence, it seemed to me this "scandalous reality" of unexpressed thought (or rather unexpressed *experience*, for I see it as including feelings, sensations, intuitions etc.) was as much ignored in person-centred contexts as anywhere else. I found little affirmation in the literature, my training or my colleagues of the swarming, seething subterrain evoked by Spice. But here the non-acknowledgment felt more problematic than in everyday environments because of all the emphasis on being real, open, whole, transparent. This last word was the one I really snagged on. For me, "transparency" implied a see-through window on one's inner world: if not that everything be actively displayed, then at least that it be available for viewing and not actively concealed. If these writers and practitioners were so transparent, where were all the bats?

Radical self-disclosure

A neglected need

The above and other questions were alive for me as I devised my MA study of 2012–13, "Saying Everything: Exploring Possibilities for Radical Self-Disclosure". My interest in the subject had a history. In my teens and twenties I had struggled greatly with the matter of how far I could go in speaking out my secret thoughts, suffering and causing others to suffer considerable pain as seemingly I went too far. When I started person-centred training in my thirties, the promise of environments that aimed to liberate expression, facilitating fuller, deeper interchange that could welcome "unacceptable" thoughts and feelings, was a central motivation.

This wasn't an outlandish hope but was right there at the heart of therapy as Rogers understood it. In one of his last books, after more than forty years of practice, Rogers (1978, p. 231) summed up the essence of many people's difficulties in a single, simple sentence: "The commonest theme in therapy is this: 'If you really knew me, my horrible thoughts and feelings, you couldn't accept me, and would confirm my fear that I am insane and/or hopeless.'"

The way of helping he developed was founded on a recognition that what goes on in us is trustworthy, and that spaces where we may be known and valued in our fullness, with all our "horrible thoughts and feelings", are healing spaces. The longing to be fully seen and still accepted – captured for me by a friend who said, "I want to stand before people in all my ugliness and for that to be OK" – would seem to be a fundamental human one and central to the therapeutic project.

How then, I was asking at the outset of my study, could the inheritors of Rogers' legacy lose sight of it? By leaving so much unacknowledged, by not supporting comprehensive revelation and expression, the person-centred contexts I had known appeared to disregard the core concern of therapy.

What were we not saying?

In the phrase "radical self-disclosure", the word "radical" was intended to mean *complete* or *thoroughgoing*, and to distinguish the kind of self-disclosure in which I was interested from self-disclosure which seemed partial and selective – such as most of the self-disclosure I had seen or read of being practised in person-centred contexts. I meant it to suggest some kind of consummate transparency about one's unfiltered inner experience.

My most ready model of radical self-disclosure was supplied by Freud and his technique of free-association. Freud (1909, p. 40) asked clients to say everything that came into their heads without excluding or selecting, even if it were unpleasant to them or seemed unimportant, irrelevant or senseless. This included thoughts, feelings, fantasies etc. about the therapist. The material this method brought to light helped me to get more specific about some aspects of experience which purportedly transparent person-centred spaces left in the dark.

First, there was *"extreme" or "unacceptable" material*, such as violent and/or sexual thoughts and fantasies. In Freud's (1909, pp. 47–48) famous case study, the "Rat Man" is so named because he is tormented by the thought of rats burrowing their way into a beloved woman's anus. It was almost inconceivable that I would ever find such stuff discussed in any person-centred literature or group! In these contexts there was also little overt traffic in more routine "nasty" feelings such as cruelty, contempt, lasciviousness, derision, repulsion, vanity and cowardice.

Second, there was *irrelevant-seeming material*, which according to Christopher Bollas (2002) was valued by Freud above all else. In contrast, Mearns and Thorne (2007, p. 140), again talking specifically of therapist-to-client communication, make relevance a guideline for what the therapist expresses and remark that she "would not do anything about a mild feeling of irritation that drifted in and then out of her awareness, or a brief flash of annoyance in relation to one particular thing that the client said" – thus discounting whole areas of experience which might be fruitful to explore. I was interested in openness not only about "extreme" material but also about "mundane" material which seemed to form a constant but unspoken part of inner life.

Third, there was *contrary and tricky material* or modes of being, again exemplified in Freud's Rat Man case and powerfully evoked for me by such relentlessly self-outflanking authors as Dostoevsky and Nietzsche. Our thoughts and feelings often are not reasonable, consistent, easily delineated, but ambiguous, eruptive, contradictory. "I find it somehow unseemly to love only well-being," says Dostoevsky's (1972, p. 41) Underground Man.

> Whether it's a good thing or a bad thing, smashing things is also sometimes very pleasant. I am not here standing up for suffering, or for well-being either. I am standing out for my own caprices and for having them guaranteed when necessary
>
> *(ibid.)*

Opening to the compulsively wayward complicates another Mearns and Thorne (2007, p. 142) guideline for appropriate therapist communication, i.e. that the therapist communicates only what is "relatively *persistent* or *striking*", for we see that parts of our experience may become persistent or striking precisely because they are "inappropriate" – just as the imperative to transparency may give rise to impulses and imaginings about which it might seem we couldn't possibly be transparent. Such sinuous and slippy subjectivity was not well represented in the person-centred world, leading me to wonder if I needed to be more straightforward in my experience and my expression to be welcome there.

Fourth, there was *material about the person to whom one was disclosing*. For me, genuinely radical self-disclosure needed to be able to include this, as a key distinguishing feature from our usual habits of disclosure. Generally we may have little difficulty disclosing thoughts and feelings about a person to someone else, but to share them with the person we are having them about is oftentimes taboo. The breaking of this taboo in Freudian analysis is supported by its understanding that the feelings clients have about the therapist may be repetitions from their other relationships, and thus not much about the therapist at all. It is "along the painful road of transference", says Freud (1909, p. 89), that the Rat Man begins "heaping the grossest and filthiest abuse upon me and my family" (ibid.) and is thus enabled to admit the fury he had felt towards his father.

Potential person-centred contributions

This list isn't meant to be exhaustive, nor is it meant to set psychoanalysis on some pedestal above person-centred therapy. Rather, I am using the comparison to illuminate some domains of experience and possibilities for expression which do not seem particularly available in person-centred contexts. Yet as Meg-John Barker and Julia Scheele (2016, p. 72) point out, paraphrasing Foucault, "It's always worth asking both what is closed down and what is opened up by any particular discourse". And where radical self-disclosure is concerned, it seems to me that new perspectives might be opened up by person-centred understandings of experience and process.

While Freud and early Rogers tended to conceive experience in terms of fixed, fully formed entities "inside" us that might be moved or represented "outside" in acts of communication (Ellingham, 2001), late Rogers and some more recent person-centred thinkers tend to look on it as fluid, indefinite and modified through being communicated (Gendlin, 2003; Greenberg and Geller, 2001; Rogers, 1961a). This shift is bound up with a broader movement from what might be called a modern-realist worldview, in which the truth is "out there", discoverable and potentially exhaustible, to a more postmodern-constructionist one, in which the truth is (at least partly) created, plural and ultimately ungraspable. The whole idea of "saying everything" is destabilised by this later outlook – for how can we say everything when "everything" will always be elusive? The very word implies a fixedness and exhaustibility which does not reflect the depthless, ever-changing nature of experience.

Radical self-disclosure in a person-centred framework might be seen as more about communicating one's experiential flow than retrieving mental objects from some place out of consciousness or awareness. While Freud might have prized "saying everything" for the interpretations he could make from disclosed material, person-centred practitioners might prize it for the more immediate possibilities for experiential "loosening and flowing" (Rogers, 1961a, p. 135) afforded by disclosing oneself to a receptive other and being accepted in that disclosing. Radical self-disclosure, then, could have direct experiential – as well as indirect interpretive – value. This perspective might place less emphasis on the *content* than on the *process* of disclosure.

Seeing our experience in process terms might also make such free communication easier to practise, and enable some defusing or normalising of material which feels difficult or even dangerous to avow when we hold to a more static view. Looking at experience in terms of relatively stable thoughts and feelings, lying around inside us waiting to be expressed, conceivably supports a certain solidifying and identifying with disclosures, while the alternative view says no disclosure can encapsulate the final truth of me or anybody, but rather each one occupies a place in an immeasurable, ongoing process.

I offer these as just a few ideas about perspectives on, and possibilities for, radical self-disclosure that might be opened up within a person-centred paradigm.

Keeping silence

> Everyone knows that there is much more going on than what enters the public domain, but the smooth functioning of that domain depends on a general non-acknowledgment of what everyone knows.
>
> *(Nagel, 1998, p. 7)*

Why do certain aspects of experience go unacknowledged in the person-centred world, despite its seeming openness? In a stimulating article on the social context of person-centred therapy, Sarah Hawtin and Judy Moore (1998) suggest this happens not *despite* its openness, but *because* of it – or more precisely, because of its particular *kind* of openness. Employing the term "client-centred" instead of "person-centred", the authors start the article as follows:

> The client-centred approach appears to be utterly benign. It does not suggest that our essential natures are anti-social or destructive. Within the therapeutic context, it does not attempt to classify or define the experience of the individual, but to support self-definition and self-understanding.
>
> *(Hawtin & Moore, 1998, p. 91)*

A few sentences on, however, and they admit to possessing "a feeling of discomfort with the apparent neutrality of client-centred theory towards personal experience and a sense that this neutrality could result in a failure to address, or even be aware of, important issues" (ibid., p. 91).

A central theme of the article is that of *discourse*, alluded to above and understood by Hawtin and Moore to mean "communication of thought by speech", and to relate to "language in use as opposed to language as an abstract system". They also understand the term along Foucauldian lines, regarding discourses as "'large groups of statements' within a given area (for example 'medicine', 'the family') that establish rules and conventions about how that area is discussed and by whom" (ibid., p. 91). They elaborate:

> All societies have procedures whereby the production of discourses is controlled to preserve the structures and conventions of that society. The process is reinforced by our everyday use of language so that the assumptions embedded in our consciousness are repeated in our most mundane utterances ... It is with the effect of these embedded assumptions that we are most concerned.
>
> *(ibid., pp. 91–92)*

The authors' main contention is that by failing adequately to appreciate the power of discourse in conveying personal, cultural and social values, the person-centred approach may leave unacknowledged and unchallenged many of the embedded assumptions that determine our perceptions, awareness and symbolisation, thus running the risk of colluding with oppressive structures in the wider culture and itself becoming oppressive. As such person-centred therapy "only presents us with a potentially neutral space, one in which our own cultural beliefs rather than theoretical dogma may lead us into misleading assumptions" (ibid., p. 100). As counsellors, they suggest,

> we are beholden to develop our recognition of the impact of society in the construction of our selves. Lack of recognition leaves us open to *perpetuating the silences that our clients bring*, to limiting the potential both for individual growth and social transformation ... [What is required of the counsellor is] a willingness to give conscious recognition to aspects of experiencing which risk being taken for granted by both client and counsellor: unaware acceptance may lead to *a dropping away of elements of experience within the client* that have begun to arise, for neither the counsellor nor the client may register their full significance.
>
> *(ibid., p. 101, my italics)*

Giving "conscious recognition" means giving attention to the *specifics* of experience; that is, being explicit and precise about the aspects of experience which risk being taken for granted ("embedded assumptions"), as well as other aspects which may in consequence remain less than fully acknowledged. In the group of people whom I interviewed for my study (half a dozen person-centred therapists), more than one said that when it comes to sharing thoughts and feelings that are generally considered unacceptable to voice, a simple invitation to express oneself is insufficient: my colleagues in my training group, or my therapist in therapy, might tell me I'm at liberty to say anything I like – but how can I be sure they are prepared for literally *anything*? A more specific invitation, perhaps involving outright naming of material that is welcome, might be necessary for me to trust that something different from expected conventional communication is permitted.

Precision, explicitness and specificity would appear to be facilitating for expression, and awareness, of experience in general, not just what is "unacceptable". Non-violent Communication trainer Thomas D'Ansembourg (2007, p. 143) tells of teaching in a poorly heated classroom in the middle of winter and, at the end of the morning, asking a student, "How are you? How are you feeling?" When she answers merely "all right", D'Ansembourg proceeds to ask her in succession, "Are you thirsty?", "Are you cold?", "Are you hungry?" – to each of which she replies in the affirmative. D'Ansembourg uses what has happened to make the following pedagogical point:

> You see that if I ask you more precise questions, you observe that you aren't all that well after all. I didn't force you to be hungry, cold, or thirsty. What I did do, though, was to invite you to check if you were in touch with those needs. You might well have answered no to my three questions or have added, "But I do feel tired" if that had been the case. I threw a line to invite you to pay greater attention to yourself rather than answer in some automatic way. That is what empathy proposes – listening to oneself in the right place.

Some might question whether D'Ansembourg is not in some sense "forcing" his interlocutor here, being "directive". But what imputations of directivity may overlook is that we are effectively "directed" before the therapist (or whoever) even opens their mouth; unknowingly directed, for the most part, by "the assumptions embedded in our consciousness" about which parts of our experience we may share – and even be aware of – when communicating with others.

Thomas Nagel (1998, p. 4) speaks of the "conventions of reticence" which operate in the majority of our interactions, such that we "leave a great range of potentially disruptive material unacknowledged and therefore out of play" (ibid., p. 6), concealing "feelings and opinions which we would find unacceptable if they were expressed publicly" (ibid., p. 8). Again, however, such leaving-out-of-play applies not just to what is "unacceptable": as D'Ansembourg's "How are you?" episode shows, our customary ways of talking can tend to cover up experience in general, sometimes by what seems to be an innocently bland attempt to call it forth. Hawtin and Moore (1998, pp. 101–102) make reference to an article in which

> Michele Crouan examines the experience of lesbian women trainees on [counselling] courses which do not actively integrate a lesbian perspective into training. She believes the likelihood is that lesbian issues will be "dealt with in the 'alternative sexualities' slot" and that a lesbian training on such a course will have to "state her sexual orientation to be fully recognised. Repeatedly having to come out means repeatedly risking rejection". This clearly illustrates how passive acceptance allows for the reproduction of social norms.

The point here is that "passive acceptance", the kind of non-classifying openness these authors find in person-centred spaces, can make for non-acceptance of a person in their particularity, since the particulars are not distinguished. It may not be enough for somebody's experience to be acknowledged implicitly or in an abstract way, e.g. by our speaking only of "alternative sexualities" without describing what this might include. Unless we throw a line to somebody's distinct experience, they may not know if it is welcome and accepted, or somehow out of bounds. Going back to Rogers' (1978, p. 231) notion of "the commonest theme in therapy", as a client I do not want to know it is acceptable to have "horrible thoughts and feelings" in general – I want to know it is acceptable to have *my* horrible thoughts and feelings in particular.

If "openness to experience" (Rogers, 1961b, p. 115) is inherent to our way of working, what are we to make of the near-total nonappearance in person-centred therapy (at least the person-centred contexts I have known) of features of subjective life which, even if they aren't as all-pervading as Freud and others may suggest, would seem nonetheless to be a part of our humanity and which most of us at least admit are there? The idea I have been unfolding in this section is that conventions from the wider culture about what is valid and acceptable to say are carried largely uninterrogated into person-centred spaces, are re-inscribed there, and that this situation is upheld by a lack of explicitness and specificity about material that might be welcomed in these spaces. As Hawtin and Moore's article conveys, it is not only saying *nothing*, and not only saying *"no"*, in regard to certain aspects of experience that can perpetuate silences and reproduce oppressive norms; it is also saying *"yes" in an insufficiently precise way* – that is, without specifying what exactly one is saying "yes" to.

Breaking silence

An important characteristic of conventions of reticence is the *double* non-acknowledgment, or twofold speechlessness, they install: first, we do not say many of the thoughts and feelings we experience; and second, we do not say that we do not say them. This second piece of speechlessness is arguably the more problematic, draping as it does a shroud of silence over the whole issue of unexpressed experience, isolating people who might wish to communicate such experience by effectively denying that it even exists.

When I used to raise the matter of saying everything and unexpressed experience with others, including person-centred practitioners, it perplexed me that I seemed to meet with little interest or engagement. It was as though this issue, so urgent and alive for me and (if Rogers' observation on the "commonest theme" were right) central to so many people seeking therapy, were a sort of non-subject, one that other people barely even registered. I often felt the loneliness described by Nietzsche (1974, p. 76) of "the person who questions":

> Everybody looks at you with strange eyes and goes right on handling his scales, calling this good and that evil. Nobody even blushes when you intimate that their weights are underweight; nor do people feel outraged; they merely laugh at your doubts.

Person-centred contexts place a lot of emphasis on being real, open, whole, transparent. And yet quite clearly people in those contexts are not sharing everything they think and feel. When pressed on this apparent inconsistency, practitioners tend to respond along the lines of Brodley, and Mearns and Thorne, above, basically retorting, "Of course we don't say everything we think and feel! Everyone knows you can't do that!" I find this response unsatisfactory, for two reasons.

First, there is a disingenuousness about it which reflects a kind of double bind (Bateson, 1956). On the one hand is an explicit, non-normative encouragement to be openly oneself; on the other is an implicit, normative understanding that we shall not speak completely freely; and sealing in the conflict is the general unavailability of metacommunication about this state of affairs. In my experience, newcomers to the person-centred world feel much confusion about "congruent communication". Beyond the fertile confusion that may be part of grappling with this elusive concept, there is perhaps a more avoidable confusion engendered by the non-acknowledgment in person-centred contexts that we are not sharing everything, that a great deal of experience goes unexpressed, that we are often rather *blind endorsers of society's assumptions*. I suspect that it could spare us some bewilderment to bring into view the fact that everything is not in view. This is only half the task, however – which brings me to the second reason that I find the "everyone knows you can't say everything" response unsatisfactory.

After bringing into view the fact that everything is not in view, we hopefully can move into a space where some of what is not in view can be so; where conventional communication and its entrenched assumptions can be questioned, and alternatives explored. Saying "everyone knows" can shut down other possibilities, as well as other people who do not "know", and suggest the status quo is unassailable. Nagel (who begins the article I've quoted with these very words) has incisive things to say about the benefits of non-expression and the drawbacks of expression, but I'm dismayed by his conservatism. It may be true that "civilization would be impossible" (Nagel, 1998, p. 4) if all our feelings and opinions were in view; but I would like it if this prompted us to question – and to think outside the frame of – "civilization" rather than resignedly perpetuate its silences. I desire wider, deeper, fuller life; and I desire therapy that helps me be alive, not just "civil". Our task then, I'm suggesting, is not only to acknowledge there are limits to our discourse, but to clarify and look beyond those limits.

In the group of people whom I interviewed, it appeared to me that two broad hopes and fears about radical self-disclosure were held in common. First, people wanted something like radical self-disclosure for themselves, and experienced relief when they imagined being able to do it; but they didn't feel it currently occurred in person-centred contexts or the wider culture. Second, people were apprehensive about what radical self-disclosure might entail, and disinclined to consider it could be possible or desirable beyond a few specialised environments. At the end I was left asking whether some need in us to maintain the status quo means we will not open our minds to the profound personal and social changes that might be necessary in a world where parts of ourselves we customarily keep hidden could be out in the open.

One aim of the study had been to find out what might be facilitating factors for radical self-disclosure – for saying *more*, if not saying everything. Already I have spoken of precision, explicitness and specificity about what may be expressed. There isn't space to comment on them here, but for readers who are interested I shall list some further helpful factors that stood out from the interviews (more detailed consideration of the dynamics of self-disclosure may be found in Jourard, 1971):

- Seeing other people self-disclose, or seeing them attempt to do so
- Permission from the other(s) to disclose
- An agreement or a 'contract' between people to be self-disclosing
- Trusting that the invitation to express oneself is made in good faith
- Other people showing enthusiasm for such expression
- Other people not reacting with hostility to expression

- Some kind of immunity from the wider social context and its laws of interaction
- Collective recognition when disclosing that people can be hurt – shared responsibility and maturity of commitment in a group
- Trusting everybody in a group is committed to the growth experience
- Recognition of, and openness to, the symbolic dimension of relationship – possibility of occupying an imaginative territory
- Creativity and playfulness in communication.

Free communicating, free conceiving

In the last few sections of the chapter, I have been connecting the apparent silences in person-centred contexts with ideas about discourse and conventions of reticence. I have spoken of silences about certain sorts of material or domains of experience; of quite glaring silences around material with which most of us will be familiar, but against which there are strong taboos; and of more subtle yet pervasive silences that are maintained not so much in virtue of distinct proscriptions, but of our use of language, which repeats and reinforces various assumptions, preventing us not simply from expressing parts of our experience but even from becoming conscious of them.

I have spoken too of silences about the silences: the way we mostly don't acknowledge all these non-acknowledgments, don't acknowledge our compliance with convention, don't acknowledge we are caught up in the sweep of larger trends and systems. This connects to comments I have made elsewhere about the need to keep our thinking open to the outside (Biles, 2016). When in this chapter I speak of "opening the discourse to other possibilities", I am interested in both opening the discourse *in* person-centred therapy (i.e. expanding the range of what and how we may communicate when in its spaces, such as training groups and individual counselling) and opening the discourse *of* person-centred therapy (i.e. expanding the range of ideas, practices and possibilities that are in play when we imagine and conceive our work).

Like the different kinds of silences, these different kinds of openings are intimately linked. The way that we conceive of therapy affects the way that we communicate in therapy, as well as what we recognise as valid and acceptable communication from clients. And the way that we communicate in therapy affects the way that we conceive of it. Open imagining and conceiving, open awareness and open communication are seemingly inseparable. In one place Rogers (1961c, p. 330) frames awareness, and the whole activity of therapy, in terms of good communication:

> The task of psychotherapy is to help the person achieve, through a special relationship with a therapist, good communication within himself [sic]. Once this is achieved he can communicate more freely and more effectively with others. We may say then that psychotherapy is good communication, within

and between men [sic]. We may also turn that statement around and it will still be true. Good communication, free communication, within or between men, is always therapeutic.

For Rogers, interpersonal loosening and flowing, freedom of communication with (an)other(s), both begets and is begotten by intrapersonal loosening and flowing, freedom of communication with oneself. Indeed, in situations that are therapeutic, the very boundary between interpersonal and intrapersonal, between communication and awareness, imagining, conceiving becomes porous, as both these realms are permeated by a single unitary process of "free communication". Expanding what and how we may communicate (what I've called opening the discourse *in* therapy) and expanding ideas, practices and possibilities (opening the discourse *of* therapy) are fundamentally the same endeavour.

It is tempting at this point to shift my focus from the former to the latter and describe some different practices and possibilities that are in play in my current life and work, impacting on the way that I communicate – but that would be another chapter.

Conclusion

When I started training, the dearest hope I had of therapy – both for others and myself – was that of being fully seen and known. At the time, I more or less equated this with saying everything; and with the value that it placed on congruence, I thought that person-centred therapy might answer to this longing. I quickly realised that the openness I found in person-centred contexts was not at all the openness I sought.

As my thinking and my practice have developed, I have become less fixed on saying everything as the way for people to be known. Nonetheless, the places which invite some form of comprehensive revelation, such as spiritual confession and psychoanalytic free association, still feel exciting to me. The possibility of radical self-disclosure answers to that basic longing to be known and unconditionally accepted. Engaging in communication of this kind potentially expands our sense of what is sayable and unfolds domains of experience which conventionally remain concealed. I don't think it should be dismissed. Yet I have come to think of openness or being known as something more than verbal self-disclosure.

In the time since starting training, I have become clearer on the difficulties involved in saying everything: not just the ethical considerations that are often raised, but also philosophical considerations, which unsettle our ideas of what disclosure even means. I have also pursued other ways of working where communication of experience by speech is not so prominent – not because it's unimportant, but because the context is more spacious. There is so much more to life than speech, and communication is more complex. At the same time, speech and words are hugely influential in our lives, shaping our perceptions and inscribing social norms. When we do not recognise their power, the silences we can perpetuate affect not just verbal expression, but expression and experience of every kind.

So what do I think openness consists of now? What would a genuinely open therapy look like? Perhaps it would involve some integration of the other ways of working I've just mentioned. But I suggest a first step towards greater openness would be simply *to admit we are not fully open* – rather than relentlessly to talk the talk of openness, yet obviously fail to walk the walk. Maintaining that there are no limits to our discourse prevents us from examining those limits and exploring what might help expand it. The double silencing that happens in the wider culture as our customary ways of talking both cover up experience and cover up the cover up, prohibiting acknowledgment that any cover up is taking place, is reproduced within the very place that promises an end to silence.

Unless we recognise explicitly that realms of unexpressed experience exist, and that we may collude in their suppression, the whole endeavour to be welcoming of people in their wholeness is negated from the start. If person-centred therapy sincerely wishes not to reinforce the silences its clients bring, it needs to recognise the silences within itself.

I began this chapter with a quote from Thomas Merton, talking of the book he always wished to write – not a book that covered everything, but a book in which everything could go. These words evoke the kind of openness that I think I am ultimately seeking, the kind of space that people come to therapy to find: a space where nothing of us is excluded, where no part of our lives comes knocking at the door and finds it barred. This may not be a place in which everything is said; but perhaps it is a place in which everything can go.

Acknowledgments

Thanks to Adam Biles, Charlotte Carter, Clare Raido and Susanne Wardle, who read earlier versions of this chapter. Special thanks to Adeline Darling, who discussed it with me indefatigably.

References

Barker, M.-J. and Scheele, J. (2016) *Queer: A Graphic History*. London: Icon Books.
Bateson, G. (1956) Toward a Theory of Schizophrenia, in G. Bateson (1972), *Steps to an Ecology of Mind*, New York: Ballantine, pp. 201–227.
Biles, D. (2016) Reapproaching Rogers: Looking to the Source to Show Us where We Are Going Wrong, *Person-Centered & Experiential Psychotherapies*, 15(4), pp. 318–338.
Bollas, C. (2002) *Free Association*. Cambridge: Icon Books.
Brodley, B. (2001) Congruence and its Relation to Communication in Client-Centered Therapy, in G. Wyatt (ed.), *Rogers' Therapeutic Conditions: Evolution, Theory and Practice, Volume 1: Congruence*, Ross-on-Wye: PCCS Books, pp. 55–78.
D'Ansembourg, T. (2007) *Being Genuine*. Encinitas: PuddleDancer Press.
Dostoevsky, F. (1972) *Notes from Underground*. London: Penguin.
Ellingham, I. (2001) Carl Rogers' "Congruence" as an Organismic, Not a Freudian, Concept, in G. Wyatt (ed.) (2001), *Rogers' Therapeutic Conditions: Evolution, Theory and Practice, Volume 1: Congruence*, Ross-on-Wye: PCCS Books, pp. 96–115.

Freud, S. (1909) Notes upon a Case of Obsessional Neurosis (The "Rat Man"), in A. Richards (ed.) (1979), *Case Histories II*, London: Penguin, pp. 225–366.
Gendlin, E. (2003) *Focusing*. London: Rider.
Greenberg, L. S. and Geller, S. M. (2001) Congruence and Therapeutic Presence, in G. Wyatt (ed.), *Rogers' Therapeutic Conditions: Evolution, Theory and Practice, Volume 1: Congruence*, Ross-on-Wye: PCCS Books, pp. 131–149.
Hawtin, S. and Moore, J. (1998) Empowerment or Collusion: The Social Context of Person-Centred Therapy, in B. Thorne and E. Lambers (eds), *Person-Centred Therapy: A European Perspective*, London: Sage, pp. 91–105.
Hesse, H. (2001) *Steppenwolf*. London: Penguin.
Jourard, S. M. (1971) *The Transparent Self*. New York: Van Nostrand Reinhold.
Laing, R. D. (1990) *The Divided Self*. London: Penguin.
Mearns, D. and Thorne, B. (2007) *Person-Centred Counselling in Action*. London: Sage.
Merton, T. (2006) *The Intimate Merton*. Oxford: Lion.
Nagel, T. (1998) Concealment and Exposure, *Philosophy & Public Affairs*, 27(1), pp. 3–30, available at http://www.nyu.edu/gsas/dept/philo/faculty/nagel/papers/exposure.html (accessed 15 June 2017).
Nietzsche, F. (1974) *The Gay Science*. New York: Vintage.
Rogers, C. R. (1961a) A Process Conception of Psychotherapy, in *On Becoming a Person*, London: Constable, pp. 125–159.
Rogers, C. R. (1961b), What It Means to Become a Person, in *On Becoming a Person*, London: Constable, pp. 107–124.
Rogers, C. R. (1961c) Dealing with Breakdowns in Communication – Interpersonal and Intergroup, in *On Becoming a Person*, London: Constable, pp. 329–337.
Rogers, C. R. (1978) *On Personal Power*. London: Constable.
Rosenberg, M. B. (2003) *Nonviolent Communication*. Encinitas: PuddleDancer Press.
Spice, N. (2004) I Must be Mad, *London Review of Books*, 26(1), pp. 11–15, available at https://www.lrb.co.uk/v26/n01/nicholas-spice/i-must-be-mad (accessed 14 June 2017).
Updike, J. (1990) *Self-Consciousness*. London: Penguin.

24
A PERSON-CENTRED POLITICAL CRITIQUE OF CURRENT DISCOURSES IN POST-TRAUMATIC STRESS DISORDER AND POST-TRAUMATIC GROWTH

Deborah A. Lee

Introduction

The American Psychiatric Association (APA) *Diagnostic and Statistical Manual of Mental Disorders* (DSM-5) (APA, 2013) currently understands what it calls "post-traumatic stress disorder" (PTSD), a diagnosis which first appeared in DSM-III to involve:

> exposure to actual or threatened death, serious injury, or sexual violence ... [the] presence of one or more ... intrusion symptoms ... persistent avoidance of stimuli associated with the traumatic event(s) ... negative alterations in cognitions and mood associated with the traumatic event(s) ... marked alterations in arousal and reactivity associated with the traumatic event(s) ... [for] more than one month ... [causing] clinically significant distress or impairment in social, occupational or other important areas of functioning.
> *(pp. 271–272)*

The concept of post-traumatic growth (PTG), which first emerged in the mid-1990s, encompasses many manifestations of post-traumatic "positive change" (Joseph, 2015, p. 180).

This chapter offers a person-centred political critique of some directions identified in the current PTSD and PTG research discourses – research discourses which will increasingly effect practitioner and public understandings of PTSD and PTG and which are, therefore, highly political.

Person-centred approaches (PCAs) seem not to always have an entirely clear position in relation to politics. Carl Rogers (see, for instance, Rogers, 1978) wrote politically, and yet, as Proctor (2006, p. 1) says, PCAs have been accused of being "individualistic". I speak as an academic/activist sociologist and person-centred psychotherapist-in-training, recognising both unique individuals and their location in the social structures of society, such as power dynamics present in the field of psychopathology.

In this chapter, I argue that such power dynamics are evident in individualising and pathologising emerging notions of PTSD. This is because the latter notions are being linked to faulty brains (Bell, 2007), faulty femininity (Lilly et al., 2009), lower resilience (Regel & Joseph, 2010), and lower intelligence (Bomyea et al., 2012), and that the more person-centred language of PTG is being enabled to develop in similar ways (Joseph et al., 2012; Joseph, 2015).

Drawing upon neuroscientific contributions which suggest the presence of faulty brains, I contend that what is happening now to PTSD has parallels with how what is currently understood as borderline personality disorder (BPD) has developed (see Shaw & Proctor, 2005), and that this is not being noticed either by psychotherapists or wider society. BPD is attracting more public criticism (e.g. Watts, 2016), and, if we are not careful, this particular wheel will need inventing again soon for PTSD.

My feeling is that PCA practitioners need more confidence if they are to intervene in the current PTSD conversation. They do have a place there, as evidenced by practice in this field (e.g. Murphy et al., 2013; Murphy & Joseph, 2014; Joseph, 2015); they can have what Proctor (2002) called the "power of individuals within a group of equals, to suggest and be listened to" (p. 37).

PCA practitioners could insist that incongruence is actually "universal" (Biermann-Ratjen, 1998, p. 114), that no-one at all is fully-functioning, and that what is currently called PTSD is really one incongruence amongst many, rather than a psychopathology encountered by some (deficient) people who need experts to treat them and make them whole again.

Such argumentation would draw clearly upon Rogers' (1978) contentions that people do not need to be "guided, instructed, rewarded, punished and controlled" because they have the tendency to actualise, "to move towards growth" (p. 8). Given that practitioners of PCAs have increasingly sought to enter the psychopathology field on *its* terms rather than person-centred terms, more important to progress in this field is that they themselves become more person-centred, perhaps by revisiting the relevance of existentialism in our work, and by recognising that what some call pathology is merely a reminder of our aliveness in the world.

The chapter starts by introducing psychopathology and its relationship with PCAs. A critical analysis of PTSD is then offered. In the UK, the National Institute for Health and Care Excellence (NICE), an organisation which gives "national guidance and advice to improve health and social care" (NICE, 2005, p. 4), currently recommends trauma-focused cognitive behavioural therapy (T-FCBT) and eye movement desensitisation and reprocessing (EMDR) as psychotherapeutic treatments for PTSD; consequently, they are then explored in comparison with PCAs, which are not mentioned by NICE (2005). Murphy et al. (2013) reveal that PCAs *are* now increasingly available in specialist trauma services in the UK; and Murphy and Joseph (2014) show the efficacy of PCAs with PTSD, declaring the approach a "radical ontology for trauma" (p. 12). This more practice-based material is explored in order to show that there is an increasingly strong place from which PCAs can intervene into the PTSD conversation in the ways proposed in this chapter.

Psychopathology and PTSD: critiques and connections

Lemma (1996) stated that "psychopathology generally refers to patterns of maladaptive behaviour and states of distress which interfere with some aspect of adaptation" (p. 1), and Joseph and Worsley (2005) wrote that "psychopathology refers to the study of unusual, distressing and dysfunctional psychological conditions" (p. 1).

Notions of a condition being considered unusual clash with Murphy et al.'s (2013, p. 435) observation that PTSD diagnoses are "increasingly common", and references to maladaptive behaviour obscure how people are much more than one of their perceived behaviours.

Furthermore, "diagnostic heterogeneity" (Kroes et al., 2011, p. 526) needs to be recognised. Curwen and Ruddell (2008) explain that a process of "ruling out" happens, and "when all other diagnoses in the differential diagnosis have been ruled out the correct diagnosis is presumed to remain" (p. 16). As Lemma (1996) said, there is "mystery" (p. 1) here.

Not all diagnosis is led by psychiatry. For instance, PTSD first appeared in 1980 with reference to war veterans (Humphreys & Joseph, 2004), who wanted and welcomed this diagnosis so that they would be entitled to access treatment (Burstow, 2005, p. 430). Following feminist lobbying in the 1980s and early 1990s (Humphreys & Joseph, 2004, p. 561), in DSM-IV (APA, 1994), PTSD encompassed abuse survivors (Burstow, 2005, p. 432), whose pain also needed to be acknowledged in a public way.

Diagnosis can, therefore, be meaningful. A client of Rutherford (2007) saw the term PTSD as "an anchor amidst her experience of disintegration" (p. 160). On the other hand, Harper and Speed (2014) point to diagnosis leading to a "devalued [identity]" (p. 40).

PCAs have been viewed as having "little or no relevance" to psychopathology (Joseph & Worsley, 2005, p. 1). The same authors considered that PCAs have been "isolated" from psychiatry, causing their marginalisation, and consider that, as PCA practitioners, "we have a duty to understand our psychological and psychiatric colleagues" (ibid., 2005, p. 2). I agree, and suggest that reading Freeth (2007), a psychiatrist and psychotherapist, may prompt empathy with psychiatrists; amongst other things, she says that while psychiatrists "are expected to take responsibility", they are also "condemned for being controlling" (p. 102).

Perhaps most compelling from the psychiatry literature, in my view, is what is termed "post-psychiatry". Tseris (2013) explained this as aiming "to grapple with issues of context and meaning, challenging the primacy of biological explanations and yet not denying that mental distress is an embodied experience" (p. 161). This suggests some common ground with PCAs, for as Sanders and Tudor (2001) said,

PCAs can make a "specific contribution to the [psychopathology] debate in viewing personality as a process rather than as a structure" (p. 153). Tudor and Worrall (2006), for instance, offered a vignette in which a client who "describes alienation from her species", i.e. human beings, comes alive when birds fly past the window, enabling her therapist to "refocus on her vitality and authenticity" (p. 159).

Joseph (2005) carefully explores how person-centred personality processes, behaviour and defence can be applied to PTSD, suggesting that: "PTSD symptoms are ... another way of talking about ... the breakdown and disorganisation of the self-structure" (p. 192). People experience a "denial to awareness of existential experiences" (p. 192) and "trauma shows us the limits of the human condition" (p. 194). PTSD intrusion/avoidance symptoms can be understood as the person "[attempting] on the one hand, to accurately symbolise in awareness their experience (intrusion) and on the other, to deny their experiences and hold onto their pre-existing self-structure (avoidance)" (Joseph, 2005, p. 194). While Joseph (2005) accounts for the diagnosis of PTSD in a way that can be followed by PCA practitioners, that should not mean that PTSD itself should be accepted uncritically by them. We need to look more deeply at the implications of embracing PTSD as it is currently constructed.

In the latest DSM, DSM-5 (APA, 2013), "Anxiety Disorders have been redistributed into three ... classifications [including] Trauma- and Stressor-Related Disorders" (Reichenberg, 2014, p. 35). This renders PTSD more *descriptive*. Even in previous DSMs, PTSD was "one of only a few diagnoses ... whose symptoms [were] attributed to situational causes alone" (Hodges, 2003, p. 409). This way of seeing has obscured a more important point made by Hodges (2003) according to which "PTSD ... cannot be conceptualised as a 'normal' response to trauma and simultaneously be called a 'disorder'" (p. 411). Indeed, Burstow (2005) explores whether PTSD responses are "disordered" at all. She says "it is unclear what makes ... responses symptoms of a disease, it is not even clear that these are unfortunate or unwise responses. It depends on the context" (p. 434). Furthermore, DSM-5 (APA, 2013) introduces three new symptoms to PTSD diagnosis, including "persistent and distorted cognitions that lead the person to blame self or others" (Reichenberg, 2014, p. 48). This seems ripe for an implication that anything that happens to individuals is their own responsibility.

For Regel and Joseph (2010), "there are no 'right' and 'wrong'" (p. 3) trauma reactions. This feels untrue as they also say that "some people may be less resilient" (p. 1). Furthermore, as research starts to identify types of intrusive thoughts, a position is now being reached where there are right and wrong intrusive thoughts: "brooding is thought to impede cognitive processing ... reflection is thought to facilitate cognitive processing" (Stockton et al., 2011, p. 85). While it is very important to explore the nuances of PTSD in order to fully understand its dynamics, one must also recognise that some pathologising is taking place here; for people cannot easily choose which intrusive thoughts to entertain, and it is likely to be distressing/stigmatising to learn that one's intrusive thoughts are of the wrong sort.

Traps for the unwary

PTSD has a gendered nature: "men tend to experience more traumatic events than women, but women often tend to experience higher impact of events" (Regel & Joseph, 2010, p. 22). Hodges (2003) notes that PTSD is "deemed pathological because it persists" (p. 414); women's emotional distress has historically been viewed as tiresome (Chesler, 2005). Lilly et al. (2009), in a study of 157 female police officers and 124 female civilians, note how "peritraumatic dissociation is one of the strongest correlates of PTSD" (p. 767), but that women police, for whom "the cost of openly expressing fear and helplessness may be great" (p. 772), experience less peritraumatic dissociation and less PTSD than female civilians. Lilly et al. (2009) want to "design interventions" to change civilian women (p. 772). This way of thinking provides a contemporary example of some women being perceived as faulty and in need of fixing by experts with interventions; it is an example of a mode of thinking according to which it is some women's own fault that they responded to trauma in particular ways; if only they were more like men …

Although Regel and Joseph (2010) identify many "pre-trauma risk factors" (p. 25), intelligence is appearing in the PTSD discourse. Bomyea et al. (2012) link "lower intelligence prior to trauma exposure [to] PTSD development" (p. 634); "one hypothesis is that those with higher intelligence are better able to use effective problem solving strategies to cope with symptoms" (p. 634). More research is said to be needed (Bomyea et al., 2012), but this argument has potential to pathologise groups with a higher prevalence of PTSD – women and particular ethnic minority groups (e.g. Perez Benitez et al. (2013) study Latinos) and it in fact already stigmatises anyone experiencing PTSD as potentially lacking intelligence.

Similarly, Kroes et al. (2011) say that studies have explored "brain variation" and have found "abnormalities" which are "similar to those implicated in major depressive disorder, raising the question of whether they … reflect common difficulties, for example in emotion regulation" (p. 525); Bell (2007) makes it clearer: "it is still unknown whether smaller hippocampal volume predisposes persons to PTSD or whether it is an effect of the disorder" (p. 29).

Such material on brains has parallels with some research exploring BPD – also a psychopathology disproportionately applied to women (see Shaw and Proctor, 2005). Women diagnosed with BPD are pathologised as being faulty, for instance being declared manipulative of others (Watts, 2016). Berdahl (2010) explains that "functional magnetic resonance imaging (fMRI) and positron emission tomography (PET) [have been used] to gain some insight into how the BPD brain works" (p. 177) and that "studies do converge on the general impression that the BPD brain has some sort of dysfunction in limbic and prefrontal areas" (p. 177).

This research introduces a notion of the "BPD brain" and the research mentioned above starts to suggest the "PTSD brain". This is highly problematic, for it has potential to locate the trigger for a perceived psychopathology in the being of the person affected rather than in the trauma that the person has experienced, rendering PTSD no more neutral than BPD. Machizawa-Summers (2007), for instance, already questions the reality of people diagnosed with BPD, saying "it is important to assess whether the BPD patients' perceptions of parental behaviours and traumatic experience are coloured by their pre-existing psychological problems or whether these negative childhood experiences facilitate development of borderline pathology" (p. 271). This parallel alone should prompt caution in embracing the PTSD discourse.

Joseph (2005) says that person-centred theory enables understanding of PTG: "as the client comes more to develop a self-structure that is congruent between self and experience, they should also become more fully functioning and able to engage in organismic valuing" (p. 197). However, drawing upon Harper and Speed (2014), it is clear that such progress is built upon "deficit" (p. 41). Indeed, current research into PTG does highlight personal deficiency: Joseph et al. (2012) report that "greater PTG is associated with … emotional stability; extraversion; openness to experience; optimism; and self-esteem" (p. 320). Likewise, there is an "optimum" level of PTSD needed for PTG: "moderate" (Joseph et al., 2012, p. 320), for then "the individual's assumptive world has in some way been challenged, triggering the intrusive and avoidant experiences, but the person remains able to cope … and engage sufficiently in the necessary cognitive processing needed to work through" (Joseph et al., 2012, p. 320). Thus, even a concept that feels positive contains traps for the unwary – notions that people did not experience sufficient PTG because they lacked particular, currently prized, personal qualities to begin with.

Overall, PTSD originally appeared to be a helpful diagnostic classification (Burstow, 2005), but *the current direction of the PTSD discourse*, and the PTG discourse which has followed it, *has problematic elements*, particularly when a strong parallel with BPD is recognised.

PCA practitioners are well-placed to offer a critique of the current discourses because they recognise, and could much more clearly insist, that incongruence is actually "universal" (Biermann-Ratjen, 1998, p. 114), rather than a psychopathology encountered by some (deficient) people who need fixing by experts. But PCAs can only intervene in the debate if they have a place there. The next section explores treatments for PTSD and how PCAs are positioned amongst them.

Trauma-focused cognitive behavioural therapy, eye movement desensitisation and reprocessing and person-centred approaches

As indicated above, the UK's National Institute for Health and Care Excellence (NICE) (2005) proposes trauma-focused cognitive behavioural therapy (T-FCBT) or eye movement desensitisation and reprocessing (EMDR) for PTSD, as well as medication, though it acknowledges that this "should not be used as a routine first-line treatment for adults" (p. 4).

T-FCBT implicitly holds a position of personal deficit. Techniques include "exposure": "prolonged imaginal exposure requires the individual with PTSD to vividly imagine the trauma for prolonged periods" (Harvey et al., 2003, p. 502); "cognitive restructuring", which "involves teaching patients to identify and evaluate the evidence of negative automatic thoughts ... [and] anxiety management training" (ibid., p. 503). Burstow (2005) made it clear that the "context" matters in deciding if "fear" is "unwise" (p. 434). Tseris (2013) argued that "standard CBT strategies" can "offer only superficial and inadequate support" (p. 160) for interpersonal trauma; "re-traumatisation" is also possible via "exposure" (Seidler & Wagner, 2006, p. 1512).

Regel and Joseph (2010) explain that T-FCBT is about "helping the sufferer challenge and change problematic thoughts and meanings" (p. 52). Harvey et al., (2003) declared that this begins with "psycho-education", which aims "to legitimise the trauma reaction, to help the patient develop a formulation of their symptoms, and to establish a rationale for treatment" (p. 502). The idea of "legitimising" (ibid., p. 502) feels respectful, but Guilfoyle (2008) also noted how CBT "patronises" (p. 198). He also says that "CBT's complicity with contemporary power arrangements is ... blatant" – the intention is for people to return to work quickly (ibid., p. 197; see also Royal College of Psychiatrists, 2015).

EMDR may be an alternative, although not for everyone – Tarquinio et al. (2012) reported excluding participants with "health issues, neurological disorders, eye disorders/pain, dissociative disorders, etc." (p. 207), and Coffeng (2004), a Focusing-oriented therapist, noted that a client's PTSD "had become worse after a treatment with EMDR" (p. 284).

While T-FCBT requires an instrumental therapeutic alliance (Polak et al., 2012, p. 4), EMDR "[lets] the process of therapeutic change organically unfold" (p. 402). However, it is the protocol that is figural in the understanding of EMDR for PTSD (Marich, 2012, p. 405), a perspective which, again, positions clients as objects upon whom to practise interventions.

Pilgrim (2009) observed that, while current guidance about treatments for PTSD "is informed by evidence ... not all evidence is being used" (p. 336). The "common factors" approach, as outlined by Hubble et al. (2010, pp. 35–39), draws attention to "client and extratherapeutic factors", "the therapeutic relationship/alliance" and "therapist factors". Hubble et al. (2010) reflected that "it is no longer a matter of which therapeutic approach is best. Rather, it is about showing that a treatment, conducted by a given therapist with a particular client at a specific time and place yielded positive results" (p. 39).

Benish et al. (2008) conducted a meta-analysis of a range of psychotherapies and demonstrated that "bona fide psychotherapies produce equivalent benefits for patients with PTSD" (p. 746), but the meta-analysis did not include PCAs. As Joseph (2015, p. 180) observes: "practitioners of the PCA are marginalised in clinical practice because of the perception that they lack the knowledge or skills to work with traumatised individuals". PCA practitioners need to be more visible – and increasingly they are becoming so.

Murphy and Joseph's (2014) experience is that PCA practitioners step in when T-FCBT/ EMDR have failed: people go "'through the system' several times" with a focus upon "symptoms" (as described above) and are "missed ... as a person" (p. 5). Tseris (2013) argued that interpersonal trauma needs more than "standard CBT"

(p. 160). Murphy and Joseph (2014, p. 90) suggested that "clients who have experienced neglect, abuse or domestic violence especially benefit from the genuine warmth and prizing of the social environment created in person-centred therapy". This is respectful, rather than explicitly about personal deficit. PCAs are not entirely distinct, however: exposure therapies also require "accurate symbolisation" and "what PCT adds is ... that there is no need ... to push the client because the client will be intrinsically motivated to increase congruence between self and experience" (Joseph, 2005, p. 196). PCAs allow for individual differences more respectfully than behavioural approaches (Joseph, 2005).

Nonetheless, the PTSD discourse can sometimes lead PCAs away from "the uniqueness of the experience" (Schmid, 1998, p. 75), and into the realms of potential "power over" – "domination, coercive authority", as Proctor (2002, p. 37) puts it – thereby almost bringing PCAs alongside some ways of conceptualising CBT/EMDR. Nevertheless, there is also sensitivity/creativity in current PCAs for PTSD, allowing for an arising of "power-from-within ... an inner strength" (ibid., p. 37).

Murphy and Joseph (2014) adopt a "principled non-directive approach" (p. 3) which is very respectful – though, in one instance, their focus on not responding to the question of a client diagnosed with PTSD (when she sought reassurance) reminded me of Totton's (2012) point that "there are many subtle ways in which the therapist can imply that they know better than the client" (p. 29). I contrast this with Hawkins' work (Hawkins, 2014) with a client who is experiencing flashbacks in which she does not deploy the term PTSD: she fully connects, person to person. Is there something about the absence of the language of PTSD that enabled this, I wonder?

What I feel matters most in the person-centred field now is not how incongruence may be mapped to PTSD to explain, in person-centred terms, a psychopathology encountered by some people (but not others) for individual reasons – which can then be approached in person-centred ways. Instead, we should properly recognise that the fully-functioning person who is "never really endangered by new experience [and has] no need to defend against any form of self experience" (Biermann-Ratjen, 1998, p. 114) does not exist and never will. So we can fully embrace the idea that everyone has a psychopathology of some sort or another, and one (PTSD included) is not better or worse than another. We can then enter the psychopathology debate on humane, equalising terms, rather than on psychopathology's own often-objectifying terms of disorder and deficit. PCAs already do recognise that people can be "trusted" (Rogers, 1978, p. 8), that they can flourish in a "growth-promoting climate" (Rogers, 1978, p. 9) which offers empathy, unconditional positive regard and congruence. We need to say that more confidently, and share more evidence of PCAs' effectiveness, as precursors to challenging psychopathology's language. This may be difficult for some PCA researchers and practitioners who engage with psychopathologies as currently understood, but it is consistent with the theory, philosophy and practice of our encounters with people. "New form[s] of communication" (Totton, 2012, p. 107) are important in the work envisaged in this chapter, for instance Warner's (2005, 2014) research on "difficult process", which Tudor and Merry (2002) linked to personality disorders. For Warner (2014), difficult process describes "descriptions of some common client experiences rather than diagnostic categories" (p. 122). Some PTSD experiences feel consistent with difficult process. There is a long-term project here, for as Warner (2005) says, "if, as PC theorists, we are able to clarify ... an overall model of health and pathology, we may also be able to increase our effectiveness in critiquing and offering constructive alternatives to current systems of mental health services" (p. 91).

Conclusion

As Humphreys and Joseph (2004) noted, "some aspects of the PTSD discourse are developed and others disregarded" (p. 564). In this chapter, instances have been shown where there is as yet insufficient recognition of the individualising/pathologising nature of some current PTSD and PTG discourses – ascribing "faults", whether to brains, to gender, to low(er) intelligence, to lower resilience or personal deficits. Some troubling parallels with the development of the BPD discourse have been shown.

I have argued that practitioners of PCAs need to be more politically aware and engaged, more willing to influence the direction of the PTSD conversation than to seek permission to listen to it. PCAs are increasingly showing their relevance to PTSD and can increasingly claim a place alongside more established psychotherapies for PTSD, acquiring the "power of individuals within a group of equals, to suggest and be listened to" (Proctor, 2002, p. 37). I have suggested how this power may be used to good effect, by challenging discourses which feel problematic.

Williamson (2010) argues that intimate partner violence (IPV) can lead to "responses" which "mimic" PTSD; she says that "we know far too little to assume that ... [IPV] ... inevitably results in a diagnosable psychiatric condition, as opposed to creating confusion" (p. 1416). It may eventually be that practitioners of PCAs will reject the term PTSD altogether, and call for others to do likewise. Certainly, arguments against the label BPD are currently gathering pace in a public psychotherapy (see Watts, 2016, for instance).

In the meantime, as PTSD can be helpful to people making meaning of symptoms, it does feel appropriate to seek to work with PTSD. PCAs are a refreshing alternative in this field to forms of psychotherapy where experts seek to help stigmatised others – but let us always keep a critical eye upon research findings and their implications.

Note

A version of this chapter was originally published as: Lee D.A. A person-centred political critique of current discourses in post-traumatic stress disorder and post-traumatic growth.

Psychotherapy Politics Int. 2017;15:e1411. https://doi.org/10.1002/ppi.1411 Copyright (c) 2017 John Wiley & Sons Ltd.

References

American Psychiatric Association (APA). (1994). *Diagnostic and statistical manual of mental disorders: DSM-IV^{TM}* (4th ed.). Arlington, VA: American Psychiatric Publishing.

American Psychiatric Association (APA). (2013). *Diagnostic and statistical manual of mental disorders: DSM-5^{TM}* (5th ed.). Arlington, VA: American Psychiatric Publishing.

Bell, J. (2007). Preventing post-traumatic stress disorder or pathologising bad memories? *The American Journal of Bioethics*, 7(9), 29–30. doi:10.1080/15265160701518540.

Benish, S., Imel, Z., & Wampold, B. (2008). The relative efficacy of bona fide psychotherapies for treating post-traumatic stress disorder: A meta-analysis of direct comparisons. *Clinical Psychology Review*, 28, 746–758.

Berdahl, C. (2010). A neural network model of borderline personality disorder. *Neural Networks*, 23, 177–188.

Biermann-Ratjen, E.-M. (1998). Incongruence and psychopathology. In B. Thorne & E. Lambers (Eds.), *Person-centred therapy: A European perspective* (pp. 119–130). London, England: Sage.

Bomyea, J., Risbrough, V., & Lang, A. (2012). A consideration of select pre-trauma factors as key vulnerabilities in PTSD. *Clinical Psychology Review*, 32, 630–641. doi:10.1016/j.cpr.2012. 06. 008.

Burstow, B. (2005). A critique of posttraumatic stress disorder and the DSM. *The Journal of Humanistic Psychology*, 45(4), 429–445. https://doi.org/10.1177/0022167805280265.

Chesler, P. (2005). *Women and madness*. Basingstoke, England: Palgrave Macmillan.

Coffeng, T. (2004). Trauma, imagery and focusing. *Person-Centred & Experiential Psychotherapies*, 3(4), 277–290. doi:1477-9757/04/04277–214 2.

Curwen, B., & Ruddell, P. (2008). Diagnosis. In S. Palmer & R. Bor (Eds.), *The practitioner's handbook* (pp. 33–49). London: Sage.

Freeth, R. (2007). *Humanising psychiatry and mental health care: The challenge of the person-centred approach*. Oxford: Radcliffe.

Guilfoyle, M. (2008). CBT's integration into societal networks of power. *European Journal of Psychotherapy and Counselling*, 10(3), 197–205. doi:10.1080/13642530802337884.

Harper, D., & Speed, E. (2014). Uncovering recovery: The resistible rise of recovery and resilience. In E. Speed, J. Moncrieff & M. Rapley (Eds.), *De-Medicalising misery II* (pp. 40–57). Basingstoke: Palgrave Macmillan.

Harvey, A., Bryant, R., & Tarrier, N. (2003). Cognitive behaviour therapy for posttraumatic stress disorder. *Clinical Psychology Review*, 23, 501–522. doi:10.1016/S0272-7358(03)00035-7.

Hawkins, J. (2014) Person-centred therapy with adult survivors of childhood sexual abuse. In P. Pearce, & L. Sommerbeck, (Eds.), *Person-centred practice at the difficult edge* (pp. 14–26). Ross-on-Wye, England: PCCS Books.

Hodges, S. (2003). Borderline personality disorder and posttraumatic stress disorder: Time for integration? *Journal of Counselling and Development*, 81, 409–417. doi:10.1002/j.1556-6678.2003.tb00267.

Hubble, M., Duncan, B., Miller, S., & Wampold, B. (2010) Introduction. In B. Duncan, S. Miller, B. Wampold, & M. Hubble (Eds.), *The heart and soul of change* (2nd ed.). Washington, DC: American Psychological Association.

Humphreys, C., & Joseph, S. (2004). Domestic violence and the politics of trauma. *Women's Studies International Forum*, 27, 559–570. doi:10.1016/j.wsif.2004. 09. 010.

Joseph, S. (2005). Understanding post-traumatic stress from the person-centred perspective. In S. Joseph & R. Worsley (Eds.), *Person-centred psychopathology: A positive psychology of mental health* (pp. 190–201). Ross-on-Wye: PCCS Books.

Joseph, S. (2015). A person-centred perspective on working with people who have experienced psychological trauma and helping them move forward to posttraumatic growth. *Person-Centred & Experiential Psychotherapies*, 14(3), 178–190. doi:10.1080/14779757.2015.1043392.

Joseph, S., & Worsley, R. (2005). Psychopathology and the person-centred approach: Building bridges between disciplines. In S. Joseph & R. Worsley (Eds.), *Person-centred psychopathology: A positive psychology of mental health* (pp. 1–8). Ross-on-Wye: PCCS Books.

Joseph, S., Murphy, D., & Regel, S. (2012). An affective-cognitive processing model of post-traumatic growth. *Clinical Psychology and Psychotherapy*, 19, 316–325. doi:10.1002/cpp.1798.

Kroes, M., Whalley, M., Rugg, M., & Brewin, C. (2011). Association between flashbacks and structural brain abnormalities in posttraumatic stress disorder. *European Psychiatry*, 26, 525–531. doi:10.1016/j.eurpsy.2011. 03. 00doi:2.

Lemma, A. (1996). *Introduction to psychopathology*. London: Sage.

Lilly, M., Pole, N., Best, S., Metzler, T., & Marmar, C. (2009). Gender and PTSD: What can we learn from female police officers? *Journal of Anxiety Disorders*, 23, 767–774. doi:10.1016/j.janxdis.2009. 02. 01doi:5.

Machizawa-Summers, S. (2007). Childhood trauma and parental bonding among Japanese female patients with borderline personality disorder. *International Journal of Psychology*, 42(4), 265–273.

Marich, J. (2012). What makes a good EMDR therapist? *Journal of Humanistic Psychology*, 52(4), 401–422. doi:10.1177/0022167811431960.

Murphy, D., Archard, P., Regel, S., & Joseph, S. (2013). A survey of specialised traumatic stress services in the United Kingdom. *Journal of Psychiatric and Mental Health Nursing*, 20, 433–441. doi:10.1111/j.1365-2850.2012.01938.

Murphy, D., & Joseph, S. (2014). Understanding posttraumatic stress and facilitating post-traumatic growth. In P. Pearce & L. Sommerbeck (Eds.), *Person-centred practice at the difficult edge* (pp. 3–13). Ross-on-Wye: PCCS Books.

National Institute for Health and Care Excellence (NICE). (2005). *Post-traumatic stress disorder (PTSD): The management of PTSD in adults and children in primary and secondary care*. NICE Clinical Guideline 26. London: Author.

Perez Benitez, C., Zlotnick, C., Gomez, J., Rendon, M., & Swanson, A. (2013). Cognitive behavioural therapy for PTSD and somatisation: An open trial. *Behaviour Research and Therapy*, 51, 284–289. doi:10.1016/j.brat.2013.02.005.

Pilgrim, D. (2009). CBT in the British NHS: Vague imposition or imposition of vagueness? *European Journal of Psychotherapy and Counselling*, 11(3), 323–339. doi:10.1080/13642530903230459.

Polak, A., Witteveen, A., Visser, R., Opemeer, B., Vulink, N., Figee, M., Denys, D., & Olff, M. (2012). Comparison of the effectiveness of trauma-focused cognitive behavioural therapy and paroxetine treatment in PTSD patients: Design of a randomised controlled trial. *Psychiatry*, 12, 166, 1–11.

Proctor, G. (2002). *The dynamics of power in counselling and psychotherapy*. Ross-on-Wye: PCCS Books.

Proctor, G. (2006). Introduction. In G. Proctor, M. Cooper, P. Sanders, & B. Malcolm (Eds.), *Politicising the person-centred approach*. Ross-on-Wye: PCCS Books.

Regel, S., & Joseph, S. (2010). *Post-traumatic stress: The facts*. Oxford: Oxford University Press.

Reichenberg, L. (2014). *DSM-5 essentials*. Hoboken, NJ: Wiley.

Rogers, C. (1978). *Personal power*. London: Constable.

Royal College of Psychiatrists. (2015). *PTSD factsheet*. Retrieved from http://www.rcpsych.ac.uk/healthadvice/problemsdisorders/posttraumaticstressdisorder.aspx.

Rutherford, M. (2007). Bearing witness: Working with clients who have experienced trauma – Considerations for a person-centred approach to counselling. *Person-Centred & Experiential Psychotherapies*, 6(3), 153–168. doi:1477-9757/07/doi:03153–116.

Sanders, P., & Tudor, K. (2001). This is therapy: A person-centred critique of the contemporary psychiatric system. In C. Newnes, G. Holmes & C. Dunn (Eds.), *This is madness too* (pp. 147–160). Ross-on-Wye: PCCS Books.

Schmid, P. (1998). On becoming a person-centred approach: A person-centred understanding. In B. Thorne & E. Lambers (Eds.), *Person-centred therapy: A European perspective* (pp. 38–52). London: Sage.

Seidler, G., & Wagner, F. (2006). Comparing the efficacy of EMDR and trauma-focused cognitive-behavioural therapy in the treatment of PTSD: A meta-analytical study. *Psychological Medicine*, 36, 1515–1522. doi:10.1017/S0033291706007963.

Shaw, C., & Proctor, G. (2005). Women at the margins: A critique of the diagnosis of borderline personality disorder. *Feminism and Psychology*, 15(4), 483–490.

Stockton, H., Hunt, N., & Joseph, S. (2011). Cognitive processing, rumination, and post-traumatic growth. *Journal of Traumatic Stress*, 24(1), 85–92. doi:10.1002/jts.20606.

Tarquinio, C., Brennstuhl, M-J., Rydberg, J., Schmitt, A., Mouda, F., Lourel, M., & Tarquinio, P. (2012). Eye movement desensitisation and reprocessing (EMDR) therapy in the treatment of victims of domestic violence: A pilot study. *Revue europeenne de psychologie appliqué*, 62, 205–212. doi:10.1016/j.erap.2012. 08. 00doi:6.

Totton, N. (2012). *Not a tame lion*. Ross-on-Wye: PCCS Books.

Tseris, E. (2013). Trauma theory without feminism. *Affilia*, 28(2), 153–164. doi:10.1177/0886109913485707.

Tudor, K., & Merry, T. (2002). *Dictionary of person-centred psychology*. Ross-on-Wye: PCCS Books.

Tudor, K., & Worrall, M. (2006) *Person-centred therapy: A clinical philosophy*. London: Routledge.

Warner, M. (2005). A person-centred view of human nature, wellness and psychopathology. In S. Joseph & R. Worsley (Eds.), *Person-centred psychopathology: A positive psychology of mental health* (pp. 91–109). Ross-on-Wye: PCCS Books.

Warner, M. (2014). Client processes at the difficult edge. In P. Pearce & L. Sommerbeck (Eds.), *Person-centred practice at the difficult edge* (pp. 121–158). Ross-on-Wye: PCCS Books.

Watts, J. (2016). Borderline personality disorder: A diagnosis of invalidation. *Huffington Post*, September 26. Retrieved from http://www.huffingtonpost.co.uk/dr-jay-watts/borderlinepersonality-di_b_12167212.html.

Williamson, E. (2010). Living in the world of the domestic violence perpetrator. *Violence Against Women*, 16(12), 1412–1423. doi:10.1177/1077801210389162.

INDEX

'accidental mystic', Carl Rogers as 167, 169
accidental therapy 3
acknowledgement *see* unconditional positive regard (UPR)
actualizing tendency: *Buen Con-Vivir* (good-living-with-others) 95, 106; directional facet 94; examples 97; importance 107; interactional facet 94; introduction to 93; non-actualization of negative capacities 94; rejection of 132
Adomaitis, R. 179, 182
affection *see* storge
affective turn xix
Agamben, Giorgio 116
agape (benevolence, charity, delectation): Biblical concept of 35, 198, 204, xviii; as big love 235; as 'Buddha nature' 36; characteristics of 35, 198; congruence and 174, 190; definition of 35; as divine love 36; eros and 35, 36; faith and 35; philia and 198, 200, 204; presence as 185; and self-gratification 199; therapy as 198, 200, 205; trust expressed as 71; unconditional positive regard as 198, 200, 201
alienation and empathy 52
Allen, Frederick 46
Amatuzzi, M. M. 63
American Psychological Association 252
amity *see* philia
Andersen, Hans Christian 252
animality of therapist 14
anthropocentrism of PCT 29
anthropomorphic understanding of God 35
apophasis 242
Argentina, therapy and politics in: neoliberal psycho-political domination 17; politics and psychotherapy 20; therapy as political act 17
Aristotle 197
Ashtanga yoga 305
attitude of respect, therapist's 133
audacity of therapist 14
authentic connections 213
Ayckbourn, Alan 212

Barker, Meg-John 320
Barrett-Lennard, G. 218
Bazzano, Manu 30, 31, 32, 39, 40, 49, 81, 114, 115, 135, 152, 221, 270, 296
beastly love 42
beautiful soul syndrome 28, 31, 34, 42
Beauty and the Cyborg: anthropocentrism of PCT 29; beastly love 42; beautiful soul syndrome 28, 31, 34; Beauty becoming Cyborg 28, 36, 40; comic faith in technofixes 31; emancipatory technofixes 38; empathic manipulators 39; introduction to 28; love and 'the Powers' 36; necessarily insufficient therapy 41; taxonomy of love 34
benevolence *see* agape
Benish, S. 336
Berardi, Franco 18
Berwick, Donald 252
Bio-Spiritual Focusing 174, 180, 182, 186

Bodhidharma xxi
bodily process, experience as 120
bodily-felt process of congruence 184
body wisdom *see* organismic wisdom
Bollas, Christopher 319
Bourriaud, N. 211
Bozarth, Jerrold 50, 52, 281, 292
British Association of Counselling and Psychotherapy 269
Brodley, Barbara Temaner 52, 87, 132, 133, 134, 135, 302, 316, 324
Buber, Martin 33, 36, 66, 279, 303
'Buddha nature', agape as 36
Buddhism 194, xxi
Buen Con-Vivir (good-living-with-others) 95, 106
Bugental, James 154, 308, 312
Burrell, Gibson 50
Burstow, B. 336
Byung-Chul 18

Cameron, William Bruce 254
Campbell, Peter 174, 180, 183, 185, 187, 189
canine-human relationships 266
cantus firmus ('firm song'), storge as 200
capitalism, neoliberal 17
Caputo, John 244
Caravaggio, Michelangelo Merisi da 42
Carter, Angela 42
case studies: beginning phase 217; client's experience of new levels of personal change 218; genres 214; middle phase 218; theoretical approaches 211
CBT *see* cognitive behavioural therapy
celebrity and access to presence 307
Centre for Counselling Studies 188
CEP *see* co-experiencing psychotherapy
change: meaningfulness 259
Chaos theory, mysticism and 172
charity *see* agape
childhood: childhood personality and adult health in relation 293; experience 103, 137, 149, 258, 335; family 258, 278; love 89; re-experience of 137; therapy 47
China: Bodhidharma's journey to xxi; Carl Roger's journey to 281
choice, meaningfulness of 252
Christianity: Bio-Spiritual Focusing 174, 180, 182, 186; Centre for Spirituality and Religion 187; community 185; congruence 182; experience xvi; immanent theology 37; love 36, 37, 194; morality 31, xvi; theology xvi; worldview 29, 36

client-centered therapy *see* person-centred therapy
clients: client-centredness of PCT 48; client-therapist connection 218; diagnosis as label 293; perceptions of distress 292; right to self-direction 133; trust in 205, 206
co-experiencing psychotherapy (CEP) 79
cognitive behavioural therapy (CBT): as evidence-based practice 249; presence 219; PTSD and PTG 335; thinking-feeling-behaviour triangle 248
Collins, Bill 259
comic faith in technofixes 31
community: as aim of therapy 21, 316; Christian 185; eros and 201; of friends 25; God as 194; inclusion in 100; international 31; love and 201; meetings 232; person-centred 238, 239, 246, 281, 300, 306; philia and 197, 200; relationships and 49
concealment: experience 327; feelings 323; love and 89; openness and 315, 317; thoughts 317, 323
conceptual relationships 97, 141, 238
conditioned worldview 243
congruence: *see also* incongruence; agape and 174, 190; bodily-felt process of 184; concept of 145; congruent communication in therapy 316; as core condition 174, 179, 182, 300, 301; cosmic *see* cosmic congruence; definition of 180; differing views of 147, 185; experience and 178; between inner and outer 147; not definable as explicit symbolization 177; to organismic experiencing xvii; presence as 179; process of 182; between self and experience 145
connections: *see also* relationships; aspiration for 258; authentic 213; client-therapist 218; empathic 270; existence 308; to food 305; *idearum* 22; inner 203; loss of 281; making 9, 12, 131; meaningfulness 308; possibility 220; presence and 303, 311; relational 'betweenness' of 239; self and other 219; self-acceptance 306; self-care 306; therapy 219, 270; with universe 198
Cooper, Mick 157
core conditions: congruence *see* congruence; in person-centred therapy 128, 301; and practitioner training xxi; presence and 23, 204
cosmic congruence: on becoming a person 175; Bio-Spiritual Focusing 182;

congruence not definable as explicit symbolization 177; ending of research 187; introduction to 174; presence as agape 185; presence as congruence 179; social dimension 186
Coyne, James 254
creative contaminations xvii
Creswell, Robyn 37
Crouan, Michele 323
Cyborg *see* Beauty and the Cyborg

D'Ansembourg, Thomas 322
Darwinism 21
Davis, Elizabeth 46
de Carvalho, Roy 282, 283, 284
deconstruction of knowledge theories 241
delectation *see* agape
Deleuze, Gilles 30, 37
Derrida, Jacques 69, 241
Descartes, René 34, 147
di Giovanni, Norman Thomas 114, 125
diagnosis: Carl Roger's critique 53, 55, 290, 298; contingency of 249, 252; differential 332; experience and 292; incongruence and 294; as label 293; meaningfulness of 332; PCT and 290; presentation of 212; primacy of 292; problem with 10; relevance to psychotherapy 290; scientific search for cause 292; therapy as 292
difference, openness to 71
Dilthey, Wilhelm 195
direction: client's right to self-direction 133; directional facet of actualizing tendency 94; directivity and non-directivity in relation to presence 308; nondirective attitude of therapist 133; PCT as non-directive therapy 134
discursivity, PCA as 110
distorted perception, concept of 52
distress, client perceptions of 292
divided brain, theory of 239
divine love, agape as 36
divine madness *see* eros
Dōgen xx
dogs and humans 266
Dostoevsky, Fedor 316, 319
dualistic worldview 140
Duncan, Barry 257
Dunne, J. 285
dysfunctional families 234, 236

Edgar, D. 219
Ellingham, I. 53, 111
Elliott, R. 213
emancipatory technofixes 38

EMDR *see* eye movement desensitisation and reprocessing (EMDR)
emotion-focused therapy (EFT): development of 156; experiencing in 157; meaning in 156; reconfiguring of relationships 157
empathy: alienation and 52; connections 270; as core condition 300, 301; empathic manipulators 39; empathic understanding 130; openness to Other 71; as process 177; relationships 284; storge and 196; strangeness and 70; and unconditional positive regard 122, 130, 135, 196, 303
empiricism, scientific 138
encounter groups, presence and 310
Enginger, Bernard (Satprem) 170
envy towards friends 89
eros (divine madness, passion): agape and 35, 36; beliefs and concepts 193; Biblical notion 35; community and 201; form of love 194, 200; Freud 194; pedagogic 195; Plato 195, 197; primacy 36; psychotherapy 195; in therapeutic process 204, 205; and unconditional positive regard 196
ethics: client's right to self-direction 133; ethical therapy 128; freedom as ethical premise for practice 131; minoritarian ethics 37; openness of ethical therapy 133; PCA and 60, 63; PCT and radical ethics 13; of radical alterity *see* radical alterity; of relationships 215; Rogerian psychotherapy 63
event, theology of 244
evidence-based practice (EBP): Common Elements Treatment Approach 248, 250, 253; common factors in models 256; introduction to 247; looking along and looking at 259; models claiming to be 250; overtechnical approaches 260; paradox within 257
existence and experience 143
experience: *see also* organismic experiencing; as bodily process 120; characteristics of experiencing 146; childhood 103, 137, 149, 258, 335; co-experiencing psychotherapy 79; concealment 327; congruence and 178; diagnosis and 292; dialectics of person and experiencing 79; and emotion-focused therapy 157; empiricism and 138; existence and 143; Experiential Learning Cycle 240; Experiential Phenomenology 140; experientially referring concepts 140; is

life 118; of life 118; openness to 155, 323, 335; PCT and experiencing 137; pedagogic eros 195; potential person-centred contributions 320; process as becoming of 118; re-experience of childhood 137; role of experiencing 145; self and 145; as 'strange consciousness of living' 42; and therapy research 280; trust in 101, 238; of unconditional positive regard 68, 130, 135, 186, 202; unfolding process of 119; words, limitations of 142
experiential-existential psychotherapy: concept of 153; EFT *see* emotion-focused therapy (EFT); existential roots of experiential therapies 154; facing own existential challenges 153; FOT *see* focusing oriented therapy (FOT); introduction to 151; therapist as fully implied 158
eye movement desensitisation and reprocessing, treatment of PTSD and PTG 335

faith, agape and 35
family: childhood 258, 278; conceptual integrity of 80; dysfunctional 234, 236; importance given to 11, 12; lack of support from 104; life 80, 94, 104; philia 197; relationships 96, 240; shame and 103; storge 196; talking about 87, 319, 321; transcendence of 25, 116; worldview 105, 278
Farid ud-Din Attar 37
feelings, concealment of 323
Ferenczi, Sándor 42
Figueiredo, Luiz Cláudio 60, 63, 64, 68
'firm song' (*cantus firmus*), storge as 200
focusing oriented therapy (FOT): development of 141, 156; as experiential-existential therapy 154; PCT as 121
food and self-care 305
Forster, E. M. 8
Foucault, Michel 112, 116, 123
freedom as ethical premise for practice 131
Freeth, Rachel 291, 296
Freire, José L.F. 70, 72, 73, 97
Freud, Sigmund: *see also* psychoanalysis; discursivity 123; eros 195; experience 320; importance 4; irrelevant-seeming material, value of 319; looking along and looking at 260; Rat Man case 318
Friedberg, Robert 213
friends: community of 25; concealed thoughts 317; creation of 114; envy towards 89; interactions with 96; lack of 105; limitations of 229, 305, 306; missing of 247; support from 272
friendship: eros and 194, 195, 196; form of love 193; fragility of 281; philia *see* philia; storge and 196; therapy as 13, 197; therapy distinguished from 129, 198
Fromm, Erich 193
full presence 23

Galilei, Galileo 138, 140, 141
Gant, E. E. 69
Gantt, Henry L. 68, 69
Garcia Marquez, Gabriel 236
Geller, Shari 171, 214, 219, 302, 304
Gendlin, Eugene T.: body wisdom 102; congruence 145, 177, 180, 185; core concepts 85; emotion-focused therapy 157; empiricism 139, 140; experiencing, concept of 87, 143, 148, 177, 280; focusing oriented therapy 121, 154; micro-processes in therapy 156; pedagogic eros 195; personality change, theory of 181; philosophy of PCA 117, 123; process-skipping 184; reconfiguring of relationships 158; Rogers, Carl, and 80, 177; Vasilyuk, Fyodor E., and xxv
Genet, Jean 233
God: agape 198; anthropomorphic understanding of 35; as community 194; love 192; making God happen 244
good-living-with-others (*Buen Con-Vivir*) 95, 106
Goodman, D. 65, 68
Greenberg, Leslie 171, 214, 219, 302, 304
Grencavage, Lisa 256

Haeffner, G. 193
Haugh, S. 179
Hawtin, Sarah 321, 323
healing power of relationships 273
health: childhood personality and adult health in relation 293; paradigms 54
Hegel, Georg Wilhelm Friedrich 31
Heidegger, Martin 66, 154, 279, xx
Helpful Aspects of Therapy (HAT) 158
Hesse, Herman 316
heterotopic practice, PCT as 110, 124
Hinduism 193
Hippocratic Oath 289
Hobbes, Thomas 21
Hook, Louis 295
'how' of knowing 238, 245
Hubble, Mark 257
human beings: as person 200; trust in 93

human development, release from social constraints on 52
humanism, PCT as radical 52
Humphreys, C. 338
Hurtado, S.A 19
Huxley, Aldous 140

idearum connections 22
immanent theology 37
implicit meaningfulness 146
inclusion in community 100
incongruence: diagnosis and 294; between self and experience 145; and unconditional positive regard 196
inner connections 203
inner relationships 157, 160
international community 31
irrelevant-seeming material, openness to 319
Islam 194

Jaspers, Karl 289, 291, 296
Joseph, Stephen 296, 336, 338
Jourard, S. M. 325
Juarroz, Roberto 24
Judaism 194
Judeo-Christian *see* Christian

Kafka, Franz 231
Kahneman, Daniel 40
Kant, Immanuel 259
Karyagina, Tatiana 79
Keltner, Dacher 303
Kepes, György 137
Keys, Suzanne 34, 36
Kierkegaard, Søren 36
Kinget, G. M. 63
Kirschenbaum, Howard 282
Klagsbrun, Francine 155
Klein, M. H. 155
knowledge, theories of: apophasis 242; deconstruction of 241; divided brain 238, 239; Experiential Learning Cycle 240; introduction to 237; knowing, 'what' and 'how' of 238, 245; theology of event 244
Kolb, David 240
Kövecses, Zoltán 111
Kuhn, Thomas 50, 54

label, diagnosis as 293
Laing, R. D. 291
Lambert, Michael 256
language and openness 67, 243
Larner, G. 69
Lasagna, Louis 289

'lawfulness' of relationships 49
learning *see* knowledge, theories of
Leicester, Graham 280
Leijssen, M. 156, 157
Lem, Stanislaw 138
Levinas, Emmanuel 33, 36, 60, 65, 68, 71, 197, 242, 279
Lewis, C.S. 260
life: client's right to self-direction 133; experience is life 118; experience of life 118; family life 80, 94, 104; as process 119
Lilienfeld, Scott 251
looking along and looking at 260
loss: of connections 281; of meaningfulness 258
love: agape *see* agape; art of acknowledgement 202; basic facts about 193; beastly love 42; beautiful soul syndrome 34; childhood 89; community and 201; concealment and 89; eros *see* eros; forms of 193, 194, 196, 200; 'framework for love in therapy' 34; meaning of 192; person-centred approach 201; philia *see* philia; philosophies, ancient and modern 194; relationships and 194, 206; storge *see* philia; storge; taxonomy of 35; and 'the Powers' 36; theory of 34; therapy through *see* therapy through love; unconditional 174, 198, 229; as unconditional positive regard 71

Macleod, R. 213
MacMurray, John 280
macro-processes in therapy 156
Maddi, S. R. 48
Madison, G. 154
madness, divine *see* eros
Manning, Erin 120
Marx, Karl 123
Maslow, Abraham 69
Massumi, Brian 120
Mathieu-Coughlan, P. 155
Max-Neef, Artur Manfred 95, 106
McGilchrist, Iain 238, 239
McLeod, J. 211, 213, 214
McMahon, Edwin 174, 180, 183, 185, 186
McNamara, Robert 254
meaning in EFT 156
meaningfulness: change 259; choice 252; conceptual relationships 97; connection 308; diagnosis 332; implicit 146; loss of 258; people 71; personal 280, 310; therapy 55; thoughts 307; worldview 156
Mearns, Dave 157, 316

medical-model concept of therapy 131, 294, 297
memory, childhood re-experienced 137
Merry, T. 338
Mertens, R. 283
Merton, Thomas 328
meso-processes in therapy 156
micro multitude, therapy as 17, 21
micro-processes in therapy 156
Mill, John Stuart 81
Miller, Scott 257
minoritarian ethics 37
Missiaen, Claude 155
modern self as 'internal discourse' 115
modernistic worldview 111, 320
modernity: modern/postmodern divide 116; and person-centred discourse 110, 116; questioning of 65; self-centered individual 61, 65, 66
Moon, Kathryn A. 128
Moore, Judy 321, 323
Morfino, V. 22
Morgan, Gareth 50
multitude, politics of 17, 21
Murphy, David 295, 336
mysticism: 'accidental mystic', Carl Rogers as 167, 169; and Chaos theory 172; introduction to 167; mystical moment 171

Nagel, Thomas 323, 324, 325
Najmanovich, Denise 101
narratives as creative contaminations xvii
necessarily insufficient therapy 41
Nelson, Maggie 265
neoliberalism 17
neurodiversity xix
Nietzsche, Friedrich 238, 319, 324
Nimatullah Wali, Shah 171
Nobel Peace Prize, Carl Rogers nominated for 167
Nohl, Herman 195
nondirective attitude of therapist 133
Norcross, John 256
Nurbakhsh, Javad 170, 171
Nygren, Andres 35

O'Hara, Maureen 280
openness: acceptance of 124; concealment and 315, 317; to difference 71; between disciplines 297; of ethical therapy 133; to experience 155, 323, 335; to irrelevant-seeming material 319; language and 67, 243; as more than verbal self-disclosure 327; offer of 24; to organismic experiencing 42; of person-centred therapy 321, 323, 327, 328; to symbolic dimension of relationship 326; unconditional 6; and unconditional positive regard 231
organismic experiencing: congruence to xvii; openness to 42; unconscious 41
organismic psychology, PCT as 29
organismic wisdom: complexity 106; examples 102; importance 107; introduction to 93; non-actualization of negative capacities 94; and understanding of world 101, 107
other person: acknowledgement of 203; empathy towards 71; PCA and otherness 116; responsibility for 66; self and 66; trust in 218, 306
outer relationships 157, 160

paradigm analysis 51
paradigms 50, 54
partners, trust between 196
passion *see* eros
PCA *see* person-centred approach
PCT *see* person-centred therapy
pedagogic eros 195
people: meaningfulness 71; notion of 21
perception, distorted, concept of 52
person: becoming 168, 175, 187, 189, 241, 258; and experiencing, dialectics of 79; human being as 200; meaning of 203; Rogers' view of 128
personality: change, theory of 181; childhood personality and adult health in relation 293
'personality disorder', definition of 293
person-centred approach (PCA): actualizing tendency 93; attitudes to medical model of therapy 294; current study approach xxii; as discursivity 110; ethics and 60, 63; future for 297, 311; Gendlin's process philosophy 117; history of 80; introduction to 110; knowledge and *see* knowledge, theories of; love 201; modern self as 'internal discourse' 115; modernity and 110; and other therapies xix; person-centred discourse 112, 123; person-centred particularity 116; presence and *see* presence; psychopathology and *see* psychopathology; and radical alterity *see* radical alterity; receptiveness of medical model 297; reinvention of, need for 110; related approaches 312; strangeness in 67; 'tribes' within 300; unconditional positive regard in 115

person-centred community 238, 239, 246, 281, 300, 306
person-centred discourse: modern self as 'internal discourse' 115; modernity and 110, 116; in PCA 112, 123
person-centred therapy (PCT): animality of therapist 14; anthropocentrism 29; audacity of therapist 14; beautiful soul syndrome 28, 31, 34; Beauty and the Cyborg *see* Beauty and the Cyborg; on becoming a person 168, 175, 187, 189, 241, 258; bridge between modern and postmodern 116; case studies *see* case studies; client-centredness 48; client's right to self-direction 133; communication 326; core conditions *see* core conditions; critiques of xvi; current study approach xxii; description 129; ethical therapy 128; and evidence-based practice *see* evidence-based practice; experience and 137; as focusing oriented therapy 121; future for 315; future of 53, xvi; Gendlin's process philosophy 117; as heterotopic practice 110, 124; knowledge and *see* knowledge, theories of; love, therapy through *see* therapy through love; necessarily insufficient 41; as non-directive therapy 134; openness of 321, 323, 327, 328; as organismic psychology 29, 30; paradigms 50, 54; political naivety xxii; as political practice 20, 24; Positive Psychology 40; positivism 30; potential person-centred contributions 320; power and 15; as present-centred therapy 47; psychopathology and *see* psychopathology; PTSD and PTG *see* post-traumatic stress disorder; radical ethics 13; as radical humanism 52; radical roots 46; research, revisioning of 277; silence, breaking 324; silence, keeping 321; storytelling 15; supervision relationship *see* supervision relationship; theoretical basis 49; theory 5; trust in 132
phenomenological relationships 141
philia (amity, friendship): *see also* friendship; agape and 198, 200, 204; Aristotle 197; community and 197, 200; family 197; form of love 35, 36, 197, 200; therapy as 197, 205
Pilgrim, D. 336
Pinheiro, Francisco P.H.A. 72, 73
Plato 35, 195

Poggesi, Rosa 213
Poirié, F. 65, 66
politics: client-centred practice as political practice 20; community of friends 25; multitude 17, 21; narratives xvii; neoliberal psycho-political domination 17; political naivety of PCT xxii; psychotherapy and 20; of relationships 20; therapy as political act 17
Positive Psychology 40
postmodernism *see* modernity
post-traumatic stress disorder (PTSD): cognitive behavioural therapy 335; eye movement desensitisation and reprocessing 335; introduction to 330; potential problem areas 334; psychopathology 332
power: love and 'the Powers' 36; therapy and 15, 129
presence: agape as 185; and beautiful soul 42; CBT 219; celebrity and access to presence 307; as congruence 179; connections and 303, 311; as core condition 301, 302, 312; and core conditions 23, 204; current state of PCA 300; directivity and non-directivity in relation to 308; encounter group process 310; as foundation of unconditional positive regard 217; as fourth condition 301; full 23; importance for future of PCA 311; person-centered core conditions 301; as relational 303; relationships and 204; Rogers' unrecognized path to 309; and self-acceptance 306; self-care, need for 304
present-centred therapy, PCT as 47
primacy of encounter above form 22
process: as becoming of experience 118; of congruence 182, 184; empathy as 177; experience as bodily process 120; Gendlin's process philosophy 117; life as 119; macro-processes 156; meso-processes 156; micro-processes 156; Rogers' model 4; skipping 184; successful 71; trust in 217, 278, 294, 322; unconditional positive regard as 121; unfolding process of experiencing 119
Proust, Marcel 233
Prouty, Garry 281
psychiatry, openness and partnership with other disciplines 297
psychoanalysis: *see also* Freud, Sigmund; 'all about sex' 3; and client-centered

therapy 4; traditional model of 170
psychology *see* therapy
psychopathology: client perceptions of distress 292; future for PCA 297; introduction to 289; 'personality disorder', definition of 293; person-centred attitudes to medical model of therapy 294; PTSD and PTG 332; receptiveness of medical model to PCA 297; Rogers, Carl, and 290
psychotherapy *see* therapy
Purton, C. 146, 147

'radical', meaning of 50
radical alterity: ethics of PCA 63; Figueiredo's philosophy of science 60; introduction to 60; Levinas's ethics of 65; Rogers and 72; strangeness in PCA 67
radical ethics, PCT and 13
radical humanism, PCT as 52
radical reciprocity 21, 22
radical roots of PCT 46
radical self-disclosure 317, 320
Rank, Otto 41, 46, 154, 277, 282
Raskin, Nathaniel 282, 284
Rat Man case 318
reactions, trust in 48
Read, Herbert 137
realistic worldview 320
reason and understanding 259
Regel, Stephen 336
relational depth 157
relationship therapy, turn to 47
relationships: *see also* connections; allusions to 96; better understanding of 176, 269; 'betweenness' of connections 239; canine-human 266; changes 260; community and 49; conceptual 141, 238; difficulties in establishing 105; empathy 284; ethics of 215; family 96, 240; healing power of 273; infinite 24; inner 157, 160; 'lawfulness' 49; living in 97; love and 194, 206; maze of 24; multitude 21; outer 157, 160; paradigms 50; phenomenological 141; politics of 20; presence and 204; reconfiguring in EFT 157; relational depth 157; therapeutic 49, 196, 284, 312, 319; wider influences on 95
religion: *see also* Christianity; Centre for Spirituality and Religion 187; comic faith in technofixes 31; love 193
Rennie, David 280
research, revisioning of 277
responsibility for the Other 66

revealing *see* openness
Rice, Bert 128
Richard of St. Victor 197
right of client to self-direction 133
Rilke, Rainer Maria 259
Rogerian psychotherapy *see* person-centred therapy
Rogers, Andy 188
Rogers, Carl: as 'accidental mystic' 167, 169; actualizing tendency 93, 96, 132; affective turn xx; agape, presence as 185; agape as UPR 198, 201; alterity 72; on becoming a person 168, 175, 187, 189, 241, 258; Buber, Martin, and 68, 303; celebrity status 308; China journey 281; client-centred practice as political practice 20, 24; client-centred therapy 48, 129; communication 326; congruence 145, 185; core conditions 301; empathy as process 177; ethics 63; existential therapy 159; experience 140, 145, 320; founding of client-centered therapy 4; future of PCT 53; Gendlin, Eugene T., and 177; Jaspers, Karl, and 289; legacy of xviii; Levinas, Emmanuel, and 60; macro-processes in therapy 156; McMahon, Edwin, and 180; mysticism *see* mysticism; Nobel Peace Prize nomination 167; organismic wisdom 93; PCT's inherent positivism 30; pedagogic eros 195; person and experiencing 80; person-centred discourse 124; presence as agape 185; presence as congruence 179; presence as fourth condition 300; psychopathology 290; psychotherapy as organismic psychology 30; radical humanism 52; Rank, Otto, and 41, 46; relationship therapy, turn to 47; as researcher 277; selection of therapists 267; Skinner, B. F., and 63; storge 197; successful therapeutic process 71; therapeutic process model 4; and Vasilyuk, Fyodor E. xxiv, xxvi; view of the person 128; Zen tradition xxi
Rose, Gillian 35
Rose, Michael 38
Rosenberg, Marshall B. 315
Rosenzweig, Saul 256
Russell, David 53

Sanders, Pete 295, 296, 300
Sapriel, L. 49
Satprem (Bernard Enginger) 170
Scheele, Julia 320
Schiller, Friedrich 32
Schlien, John 295

Schmid, Peter 55, 69, 70, 73, 279
Schön, Donald 279
Schopenhauer, Arthur 195
Schulze, Alfred Otto Wolfgang (Wols) 137
science: comic faith in technofixes 31; diagnosis and 292; empiricism 138; experience and 137; Figueiredo's philosophy of 60; mysticism and 167; paradigms 50; 'scientific imperialism' 291; worldview 138
'scientific imperialism' 291
self: connections 219; experience and 145; modern self as 'internal discourse' 115; and Other 66; trust in 175, 203, 205, 221, 226, 244
self-acceptance: connections 306; presence and 306
self-care: connections 306; presence and 304
self-centered individual, modernity and 61, 65, 66
self-direction, client's right to 133
self-disclosure: dynamics of 325; openness as more than verbal 327; radical 317, 320
self-gratification, agape and 199
Sells, Michael 242
Shakespeare, S. 241
shame, family and 103
Shaw, Tamsin 39
Shlien, John 48, 310
Shorey, Ryan 212
silence, breaking 324
silence, keeping 321
Simondon, Gilbert 22
Skinner, B. F. 63
Smail, David 312
Smith, Adam 280
Smith, Philip B 106
social constraints on human development, release from 52
social dimension of cosmic congruence 186
social science paradigms 50
Sommerbeck, Lisbeth 290, 296
space for trust 25
Spice, Nicholas 317
Spinoza, Baruch 17, 21, 22, 24, 25
spirituality: *see also* mysticism; Bio-Spiritual Focusing 174, 180, 182, 186; Centre for Spirituality and Religion 187; comic faith in technofixes 31; narratives xvii; spiritual bypass 35; trust and 245
Sri Aurobindo 170
Stein, Gertrude 20
Stern, Daniel 47
storge (affection): as *cantus firmus* ('firm song') 200; empathy and 196; family 196; form of love 35, 196, 200; in therapeutic relationship 196; therapy as 205; trust and 203
storytelling as therapy 15
'strange consciousness of living', experience as 42
strangeness in PCA 67
Stuart, Gregory 212
Sufism 36
supervision relationship: example 271; introduction to 265; personal/professional double bind 267, 269; rigid formalisation 265; room for important questions 272; vicarious trauma 269
symbolic dimension of relationship, openness to 326
symbolization, congruence not definable as explicit 177
Syvanen, Michael 38

Tabbarah, Sarah 213
Taft, Jessie 46, 281, 283
taxonomy of love 35
technofixes: comic faith in 31; emancipatory 38
Teilhard de Chardin, Pierre 180
theology: of event 244; immanent 37; love 193
'therapeutic', meaning of 68
therapy: accidental 3; agape 198, 200, 205; aim of 175; animality of therapist 14; attitude of respect 133; audacity of therapist 14; childhood 47; client perceptions of distress 292; client's right to self-direction 133; communication 326; community as aim 21, 316; congruent communication 316; connections 218, 219, 270; definition of 129; as diagnosis 292; eros 204, 205; ethical 128; 'framework for love' 34; freedom as ethical premise for practice 131; as friendship 13, 197; friendship distinguished from 198; Helpful Aspects of Therapy (HAT) 158; love, therapy through *see* therapy through love; macro-processes 156; meaningfulness 55; medical model 131, 294, 297; meso-processes 156; as *micro multitude* 17, 21; micro-processes 156; necessarily insufficient 41; nondirective attitude 133; person-centred attitudes to medical model 294; philia 197, 205; politics and *see* politics; power and 15; power relationship 129; primacy of encounter above form 22; psychopathology *see* psychopathology; radical reciprocity 21,

22; as relationship 49, 196, 284, 312, 319; selection of therapists 267; storge 196, 205; storytelling as 15; successful therapeutic process 71; therapist as fully implied 158; trust 217, 278, 294, 322
therapy through love: basic facts about love 193; forms of love 194, 199; human being as person 200; introduction to 192; love and art of acknowledgement 202; love in psychologies 193; meaning of love 192; PCA and meaning of love 201; PCA and power of love 202; UPR as agape 201
thinking-feeling-behaviour triangle 248
Thorne, Brian 174, 278, 281, 316
thoughts: concealment 317, 323; meaningfulness 307
Tolstoy, Leo 89
tradition: adaptation xvii; creative contamination xvii; keeping alive xvii; preservation xvii
transparency *see* openness
trust: in client-centered therapy 132; in clients 205, 206; in experience 101, 238; expressed as agape 71; in human beings 93; in other person 218, 306; between partners 196; in reactions 48; in self 175, 203, 205, 221, 226, 244; space for 25; spirituality and 245; storge and 203; in therapeutic process 217, 278, 294, 322; as unconditional positive regard 71
Tudor, K. 338
Tversky, Amos 40

unconditional: acceptance 23, 186, 237, 307, 327; assertion of being 244; as event 244; hospitality, therapy as 32; love 174, 198, 229; openness 6; support 307
unconditional positive regard (UPR): as acknowledgement 204; as agape 198, 200, 201; for all 233; aspiration for 13; as core condition 300, 301, 302, 327; definition of 130; empathy and 122, 130, 135, 196, 303; eros and 196; experience of 68, 130, 135, 186, 202; incongruence and 196; love as 71; notion of 34; openness and 231; in person-centred approach 115; presence as foundation of 217; as process 121; in therapeutic process 70; by therapist 48, 130; trust as 71
unconditional support 307
unconscious, organismic experiencing of 41
understanding: empathic understanding 130; and organismic wisdom 101, 107; reason and 259
unfolding process of experiencing 119

United Kingdom: medical-model concept of therapy, dominance of 292, 294, 295; person-centred approach 290, 296, 297; person-centred research 277; PTSD therapies 335; 'scientific imperialism' 291
universal worldview 33
universe, connection with 198
Updike, John 317
UPR *see* unconditional positive regard

Van Deurzen, E. 213
Vasilyuk, Fyodor E. 80, xxiv
verbal self-disclosure, openness as more than 327
vicarious trauma 269
Vieira, R.D. 70, 72, 73
Vygotsky, L.S. 88, 118, xxvi

Warner, M. 338
Warner, Margaret 281, 295
Webb, Julie 30
wellbeing *see* health
Wessely, Simon 294
'what' of knowing 238, 245
Whitehead, A. N. 118, 139
Williams, Whiting 68, 69
Williamson, E. 338
wisdom *see* organismic wisdom
Wittgenstein, Ludwig 285
Wols (Alfred Otto Wolfgang Schulze) 137
Wolter-Gustafson, Carol 279
words, limitations of 142
World Association for Person-centered and Experiential Psychotherapy and Counseling (WAPCEPC) 312
worldviews: *see also* paradigms; adaptation 28; assumptions 176; Christian 29, 36; conditioned 243; criticism of 243; dualistic 140; family 105, 278; incompatible 41; meaning and 156; modernistic 111; modern-realist 320; organismic wisdom and 101, 107; scientific 138; static 140; universal 33
Wu, emperor xxi
Wucherer-Huldenfeld, Augustinus 197

Yankelovich, Daniel 254
Yoder, John Howard 37
yoga, Ashtanga 305

Zeldin, T. 211
Zen Buddhism xxi
Zeno 142

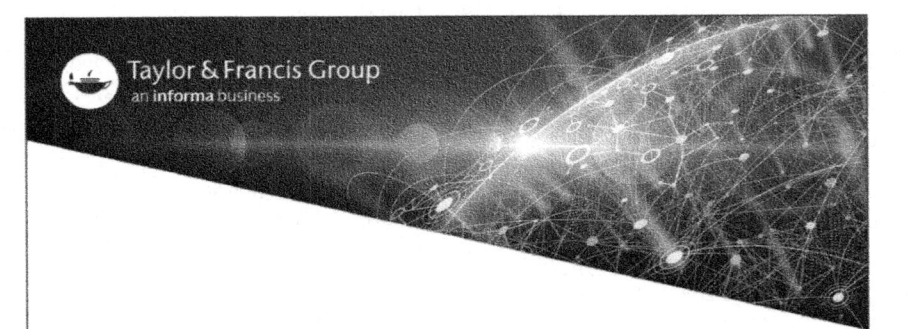